A. Mary F. Robinson

A. Mary F. Robinson

*Victorian Poet and
Modern Woman of Letters*

PATRICIA RIGG

McGill-Queen's University Press
Montreal & Kingston · London · Chicago

ISBN 978-0-2280-0883-5 (cloth)
ISBN 978-0-2280-0884-2 (paper)
ISBN 978-0-2280-1013-5 (ePDF)
ISBN 978-0-2280-1014-2 (ePUB)

Legal deposit third quarter 2021
Bibliothèque nationale du Québec

Printed in Canada on acid-free paper that is 100% ancient forest free (100% post-consumer recycled), processed chlorine free

This book has been published with the help of a grant from the Canadian Federation for the Humanities and Social Sciences, through the Awards to Scholarly Publications Program, using funds provided by the Social Sciences and Humanities Research Council of Canada. Funding was also received from Acadia University.

Funded by the Government of Canada   Financé par le gouvernement du Canada   Canadä   Canada Council for the Arts   Conseil des arts du Canada

We acknowledge the support of the Canada Council for the Arts.
Nous remercions le Conseil des arts du Canada de son soutien.

Library and Archives Canada Cataloguing in Publication

Title: A. Mary F. Robinson : Victorian poet and modern woman of letters / Patricia Rigg.

Names: Rigg, Patricia, 1951- author.

Description: Includes bibliographical references and index.

Identifiers: Canadiana (print) 20210203439 | Canadiana (ebook) 20210203552 | ISBN 9780228008835 (cloth) | ISBN 9780228008842 (paper) | ISBN 9780228010135 (ePDF) | ISBN 9780228010142 (ePUB)

Subjects: LCSH: Robinson, A. Mary F. (Agnes Mary Frances), 1857-1944. | LCSH: Authors, English – 19th century – Biography. | LCGFT: Biographies.

Classification: LCC PR4629.D18 Z85 2021 | DDC 821/.8 – dc23

This book was designed and typeset by Peggy & Co. Design in 11.5/14 Adobe Caslon Pro.

For Adrienne, Danielle, and Nève;
for Gabriel;
for Christian and Olivier

Contents

�֍

Preface and Acknowledgments

My work on A. Mary F. Robinson has taken me to archives in England, Scotland, France, Italy, the United States, and Canada, where she has an extensive archival presence that indicates her importance as a poet and prose writer in the nineteenth and twentieth centuries. Robinson had a wide circle of friends who attended her popular salons in London and in Paris, and she was a prolific letter writer, corresponding regularly with literary and artistic friends, with publishers, and with family members. She left annotated books and manuscripts, as well as personal documents in these official archives and in the Duclaux family home in Olmet, a village outside Aurillac in the Auvergne, where she died in 1944. Working on a Victorian writer who lived until the middle of the twentieth century has been a unique experience for me as a nineteenth-century specialist, particularly since I have had access to family papers and was able to develop a friendship with Robinson's great-granddaughter by marriage, Jacqueline Bayard-Pierlot, who died in February 2021 and whose grandfather, Jacques Duclaux, was the elder son of Robinson's second husband, Émile Duclaux. Jacqueline and I met in Paris in January of 2016, and the following June she invited my husband and me to stay with her at the family home that Robinson had shared with Émile Duclaux. After Émile's untimely death in 1904, Robinson continued to stay at the house regularly, and during the Second World War, when the whole family had to leave Paris, Jacqueline lived there for periods with Mary and her sister Mabel. Jacqueline was old enough to remember the idiosyncrasies of the elderly ladies.

Spending time in Robinson's house at Olmet, using her library of books, and making my way through the personal papers and documents left there was a rare gift. It became clear to me that Robinson's poetry and prose are deeply connected to and reflective of how she experienced her life and that a critical biography would tell her story as fully as possible. To that end, I have organized the book chronologically, with each chapter highlighting significant points of transition in Robinson's life and focusing on representative poems and prose – biographies, histories, literary essays, and critical reviews – in order to understand the events of her life that inspired her and in order to trace her development as a writer.

In addition to Jacqueline Bayard-Pierlot, I have many people to thank for their help and their support. I am grateful to Acadia University for a combination of internal grants and SSHRC Institutional Grants that made it possible for me to carry out research overseas and across North America. This funding also made it possible for me to participate in conferences that gave me access to the wide international community of Victorian scholars. It is humbling and gratifying to be able to count myself a member of a community of academics who are always so generous with their time and their resources. I particularly want to thank Dr Sophie Geoffroy and Dr Roger Lewis for sending me letters pertinent to my work on Robinson. Many thanks to Mark Abley at McGill-Queen's for steering me through the reviewing and revising processes, and to Kyla Madden and Elli Stylianou for seeing me through the rest of the process. Elli Stylianou was particularly helpful with preparing the photographs for the book. Thank you to Shelagh Plunkett, copy editor, and all the other members of McGill-Queen's who made this book possible. Specifically, I owe a great deal to the three anonymous reviewers who did me an enormous service in directing the revision processes of the manuscript. All of these professionals have made this a much better book than it would otherwise have been.

Library staff at the numerous archival depositories I visited over the course of ten years made my research go smoothly. In the UK, I would like to thank the staff at the British Library, Elizabeth D. Harris at City University London, and Dr Anne Manuel at Sommerville College Library, as well as staff at the Brotherton Library, and at the National Library of Scotland. Staff at the Bibliothèque Nationale de France and Mme Dominique Dupenne of the Pasteur Institute in Paris were patient and very helpful, as was Alyson Price, archivist at the Harold Acton Library at the British Institute in Florence. In the United States, I owe a special thanks to Patricia Burdick at Colby College, as well as staff at the New York Public Library and the Library for the Performing Arts at the Lincoln Centre, the Library of Congress in Washington, and the Huntingdon Library in California. Thank you as well to the staff at the University of British Columbia Library in Vancouver, Canada. The technical staff at the Bibliothèque National de France, Maggie Libby at Colby College Library, and Vincent Grovestine at Acadia Vaughan Memorial Library helped with formatting the images for this book.

Thank you to the following journals for permission to reprint portions of my published articles: "Gendered Poetic Discourse and Autobiographical Narratives in Late Victorian Sonnet Sequences," *Victorian Poetry*, a special edition edited by Veronica Alfano and Lee O'Brien, 57 no. 2 (2019): 201–23; "A. Mary F. Robinson's *The New Arcadia:* Aestheticism and the Fin-de Siècle Social Problem Poem," *Papers in Languages and Literature* 51 no. 2 (2015): 170–94; "'Tell me a story, dear, that is not true': Love, Historicity, and Transience in A. Mary F. Robinson's *An Italian Garden*," *Australasian Victorian Studies Journal* 17 no. 1 (2012): 1–14; "'War Work' and the Philosophy of Heroism: A. Mary F. Robinson Duclaux's Friendly Fire with Marie Lenéru and Vernon Lee," *Vernon Lee and Radical Circles*, edited by Sophie Geoffroy, Paris: Michel Houdiard, 2016; Dr Dino Franco Felluga for permission to include sections of my entry on Robinson for *The Encyclopedia of Victorian Literature*, edited by Dino Felluga, Wiley-Blackwell, 1st edition, 1 August 2015. Thank you to the trustees of the National Library of Scotland for permission to quote from the letter of Mary Duclaux to Cunningham Graham.

Finally, my thanks to my husband Christopher Rigg, who not only keeps my life humming along smoothly during my excursions into the nineteenth century – even during a pandemic – but who read and offered advice on several versions of this manuscript. He is patient, perceptive, and eagle-eyed, and after thirty-nine years of marriage continues to inspire me.

A. Mary F. Robinson. BNF Fonds Anglais 252 f. 54.

Robinson at the British Museum Library. Vernon Lee Collection, Colby College Library.

A. Mary F. Robinson. Vernon Lee Collection, Colby College Library.

Robinson carte de visite. Vernon Lee Collection, Colby College Library.

James Darmesteter. In *English Studies* by James Darmesteter, trans. Mary James Darmesteter (London: T. Fisher Unwin, 1896), inside front cover.

Mary James Darmesteter, 1893. BNF Fonds Anglais 252 f. 55.

Mary Duclaux. Vernon Lee Collection, Colby College Library.

Émile Duclaux, photographed by Pierre Petit. Wellcome Images,
Wellcome Trust.

Mabel Robinson, Mary Robinson, and Erma (a friend). Family Archives of Jacqueline Bayard-Pierlot, Olmet.

Mary Duclaux passport photo, 1927. Fonds Anglais, 243, f 122, Bibliothèque nationale de France.

Émile and Mary Duclaux's tomb in Aurillac. Photograph by Patricia Rigg.

A. Mary F. Robinson

Introduction:
An Anglo-French Life

Part One: An Anglo-French Life

Primarily known to English readers as a late Victorian poet and to French readers as a twentieth-century biographer, reviewer, and essayist, Agnes Mary Frances Robinson lived in England, mostly in London, for the first third of her life; however, she spent the next two-thirds in France, mostly in Paris, where she experienced two happy marriages, the Dreyfus affair, the cultural height of the belle époque, and both world wars. Her fluency in French enabled her to publish essays and reviews in major French journals, as well as place histories and biographies with respected French presses. Although she did not publish poetry in French, she wrote a number of poems in French; in fact, the poem thought to have been her last is written in French. It is my aim in this book to reconcile the English poet and the French woman of letters through a biographically informed, comprehensive study of the poetry and prose of A. Mary F. Robinson, who subsequently published under her married names Mary James Darmesteter and Mary Duclaux. In considering the ways in which Robinson developed as a poet when she left her London context for a more cosmopolitan life in Paris, as well as the ways in which her poetics and her historical and biographical writing become increasingly integrated in style and content, we can better understand and appreciate the significant contribution Robinson made to literature and letters during the shift from Victorianism to modernism.

As a biographer herself, Mary Robinson well understood the importance of personal documents and archived materials to biographers of the future. When I wrote my "biographically informed"

book on Augusta Webster, published in 2009, I was hampered by a
dearth of existing correspondence, manuscripts, and personal documents, and I depended in large part on public documents, records of
the London Suffrage Society and the London School Board, as well
as publishers' records, to supplement the few personal letters that
remain. Robinson, on the other hand, was not an activist and left few
documents in public records. She expressed social and political views
in poetry, biography, and essays. She also corresponded regularly with
many literary and artist figures in England and France, and, in contrast to Webster, she left personal letters and annotated documents
in archives in England, Scotland, France, Italy, the United States,
and Canada, as well as the family papers now held by Jacqueline
Bayard-Pierlot's estate.

Robinson's eight biographies were all well received, both in
France and in England. Through biographical writing, she built
her reputation as a perceptive analyst of human nature, and, since
the seven biographies that followed *Emily Brontë* focus on French
subjects and were written originally in French, Robinson developed
a sensitive and nuanced understanding of the French language and
French culture, enabling her to facilitate a transnational literary
discourse with her English readers. In the nineteenth-century context
of biographical "theory" Robinson stands out because she approached
biography as she approached poetry, looking for language that would
convey the truth about her subject and yet appeal to the reader interested in drawing independent conclusions about the same subject,
and her success in the genre is remarkable, given the dual context,
language, and readership with which she was concerned. She might
be described as a subjective biographer who interspersed her personal
assessment of people and events with the "facts" as she was able to
find them. Her biographer friend Edmund Gosse wrote in 1903, "the
adventurer in biography has to make up his mind to the commission
of certain sins of indiscretion," and Robinson seems to have written
consciously aiming to reveal rather than conceal.[1] In 1915 her friend
Maurice Barrès suggested to her that all biographers inevitably
engage in hagiography and produce distorted representations of
their subjects as they embellish and enrich details.[2] The perspectives
of Gosse and Barrès are late nineteenth-century and early twentieth-
century articulations of the basic issues of biographical writing

related to all representations of past lives that remain pertinent to biographers today, and reviewers of Robinson's biographies are united in their praise of her for resisting strategies that would compromise the integrity of her work. A tributary article upon her death published in the *Times Literary Supplement* reiterates that not only did she treat her subjects with "fairness" but that this "perspective seems to be part of her natural sight."[3]

In essential ways, the theoretical implications of biography, of life writing, and of the complex nature of the relationship between biographer and subject have not changed over the years, and they have certainly not changed in the past twenty years of my attempts to carry out biographical research and writing.[4] I am still conscious of and interested in the ways in which history, historicism, and historicity paradoxically interfere with and aid the process of biographical recovery and reconstruction. Charles Baudelaire, whom Robinson admired as a poet and about whom she wrote in English and in French, expresses this paradox through his understanding of *modernité*, which, when applied to art, he suggests, refers to "the transitory, the fleeting, the contingent, half of art whose other half is the eternal and the immutable."[5] The challenge for Baudelaire is that art is ultimately connected to the context in which it was produced, a context lost in essence with passing time. However, as Erin O'Connor writes in her discussion of Byatt's *The Biographer's Tale*, it is "no matter that we can never *really* imagine our way into another's world, or life, or work. What's important is that we try" [emphasis O'Connor's].[6] Nigel Hamilton situates this importance more specifically, arguing "that the pursuit of biography, controversial in its challenge to received ideas of privacy and reputation since ancient times, is integral to the Western concept of individuality and the ideals of democracy, as opposed to dictatorship or tyranny."[7] These are large claims but precisely the context we should keep in mind, I think, when we attempt to situate biographical criticism logically in the contemporary world. Generally, most recent work on biography as a critical discipline has developed along the lines that its importance is magnified in a volatile world in which we learn about and react to events with sometimes shocking immediacy – an age of social media and "fake news." As Sabina Loriga explains, the biographer must not only sort and sift biographical details and make decisions about what to include and what to omit, as has always been the case, but he or she must also consider "the relationship between biography and history" and the broader thorny issue of whether "the life of an individual [can] illuminate the past" and, implicitly, of course, the present.[8] Loriga makes these remarks in the most recent comprehensive study of biographical criticism, *Theoretical Discussions of Biography: Approaches from History, Microhistory, and Life Writing*, edited by Hans Renders and Binne de Haan. The interesting feature of this collection of essays is its demonstration of the diversity of ways in which biography intersects with other methodologies to examine how the social, cultural, and political climates within which an author experiences life are reflected in his or her writing and how our climates affect our reading of history.[9] In each of Robinson's biographies, I suggest, we gain insight not only into her subject but into Robinson herself, for in shaping the narrative of her subject's life, she reveals her own interests, her learned approach to writing, and, of course, her personal biases.

Robinson's breadth in her prose writing accounts for her success as a transnational member of the Anglo-French literary community, for, in addition to biography, she authored history articles and books in both languages, and, during two specific periods when she had opportunities as a married woman to travel in France, she experimented with writing travel articles for her English readers. As a biographer and as a historicist, she is adept at treading the line between conveying facts and interpreting what the facts suggest, thereby combining what Barrès implies is historical fiction with what Hans Renders argues is the desired form of modern journalism, the "one characteristic that binds all biographers together." Renders reasons that "this association becomes apparent in their striving to write readable stories, in their setting of high ethical standards regarding their inter-action with research materials (a characteristic they share with scholars and scientists), and in their choice of sources."[10]

There have been two biographies of Mary Robinson, both written in French and both focusing only on her life as an English poet. Sylvaine Marandon worked her 1960 doctoral thesis into a book, which she published in 1967, and Jacqueline Bayard-Pierlot self-published a similarly focused biography of her great-grandmother by marriage in 2015. Robinson expressed herself most intimately in poetry, but her prose contributes to our understanding of the integration of intellectualism and aestheticism that defines an oeuvre impressive in its range and diversity of poetic genres. In this respect, Robinson's work reflects her status as a woman of transitions – she was a citizen of two countries who was twice married to French men and twice widowed, a woman much admired in London, when she moved from her place of prominence in British aestheticist circles to an important place in twentieth-century French intellectual and literary circles in Paris. She held and attended successful salons in both London and Paris, gaining prominence in each society as a writer and as an independent thinker whose iron will now and again surprised family and friends – defying her parents and Vernon Lee to marry James Darmesteter, for instance, and later setting herself in opposition to friends in France, first as a committed Dreyfusard and then as a firm believer that heroic action rather than pacifism was needed in times of war. Her impressive historical knowledge, particularly with respect to the medieval period in both England and France, her wide-ranging literary interests, her ability to read and write in Italian and German as well as in French and English, and her foray into the female intellectual circles of Greek translation make her of particular interest to scholars of British aestheticism, the Anglo-French community, and the ways in which twentieth-century literature is informed by its Victorian past.

Throughout her long life, Robinson sought to reconcile her yearning for a spiritual life that would prepare her for an abstract and undefined afterlife with her intellectual conviction that she would not find such preparation by following any formal religion. She was confirmed into the Anglican Church at age fifteen when she was at school in Brussels, but she does not seem to have ever practiced formally, either with her family or on her own.[11] By the age of twenty-one, as she confided to John Addington Symonds, she had decided that the form religion would take in her life was that of helping the world and using poetry to inspire others to do good works.[12] The tension between head and heart in this respect caused her a great deal of anxiety, particularly after the death of James Darmesteter and during her own aging process. Her poetry in particular reflects the influence of her friend Walter Pater and his dismay at the "awful brevity" of human existence.[13] She strives to poeticize what Pater defines as the fragmentary moments of human experience – the experience of hearing music, of viewing art, of walking outdoors, or of the terrible reality of war, and through her poetry she invites us to participate in an aesthetic community of individuals with similar concerns. Her poetry evokes the aestheticist mantra that "one does not step twice into the same aesthetic stream; each encounter is new and transformative."[14] Yet, in making her own encounter with such contemplative moments available to us, she compels us to experience similar moments shaped by our time and our experience of the world around us. Robinson develops themes common to us all – love, death, the yearning for transcendence of death through love, and the importance of nature, both as a means of enhancing aesthetic pleasure and as a source of insight into the individual life experienced in fragments and significant moments. For all of these reasons, Mary Robinson is indeed what Vernon Lee called "a born poet," but she is also a technically astute poet who trained herself by experimenting with poetic form in innovative and interesting ways without compromising the principles associated with specific poetic genres.[15] Paradoxically, as she grew older and her myopia became more severe, her poetics matured and she seemed more and more able to "see" details in nature by virtue of being compelled to view the large picture – the panorama – in minute parts close up.

The context within which Robinson developed as a poet, then, was late nineteenth-century aestheticism, the literary and artistic movement that Karl Beckson defined in broad strokes nearly forty years ago in terms that remain pertinent today: aestheticism "implies certain attitudes rather than forms of behavior, attitudes associated with the concern over aesthetic form and experience divorced from moral judgment."[16] However, although Robinson grew up in an aestheticist household, she is not an "art for art's sake" poet, and she did not accept the extreme aestheticist position, which, as Gene Bell-Villada puts it, assumes that "we 'learn' absolutely nothing about life or about values from literature."[17] Her close friend Vernon Lee records discussions with Robinson about what can and should be learned through writing and reading poetry in "A Dialogue on Poetic Morality," published in *Belcaro*, which Lee dedicated to Robinson in 1881. Lee explains, as Emily Harrington aptly puts it, "how the acts of producing and consuming art could themselves be moral by creating pleasures that approached the feeling of sympathy."[18] The fact is that Robinson's aestheticist culture has its own set of values that are frequently of a social and political nature and that appear in poetry and in prose that asks us to examine all aspects of our lives, material and spiritual. She experimented with a diverse number of poetic forms – lyric, dramatic, and narrative – and she experimented as well with themes that were at times politically focused, at times historical, and at other times contemplative and abstract.

Mary Robinson grew up in a family confident that individual desires could be reconciled with universal needs and that young women like Mary and her sister Mabel should be encouraged to achieve this reconciliation by reading extensively, both at home and more formally in the classroom. Her father, George Robinson, was a journalist and an architect, professions that blend the creative–cultural perspective with material and sociopolitical concerns. George Robinson lived according to the aestheticist principle that Ruskin articulates in an 1859 lecture: "beautiful art can only be produced by people who have beautiful things about them."[19] He made sure that his daughters grew up surrounded by literature and art through which they developed not only an appreciation of beauty but also a thirst for knowledge about the historical and philosophical contexts in which these great works were produced. Mary Robinson was particularly interested in religion and mysticism as records of this pursuit, but ultimately, she had a keen sense that history, historical figures, and historicism itself held the key not only to understanding the contemporary world but also to accepting the finitude of human life.

Robinson's interest in art, history, and social justice continued when she moved to France in 1888, where she became a French citizen wholly immersed in French literature, culture, and politics. She remained steadfast in her love for her adopted country, and it was in France that Robinson, like other British aesthetes, took up the more Decadent preoccupation, as R.K.R. Thornton describes it, of reconciling joy in "the world, its necessities, and the attractive impressions" of the here and now with a yearning for "the eternal, the ideal, and the unworldly" that would lead to some form of transcendence.[20] She made many attempts to delineate this two-pronged, paradoxical yearning in her poetry. She relied on friends in both countries to point the way for her to negotiate the complicated path between desire and attainment, notably Oscar Wilde, Walter Pater, Robert Browning, Edmund Gosse, and John Addington Symonds in her early years in London and Ernest Renan, Hippolyte Taine, Maurice Barrès, Paul Bourget, Daniel Halévy, and Marcel Proust in France. Like Arthur Symons, another friend, Robinson participated in the Anglo-French community, and in later life she became a mentor to young writers in both countries. She was a cofounder of the Prix Femina and served on the first jury in 1904, continuing to serve for the next thirty years. She was a loyal and dedicated friend to the difficult George Moore throughout his life. She was not a complex woman in social terms, usually, with the exception of the anti-Dreyfusards during the Dreyfus affair, able to find middle ground with those who held views opposing hers. We see in the epistolary and publication trails that she has left us that she remained essentially the same person throughout her long life, despite her transitions delineated by her marriages, as Daniel Halévy makes clear in his pointedly titled essay "Les Trois Marys." While Moore and others felt that she had compromised her literary reputation with her move to France and in publishing under three different names, it is clear that she was a successful British poet well into the twentieth century and an extremely well-respected writer of prose in both English and French until her final *Times Literary Supplement* review article in 1937. Herein, I suggest, lies the importance of Mary Robinson to the development of an Anglo-French literary culture in which she was uniquely placed to bring to English readers an understanding of French writers, both past and contemporary, and to French readers a similar understanding of English writers. A reviewer of her biography of *The Life of Racine* casts Robinson's success in biographical writing in this context, noting that her "able and sympathetic biography makes a noteworthy addition to the number of books by which she has helped English readers to understand the masterpieces of French literature."[21] Writing poetry and prose at a transitional moment in the final decades of the nineteenth century in England and the first decades of the twentieth century in France, Robinson also developed technically as a poet, moving away from her early focus on fantasy and her youthful emotional excesses to produce impressive contemplative and philosophical poetry. Although not all of her experiments with either genre were successful, Robinson's prose is often intimately connected to her poetics, and in situating her poetry and her prose in the context of how she experienced her life, we not only see more clearly biographical influences on her professional growth, but we gain insight into a writer who compels us to look beyond accepted contexts of literary periodization.

Part Two: Family Life and Early Years

Agnes Mary Frances Robinson was born 27 February 1857 at Milverton Crescent near Leamington in Warwickshire, and her sister Frances Mabel Robinson followed on 16 June 1858. George Thomas Robinson (1828–1897) and Frances Sparrow (1831–1917) were aesthetically, intellectually, and socially well positioned, as well as financially comfortable. The family stayed in Leamington for the next ten years, with George Robinson working as diocesan architect for the archdeaconry of Coventry. He also worked as a journalist for the *Manchester Guardian*, which meant travel to the continent. On one such trip in 1870, when Mary was thirteen years old, George found himself trapped in Metz as the Franco-Prussian war intensified. There is an interesting, albeit improbable, family story about his dedication to journalism at this crucial point in French history. Unable to send his correspondence home any other way, he is said to have ingeniously enclosed his reports in balloons, which he sent over enemy lines, and such stories, suggests an old family friend John Pollock, contributed to George Robinson's success in instilling a "sympathy with France" in his daughters that stayed with them their whole lives.[22]

When he returned to England, George Robinson combined his aesthetic interests in architecture and painting with his love for writing, and he became an art critic for the *Manchester Courier*, as well as editor of the *Art Monthly Review*. As a financially and professionally successful man, he gave his daughters not only access to literature and art but also the economic security needed to enjoy an aesthetic middle-class life. The young Mary, a precocious reader, took advantage of her father's extensive library from a very early age, spending significant amounts of time in seclusion reading literature, biography, and history. In his 1884 article for *Harper's New*

Monthly Magazine, Edmund Clarence Stedman writes of George Robinson's friendship with William Morris, at the time an already well-known practitioner of "decorative art," and he refers to the "literary and musical receptions in Mrs. Robinson's drawing room." George Robinson's library, notes Stedman, "is curiously rich with rare and antique volumes."[23] This rich literary foundation no doubt foreshadows Robinson's later interest in history, classics, and biography, but it also foreshadows ways in which she would integrate fact and fiction in her poetics, particularly in her ballads. However, the young Mary Robinson also developed a love for nature that became the inspiration for much of her poetry during frequent visits to her maternal grandfather in his country home in Warwickshire, where she and her sister "were suffered to run wild and taught to know all the flowers and birds in the country by their blossoms and their note, and when she and Mabel appeared unwell, their mother would offer her standard advice: 'Let them run wild for a month or so.'"[24] The country home remained in the family after her grandfather died, and Robinson returned to it often while she lived in London. It became the source of her only socially focused poem *The New Arcadia* and is featured in certain details in her only novel *Arden*.

In 1867, when Robinson was ten, the family moved to Manchester, where Mary and Mabel attended school very briefly and were then educated at home by a German governess until they moved to London.[25] In London, Mary and Mabel pursued wide ranging literary tastes and developed individual talents, both girls flourishing under the guidance of parents with foresight and liberal views beyond their time. The Robinson girls were encouraged to strive for excellence, yet neither seems to have felt unduly pressured to be successful at everything she tried. For instance, Mary was given dancing lessons from the age of four; however, although she maintained a lifelong love of art and music and continued dance lessons at the finishing school in Brussels that she and Mabel attended when Mary was fifteen and Mabel fourteen, she remained both inept at and uninterested in dance. Moreover, despite a lifelong affinity for the natural world and for country living, she generally disliked physical activity as a child, which perhaps explains in part the long hours spent in her father's library.[26] The library not only gave her countless hours of pleasure but also enabled her to develop reading and comprehension levels quite remarkable for a child so young, particularly for a girl at that time: she read Froissart at a young age and had read Dante by age twelve.[27] When she was only four years old and could read fluently but could not yet write, she composed nursery rhymes for her patient mother to write down for her. "I was very obstinate in describing things and sensations exactly as I felt and saw them, however absurd or false these descriptions appeared to grown-up people, so ... I may always have been a Preraphaelite without knowing it," she tells Countess Ballestrein.[28] On 5 January 1870, at twelve years old, she penned the poem "Sunset at Kenilworth," and it appeared three days later in the *Leamington Courier*.[29] By her late teens, "she was engaged in two histories, one of Athens and one of Etruria, a comedy, and portraits in prose of twelve 'Ideal Heroines from the Best Authors', which she intended as a present to her mother."[30] Although these projects did not come to fruition on the public market, they indicate the extent to which Robinson from an early age was interested in and devoted to a life of letters.

George Robinson's fluency in French and the German governess in Manchester ensured that Mary and Mabel were proficient in French and German before they went away to school in Brussels, and, not surprisingly, Robinson distinguished herself there in both English literature and German, although she was less successful at arithmetic, drawing, and, of course, dancing. When she and Mabel asked to return to London instead of staying on in Brussels, the sixteen-year-old Mary and fifteen-year-old Mabel were permitted to come back with the proviso that they attend University College London, where, after "a year or so" of general studies she decided to study literature.[31] Mabel entered the Slade School of Art to study under the direction of Alphonse Legros, a French painter who had by that time earned a significant reputation in England, first at the South Kensington School of Art and then at the Slade School at University College. Although Robinson's focus on literature was evidently the right choice for her, Mabel's interest in art ultimately faded and came second to her career as a novelist. Mabel also served as secretary at Bedford College, University of London's college for women. Robinson's scholarly successes and her promise were noted after completion of her first year at University College by the "Ladies' Educational Association," an organization connected to the college that presented her with a certificate of achievement dated 23 May 1874. She received First Class with Honours from Henry Morley, her professor in English literature, who noted on the certificate that she was "one of two ladies who obtained the highest number of marks in the final examination."[32]

Clearly, the environment at home was inspiring and energizing for both women, and it was certainly an environment that fostered the aesthetic presence, the literary acumen, and the intellectual interests that made Robinson memorable to contemporaries throughout her life. As a young woman, Mary Robinson knew that she lived a charmed life and that she had been denied little and given a great deal. To Arthur Symons, Robinson was the "spoilt child of literature," an apt description of her privileged upbringing and precocious literary development.[33] Writing to the family friend Edmund Gosse in 1879, she admits, "to tell the truth I am afraid I have a little too much of books and work and healthful play. But I am very fond of all three." The letter is signed "Yours in the dearest design of industry."[34] In reality, however, Robinson began at an early age to cultivate an aura of "delicacy" that she maintained through her ironically long and relatively healthy life. This persona complemented her aestheticism, her slender build, and her overall refinement, and the culture of delicacy she created influenced her worldview and the perspectvie from which she expressed that view poetically.

Robinson's physical appeal profoundly affected those she met and continued to do so when she was beyond middle age. She was, remembers Pollock, "a young woman of astonishing personal sparkle and wit ... tiny and light as a fairy she was beautifully formed. Her face was a perfect oval, her mouth the legendary cupid's bow. Under a broad forehead, surmounted by a mass of dark hair, eyes nearly as large as saucers were pools of deep, limpid, flashing light, set off by strong, straight eyebrows." Pollock goes on to note that had she been born later, she would have been a Mary Pickford, who "would have knocked Hollywood's beauties endwise, and did indeed somewhat resemble the Mary Pickford of her prime, but with a vivacity, an intelligence, and a brimming delight in things of the mind that no screen heroine could touch."[35] The sketches, paintings, and photographs of Robinson that show her as a young woman convey her awareness of her aesthetic presence as the charming child grew into a woman.

Correspondence between Robinson and her father, her mother, and her sister underscores the closely knit dimensions of the family and indeed suggests a familial conviction that an aesthetic life could only enrich and enhance an intellectual life. When she was at university, Robinson not only excelled academically but she also published poetry and fiction in the *University Magazine*, and she was elected as a member of the Women's Debating Society. In 1902, her friend Hannah Lynch links Robinson's success as a writer to an upbringing that was unusual for her time: "The girl of nineteen, who thought for herself, and went to Greece and Italy for her inspiration … has fulfilled the intellectual promise of that girlhood."[36]

The biographical resources that remain – family letters, anecdotal accounts by friends of George and Frances Robinson, and a few broadly sketched remarks by contemporaries in encyclopedia and anthology entries – suggest that Robinson had no close friends as a young girl outside her immediate family circle, and those with whom she was on friendly terms tended, she told Symonds in 1879, to be fifteen years older than Mabel's friends.[37] She developed literary relationships with Robert Browning, Edmund Gosse, and John Addington Symonds, and these much older friends mentored the young writer. She did enjoy spending time with Helen Zimmern, but it was not until she met Vernon Lee in 1880 that she found a kindred spirit, and even with Lee, Robinson was, at times, reserved. In a letter of 26 November 1884, at the height of their intense friendship, for instance, Lee refers to Robinson's reluctance to commit herself wholly to anyone, telling her, "I know that with your character it is difficult, nay impossible, to give over loving."[38] The context for this awkward remark is Lee's attempt to reassure Robinson that she appreciates what love Robinson can give and returns the feelings wholly. During the period 1880–86, letters between Lee and Robinson tend to reflect insecurities in both women about expressing and receiving love and affection. Nevertheless, the Robinson family's paradoxical ability to remain a self-contained unit while actively constructing a socially oriented life laid the foundation for how Robinson would live the rest of her life as a poet who expressed with equal force in poetry her inner thoughts and hopes and her preoccupation with human history and biography; these thematic threads were related by their tendency to underscore the transience and impermanence of all human life. She seems to have been the contemplative member of the family, the intellectual girl who was also at times introspective and even self-absorbed. However, she found relief in the aesthetic life her parents led, and, in later years, Mary Robinson hosted some of the most sought-after salons in London and in Paris to make her life as rich as possible.

The Robinsons were not a church-attending family, although they counted themselves officially as High Anglican. On returning from school in Brussels, Robinson declared that she was an agnostic, a philosophical perspective she felt was the only intellectually responsible one to adopt but one that she sincerely regretted and tried unsuccessfully to change throughout her life.[39] As she told Maurice Barrès many years later, although she had lived most of her life without a "religion extérieure," if she were to embrace any formal religion late in life, it would be the aesthetically appealing Roman Catholicism.[40] She found a substitute for the aesthetics of religion in the beauty of nature, and she found philosophical and artistic satisfaction in a wide circle of aestheticist friends in London that went beyond her three primary mentors, including William Michael and Lucy Rossetti, Richard Garnett, William and Elizabeth Sharp, William Morris, Holman Hunt, Edward Burne-Jones, Whistler, Arthur Symons, Ford Madox Brown, William Butler Yeats, and Mathilde Blind. John Singer Sargent painted her portrait and Marie Spartali Stillman sketched a very Pre-Raphaelite Robinson.

The Gower Street house was close to where the Pre-Raphaelite Brotherhood had held meetings at 7 Gower Street, and the neighbourhood remained an avant-garde area that would eventually become even more fashionable in the Bloomsbury years. As Ana Vadillo notes, Robinson's position as a published poet drew other women poets in particular to her salons, including "Amy Levy, Louise S. Bevington, Augusta Webster, Emily Pfeiffer, Elizabeth Chapman and Margaret Veley."[41] Writing to John Addington Symonds early in their friendship, she describes the William Rossettis, the Garnetts, and Mathilde Blind as "Shelley-people ... of whom the first are among my dearest friends."[42] Mary and Mabel were regulars at Blind's salons, and later Robinson introduced Blind to Vernon Lee.[43] She describes in a letter to Symonds of 10 November 1879 attending a party given by Oscar Wilde at a hotel in London. Robinson, her mother, and sister thoroughly enjoyed the lavish and excessive atmosphere that Wilde managed to achieve through lighting that left the room, she said, like a Whistler painting.[44] Precisely what she meant is not clear, but she admired Whistler and the implication is that she very much enjoyed the unpredictable nature of an Oscar Wilde fête. At an earlier gathering at the home of Frederic Myers, when Robinson was twenty, she played the role of Cassandra in Myers's informal production of the *Agamemnon*. This event led to her being invited to go to Oxford to stay with Thomas Humphry Ward and his wife, the novelist Mary Augusta Ward, where she met Walter Pater before he and his two sisters became neighbours of the Robinsons on Earl's Terrace in Kensington.[45]

In 1876, Robinson met John Addington Symonds and began an intense friendship that was mainly epistolary in nature but that had a significant influence on her development as a poet. She routinely sent many of her early poems to Symonds, asking for advice, hoping for praise, and occasionally, as in the unpublished "Far-Friendship," poeticizing the close relationship between mentor and pupil that they enjoyed.[46] Symonds was married to a woman he loved and they had four daughters whom he adored; however, he also lived a secret life with male lovers that few of his friends knew about and that he reveals fully in his memoirs. There has been speculation about Symonds's romantic interest in Robinson: Yopie Prins, for instance, sees parallels between Symonds and Robinson that cast his mentorship in the light of "a 'queer' tutelage with his passionate response to Greek literature serving as a model for Robinson to discover the passion of her own literary projections and erotic identifications."[47] Perhaps he intuited a kindred spirit, as Prins suggests, and letters between the two imply that they were each aware that they lived outside the context of conventional heterosexual desire. Symonds shocked Robinson in 1879 when he sent her the poems that were eventually collected in *Old and New* in 1880, telling her that he planned to publish them as part of *Anima Figura*, a highly autobiographical sonnet sequence. She convinced him to keep them separate from the volume, pointing out that he would not like his daughter Janet to see them in the context of *Anima Figura* one day. Her tone and her careful choice of words in this letter indicate her uncertainty about the explicit nature of the poems, but she points out, "there is nothing so dangerous as a dramatic imagination lying about when it's loaded."[48]

It is certainly difficult to believe that Symonds could have had a serious interest in Robinson other than gratification at mentoring a beautiful and talented young woman who clearly adored him personally and respected him professionally. For the most part, her letters to Symonds bespeak her adulation. During 1879 and 1880, she wrote very long letters usually signed "your very grateful little friend," and her gratitude has to do solely with his guidance in her development as a poet. She writes 25 February 1879, for instance, "you see, I am taking your advice and trying to grow out of myself. Of this I am sure – if ever I do become a Poet it will be chiefly owing to your advice and influence. I at least shall always be grateful to God that he made you a Poet – and to you that you made yourself my friend."[49] In an undated letter of the same period, she tells him, "you are my ladder up to Heaven," as she asks him to be patient until she is fully able to understand his comments and analysis of her work. She says that her "soul is newborn and feeble" and that if he becomes impatient and leaves her "there will be no one to teach it to fly."[50] She writes 4 March 1879 to thank Symonds for his comments on "Philumene to Aristides," which she would publish in the *Hippolytus* volume in the early summer of 1881: "I am so glad that you did send me the 'serious advice.' It is what I have been wanting for so long. Years ago I hoped and prayed for a friend or teacher to help me and guide me." Her youth is evident when she admits that although Helen Zimmern asked her for Symonds's "autograph," she could not bear to deface one of his letters to her.[51] On his part, Symonds seems to have accepted his position as assessor and editor of her poetry during these two years in particular, vetting many of the poems that would be published in her first two volumes of poetry. It is interesting that during the late fall of 1878 and early winter of 1879, Symonds was suffering symptoms that he describes to Gosse in a letter dated 25 November 1878 as the "'continuous fever' which is a phase of my illness." He refers to the tuberculosis from which he suffered, and he explains that the persistent cold and neuralgia he could not throw off left him depressed. "The future is very dark before me," he adds.[52]

Robinson's friendship with Symonds became more complicated when she met Vernon Lee, for Symonds and Lee were acutely at odds about nearly everything, including Robinson. Symonds was a powerful figure in literary circles and he and Lee overlapped in scholarly interest in the Renaissance, but it is difficult to understand the animosity Symonds expresses in letters to Lee in the early 1880s. As Phyllis Grosskurth notes, "Symonds's dislike of Vernon Lee was so intense that he appears to have written to her only to get news of Mary."[53] Certainly when he writes to Lee between 1882 and 1884 ostensibly to comment on her work, he refers to Robinson in nearly every letter. Perhaps, as Grosskurth suggests, there was jealousy on Symonds's part that had little to do with romantic love and more to do with his tendency to view Mary Robinson as a daughter figure slightly older than his own girls. As Ruth Holmes writes, "it is difficult to read Symonds' letters to Mary as love-letters, although they were occasionally sent with rose-petals in the envelopes."[54] The correspondence wound down as the decade progressed, but Robinson remained devoted to Symonds and interested in all aspects of his life, including his increasingly poor health. When his eldest daughter Janet died in Italy in April 1884, a concerned and sympathetic Robinson confessed to Gosse that she wrote to Symonds three times that day.[55]

Robinson's friendship with Edmund Gosse was very different in character from her friendship with Symonds. Gosse and his family were old friends of the Robinson family. He was also happily married and had three children, but he too had homosexual desires. He was determined to suppress these desires, however, and did not confess them to his friend Symonds until 1890, thereby confirming suspicions that Symonds had long entertained.[56] Symonds did not at first tell Gosse about his relationship with Robinson, dissembling on 4 February 1879 when Gosse asked him about Robinson and her first book of poetry, actually fibbing about the character and source of his friendship with Robinson. "I am amused that the rumour of my brisk interchange of letters with Miss Robinson sd have reached you: I felt so much interest in her poems that I wrote to her about them; & her answer to that letter drew me into wordy correspondence."[57] Perhaps Symonds was feeling some anxiety about the nature of this correspondence, for this letter coincides with his exchange with Robinson about his questionable poems. While she felt that the poems had aesthetic merit and could well be published separate from *Anima Figura,* Gosse suggested that Symonds "would be led into doing an unwise thing in publishing his poems" at all. Robinson argues that Symonds's "personal and ethical poetry is of real and enduring value."[58] Gosse was not above personal notes either. He wrote "A Ballad of Poetesses" for Robinson, sending it to her on 8 July 1879, and two days later she playfully urged him to write a "chaunt royale" to the memory of the "lesbian ladies."[59]

In retrospect, of course, there is a great deal of subtext in these exchanges, but the triangular relationship of Robinson and two older married men with complicated sexualities seems to have been paradoxically nurtured by her childlike, asexual disposition. To both Symonds and Gosse, Robinson had a tendency to understate her merits, and both men responded with encouragement about and appreciation of lyrics produced to reflect the Pre-Raphaelite lens of her parents' circle through which Robinson viewed the world. Gosse was helpful in practical ways, using his influence in poetic circles to further Robinson's career and bolstering her lack of confidence, not only by arranging for her to meet influential people such as Andrew Lang but also in sending her his own work for review in the *University Magazine.* She writes to him 17 March 1880, "there are no words that say how grateful I feel for your kindness and how much encouraged by it."[60] These were authoritative, yet kind father figures on whom she could depend, and they each enjoyed their relationship with her.

A third older man on whose advice Robinson relied was a poet she very much admired, Robert Browning. She could not believe her good fortune when she met Browning in 1879 on board the Dover–Calais ferry when she and her cat were on deck trying to combat extreme seasickness. Browning evidently gave her something to help with the seasickness, and they remained fast friends. Robinson considered that bout of seasickness one of the most auspicious incidents in her life, exclaiming, "Oh, Poseidon, god of the seas, thanks for having me saved by Browning."[61] In April 1879, Browning sent her a copy of *Dramatic Idylls,* and she visited him several times in the next decade before his death, introducing him as well to Vernon Lee in July 1881.[62] In later years, Maurice Barrès pressed Robinson for information on Browning and his relationship with Barrett Browning, hoping that she might remember anything

Browning might have indicated in his old age that would reveal the rigors of his married life with the older Elizabeth Barrett and that she might elaborate on his man-about-town image after her death. Robinson pointed out that when she met Browning, he was more than sixty years old and she was eighteen (she was in fact a little older) and therefore not acutely aware of such nuances. However, she says she remembers that Browning spoke of his wife constantly and that he told Robinson, "I always feel that she's just in the next room."[63] Whether Browning was always happy in his marriage, she could not say, she told Barrès, but she was very certain that he was happy in his old age each time he reflected on his marriage. She would have more to say about the Browning marriage and the crisis precipitated by their differences with respect to Elizabeth's belief in spiritualism and séances in her 1922 introduction to the publication of a volume of Browning's poetry in French. She describes a visit to Browning to see some of Pen Browning's pictures, with which Robinson was not particularly impressed. "Mr. Browning was very excited about these pictures – it is quite pathetic to see how he loses himself in his rather ordinary son," she tells Symonds. In the same letter, she writes that the following day Browning in turn visited her to see some of her books. She was particularly proud of having a first edition of Milton and reports that "he read quite a bit of Milton to Helen Zimmern and me. It was something always to remember."[64]

Robinson's friendships with other illustrious writers made her London life satisfactory. In addition to Helen Zimmern, she counted as a friend Eleanor Frances Poynter, the sister of the painter Edward Poynter, who preceded Legros at the Slade School of Art. It was Eleanor Poynter who introduced her to Symonds in Bristol in 1876 and who later translated some of her French prose into English for publication in London. She also tried to help Robinson's entry into the world of writing fiction, and, although she did not succeed in the genre, Robinson dedicated her only novel *Arden* to Eleanor Poynter. Robinson came to know Emily Sargent, the sister of John Singer Sargent, who painted both her portrait and Lee's.[65] Emily Sargent in her late years left Robinson and Mabel a small legacy to help them over financial difficulties, and, when Emily died in 1936, Robinson wrote a tributary note for the *Times* (14). By the spring of 1878, Robinson had begun lecturing at the Working Women's College in London, an experience that she found rewarding in theory but more challenging in practice. She suspected that her father, who she felt "had always looked with a discouraging eye on [her] poetical efforts," would not help her in publishing endeavours nor would he "sacrifice his Tory principles to [her] earnest desire" to lecture once a week. However, George Robinson seems to have given in on both counts, paying himself for the publication of Robinson's first volume of poetry rather than having "a dance in [her] honour" and also allowing her to lecture.[66] As she reported to Symonds in this letter, the first lecture "had cost me not hours but days of thought. I had tried so hard to make it thorough and comprehensive and simple and helpful and not too much de haut en bas. And I don't believe two people in the room understood what I wanted to convey." Nevertheless, she had favourite students that she really did feel she was helping to achieve literacy and was still lecturing in 1882, when she took Vernon Lee along one evening. Lee told her mother that there were "three nice looking young women of the well to do shop girl sort," and after describing Robinson's enthusiasm in teaching them about the Lake Poets, Lee adds, "it is worth doing, as of course Mary has to know all that, and it evidently gives them much pleasure & opens a new world to them."[67]

Robinson's life was by and large happy, even though she could be intense when she was determined to find success as a writer. Writing to Symonds in February 1880, she tells him effusively, "just lately I have been living in such a whirl of concerts, operas, theatres, dances, lectures, classes, Women's Rights meetings, and Debates that I have had scarcely time to feel or grieve [not seeing him]."[68] Her family relationships were rewarding and her friendships, although more formal than intimate, were based on common interests in literature, art, and music. She tended to present herself as a "little friend," and her family called her "mouse," but then she was by all accounts a small woman. In correspondence with Gosse and Symonds, she rarely presents herself as physically ill, although she is extremely intimate with Symonds about her emotional health. "You say it is my success (!) that has made me self-conscious – and wish that I had not published; but against this harm it is only fair to set down the good it has done me – increased happiness, sympathy with my fellow creatures, earnestness of striving after right, and most of all, your friendship," she writes not long after the publication of *A Handful of Honeysuckle*.[69] However, although she was happy to be directed in her professional life, Robinson did not allow any of those to whom she was close, including her parents and Mabel, to interfere with the major personal decisions of her life. In matters of the heart, she was always guided by her own instincts, and she could be determined and independent to an extent that shocked those who thought they knew her well.

CHAPTER ONE

A. Mary F. Robinson: "A Born Poet"

❧

A Handful of Honeysuckle

Robinson submitted her first poetry collection to Macmillan and received Frederick Macmillan's rejection 28 July 1877. Macmillan addresses Robinson by her formal first name, Agnes, instead of the preferred Mary, which indicates that he did not know her personally. "We have read the little collection of poems that you left in my hands on Thursday and have been much taken with their beauty and the true poetic feeling they contain," he writes. However, he goes on to indicate that volumes of poetry did not sell well, and, despite assurances that the Robinsons were prepared to defray expenses, the company was reluctant to enter into such an unpromising venture. He suggests that she publish 250 copies privately and offers to help her to prepare the book under these conditions.[1] Robinson declined the offer and went to Kegan Paul, who published *A Handful of Honeysuckle* at the expense of the family and in lieu of the coming out ball that had no appeal for the shy, nondancing Robinson anyway. The charge of £19 plus £4 for advertising was precisely what Macmillan predicted, so the reason for the change in publisher – other than trying her luck in finding someone more enthusiastic – is not clear; however, the volume came out 1 March 1878, two days after Robinson's twenty-first birthday.

Robinson had written many of the poems included in *A Handful of Honeysuckle* when she was still a teenager, yet the volume reflects her precocious insight into human nature and her disciplined approach to technical poetics, attributes that from the outset are defining features of the poet and her poetry. In this first volume, she is adept beyond her years, not only at working within conventional poetic forms but also at manipulating the conventions to explore abstract ideas and philosophical perspectives. These philosophical perspectives on love, death, the spiritual life, the natural world, art, and poetry are compelling, and, as Hannah Lynch writes in 1902, "though *A Handful of Honeysuckle* is a work of first girlhood, there is nothing loose or vague or unfinished about these verses; quite the contrary, we are startled by a surprising and inexplicable maturity of thought and sobriety of expression."[2] In his review for the *Athenaeum* Henry Arthur Bright highlights Robinson's technical competence: "These Honeysuckles are flowers of strangely artificial growth, but they are carefully chosen and skillfully arranged. They have an air of refinement and of fashionable culture about them."[3] The reviewer for the *Saturday Review* chides Robinson for "artistic affectation" but praises her for her "unusual command of metrical language," a response that is very similar to that of Andrew Lang writing for *The Academy* in an earlier review.[4] Although she has "a trick of unconscious imitation," Lang writes, she has "*style*" and "her collection is infinitely superior to most handfuls of lyrical honeysuckles" [emphasis Lang's].[5] The reviewer for the *Spectator* limits his review to the first poem in the volume, but even in its brevity the review itself is complimentary.[6] Ironically, this first success, although gratifying, became an albatross of sorts for Robinson, and, as the correspondence with Symonds demonstrates, she really did worry that she would not in future work be able meet the bar she had set for herself.

In essential ways, *A Handful of Honeysuckle* is very much a young woman's first volume of poetry, most particularly in the prominence of the theme of love and the speaker's idealization of love in the abstract. Jules-Ernest Tissot writes in a biographical note to his chapter on Robinson in his 1909 *Princesses de Lettres* that Robinson told him that she fantasized in her room from the age of seventeen about love. She also said that love did not come to her until her first marriage, which casts her intense relationship with Vernon Lee in an interesting light.[7] As Marandon points out, Robinson tended to highlight this theme in her poetry when she was single and not in love, but in work she produced during her two happy marriages, love recedes to the background. This pattern suggests to Marandon that Robinson was unable to write about love as she was experiencing it herself, which is consistent, I think, with Robinson's shift to more philosophical and historical themes as she grew older.[8] The poetic discourse on love in *A Handful of Honeysuckle* certainly expresses the poet's yearning to experience the unknown and reflects her ability to fuse ideas and images imaginatively. Robinson's contemporary Francis Thompson, whose poetry she admired, rates Robinson's faculty of fantasy above that of imagination and points out that Robinson's treatment of fantastical themes is a feature of her early poetry.[9] Pater confided to Gosse, who had loaned him the book, that he enjoyed *A Handful of Honeysuckle* in principle and the "Ballad of Heroes" in particular.[10] Robinson sent a copy of *A Handful of Honeysuckle* to Dante Gabriel Rossetti, who duly read it and then wrote to Robinson 31 May 1878, "I see you have some command over what belongs to fantasy; though the extremes to which you carry form seem to hamper you sometimes; and indeed the simpler poems please me best." He adds dishearteningly, "if you mean to pursue poetry, I would suggest your taking up some subject which should deal with realities, & seeing what you could make of that. This test should always be resorted to when the natural tendency lies strongly in the other direction."[11] A few years later, Gosse said something along the same lines, urging Robinson to abandon her aestheticist style in favour of something more in the way of realism, and her response to these requests was "The New Arcadia" in 1883.[12]

To develop the metaphor of the title of her first volume, Robinson frames the contents with a "prelude" sonnet titled "Honeysuckle" and a "finale" octave to conclude the collection. Left untitled, the final octave continues the "thorny internal monologue" of the opening sonnet, as Stephanie Burt and David Mikics describe the conventional rhetorical process of the sonnet form.[13] The varied nature of the honeysuckle plant – its fragrance, its mythical links to immortality, and its vining, clinging, and climbing attributes – suitably introduces this eclectic volume of poetry. Robinson learned from a fifteenth-century text in her father's library that the Druids viewed honeysuckle as the physical representation of life's sweetness and potential for beauty, an apt metaphor for the poems that follow.[14] The first line implies that the sonnets are organic, natural "flowers" that the speaker only has to "gather" up for her volume, thus focusing the poems to come in terms of the creative process that comes naturally to her; however, this first quatrain ends with the speaker's recognition of her inexperience and skills not yet mature.

I gather from the hedgerows, where they spring,
These sunshine-yellow flowers, grown sweet i' the air,
Fearing to hope that ye can find them fair,
Who at your wish could have a costlier thing.[15]

In the second quatrain, the speaker extends this apology for her poetics, made of honeysuckle rather than the "roses," "violets," and "laurel crowns" conventionally associated with poetry, and in the sestet, the speaker acknowledges that many of these poems were written some time ago and may resonate as the juvenilia they indeed are:

But these are all I have, and these I give.
True, they have languish'd since they came to town,
As music suffers in the writing down,
And well I know they have not long to live.
Yet for your sakes these left their country ways,
That, taken thence, are grown too poor for praise.

In comparing her published poetry with music that has been transformed into notes on paper, she conveys her anxiety as she turns her work over to others to interpret and assess it. These are concerns to which she returns in the closing octave, once again asking for tolerance and patience as she matures as a poet and pleading for sympathy and understanding from other poets, who have at hand "rose and lily bowers" from which to fashion the "costlier" poetry to which she refers in the opening sonnet. She seems to be speaking directly to Symonds as she pleads poetically for the patience that she was asking of him in her letters of this time. There is some irony, then, in the fact that critical reception of the volume far exceeded what Robinson anticipates in this framing poetic apology, and what "pity" she may have garnered for subsequent work, expressed both formally and informally, emphasized the trial of setting for herself such a high bar in an early work.

A Handful of Honeysuckle includes a variety of lyrics – thirteen sonnets that follow the prelude, a few ballads, and other diverse lyrical forms. Some of the sonnets no doubt issue from the young girl that Tissot describes alone in her room yearning for love and speculating on the emotions associated with the experience of romantic love and on the potential for expressing love in poetry. These sonnets

indicate how early Robinson adopted the aestheticist perspective
on love and death and regretted intensely, even in her youth, that
love could only be characterized in terms of the finite nature of an
individual life. She is at her best in managing the sonnet form when
she avoids abstraction and when she resists idealizing her subject
in vague terms. "Love's Epiphany," "A Dreamer," and the paired
sonnets "Maiden Love" and "Woman's Love," for instance, are less
successful in conveying the power of love than are the ballads of this
volume that reflect her extensive reading history. When she situates
love in more specific terms, linking it, for instance, to its role as an
enduring poetic theme, such as in the ekphrastic sonnet "The Laurel
Bearer," she is more successful. Subtitled "For a Picture," and possibly
inspired by Frederic Leighton's 1876 painting "Daphnephoria," this
sonnet reflects the integration of her astute creative imagination and
her accumulated knowledge of history and the classics. She draws
here on the complex associations of Apollo, not only with athletic
and military competition and the Greek extension of competition
to poetry, but also with Apollo's passion for Daphne, doomed by the
vengeful god of love, Eros. This history informs the context in which
the speaker in the octave, the young laurel bearer of Leighton's painting carrying the traditional tribute to Apollo, voices his confusion
about the fact that men have died for such an honour:

> The bells to-day ring welcomes through the town,
> As slowly down the sunny, crowded ways,
> Where country folk compare old holidays,
> I bear these laurels for the victor's crown.
> Strange – that for this men lay life gladly down,
> That from the cool growth of these unknown sprays,
> Their hands may grasp a weight of withering bays,
> Dead emblems of immortalized renown! (67)

The boy speaker participating in this ceremony that occurred only
every nine years has not had the benefit of history to understand the
relationship between love, death, and poetry. However, the nineteenth-
century speaker of the sestet, understanding this complex relationship
and the enduring elements of poetry and of art, urges a renewed
primacy of Apollo and the laurel crown in the context of poetry as a

vehicle of love and the laurel crown as a celebration of that context. "King Love, arise in glory and refute / These hollow claims of honour born of harm," the speaker says, and

Stand forth with life's elixir in thine eyes
God's poet, with our heart-strings for thy lute
Who changest all our sorrow to a psalm
That listening angels learn in Paradise. (67)

The religious imagery in these final lines links the mythological god to the Judeo-Christian God, thereby highlighting the tremendous power of poetry to convey the human need for love.

Robinson's focus on poetic power and poetic expression comes to fruition in one of the most beautiful sonnets in this volume, which, in 1880, Vernon Lee took as her epigraph for and quoted in its entirety to centre her argument in her essay "A Dialogue on Poetic Morality." Lee included this essay, which originally appeared in the *Contemporary Review* in January 1881, in *Belcaro* a few months later. Lee's discourse with Robinson, to whom she dedicated *Belcaro*, begins in the introduction to the volume, where Lee records the circumstances in which she conceived her ideas about art that unfold in "A Dialogue." In dedicating the whole of *Belcaro* to Robinson, she explains in the dedication itself, she hopes to "influence those young enough and powerful enough to act upon these ideas; and, this being the case," she continues, "my first thought is to place them before you: it is, you see, a matter of conversion, and the nearest, most difficult, most desired convert, is yourself." Lee expresses the significance of the day spent with Robinson, a day that inspired her to collect together essays on the aesthetics of art: "the memory of that winter day seems as real as the present reality of this summer one; and *haunts* me still, as I write these words, even as it has *haunted* me throughout the putting together of this book, which I have called, from that *haunting* remembrance, and, perhaps, a little also that the association might make it more pleasant in your eyes, by the name of that strange, isolated, ilex-circled castle villa of Belcaro" [emphasis mine].[16] The details of this "haunting" episode unfold in "A Dialogue" and have to do with Robinson's tendency to be abstract in her *Honeysuckle* volume, published, of course, before Lee actually

met Robinson. In the dedication note, Lee summarizes the fruit of
her meeting Robinson, who has led her to think "about what each
art can and cannot do, about the relations of the various arts amongst
each other and to their artists … what value, in this world of good
and evil, of doubt and certainty, of action and inaction, in this world
struggling for physical and social and moral good, what value have
æsthetical questions at all?"[17] Lee is more specific with reference to
this particular sonnet in her letter of 19 November 1880, which she
wrote soon after their original meeting: "I feel that your very noble
sonnet strikes a very resonant string in myself. But here again it seems
to me that you are carried too far by reaction. Behind every artist
there is a human being, & the human being & its human worthiness
is more important than the artist & his artistic perfection."[18] This
practicality of art and its function in the real world is indeed the
premise upon which Baldwin (Lee) builds his argument to Cyril
(Robinson) in the "Dialogue":

> The poet is the artist, remember, who deliberately chooses as
> material for his art the feelings and actions of man; he is the
> artist who plays his melodies, not on catgut strings or metal
> stops, but upon human passions; and whose playing touches
> not a mere mechanism of fibres and membranes like the ear,
> but the human soul, which in turn feels and acts; he is the artist
> who, if he blunders, does not merely fatigue a nerve or paralyze
> for a moment a physical sense, but injures the whole texture of
> our sympathies and deadens our conscience.[19]

Lee's sense that poetry originates in human emotions and is at the
same time a human expression of those emotions explains her use of
"Sonnet" as an epigraph. Robinson's poem speaks of a divine envoy
sent on a Shelleyean mission to reform the world who learns instead
how little he understands about the workings of the world.

God sent a poet to reform His earth.
But when he came and found it cold and poor,
Harsh and unlovely, where each prosperous boor
Held poets light for all their heavenly birth,
He thought – Myself can make one better worth

The living in than this – full of old lore,
Music and light and love, where Saints adore
And Angels, all within mine own soul's girth. (65)

The speaker's optimism moves quickly to an expression of hubris that
the poetic activity of creation – or re-creation – will transform God's
creation into a heavenly place. However, in the sestet, God brings
the speaker up short for this misrepresentation of heaven as an ideal:

But when at last he came to die, his soul
Saw Earth (flying past to Heaven) with new love,
And all the unused passion in him cried:
O God, your Heaven I know and weary of.
Give me this world to work in and make whole,
God spoke: Therein, fool, thou hast lived and died!

Robinson articulates poetically in the sestet the position of her alter
ego Cyril in "A Dialogue," who justifies destroying his verses in
terms of the impracticality of poetry, unable to understand, like the
youth of "The Laurel Bearer," the power of poetry to move us to
carry out great actions to make the world a better place: "You know
that since some time I have been asking myself what moral right a
man has to consume his life writing verses, when there is so much
evil to remove," Cyril comments.[20] Cyril's resentment of Baldwin for
first suggesting a perspective on poetry along these lines and then
retracting that perspective to write "in half-a-dozen letters, that the
sole duty of the artist is to produce good art, and that good art is
art which has no aim beyond its own perfection" perhaps explains
Cyril's recitation of the entire sonnet.[21] Baldwin's argument for the
aesthetic pleasure of poetry as a means of earthly "reform" indeed
reflects the text of letters exchanged between Lee and Robinson at
this time and for the years following as Robinson experimented with
poetic form and subject, as well as with prose fiction and nonfiction.
It is notable that she was thinking of these issues before she met Lee
and before Lee transformed their conversations into "A Dialogue
on Poetic Morality."

The themes that Robinson develops in this first volume encompass
various aspects of poetry and its "affect," particularly with respect to

Robinson's articulation of Pater's regret at the "splendor" and the "awful brevity" of our existence, as he writes in the Conclusion to the *Renaissance*.[22] She expresses this regret as the elusive and ephemeral "afterlife" of material things, which indirectly manifests itself in scents, sounds, and visual images that linger as evidence of transient physical objects. In "Thanksgiving for Flowers," for example, the transience of floral beauty underscores the paradoxical role of flowers as they increase the aesthetic joy of living, even as they represent death and mourning. The speaker addresses directly the one who has gifted the flowers in language that emphasizes the transience of all life, and the sonnet quickly assumes a funereal perspective:

> You bring me flowers – behold my shaded room
> Is grown all glorious and alive with Light.
> Moonshine of pallid primroses, and bright
> Daffodil-suns that light the way of the tomb. (74)

These lovely flowers "mourn for Sappho," the speaker continues, thereby linking the suicide of the primal poetess to the transience of life as it is represented in this sonnet. As she thinks of various flowers waning and fading into sad "memorials," she realizes that her existence is as temporal and temporary as these blooms:

> My flowers, my dreams and I shall lie as dead!
> Flowers fade, dreams wake, men die; but never dies
> The soul whereby these things were perfected, –
> This leaves the world on flower with memories.

The subtle shift in meaning of "on flower" in this last sentence points to the power of poetry as it represents the human soul as an unseen and intangible evidence of existence, just like the scent of flowers that lingers, first physically and then in memory. The allusion to Sappho lingers as well in this sonnet that paradoxically celebrates rather than mourns transient beauty. The speaker's "thanksgiving" of the title, then, has to do with flowers as a reminder that there are means of transcendence other than the certainty of a Christian God. Robinson's development of this theme of endurance appears in other poems: the speaker of "Past and Present," as the title suggests, likens the "great aims in youth" to "fair unfruitful flowers," and in both "At Sunset" and "A Search for Apollo," the poetic voice hopes to find resolution of the paradox of impermanence in the legacy of poetry, the former positioning the speaker both at the close of day and the close of life and the two sequenced Spenserian sonnets of the latter conceding that insight into an abstract "truth" may always be out of reach. Hence, we see how Robinson's early poetry antici-pates the conversations she would have with Lee, and Lee's rein-scription of "A Sonnet" in her "Dialogue" acknowledges Robinson's developing aesthetics.

While the sonnets "Siren Singing," "Death's Paradise," "Lethe," and "Song" are all concerned with simultaneous desire to escape and endure the pain of love and life, the five verses that make up "Octaves from Death's Gamut" explore the ways in which the breadth, the range, the spectrum, and the inevitability of death can usefully define how we tend to live our lives. These octaves are unified by the tension between compulsive yearning to transcend death and the compelling evidence of physical decay and dissolution that marks the end of life. The speaker's quest for resolution of the tension begins with implied bravado in the first octave, as though the quest itself leads to empowerment in understanding the diverse guises in which "Death" lives among us:

> I sought for Death through many nights and days,
> At last I met a minstrel tall and young
> Who by the fountain in the market place
> Played on a golden harp (with heart-strings strung)
> Whereat all hearers sang aloud his praise.
> But I who joined not in the songs they sung
> Saw 'neath each singer's smile the paling face
> And heard the death-sigh in each chord he wrung. (29)

And so the speaker aims to reveal the undercurrent of our preoccu-pation with the unknowable through a series of metaphorical "songs" that suggest the possibility of transcendence: iconic saintly images in the second octave; illnesses that bring us to the brink of death and then recovery that wipes away the temporary "faith" linked to the process of dying in the third; the experience of witnessing death that

banishes fear of the inevitable in the fourth; and in the final octave
in the doppelganger effect when, for a brief moment, the speaker
realizes that this preoccupation is in itself a kind of death in life:

> Death held a glass before my eyes; Behold,
> He cried. I saw outside a busy mart
> A miserable man alone and old,
> Worn with weary years and sick at heart,
> For none would buy the merchandise he sold. (30)

The old man, of course, is the speaker, and in the final tercet it is
revealed that in devoting his life to unearthing death, he has, like
God's emissary who attracted Lee's attention in "Sonnet," neglected to live. In this moment of truth, he sees himself as a "singing
Angel crowned with gold," as an alternative, Death suggests, to a
life devoted to denial and negation. Thus, the poem suggests, the
reasonable philosophical perspective on death is to accept that it
is inevitable and unknowable; therefore, we need to focus instead
on life.

In his review, Lang highlights "Will" as an example of excellence in Robinson's reiteration of the difficulty in negotiating this
world – the only certainty we have. Lang situates "Will" as a tribute
to Schopenhauer, and indeed, the speaker's counsel, unfolding in four
rhyming couplets that mark off the stages in the speaker's reasoning,
points to the importance of self-determination. Human will, says
the speaker, is paradoxically powerful and limiting in this respect:

> The world is a garment for me to wear
> The days are my glance and the dark my hair.
> Alone in the kingdom of space I stand
> With Hell and Heaven in either hand.
> Life is the smile, Death the sigh of me,
> Who was, who am, who shall ever be.
> Men and their gods pass away, but still
> I am maker and end, I am God, I am Will. (53)

The speaker thus views the world as a Carlylean "garment" that
gives the spiritual a human shape and form, and the world itself as

representation of one "Will" named "God." In selecting rhyming couplets to develop this complex allegory of the world as representation, Robinson uses end rhymes to underscore the ways in which it seems to her in these poems of her youth that all philosophical perspectives reflect in essential ways that of Plato, and she struggles here and in later poetry not only with a preoccupation with the tension between appearance and reality but also with the pessimism to which this duality inevitably leads. Many years later, James Darmesteter would call her his "little platonicienne."[23]

When she writes about love in the ballad form, with which she went on to have continued success, Robinson is able in the narrative patterns of the ballad to demonstrate her impressive knowledge of history. "A Rime of Two Lovers" is the only poem in the volume that the *Spectator* critic mentions, writing that it "is a little poem of such sterling value, that we need not go further to be assured of Miss Robinson's poetical capacities."[24] The poetic voice framing this story of love taken from Boccaccio's *The Decameron* dedicates the verses to "all lovers, all who are beloved" and invites them to celebrate their fortune by listening to this tale of persistence and endurance in love (1). The narrative of Constance and Martuccio, who fall in love during their childhood in ancient Sicily, is contextualized by a complex setting that is sensuous and exotic, yet at the same time pastoral, with the consequent intermingling of eroticism and innocence.

This narrative of love is not in itself distinctive: class divides the lovers when they reach adulthood, and Martuccio leaves for Barbary to win the fortune needed to ask for Constance's hand in marriage. However, Robinson's metaphors evoke the poignancy and the promise of sexual fulfillment in their concentration on the closeness of the bodies of the lovers as they prepare to part:

> Once more against the fountain side
> They lean together, breast on breast;
> Her passionate eyes are strain'd and wide,
> Her wild hair veils her crimson vest,
> And while those sad eyes seek his face,
> With claspt white hands she prays for grace,
> Leave me not, leave me not – tears drown the rest. (4)

Through these anapestic rhyming patterns, suggests Ben Glaser, Robinson ably expresses "female longing."[25] The rest of the story – the mistaken news a year later that Martuccio is dead, Constance's attempted suicide and subsequent fortuitous arrival at Barbary, where Martuccio has survived a shipwreck to become "the most powerful prince" – emphasizes the strength of their love. In eliminating a character central to Boccaccio's tale, the serving woman Carapresa, who in Boccaccio is essential to the reunion, Robinson emphasizes the mystical and fantastical elements of chance and coincidence upon which "true love" depends. Constance's assumption that she and Martuccio are "in Paradise" is an early example of Robinson's tendency to use that specific word to refer to an earthly rather than a heavenly state, and certainly her Pre-Raphaelite influences are clear in the physicality of Constance's final reclaiming of her lover:

> Then all her passion overcame
> A maid who knew no maiden's art,
> And calling on Martuccio's name
> She threw herself upon his heart. (13)

Robinson successfully subverts the didacticism inherent in the ballad form and uses this convention to highlight and champion Constance's directness, honesty, and daring in matters of love.

A second ballad, "Queen Rosalys," is more conventionally developed through the use of a refrain, a strategy that Andrew Lang criticizes in his review for the *Academy* as "not only superfluous but now positively unfashionable."[26] Arguably, however, the refrain not only enhances the musicality of this ballad of thirty-eight stanzas but also creates an insidious contrast between Rosalys's outer manifestation of love and a darker, meaner side that love brings out in her. The two refrains repeated in alternate stanzas pair "fair" with "beware" and "rare" with "snare" to highlight this contrast in the first two stanzas and act as a unifying thread as the ballad narrative unfolds:

> Queen Rosalys was in her tower
> *(And hey but she was fair!)*
> Her mouth was red as any flower
> And soft her voice as a summer shower.

(But 'ware my bird and beware)
Queen Rosalys look'd east and west,
(Red rose and lily rare)
She sought the lover she loved best,
She gave her shining eyes no rest.
(Fine flowers cover a snare.) (14, italics Robinson's)

The warnings are for Queen Rosalys's lover, Sir Edward, who not only arrives late for their "tryst" but tells Rosalys that he is returning to his "Lady" in England. Rosalys's revenge in the form of a curse on "the woman my love loves best" ultimately and ironically becomes a curse on Rosalys herself, thereby recasting the didactic impulse of the refrain to highlight love as a potentially self-destructive force. Robinson uses the refrain and repetition as a unifying balladic feature to great effect in "Cockayne Country," the title of which refers to the form of satire attributed to Lucian in the second half of the thirteenth century in Ireland. Lucian describes an ideal land, where life is easy and luxurious, with wonderful, exotic foods and a liberal sexual life available to all; Robinson describes through the rhyming couplets an ideal island off the west coast of Spain that offers a "wel of goodness," as the epigraph promises, to those who can imagine it. In concluding each of the four octaves with the parenthetical reminder "(But it is far away)," she highlights the elusive nature of the fantasy possible in the imagined Cockayne country, where "all poets live at peace, / And lovers are true they say" (58).

Rossetti found poetic realism lacking in this volume, and the fact is that the socially grounded "Lover's Lane" and "The Street Singer," both which develop the fallen woman theme, are less technically convincing than when she works within the world of romance. It may be that the context of romance itself seemed to offer endless possibilities to the youthful poet, enabling imaginative freedom that also enabled technical experimentation. "To a Dragon Fly," for example, which is written in the distinctive rhyming patterns of the Welsh Cyhydedd Hir, stands out in this volume, notes the *Spectator*.[27] In this technically sophisticated poem, Robinson condenses the usual pentametre lines of the Cyhydedd Hir to tetrametre lines, which, along with the tight rhyming patterns aaabcccb, emphasizes the speaker's feeling of restriction and limitation in having entered into the material, adult world of love. The poem opens with the speaker's recognition of the dragonfly as a kindred spirit that has emerged, like she, from the world of romance:

> You hail from Dream-land, Dragon-fly?
> A stranger hither? So am I,
> And (sooth to say) I wonder why
> We either of us came,
> Are you (that shine so bright i' the air)
> King Oberon's state-messenger?
> Come tell me how my old friends fare,
> Is Dream-land still the same? (23)

The speaker names the inhabitants of this world in subsequent stanzas, citing King Arthur, the Red-Cross Knight, Caliban, Guinevere, and others of medieval romance, thereby reflecting Robinson's interest in medieval life and medieval history. As Marandon points out, the shape of the dragonfly is reminiscent of a chivalric knight.[28] This remarkably agile insect of modern day moves quickly in all six directions and sees equally well from all perspectives, thereby evoking its formidable mythical ancestor, the dragon. The dragonfly is associated with nuanced perception of change in its environment as it skims along the water, perception that in literary terms symbolically represents the understanding of life that comes with maturing and that in this poem is linked to the responsibility associated with love. This theme is given context in the final stanza with the speaker's rejection of love in this transitional world and her vow to return to the fantasy land and the idealized love of medieval romance:

> Ah, I have been too long away!
> No doubt I shall return some day,
> But now I'm lost in love and may
> Not leave my Lady's sight.
> Mine is, (of course), the happier lot,
> Yet – tell them I forget them not,
> My pretty gay compatriot,
> When you go home to-night. (24)

Hence, the real "home" of the speaker is the fairy world, and she patiently accepts her place in the transitional and transient world of human experience because she is only temporarily away from the world to which she belongs. Several years earlier, in July 1876, Robinson responded to a gift of a sketch of a dragonfly from Margaret Symonds, the third daughter of John Addington, with a poem she titled "A Fable: To Madge" and it serves as a prototype for this version in *Honeysuckle*.[29]

Robinson was also at this early stage quite familiar with the French ballade, a form with a complicated rhyme scheme more difficult to maintain in English than in French. Robinson's "A Ballad of Lost Lovers" and "A Ballad of Heroes" both modify the conventional rhyme scheme, but they are nevertheless successful ballades of four eight-line stanzas, the last line of each an italicized refrain, and a final four-line envoy. Both poems in this collection reflect her preoccupation with the transience – with the brevity – of life as it is represented in poetry. The great loves depicted in "A Ballad of Lost Lovers" are now, as the refrain indicates, "*half-remembered and half-forgot*," and the heroic acts of myth and history depicted in "A Ballad of Heroes," are, as the refrain suggests, similarly obscured by the passage of time: "*Now all your victories are in vain*" (61, 76). In the former poem, the grand lovers of literature remind us of the transience of human love and human memory, and in the latter, Walter Pater's favourite, this same sense of impermanence is developed in terms of historical significance. So many heroic deeds performed in history, the speaker suggests, are now completely meaningless, and wars fought long ago are forgotten. The Envoy underscores the futility of such acts in the long run:

O kings, bethink how little is
The good of battles or the gain –
Death conquers all things with his peace
When all your victories are in vain. (77)

One of the more interesting ballads in this collection, however, alternates modern French with old French in a four-line refrain at the end of each of the three stanzas. The first stanza of "In Apollo's Garden" demonstrates the effect of this intricacy of diction and form:

In King Apollo's garden
About the summer's prime,
When plums and peaches harden
Before their melting time,
I love to stray the live-long day because no otherwhere
The paths are made so dark with shade, the plots so fresh
    and fair.
Where the coolest shade is,
Where clear the waters flow,
Poets lead fair ladies
They sang of long ago;
Sont tous amans fidèles
Chantant au bord des eaulx,
Les belles damoiselles,
Les Beaulx damoiseaulx. (42; italics Robinson's)

The fruit at its peak in the first stanza suggests the ironic paradox
that Robinson's admired Robert Browning repeatedly develops –
fruition not only marks the end of anticipation but also heralds decay,
deterioration, and death. The speaker is led in the next lines to see her
surroundings as a source of poetic inspiration, and she slips into old
French in a refrain that depicts men and women inspired as well to
express their love in the midst of such beauty. In the second and final
sections, the refrain continues to act as a liaison between past and
present, bringing the speaker to consciousness that, just as the seeds
of the plants that grow in her nineteenth-century garden are blown
on the wind to transform and transfigure this place of beauty, so she
too has been brought to this point by an unknown, metaphorical
"wind," and, like the lost "damoiselles" and "damoiseaulx," she does
not know where it will ultimately take her: "But what wind brought
me hither," she concludes in the last lines preceding the final refrain,
"And whither shall I go?" (43). The garden has served its purpose in
reminding her of her own place in the passage of time.

    In other poems, this consciousness of passing time is linked not
to a nostalgic evocation of the past but to an abstract yearning for
transcendence of the present. Robinson effectively uses synesthesia,
the intermingling of the senses, to replace the refrain of longer poems
in short lyrics such as "Dawn-Angels," "Dawn," "Spring Song," and

"Rejoice" in order to convey the speaker's imagined immaterial world. In "Dawn-Angels," for example, the shifting ethereal images belonging to the interstices of day and night simultaneously herald the day even as they cling to the last vestiges of night, and in "Dawn," these same interstitial spaces are particularly nuanced in the opening lines:

> There is no bird as yet awake,
> The earth is drunk with night,
> The hollow heavens hold in check
> A wave of opal light. (52)

Hannah Lynch comments on the sophisticated restraint in this poem that distinguishes Robinson from established poets, even, she notes, Rossetti: "Not a word here is used for the mere pleasure of eye or ear, which is a signal proof of wisdom at twenty."[30] A good example of this artistry appears in the second stanza, where "shine" not only suggests the physical "unearthly" nature of the dawn light but also underscores the speaker's spiritual connection to the divine in this moment:

> Unearthly light! The stars are set
> That saw the moon's decline,
> The sun is not arisen yet,
> And still these heavens shine!

When the sun appears in the third and final stanza, it seems to the speaker to be a "flaming sword" that cuts through this magical light, and again diction in the final line of the poem to herald the "re-arisen Day" rather than the more conventional "new day" situates the cyclical nature of worldly existence in an allusion to the Christ figure that promises renewal of a spiritual life as well.

When Robinson alludes in her early poetry to heavenly elements such as these, she does so less in the context of formal religion than in the context of Baudelaire and his system of correspondences between the real world and an imagined ideal paradise, a perspective closely related to the English Romanticist view of God as orchestrator of the ways in which the natural world offers insight into a spiritual ideal. In "A Vision of Storm," for instance, the mystical experience of transience originates in the speaker's contemplative gaze at large grey rocks that hold the "unrecorded monuments / of a forgotten world" (27). In the mind of the speaker, these "monuments" take the shape of a Titan woman, the mythological female goddess of the giants who ordered heavenly cycles. Not having participated in the war against the Olympians, she retained a great deal of her power and influence when the war was lost, and Robinson casts the wild seas under her control. She is, therefore, a gendered symbol of the strength of neutrality and reason, with the rising and receding metrical patterns suggesting the timeless and enduring force of nature, for "in her eyes that never weep / lightnings are laid asleep" (27). In other poems, the poetic perspective is more subtly infused with the emotional lens through which the speaker gazes. In "A Grey Day" internal couplets and tetrametre lines depict a landscape of grey in both sea and sky that eventually permeates the speaker's consciousness:

> I wait alone in a stranger's land,
> By unremembered floods I stand,
> Whose shores unhaunted are.
> I sorrow and who shall comfort me?
> The wide grey sky or the wide grey sea,
> Or Love that lingers afar? (47)

Rhyme links the speaker's loneliness for someone not with her to the grey seascape that stands between her and the one who implicitly chooses to stay away. The synesthetic power of the colour grey lies as well in the implied muted and unresponsive landscape that increases the speaker's feelings of isolation. Robinson achieves the same effect in "Foreboding," with rhyming patterns alternating in the first four lines and couplets in the last four to develop the familiar paradox of anticipation and fruition – while spring promises the joy of summer, it also reminds the speaker that autumn is in sight as well; this seasonal governance of poetic mood emerges again in "Winter and Spring," as the trochaic first lines of each of the two stanzas give urgency to the speaker's request to sing for the arrival of spring: "Shout and sing for the Spring is here! / Laugh and dance, for Winter's away," the speaker says enthusiastically in the first of the two stanzas; however, by the second stanza the speaker is more subdued as she realizes the broader philosophical implications of transitional phases in the natural world: "Sing if you will that Spring is here, / But heave a sigh for Winter away; / Poor Winter that was Spring last year" (60). We find perhaps the most successful integration of the Romanticist perspective on the paradoxical duality of nature as both awe inspiring and fearsome in its inexorable and unpredictable force in "Song of a Stormy Night." The conflation of the speaker's mood with the intensifying storm is conveyed through rhyming couplets. This rhyming pattern suggests the speaker's increasing panic as the anticipatory moments of the storm and its climax seem to her to mirror a similarly inevitable climax of life in death:

> In my pale garden yesternight
> The statues glimmered ghastly-white,
> The brooding trees that haunted me
> Flapped dusky wings despairingly.
> Both air and sky death-heavy were,
> But oh my heart was heavier,
> For life (I said) is useless grief,
> And death an undesired relief. (78)

The rest of the poem unfolds in the vein of these opening lines, which, Ana Vadillo points out, are equally expressive of how the speaker sees the landscape and her state of mind.[31] As the storm rages in the next two stanzas the speaker, in perfect union with the wild elements, undergoes a type of exorcism until, at the conclusion of the fourth stanza, she feels that her "heart was freed / from the storm of desire" (79). In the final stanza, iambic tetrametre couplets now have a different effect and indicate a new calm, with speaker and nature cleansed by the parallel storms:

> My lilies passion-sweet are dead,
> Love's purple, royal roses shed,
> But heart and garden are besprent
> With flowers of patience and content.

As Marandon recognizes, Robinson's use of the archaic "besprent" to mark the cleansing effect of the storm works in accordance with her nuanced description of the age-old response to natural and human passions as transformative processes.[32]

In his review for the *Athenaeum*, Bright objects to what he calls "affectations" in Robinson's style; however, in "Paradise Fancies," which the friendlier Lang calls "pretty and scrappy" in his review for the *Academy*, Robinson arguably develops a sophisticated metaphor through an apple with which the angels play and which they lose as it goes out of bounds and lands beside a chapel on earth.[33] The theme of this poem is religious hypocrisy, not a particularly innovative theme, perhaps, but the poem foreshadows Robinson's later fascination with and personal interest in Renan and in the concept of truth. There is a Rossetti-like suggestion of the sacrilegious in this depiction of a heavenly love in the opening stanza:

> Last night I met mine own true love
> Walking in Paradise,
> A halo shone above his hair
> A glory in his eyes.
> We sat and sang in alleys green
> And heard the angels play,
> Believe me, this was true last night
> Though it is false to-day. (48)

In 1889, Amy Levy recognized Robinson's perceptive and subtle play on words in this first section and took the last two lines as her epigraph for "The Dream," published in *Plane Tree and other Verse*. These lines highlight the paradox of the dream world that is in the absolute sense "true" while it unfolds within the subconscious; however, as a "dream" this world is "false" in its real-world context. The ambiguous nature of the love that Robinson depicts – whether it is a dead love remembered or a wholly fantastical ideal – is central to our understanding of the powers of fantasy, for only in an imagined paradise, the speaker demonstrates in the rest of the poem, can we find a world that permits a perfect synesthetic integration of the senses through colour, music, and scented flowers as the angels play with the iconic apple that they have taken from the "Tree of Life." Marandon suggests that this poem demonstrates Robinson's ability to use traditional flowers to evoke a mood or melody and she suggests as well that "Paradise Fancies" is a prototype of Robinson's dominant style of fantasy.[34] When the apple leaves the boundaries of the angels' game and rolls into the world, the "old priest" who finds it sees only a "battered apple" that needs to be tossed far away from the chapel. Therefore, this agent of the church who is meant to be an intermediary between earth and paradise fails to recognize this Baudelairean "correspondence."

Lang also has much to say about "In the Organ Loft," another poem about the intersection of heavenly and earthly realms. This is the first of several poems that Robinson would subsequently write in which music is the intermediary through which the speaker, successfully this time, enters into a state of spiritual awakening. Lang praises particularly the opening stanzas, writing, "these lines, full of melody and sentiment, are the key-note of the poems, which themselves are rich with the long sunsets and lingering visions of youth."[35]

> In the brown old organ-loft,
> Rose and gold with sunset fire,
> I sat playing loud and soft
> Dreaming out my heart's desire.
> Till the room was filled with sound
> Thrilled with music glad and strong,
> Sad and long, it swelled around,
> Burst and blossom'd into song. (37)

The organ-playing speaker in an enclosed church loft is transported through music to a spiritual reunion with his dead loved one. The church setting, the organ, and the implied transcendence through the impermeable divide between the finite and the infinite all suggest that the speaker attains the impossible – union with the divine. The poem hinges, however, not on a successful transcendence of this nature but on the speaker's disappointment in discovering that this divide is formed not only by the death of the woman he loves but also by her liaison with God. He "finds" her, so to speak,

Long white hands clasp'd prayerfully,
Eyes that love not but adore,
Seeing God, forgetting me,
Evermore and evermore. (39)

It is telling that when the speaker tries to transcend this boundary between the infinite and the finite by praising God himself, the connection is broken and

All was gone
And the silence seemed to be
Thunder, where I sat alone.

The image with which we are left is that of Rossetti's "Blessed Damozel" leaning over the bar, as in the final quatrain of the poem the speaker emerges out of this moment of epiphany and is unable to "bring that vision back again" even though he plays the music all night long.

The idea of transcendence, then, takes a number of conventional forms in this first volume of poetry – religious transcendence, transcendence through nature ("A Pastoral"), and transcendence through idealized love ("Love Stronger than Death"). Although these lyrics are less distinguished than "In the Organ Loft," the general idea of replacing religious conviction with some philosophical perspective on the human condition was clearly a preoccupation of the young Mary Robinson. On the other hand, some of Robinson's more philosophical poems of this time foreshadow the intellectual writer and poet into which she developed steadily in both English and French. The poetically complex "A Dialogue," for example, uses the natural world to contrast gendered perceptions in verses of seven lines each, within which a woman speaks in alternating rhyme and the man in a couplet, which is then followed by a return to the original rhyme. Moreover, the first six lines of each stanza follow the rhyming pattern of the English sestet but the added seventh line, with its link to the first line of the poem, brings the verse full circle to close the dialogue. This rhyming pattern sets the woman's extended aesthetic response to the natural world in contrast to the man's terse practical response. In the opening four lines, the woman conveys through her parenthetical "alas" her regret that natural cycles, in this case dandelions and ladysmocks, must come to an end:

> *She.* The dandelions in the grass
> Are blown to fairies' clocks,
> On this green bank I pluckt (Alas)
> The last of lady-smocks.

The man is pragmatic in his response:

> *He.* Let them die,
> What care I?
> Roses come when field flowers pass.

In the second stanza, the rhymes of "hours" and "flowers," as well as alliteration, convey the woman's elevated anxiety about the transient nature of the flowers that have become for her representative of all living things:

> *She.* But these sun-sated sultry hours
> Will make your roses fall,
> Their large wide-open crimson flowers
> Must die like daisies small.

Once again, the man replies in shortened metre and the tightened rhyme of a couplet that emphasizes his view that this passing of natural life is insignificant because nature inevitably renews itself:

> *He.* Sweet as yet!
> I'll forget
> (When they die) they lived at all! (40)

In situating this discourse on nature as a means to a more philosophical discussion of transience in terms of gender, Robinson highlights the relationship between gender and perspective in even the simplest human experience of the natural world.

The young and insightful Robinson's ability to present even the most playful lyrics in technically astute metrics foreshadows

the mature poet. In the historically inspired "Fiametta: A Sequence,"
Robinson recasts Boccaccio's novel, transforming the young, married
Fiametta from the woman who gives a first-person account of her
illicit love of Panfilo, a merchant of Florence, into the "little flame"
that her name suggests. The poetic perspective of this triolet sequence
of twelve stanzas is that of the man who has fallen in love with this
"angel," as he calls her in the first stanza:

> Behind the Rector's lily-bed
> I saw an Angel pass,
> A halo shone behind her head
> Behind the Rector's lily-bed,
> It was the sun blushed fiery red.
> So very fair she was!
> Behind the Rector's lily-bed
> I saw an Angel pass. (81)

The relatively unusual triolet, with which Robert Bridges, Henry
Austin Dobson, and William Ernest Henley were experimenting
in the late 1870s as well, employs a tight two-rhyme pattern consistent with the theme of Petrarchan love that remains unattainable.
Rossetti's 1878 painting, for which the painter Marie Spartali Stillman
was the model, and Rossetti's accompanying sonnet, may well have
inspired Robinson's work, and it is worth noting that Stillman herself, who completed a Pre-Raphaelite-style painting of the young
Robinson, also produced two paintings on the same subject.[36] The
fact that Robinson adopted a form originating in medieval French
literature earned Lang's praise, who writes, this poem has "highest
poetical merit, the most touching lyrical cadence."[37] It is also a poem
with sexual connotations that indicate the lover's arousal through
repeated invocations of "flame" and "fire" associated with Fiametta,
and, as the poem unfolds, the speaker's desire is intensified for this
"angel" no longer of this world.

A final poem of note, "Tryst," possibly inspired by Arthur Hughes's
1860 painting, integrates themes of gendered perspective, of love, and
of the sequenced moments of transience and impermanence that for
the aestheticist Robinson defined the human condition. The first
stanza of nineteen lines traces the transformation of the speaker's

anticipation of and excitement about an upcoming meeting with the woman he loves into despair that she will not come, despair that increases with each moment he waits. This shift in mood suggests his inner, residual uncertainty about her love. Alliteration and assonance in the opening lines highlight his inner struggle, with the repeated "s" sounds and "m" sounds also acting as onomatopoeia:

> Low, low in the marshy meadows
> The soughing aspens under,
> Where murmuring waters wander,
> 'Mid sagging rushes and reeds and sedges,
> 'Mid rank lush hedges and growing bushes,
> 'Mid sweet rooted galingales,
> There lies a drowsy shallow, (86)

The first section continues in this vein, and the rhyming patterns formed primarily by couplets suggest the uncontrollable bubbling up of natural elements that mimic the speaker's rising anxiety. Most of the end rhymes are two syllable feminine rhymes, with "ing," "er," and "es" conveying his excitement and the activity within as he tries to manage his anticipation of what her arrival will bring. The final one-line complete sentence of the stanza indicates his despair as he waits "till hope deferred grows faint and fails." In the relatively brief second stanza of eight lines that focuses on her arrival, the natural movements around the speaker are softer and more welcoming as the birds seem to sing more loudly, the flowers bloom with greater intensity, and the wind causes the boughs of the trees to bow down as though to a royal arrival: "Sing louder birds and clearer, / Blow sweeter flowers and fairer," the speaker urges the natural world as he senses her arrival. The rhyme scheme tightens to three rhyming patterns in these eight lines, with the rhymed tercet near the end of the poem integrating the loved one into the natural scene through a return to the "lush"-ness implicit in "blushes," "flushes," and "rushes" that include her in the speaker's perception of natural wonder and beauty. "My lady is come through the vales," he exclaims in joy and relief (87). Yet, it is his anxiety that has focused this moment and that has become the theme of the poem, for his is an emotional condition familiar to most of us living in a transient world defined by uncertainty.

The aestheticist themes of transience and impermanence that Robinson develops from the perspective of love, death, nature, music, and art explain the now well-known *Punch* cartoon of 1885, which features a caricatured Robinson as the lone female reader among a throng of male readers in the British Museum. She is posed as a "femme fatale" figure with her hand on a copy of *A Handful of Honeysuckle*. The satirical intent of the cartoon aside, the mere fact of Robinson's appearance in such a venue is a testament to the stir *A Handful of Honeysuckle* created on its publication, and it suggests the integration of poetic personality and poetic voice that typifies so much of her poetry.

Other Early Writing

As she prepared poems for journal publication with a view to creating a second poetry collection, Robinson was also working on her translation of Euripides and produced several miscellaneous pieces in the *University Magazine* in 1879. The essay "Michael Drayton" in July and the two poetry translations, Aristophanes's "An Address to the Nightingale" in November and Euripides's "The Sickness of Phaedra" in December come directly from her student days. "Michael Drayton" is a fairly long essay with an extensive review of Drayton's popularity in his time and an assessment of his currency in the late nineteenth century. The significance of the essay lies in its foreshadowing of later prose work as Robinson not only offers an analytical review of his work but also reveals the man behind the work, a technique that would become a trademark of her biographical and historical prose and that ensured her popularity with critics and readers. This strategy highlights Robinson's insight into the modern biography as a genre that appealed to a popular reading audience. She depicts Drayton, for example, as cursed – and blessed – with a charming but irascible nature and difficult personality that informs the songs and pastorals, the best of his work (56). In December 1879, she published "Dante Gabriel Rossetti" along similar lines in German in *Unsere Zeit*, one of a series of papers on contemporary English poetry on which she was working for the magazine. "Lately, I have also been writing two or three hours a day for Unsere Zeit and that and my verse-making and music keep me pretty well employed," she tells Symonds.[38] The Rossetti article, along with articles each on Tennyson and Browning, seem to have been all that she refers to as a potential series that she mentions to Countess Ballestrein in 1879.[39] In the spring of 1880, "Shadow Lovers" was published in the *University Magazine*. This poem begins with the speaker's implicit regret that the figures of poetry, history, and art that guided her life when she was younger have been replaced by the worldview of the adult:

> All my lovers are estranged,
> Shadow-lovers without end;
> But last night they were avenged. (144)

The form of their revenge is to visit her in a dream to reinforce the poignancy of her loss even as they urge her to turn her attention away from the world of reverie and look instead to the material world and its offerings of love:

> For all went and left me there,
> Sighing as they passed me by;
> Ah, how sad their voices were,
> I shall hear them when I die.
> "Fare-thee-well" (they said) "we go
> Scorned as shades and dreams. Adieu!
> Love thine earthly friend, but know
> Shadows still thou dost pursue." (145)

In its emphasis on transition and its juxtaposing an ideal dream world with the world of daily life, this poem is consistent with several poems in the *Honeysuckle* volume, but Robinson would repeat the whole poem as the first section of "On a Reed Pipe" in her next collection of poems for the *Crowned Hippolytus* volume, and she would reprint in its entirety "An Address to the Nightingale" as well, another poem influenced by her classical studies. The rhymed couplets of "An Address to the Nightingale" complement Robinson's mimicry of the original "Call of the Nightingale" from Aristophanes's *The Birds*, which was performed in 414 BC. In Aristophanes, the birds that gather to oversee humans and gods as they build a city in the sky are called into action by a female nightingale. This lovely songstress stays off stage throughout the play and sings unseen, literally defined only by her voice as she calls on her mate to inspire others. Robinson's forceful and measured trochaic and spondee lines in the first section of the poem, when the speaker urges the nightingale to sing, are in striking contrast to the sweet anapestic rhymes of Philomena in the second section.

During the spring of 1880, Robinson was corresponding with Philip Marston, who became a good friend and for whom Robinson spearheaded a campaign to help him financially when he became ill and unable to support himself.[40] This circle included Frederic Myers, in whose salon the twenty-year-old Robinson played the role of Cassandra in his informal production of the *Agamemnon* and through whom she met Walter Pater and began her long and intimate friendship with Pater and his sisters. However, this introduction to Humphry Ward was fruitful professionally as well, since he gave her an opportunity to write critical introductions to Anna Barbauld, Joanna Baillie, and Felicia Hemans for his anthology, *The English Poets*. These introductions are not particularly distinguished, and Robinson was no doubt writing according to Ward's specifications, but they emphasize her interest in the personality behind the works and thus anticipate the biographer she would become.

Even this early in her career, Robinson situates herself as a critic with the sophisticated perspective of a well-read woman. She credits Barbauld with expressing "herself clearly and with grace," for instance, but is less positive about Barbauld's more serious religious work and her satiric long poem *Eighteen Hundred and Eleven*, suggesting that Barbauld treats the subjects of religion and history with less skill and accuracy than needed (576). About both Baillie and Hemans, Robinson is even less enthusiastic. While Baillie has "a quickness of observation that nearly supplies the place of insight; a strongly moralized temperament delighting in natural things; a vigorous, simple style," it is only when she deals with "simple and homely things," Robinson writes – borrowing this phrase from Baillie's description of herself – that she produces successful poetry (222). While today it is Baillie's dramatic work that critics tend to praise, Robinson glosses over this body of literature, saying only that her drama is lackluster, with undeveloped and uninspiring character development that fails to "cover the sins of a wandering story" (223). On the other hand, in *Fugitive Pieces*, especially "Song," "The Church and the Crow," and "Fisherman's Song," writes Robinson, we find the "best qualities of Scottish national poetry." Hemans receives little praise for "her tedious romantic tales, her dramas characterless and without invention," although some of her lyric poetry resonates with this intense young critic. As is to be expected, she criticizes the religious overtone of much of Hemans's poetry and the "looseness of style" and "incoherence of thought" of an author who she suggests did not take the care to revise her work (335). Nevertheless, she obviously admired and was inspired by Hemans's professional success, writing 17 March 1880 to Gosse that when she thought of giving up writing professionally and finding employment of some kind, "seven volumes of Mrs. Hemans smile up at me and assure me there is no need for that yet."[41]

By 1880, then, Robinson was well on her way to a promising future in letters, a natural path for a young woman with a tendency to isolate herself in studies, to read literature and history voraciously, and to live vicariously in books rather than worldly experience. On the other hand, through her parents and the circles of inspiring friends that attended the salons at the Gower Street family home, she was already proving to be a keen observer of human nature and an able contributor to the aestheticist circles in which the Robinson family moved. She admired Francis Thompson's poetry, the French writers Villon and Marot, and the painters Whistler and Manet. She was on friendly terms with William Sharp, John Payne, Arthur O'Shaughnessy, Andrew Lang, and, most notably, Oscar Wilde, in addition to the regulars at the salons. Her horizons were broadening, and, as the new decade began, she met Vernon Lee, who became her confidant and intimate friend on many complex and intriguing levels.

CHAPTER TWO

London, Florence, and Vernon Lee, 1880–82

Mary Robinson met Violet Paget, who had been known as Vernon Lee since 1875, in October 1880, when she was travelling in Italy with Frances and Mabel. Mary had admired Vernon Lee's published work for some time, Frances reminded George Robinson, who had joined his wife and daughters for a brief time and then returned to London.[1] Indeed, as Vineta Colby suggests, "for Mary Robinson, only a few months younger than Violet and herself aspiring to a writing career, [Lee] was an idol. Everything about her, even her paralyzed brother, glowed in the radiance of a Florentine autumn. Coming from a solidly prosperous family home in London furnished in solidly Victorian style, she was enchanted with the Casa Paget and its inhabitants."[2] Robinson was indeed "enchanted" with the Paget family and with Lee herself, and the trip that had begun as both a holiday and an opportunity for Mabel and Mary to complete historical research and gather material for their academic and creative pursuits in London, led to a transformative and complex relationship between the two women and their families. Letters from Frances to George indicate the extremely positive first impressions Violet Paget, along with her mother Matilda and her half-brother Eugene Lee-Hamilton, made on Frances Robinson and her daughters, particularly the earnest Mary. Lee had already shown herself to be a formidably intelligent writer with a keen interest in the Renaissance, and Fanny Robinson, as she was called in the family, instinctively liked her, telling George Robinson 24 October 1880, "if we lived in the same town I think we might become great friends."[3]

The Robinsons did become friends with the Paget family and by December Lee was accompanying Mary, Frances, and Mabel on local tours of Italy. Mary stayed on with Lee and her family in Casa Paget after her parents and sister returned to London. Later, however, Fanny's instincts would prove to have been wrong, as Frances and George came to believe that Lee had far too much influence over their daughter. The friendship between Lee and Robinson developed into what Robinson described in retrospect as "whole years of a perfect companionship. And – at any rate from 1880 to 1884 – a long friendship of absolute trust and satisfaction."[4] In this letter written shortly after her marriage and at a time when Lee was suffering her catastrophic breakdown, Robinson continues to use the language of a devoted friend, and, despite Lee's pained silence, repeatedly promises Lee that she loves her "with all my heart and soul. You who have been so long the dear glory of my life, the kindest friend, the invariable confidant – and to whom, so sadly and involuntarily I have caused such a long heartache." Lee's collapse when she learned of Robinson's decision to marry James Darmesteter was devastating in physical and emotional terms the extent of which Robinson did not fully understand; however, although the friendship never regained its intensity, it was ultimately renewed in a more mature form and continued until Lee's death in 1935.

Robinson was drawn to Lee's intellectual approach to aesthetics, specifically to her grasp of the nuanced ways in which aural, visual, and literary arts were integrated, not only as cultural representation but as cultural stimulus. Lee's *Studies of the Eighteenth Century in Italy* was successful and marked the twenty-four-year-old as the kind of scholar that Robinson herself was already becoming. Very soon, though, the two women developed a friendship that was more encompassing and that was highly emotional. The precise nature of this relationship with Lee during the 1880s continues to intrigue critics and invite speculation about a physical and sexual dimension to their love for one another. However, letters between the two record a narrative of love and devotion between soul mates, literary companions, and intellectual comrades that was physical and intimate in some ways, but there is no indication that sexual desire or sexual gratification were features of Robinson's love for Lee. Indeed, although the exchanges between the women are passionate and romantic, they are markedly nonsexual, despite Lee's declaration on 25 January 1881, a few months after meeting Robinson, "I sometimes think what a pity ... I was not born a man. I should have asked you to marry me."[5] This letter took Lee several days to compose, but a few weeks later, 19 February 1881, Lee writes with more confidence that she had not known the merits of Robinson's poetry when they first met and had actually been put off by Robinson's reputation as a "fashionable woman."[6] In August 1881, Lee sent Robinson "a little silver *alliance* [wedding ring], similar to the one I have just got myself," and explains that the peasants of Italy wore such a ring in the past.[7]

Correspondence held in the Bibliothèque Nationale in Paris and in the Vernon Lee collection at Colby College, as well as Robinson's letters in other archives, gives us insight into a friendship that tended to unfold in consistent and characteristic ways, as the young, beautiful, but immature Robinson expresses in flowery language her undying love for, her need of, and her commitment to Lee, while the desperately lonely, lesbian Vernon Lee demands more concrete evidence of Robinson's devotion in terms of visiting Florence more often. Lee's possessiveness and the fact that she was less able financially to travel brought out the worst in both women at times, as demands that Robinson visit Florence for extended periods led Robinson to manipulate and prevaricate, citing her health and family responsibilities as impediments to travelling to Italy. Nevertheless, Robinson did indeed spend considerable time in Florence with the Paget family and Lee travelled to London once a year, usually arriving in June. During these summer visits, Robinson's ill health, Frances's ill health, and family commitments that had caused Robinson to postpone and sometimes cancel extended holidays in the Lee household seemed to disappear.

In the epistolary record of this relationship, Lee assumes the dominant position and refers to Robinson regularly as "child," a role that Robinson seems to be happy to play and one that she assumes very early. This "romantic friendship," as Vineta Colby aptly terms it, unfolds as each woman positions herself ironically in a parody of a heterosexual relationship.[8] In her letter of 10 August 1881, for instance, Lee reassures Robinson that she could never lose interest in her, writing, "my love, how can you think that I can for a moment forget you, when I love you more and more, and the thought of you is my constant companion. Indeed, my child, I love you as much as it is possible for me to love anyone, as much as I can love anyone."[9] On the basis of amatory expressions in letters exchanged between their meeting in 1880 and the unravelling of the friendship in August of 1887, when Robinson dropped the devastating bomb of her intention to marry James Darmesteter, it would seem that Robinson was uninterested in sexual relations of any kind and that Lee suppressed her own lesbian desire. In fact, extant letters make clear that both of Robinson's heterosexual marriages were celibate.

Perhaps, then, the intimacy that Lee and Robinson shared is best characterized not in sexual terms but in intellectual, emotional, and physically companionate terms: they embraced, and they kissed as women kiss other women they love, and they enjoyed being in close physical proximity to one another. In 1929, Robinson reminds Lee of the joy "when we first made acquaintance, and our minds rushed together in such enthusiasm that all the ups and downs of fifty years have not really divided what came together then; I, at any rate, can not imagine my life with Vernon omitted from it."[10] A month later, Lee characterizes this period in romantic terms, describing Robinson in a photograph that Robinson gave her in 1880 and that she still kept in her writing case, a gift that came with the photograph. She describes the young girl in a "spring liberty brocade dress" and concludes the letter with the observation, "we were rather ashamed, weren't we? of not really belonging to the past, which alone was romantic."[11] Colby expresses the nature of this "romantic" friendship in terms of Robinson's offering Lee "a release for her long repressed hunger for love and affection," but for Robinson, Lee provided not only the intellectual stimulation of a peer but also an opportunity to move in aesthetic circles outside the London circles that were the purview of her family. Colby adds, "that their relationship was and remained nonsexual in the physical sense is beyond doubt."[12] When Lee reacted so adversely to her marriage, Robinson confided to Emily Sargent that she was "often tormented with the thought of Vernon's illness and estrangement," and furthermore, "it is all some dreadful misunderstanding – and one that, of course, it is impossible to explain away. The best way is <u>not</u> to explain!" She continues, however, "I owe her so much of the best of my life. I love her so unalterably ... I cannot imagine that we shall always be separated or that any other friend will ever be to either of us what each was to the other. And why should it ever be different? I don't love Vernon any less, God knows, because I am a married woman who loves her husband."[13] Unfortunately, although Robinson worked to regain Lee's love, Lee alternated for many years between hostility and cautious comradeship. They had another falling out during the First World War, when the pacifist Lee resented Robinson's aggressive support of heroic action and her work in print to further the war effort.

During the early 1880s, however, Robinson and Lee were literary sisters, and this is the image that Robinson cultivated in retrospect in 1907: "We were always writing in corners, Violet and I. She at a carved table on large vellum-like sheets; I huddled in a shawl on the chimney step, my inkpot neighbouring the firedogs, a blotting-pad upon my knee" ("In Casa Paget" 936). For her part, Robinson helped the socially awkward Lee professionally by introducing her to members of the London literary community, such as Edmund Gosse, who did not at first like Lee and had to be persuaded to meet her a second time.[14] John Addington Symonds and Lee were particularly antagonistic to one another from the outset. However, the introduction to Walter Pater went well, as did introductions to Robert Browning and William Morris, both whom Lee visited in their homes. Robinson introduced Lee to William and Lucy Rossetti, Mathilde Blind, William Sharp, Theodore Watts, Leslie Stephen, and the editor of the *Athenaeum* Norman McColl, as well as the Humphry Wards. She also introduced Lee to Oscar Wilde, and he and Lee tolerated each other until the publication in 1884 of *Miss Brown*.

The Crowned Hippolytus of Euripides and New Poems

When Robinson returned to London after the trip to Italy in the fall of 1880, she went to work on preparing the final manuscript of the translation of Euripides that she had begun while she was a student at University College. This translation, along with a number of poems, would be her second major publication, and, as she explained to Marie Herzfeld in 1895, "learning Greek was the chief intellectual event of [her] life."[15] Robinson agonized over whether she should include a body of poetry with the translation. Her publisher, Kegan Paul, advised against the bundling of poetry and translation, but ultimately, she took the advice of friends and family and included twenty-nine poems that she had ready, some of which were new, as the volume title suggests, and others that had been published previously in contemporary journals. Robinson was very nervous while she waited for Kegan Paul to assess the final manuscript, and in sympathy, Gosse used his influence with the publisher to get advanced notice of its acceptance. Writing to thank Gosse 27 January 1881, Robinson confesses her worry about the book's reception: "I wish I could go to sleep and not wake up till all the reviews were published and had done their worst! Is not that a cowardly admission?"[16] As the book proceeded through the press, she continued to worry, and Gosse continued to bolster her spirits. Having sent in the final proofs, she tells him 30 April 1881 that "in type the poems looked so bad" that she had been for some time "in a low spirited condition about [her] work, thinking it had gone off so"; yet, she continued to hope for praise similar to the praise that *Honeysuckle* received.[17] *Literary World* in 1884 claimed that "in her heart" Robinson considered the poems in this volume to be "the most mature and accomplished of her various efforts."[18]

Robinson had some help in shaping her translation of the play from Professor Alfred Goodwin, who, as Yopie Prins notes, had recognized her intellectual potential but who had also cautioned her to be less "modern" in her approach to Greek literature.[19] As Prins points out as well, in publishing the translation along with her contemporary poetry, she had moved away somewhat from classical scholarship and had "invited readers to read her poetry through the lens of Euripides and Euripides through the lens of her poetry."[20] These poems deal with the broad themes of love and death in tones that are overall dark and pessimistic, making them thematically consistent with the *Hippolytus* and the extreme emotions of tragedy. She was clearly aware of the importance of diction and syntax in conveying the Greek playwright's complex integration of themes of love, passion, revenge, and fate that highlight the tragic and danger-ous intersection of powerful, uncaring gods and weak, flawed human beings. This is a play about excesses – in love, in desire, in restraint, in fear, in purity, and in familial relations.

Robinson joined several well-known Victorian women in breaking into the "learned" arena of translation: Elizabeth Barrett Browning,

Augusta Webster, and Anna Swanwick all translated Aeschylus, and
Webster also translated the *Medea* of Euripides; however, until Anne
Carson's 2006 translation of the *Hippolytus*, Robinson remained the
only woman to produce a scholarly translation of this particular play,
an interesting point in that she never attempted translation again.
Like the *Medea*, the *Hippolytus* has a gendered framework, the source
of the tragedy arising out of the young Hippolytus's rejection of the
attention of the goddess Cypris, known also as Aphrodite. The most
beautiful of goddesses, she is accustomed to very different responses
from the men for whom she expresses her desire and who she graces
with her love. Shocked at Hippolytus's insistence that he is above
sexual desire and furious with him for vowing to maintain a life
of sexual purity in a platonic friendship with the goddess Artemis,
who is associated with the moon and who is known as the virginal
protector of young girls, Cypris devises a revenge that targets this
pure and asexual relationship. In casting the spell on Theseus's wife,
Phaedra, Hippolytus's stepmother, to make her fall madly in love
with her stepson, Cypris initiates the course of action that leads to
the deaths of Phaedra and Hippolytus. It is not this "resolution"
of the tragic elements that makes this play controversial; rather, it is
the suggestive and nuanced treatment of love that deviates from the
norm that led to problems for Euripides in his time as well.

The Crowned Hippolytus is dated about 428 BC and is the second
of Euripides's versions of the legend. The original play was titled *The
Veiled Hippolytus*, and the main difference between it and the version
Robinson translated is that in the original play Phaedra approaches
Hippolytus directly and tells him that she loves him; in horror and
in shame, Hippolytus covers his head with a veil. In Robinson's
translation of the play familiar to us today, the Nurse, hoping that
Hippolytus will help to save Phaedra, approaches Hippolytus on
Phaedra's behalf, and, to emphasize his sexual purity, Hippolytus
wears the crown of Artemis during this encounter. Aristophanes of
Byzantium legitimized *The Crowned Hippolytus* as a replacement play
in his introduction to his edition in 200 BC, suggesting, explains Sophie
Mills, "that the lost play was condemned for its 'unseemly material,'
and that the second play was an attempt to make amends with the
Athenian public."[21] However, Mills is sceptical that Euripides would
rewrite the play merely to appease his audience, particularly since the

first play is truer to the role of Phaedra in Greek legend traced as far back as the sixth century BC.[22] The long history of translations and rewritings of Greek legend broadens our understanding of the limited resources available to Robinson's contemporaries, including, of course, her friend Symonds, with whom she was in constant correspondence while she translated Euripides and who suggests in "Studies of the Greek Poets" that the relatively small number of Greek sources eventually led to the erasure of Greek drama in the modern world. There were in Euripides's time, Symonds points out, three important poetic playwrights: "Aeschylus was the Titanic product of a bygone period; Sophocles displayed the pure and perfect ideal; but Euripides was the artist who, without improving on the spirit of his age, gave it a true and adequate expression."[23] In Symonds's view, "Euripides, to use a modern phrase, is more sensational than either Aeschylus or Sophocles."[24] Robinson acknowledges Symonds's influence in her dedication of the translation: "To my friend J.A. Symonds."

Although we cannot be certain, Sophocles may have written his *Phaedra* between Euripides's two versions of the *Hippolytus*.[25] We can date Seneca's *Phaedra* as 54 AD, and the only prenineteenth century revisions of the myth are Gabriel Gilbert's *Hyppolite ou le garçon insensible* in 1647, Racine's *Phèdre* in 1677, and the Trinity College, Dublin scholar Martin Tuomy's *Literal Translation of Euripides's Hippolytus and Iphigenia* in 1790. There were only two nineteenth-century versions of the Hippolytus preceding Robinson's translation: Julia Ward Howe's 1857 drama for the stage is a feminist play, but it is not a scholarly translation, and it was not staged until 1911 and not published until 1941; however, Maurice Purcell's translation in verse was published in 1867. In all versions of the play, Phaedra is a character of interest, and, as William Sale explains, "the great dramatic problem posed by the *Hippolytus* is how to maintain sufficient interest in the hero once Phaedra is dead."[26] Robinson's translation seems to have revived interest in this "sensational" playwright, for there followed a series of translations by Edward Coleridge in 1891, Gilbert Murray in 1911, Arthur Wray in 1912, Augustus T. Murray in 1931, and David Green in 1942. Most of these, with the exception of the prose translations of Coleridge and Murray, are verse translations. Anne Carson's 2006 translation indicates contemporary interest in this complex and arresting story of sexual passion and restraint.

The young Robinson seems to have followed Augusta Webster's advice that a good translator must "enter into the genius" of the original author in order to render a translation true to its source.[27] A true translation requires "*recreating* the energy, wit, irony, and pathos of the original," points out John Lauritsen, a statement that reminds us of the clear implications of the gendered perspectives of playwright and translator [emphasis Lauritsen's].[28] Euripides's reputation for "feminine lyricism," although unappealing to many of her nineteenth-century contemporaries who considered him "effeminate," as Prins points out, seems to have made him all the more attractive to Robinson, and the complexity of Phaedra, a character who scandalized Euripides's contemporaries, perhaps offered Robinson some scope to explore the character from the perspective of a woman uncertain about her own "natural" desires. Reviewing Robinson's translation for the *Athenaeum* 2 July 1881, Andrew Lang avoids these enticing elements, commenting that Robinson succeeds in producing "an English poem" but observing that she falls prey to the error of many translators and cannot resist "prettifying her original." While he cites instances of this interpretive interference, he concludes that her "version will satisfy the English reader, and bring the student back to Greek studies."[29]

Critics over time have wrestled with two major issues in the *Hippolytus*: the extent to which Phaedra is responsible for her fate and the extent to which, in his reaction to Phaedra's confession of love for him, Hippolytus is responsible for his fate. Both Phaedra and Hippolytus feel intense shame as a result of the untenable situation in which they find themselves, a situation resulting from the interaction of gods and humans. The gods are powerful and ruthless, and shame and remorse are human feelings rather than divine feelings. As Carson points out, "*Aidos* ('shame') is a vast word in Greek. Its lexical equivalents include 'awe, reverence, respect, self-respect, shamefastness, sense of honor, sobriety, moderation, regard for others, regard for the helpless, compassion, shyness, coyness, scandal, dignity, majesty, Majesty.' Shame vibrates with honor and also with disgrace, with what is chaste and with what is erotic, with coldness and also with blushing."[30] *Aidos* is complicated by gendered expectations, I suggest, for while Victorian readers expected Phaedra to feel shame at the unchaste desire she has for her stepson, they also expected Hippolytus to feel shame at his intense and, at times, unappealing chastity. This aspect of the play would have been just as important to a Greek audience: as a man Hippolytus would have been expected to desire women in a sexual way, and his resistance to both Cypris and Phaedra is overshadowed by his certainty that a platonic relationship with Artemis is in principle above all sexual relations. Phaedra, on the other hand, is a wife and mother, and as such she has successfully channelled sexual desire into socially accepted institutions. Miscommunication is at the heart of nearly all the great tragedies, and thus the story of Hippolytus and Phaedra unfolds.

I think it fair to say that the "edginess" of characterization, the classical plot, and the nuanced language of this play appealed to the young Robinson and, as Prins suggests, enabled her to "articulate a language of 'pure companionship' that she shared first with Symonds, and then with Vernon Lee."[31] This is precisely the relationship that she would go on to share with each of her husbands as well. Hippolytus is indeed "a figure for homoerotic aestheticism," as Prins suggests; however, Robinson chooses specific words to situate Hippolytus's asexual desire and his narcissism convincingly in his claim that Phaedra represents an "adulterate evil" that lies innate within "devising" women (35). While it is true that he favours the one female goddess who is masculine in her activities of the hunt, he spends his days with her in the "fresh green forest," the implicitly sexually innocent wording casting his activity of getting rid of wild beasts as an act of shaping the forest into his own homogenously ideal community (4). It is precisely this aspect of Hippolytus, particularly his restraint, that Symonds finds appealing when he casts Hippolytus's "purity" in contrast to the "fever of Phaedra" as "the pure fresh health of the hunter-hero." Specifically, argues Symonds, "in his observance of the oath extorted from Phaedra's nurse, in his obedience to his father's will, in his kindness to his servants, in his gentle endurance of a painful death, and in the joy with which he greets the virgin huntress when she comes to visit him, Euripides has firmly traced the ideal of a guileless, tranquil manhood."[32]

The Chorus of Retainers that accompanies Hippolytus characterizes him as a man of integrity because he is an androgynous huntsman, pure of heart and chaste in body and mind. The Chorus reassures us that Hippolytus has his supporters, those who value the

life he has chosen in distancing himself from lust and bodily pleasures. However, Hippolytus's men well understand what Hippolytus
does not seem to understand – the danger of antagonizing Cypris.
When Hippolytus shrugs off the implications of her presence as
she hovers outside the city gates, the male Chorus says ominously,
"Mayst thou fare well, having the sense thou lackest!" (8). These are
servants, of course, and can only in the end pray to Cypris to "hear
and forgive / The idle words of the o'er-strained mood of youth" (9).
The juxtaposition of this last warning, with the full choral exchange
that follows, introduces the connection between Hippolytus and
Phaedra. However, modern scholars are less accepting of Hippolytus's
restraint and sexual antipathy and more inclined to see Hippolytus in
terms of ambiguity and indeterminism. George Devereux points out
that "a further objectionable – and, for a Greek, almost unforgivable –
trait of Hippolytus is his lack of in-group solidarity, of civic virtue,
and citizenship."[33] Certainly his self-imposed isolation from all but
his huntsmen and Artemis has the disturbing effect of implying that
he disdains and dismisses the human world to which he belongs.

There is some consistency, then, in Robinson's approach to characterization of Hippolytus as a man who lacks self-confidence. This
blurring of the gender lines is consistent as well with her status as a
nineteenth-century classical scholar working away at her translation
in a class of young men. She writes 1 January 1879 to Symonds,

> out of politeness to me the Professor makes the unfortunate
> youths translate Euripides' diatribes against women all wrong.
> For instance that passage in the Epode of the first chorus,
> about the evil unhappy helplessness of the wayward disposition
> of women he made them translate 'the complex nature of
> females is prone to day-dreams'! At which compliment not all
> the dignity of my newly acquired womanhood could save me
> from laughing out loud.[34]

A few months later, she tells Symonds that the Women's Debating
Society at University College elected her to be a committee member,
and although she feels herself "a frivolous poet among all the learned
ladies in checked Ulsters," she hopes that she was elected "for the
sake of the Greek."[35]

Robinson's confidence in herself as a translator and her sense that such scholarly activity legitimized her as a writer in diverse ways is implicit in her willingness to differ radically from the more conservative translations of key passages, such as Hippolytus's condemnation of all women when he suggests to Zeus that in a world without women, men could purchase children with offerings to the god, which would be far better than having to live with this "female plague" (35). Robinson's depiction of a Phaedra who knows before Hippolytus speaks that he will condemn her is consistent with modern feminist readings such as that of Froma Zeitlin, who points out that Phaedra knows that "the world will judge her as it does all women, reading her divisions not as a conflictual ambiguity between self and role but rather as a generic duplicity characteristic of her sex."[36] In his translation in 1790, Tuomy renders the text in much more innocuous terms as Hippolytus simply says that it would have been better had men been able to purchase children and "dwell with freedom in their habitations without women."[37] Julia Ward Howe's 1857 script, written for the actor Edwin Booth, situates this misogyny in terms of Hippolytus's failure to decline Phaedra's invitation to dinner, even though Creon warns him not to go. "Albeit no woman's banquet pleasures [him]," he will nevertheless go out of courtesy, he says.[38] Hippolytus's refusal to acknowledge the womanly side of himself – the inner tempering of his masculine side – is subtly implicit in Robinson's depiction of Hippolytus as a man in whom what might have signalled a balance between head and heart anticipates modern readings. Sale, for instance, points out that "the great psychological problem posed by that hero is how to relate the two sides of his personality: his love of nature and his rigid, strident chastity."[39]

The two goddesses at war for this chastity frame the play, Cypris appearing at the beginning and Artemis at the end. The dichotomies of masculine/feminine, hunter/hunted, and male sexual desire/female sexual reticence are all represented in inverted forms. Cypris reasons that as a goddess, she need only, as she puts it, "honour those in turn that worship me," and she really cannot understand why Hippolytus "worships" Artemis (3). Of course, this is a conundrum that is never truly explained in the play, but it sets the play on the irreversible course of revenge tragedy. This most female of goddesses in the essential ways of outward beauty and knowledge of the joys of all things carnal is ultimately less significant than Artemis, who, in the final lines of the play, steps into her role as protector of women to bring Theseus back to a point at which he can regain his perspective on the wife and son he has been so quick to condemn. Artemis also points out that Theseus was careless in what he wished for and that he, as the son of a god, ought to have understood Cypris's motive "to satisfy her heart." He should have known, she says, "so runs the law / For gods" (69). Through his acceptance of his own complicity in this tragedy, Theseus is brought back to the point of redemption, Hippolytus given his legacy of virtue, and Phaedra remembered with pity and sorrow.

Through manipulation and nuancing of Greek and English diction, Robinson elicits our sympathy with Hippolytus despite his failure to rise to his obligations, both as a man and as a human being. Moreover, she situates his repudiation of Cypris in gendered nineteenth-century terms: "I hate / Your *clever* woman," he says and goes on to suggest that Cypris, being such a woman herself, "plants [mischief] in the minds of *clever* women" [emphasis mine] (36). Robinson's choice of "clever woman" rather than Tuomy's "philosophical lady" is telling in the context of late nineteenth-century usage of this term applied to the New Woman figure, as is her casting of Hippolytus's restraint and sexual purity in a misogynist light when he suggests that wives should have as confidents only "voiceless beasts" (36).[40] In such language choices Robinson differs significantly from the eighteenth-century Tuomy. For example, whereas Tuomy translates Hippolytus's persistent misogyny later in this passage as "I'll never be tired of detesting women," Robinson translates the same line as "I shall never get my fill / Of hating women" (37). In using stronger and more vitriolic language, she highlights Hippolytus's warring inner character, conveying the strange delight he takes in keeping his promise to the Nurse to remain silent about Phaedra's attraction to him, not for Phaedra's benefit but because he enjoys the discomfort of the Nurse and the pain of Phaedra as they carry out their duplicity to Theseus.

One can see why Robinson's Classics professor found some of her "modernisms" alarming as she delineates the ruthless and cruel aspects of Hippolytus that are at odds with the pastoral world he inhabits. Robinson succeeds in casting Hippolytus's hatred of women and of all sexual impulses – heterosexual and homosexual – to convey his reluctance to consider that Phaedra might be innocent. Unfortunately, this also prevents him from understanding that he is responsible for her suicide. As the Chorus protests, "Hapless the fate is of women, a lot that we loathe!" (37). In this respect, Robinson emphasizes the total helplessness of Phaedra as she astutely foreshadows through language Hippolytus's ultimate fate when he fulfills the prophecy of the meaning of his name, "loosed by horses," with the double sense of "unleasher of horses." Hippolytus is driven by his taste for extreme and excess, a need he articulates as he uses Phaedra's lust for him to "unleash" his own terrible secret from deep within his inner consciousness.

Modern audiences have difficulty in reconciling Hippolytus's excessive chastity – excess that interferes with our sympathy for a man who seems nothing short of cruel – with the tragic emotions of grief and pity that Aristotle identifies as our means of entry into the experience of tragedy. Only when Theseus casts Hippolytus out does Hippolytus seem human in his despair, and only then do we begin to pity him. In the final scenes of the play, Theseus adopts the same punitive attitude toward Hippolytus that the latter had shown toward Phaedra, and so Hippolytus becomes the one unjustly treated in place of Phaedra. This role reversal underscores the principle of classical tragedy that relies on misconstrued notions of power. While Phaedra dies alone and offstage, Hippolytus's tragic position is emphasized first by the messenger's dramatic account of his accident and then by his long, protracted death on stage in Theseus's arms. During the messenger's speech, we focus on the terrible pain that Hippolytus endures and the unfair pitting of the man against the powerful god who brings about the catastrophic panic of Hippolytus's beloved horses. The messenger uses figurative language to tell his story in a narrative filled with action and excitement, and while the Chorus merely affirms that "Fate and necessity may no man flee," Hippolytus himself is shocked that the "team of my chariot, fed at my hand" has brought about his destruction (65, 70).

While Hippolytus was the character central to the tragedy for the original Greek audience, Phaedra is of great interest to a modern audience and clearly figures prominently in Robinson's understanding of the gendered nature of this tragedy, including the irony that she is the victim of warring female gods. That Euripides was deliberate in his gendered context of tragedy is suggested by his revision of her character for the second version of the play, for the original Phaedra was manipulative, not only confronting Hippolytus directly instead of through the Nurse but also, upon his rejection of her, accusing him of rape. Euripides softened this aspect in the second version, never placing Hippolytus and Phaedra in contact with one another and situating her note to Theseus accusing Hippolytus of impropriety in the context of a more general fear that, as the play well demonstrates, as a woman she would be accused, tried, and found guilty after death.

In her darkest hours, just before she confides in the Nurse, Phaedra chooses Artemis, the virginal goddess, to emulate, pleading that she be sent to the mountains "where the dogs, the hunters, / Tread in the shade of the pines, / Chasing the dappled deer" (13). The Nurse does not miss the fact that this wish is very unlike Phaedra, a recognition that conveys to us the extent of Phaedra's suffering and the irony that she represents the kind of womanly attention that Hippolytus loathes. The intensity of his loathing prepares the audience for Phaedra's inevitable end, thereby redirecting the tragic emotions to Phaedra in her address to the Troezenian women, when she repeats the word "shame" eight times in different contexts to emphasize her position as victim (24–5). It is important to her that they, women representing her community, understand that she has fought a long and difficult battle: "I hoped to bear my folly well," she says, "and gain the victory through self-control" (ibid.). Of course, she is only human, and she cannot win a battle involving the gods. Her shame points to the inevitability of her death, and her careful consideration of the method of her suicide underscores the hopelessness of her situation and the paucity of sympathy for her on the parts of both her stepson and her husband. In ignoring the Nurse's warning that her death will leave her children in a precarious situation, she signals to the audience the extent of a despair that even her maternal devotion and reluctance to leave her children cannot mitigate.

The Nurse is seminal to the tragic trajectory of this play, both despite and because of her unintentional contribution to its catastrophic finale. The Nurse is in an untenable position in that she truly loves Phaedra and is at first bewildered by Phaedra's profound sadness, by her restless desire, and by her insistence that she be hidden behind a veil. All of these behaviours run counter to what the Nurse understands of Phaedra's life: that she is a happily married woman with children. When Phaedra finally confides in the Nurse in her long, self-deprecating "shame" speech, the Nurse sees with absolute clarity that Phaedra is blameless and tries to reason with her about "this passion, but hurled down from heaven on thee" (26). Robinson's use of "hurled" here creates an emphasis missing in Tuomy's rendition of this passage in which the Nurse undermines the seriousness of this event by casting it simply as "the anger of a deity light upon you" (19). The aggressive nature of Cypris's action is at the heart of Robinson's focus on the women in this tragedy, and not only she but also Phaedra, Artemis, the Nurse, and the Chorus create, manage, and mismanage the conflicts that contribute to the rising and falling actions leading to the catastrophe for Hippolytus and Theseus at the end of the play. The Nurse is convinced that Phaedra can "trust" her and that she "will do all things well," first in providing Phaedra with a folk remedy to calm her restlessness and then in approaching Hippolytus on Phaedra's behalf (30). In the context of classical tragedy, of course, the outcome is the Nurse's tragedy as much as Phaedra's, and before much longer the Nurse realizes that because we are human, "we make a coil of words" (39).

The Chorus of Troezenian women assesses the actions of the principal characters in the tradition of classical tragedy, at times commenting objectively on events and at other times expressing the deep human sympathies that Euripides hopes will surface in the audience. The Chorus is the mechanism through which we experience the cathartic emotions of fear and pity, both from a distance and from within the culture of the play. For example, the Chorus first speaks to Hippolytus's Chorus of Retainers, the men who accompany him on the hunt, spreading the news of Phaedra's illness to the Retainers but also noting Hippolytus's satisfaction with his androgynous life in a primarily male world. In the Strophe, the Chorus refocuses the audience on Phaedra's situation, taking us back to the curse of Cypris and Phaedra's construction of a statue of Cypris in honour of her love for her stepson when she and Theseus lived in Athens. Now, the Chorus points out, she has gone into exile with Theseus and does not have the statue to alleviate some of her distress. Hence, her "illness" has intensified, says the Chorus in the Antistrophe. In the "b" strophe and antistrophe, the women clearly sympathize with their "sister," albeit at this point they do not really understand the extent to which she has been victimized (10).

The Chorus's reliance on intuition occurs again when, as Richard Buxton points out, Theseus banishes Hippolytus. The Chorus tends to judge events in a context common to gods and humans when, in reality, their worlds and contexts are very different. "Nevertheless," says Buxton, "the chorus' words do at least present 'local' bafflement as the possible effect of the action upon a group of (within the dramatic context) 'ordinary' people."[41] In the Epode to this first choriambic song, the Chorus can only comment on the difficult lives of women in their "helpless ill / of child-bearing travail," calling on Artemis in her role as protector of women (10). None of their comments here are specifically related to Phaedra's plight because they do not yet understand the nature of her distress. Ben Glaser and Yopie Prins have both written persuasively on Robinson's lyrical achievement in manipulating prosody to convey Phaedra's emotional state. Glaser points out that Robinson uses the anapestic metre "to formally represent [Phaedra's] female longing" and, he adds, this metre often "approximates one of the most common English metrical forms, ballad meter."[42] Hence, Robinson integrates Greek and English lyrical forms to suggest a more contemporary, more discerning chorus and foreshadows in these moments her continued success with ballad forms. Prins suggests that Robinson's selection of lines of the Chorus for publication in the *University Magazine* attests to her awareness of the significance of what Prins terms "metrical de-cadence," which is especially significant in the exchange between Phaedra and the Nurse when the Nurse vows to "do all things well" but not, we realize, according to Phaedra's wishes for secrecy.[43] The female Chorus sympathizes with the Nurse in her dilemma and her misguided sense that she is following the choriambic advice to women to engage our sympathies within the community of women.

The Chorus's warning includes Theseus, of course, who is not a physical presence on stage until the final third of the play; he is, however, implicitly present from the moment that Phaedra expresses her shame. He is the injured husband, and she is conscious that as her tragedy unfolds, she will cause him great pain. It is significant in this respect that when Theseus is told that there has been a devastating incident at home, his first concern is for his father and then for his sons. When told that Phaedra has been found "hung in a noose she fastened round her neck," his next question is whether she was "stiff with despair or through some accident" (44). Robinson translates this crucial moment in Theseus's history quite differently than Tuomy, who has the Chorus convey the details clearly: "She tied a hanging collar and strangled herself." Theseus's response to this assertion is not a question but an exclamation that she was "wafted with grief! Or, compelled by some distress."[44] Tuomy's literal translation highlights the radiating effect of Phaedra's action, as the Chorus chides Phaedra that "the action of your desperate hands involves this house in confusion." Moreover, the Chorus of Tuomy echoes Theseus's sense that Phaedra has "ruined" him, as he says, and, therefore, he too is caught up in fate and necessity. Robinson's Theseus does indeed denounce Phaedra at this moment, referring to her as "my wife that has destroyed me in her death" (45). However, Robinson situates the source of Theseus's misfortune in a more specific context through the reaction of the Chorus to Phaedra's suicide, this more modern Chorus focusing not on Theseus but on Phaedra as the community of women sings in unison, "Alas! and I weep for thy sorrows, O Queen" (45). The Herald who announces the discovery of Phaedra's body is greeted by a chorus divided into two semichoruses to express not only shock and dismay but also fear at what this terrible circumstance might bring to the lives of ordinary people. One semichorus suggests entering the house to try to save Phaedra from her noose, while the other points out that "meddling brings no safety to our lives" (43).

These philosophical questions are integrated into the larger tragedy of the play, which unfolds through Phaedra's desperate and false accusation of sexual impropriety, which sets in motion the falling action. This is the point from which there is no recovery, and Theseus reacts by calling on his father Poseidon and exerting his half-god status. We know now that things have gone beyond the human context and Phaedra's untruth has initiated a final catastrophe because, ironically, it is the human side of Theseus that believes Phaedra, since only in thinking ill of his son can he maintain his self-respect. He can take heart in the fact that taking her own life was a feminine weakness, and it is the feminine side of Hippolytus that he finds offensive: "Wilt thou say / this folly is not in men, that women have? / I have known men as facile and weak / for all their manliness," he tells Hippolytus (52). We shift our sympathies from Theseus to Hippolytus at this point because the latter remains silent and respects the oath he has made. Significantly, when the mortally wounded Hippolytus is brought back in for the denouement and forgives Theseus, Phaedra's absence has the positive effect of refocusing the final moments of the play on the tragedy between father and son. "Woe's me, to lose a son so dear and brave," says Theseus (76). In this moment, Hippolytus, and implicitly Phaedra, die redeemed, even as the Messenger's graphic description of the destruction of his body – a body that Hippolytus has treated as a sacred temple – reinforces our unease at Hippolytus's dismissal of the power of the gods. As usual in Greek tragedy, the Chorus has the last say, thereby emphasizing the centrality of public opinion to human culture, and in its six short lines, the Chorus reinforces the inclusive pain of the community at large.

Poems in *The Crowned Hippolytus*

Robinson's concern that including poetry with the classical translation might undermine the significant contribution she was making as a woman translator was intensified by her persistent fears that the new poetry would not measure up to the successful lyrics of *A Handful of Honeysuckle.* She expresses this latter worry in the opening sonnet, subtitled "In Preface to My Second Book." In the first lines, the poet-speaker positions herself between girlhood and womanhood, her literary maturity defined but as yet too new to be judged as experience: "How deep a chasm is open, how deep and wide, / between these songs and the first songs I said / with tremulous girlish voice (81). She remains resolute in the sestet, however, to accept the truth of her inadequacies as well as her achievements, concluding, "I scorn to mock my dearth with spurious bloom / Or wrong true laurels by a tinsel crown." Reviewers obliged, finding promise in complex and compelling poems that not only integrate cultural commentary with spiritual reflection but also record the depth and breadth of Robinson's continued scholarly approach to religion and philosophy.

Although some of the poems of this volume indeed belong to the *Honeysuckle* era in terms of theme and technique, others well demonstrate Robinson's increasing sophistication in wedding form and function to create poetry technically well suited to the development of aestheticist themes. We see this shift in maturity in the seven sonnets that follow the "Preface" as Robinson uses the rhetorical process of the Petrarchan sonnet to ground the esoteric and abstract in a material context familiar to a reader of any age. The first line of "In La Sua Voluntade È Nostra Pace," for example, translates the title, which is taken from Dante's Paradiso Canto 3 (line 85): "For in the will of God we have our peace." Matthew Arnold quotes this line from Dante in "A Study of Poetry" as a "touchstone" of excellence, at least as excellent as is possible in the poetry of human beings, and Christina Rossetti uses it as an epigraph to the last verse of "Monna Innominata" to reinforce the temporary and impermanent nature of perfection, in this case female beauty.[45] The line is also a reminder of the tribute to Schopenhauer in the *Honeysuckle* poem "Will." Like Arnold and Rossetti, Robinson recognizes the divine as a source of human peace, but in the sestet of "In La Sua Voluntade È Nostra Pace," she reminds us that we are imperfect beings whose youthful ambition and idealism inevitably fade into a realistic acceptance of limitation:

> Peace from ourselves He gives us, from desire,
> From the large claims of youth, from palsying doubt;
> Let this suffice; for while the foes of the good
> Are mighty upon the earth, within, without,
> While yet there last a wrong to be withstood,
> Another rest than this must none require. (190)

Robinson confided to Symonds in 1879 her resistance to living her life under such religious direction:

> I cannot believe what I would like to believe, the religion in which I have been brought up no longer helps me and I must renounce what I have no more faith in, but I feel hurt, unhappy, even wicked at renouncing it. I cannot tell my troubles to my Mother and Sister, because I should grieve them and make them anxious. I am too shy to make confident friends.[46]

Yet, in the final lines of "In La Sua Voluntade È Nostra Pace," the speaker of 1881 finds a way out of the "troubles" Robinson expresses to Symonds by recasting religious service in more material, worldly terms to eradicate "wrong." It not surprising, then, that the word "soul" rarely appears in a religious context in Robinson's poetry, and she refers more often to the anima or inner life that is at times positive and optimistic and at other times an indication of despair and desperation. She was moving toward the pantheistic approach to God that Schopenhauer equates with atheism.[47]

In other Petrarchan sonnets, Robinson's subliminal and persistent yearning for an elusive spiritual certainty is reflected in her characterization of the material world. In "A Child-Musician," for instance, God seems to the speaker to have chosen a "simple child" to disseminate "his flaming passion that outweighs / the burden of man's blame or praise," but by the end of the sonnet it is clear that the child's private communication with God achieved through music is limited to the state of childhood (195). "The One Certainty" and "De Profundis" similarly cast desire for insight into the infinite in terms of the inevitable process of life that thwarts such desire. "The One Certainty" develops such predictability through an analogy between the limited span of earthly life and a flimsily structured summer home in which one spends little time and, therefore, invests little effort in constructing. Hence, the "one certainty" of human existence is that death will inevitably end that existence, a truism that offered no spiritual comfort to the young Robinson. "De Profundis," from Psalm 130, is the cry from the deep at the horror of an earthly life defined in these terms, a theme that Tennyson, Christina Rossetti, and numerous other poets had already developed. Robinson's first two lines situate the speaker in the same state of despair as her predecessors: "To thee, O God, I cry from this profound / Horror of gloom and vast tempestuous night" (197). The presence of these religiously themed poems bespeaks the young Robinson's persistent attempts to find ways in which she might draw some comfort, not from the formalities of religious practice but from historical and literary representations of longing for religious certainty.

In some of these poems, escape from nihilistic despair is suggested conventionally, as it had been suggested in the *Honeysuckle* volume, through transcendent love as a way to fill the spiritual void into which Robinson's speakers fall from time to time. Indeed, the two Petrarchan sonnets that comprise "Two Lovers" were published in the *Athenaeum* in 1879 and belong to the *Honeysuckle* period in this respect as Robinson personifies the extremes of human love as "Endeavour" and "Content" to highlight the dangers of complacency in matters of the heart. Endeavor is demanding and disapproving, his love couched in his awareness of the loved one's limitations, and "Content" is an undisciplined lover who leads the speaker to view life in exotic and perpetually spring-like terms, offering, therefore, a love that is unrealistic and unsustainable. In "Lover's Silence," which appeared in the *Athenaeum* a few months later, Robert Browning's influence is telling in the speaker's recognition that infinite desire is unattainable in finite existence. However, the final Petrarchan sonnet of this period, "Love After Death," which was first published in the *Athenaeum* in 1880 under the title "Unequal Souls," stands out as a poetic tribute to Dante Gabriel Rossetti. This sonnet reiterates the themes of "In the Organ Loft" and "Love Stronger than Death" of *A Handful of Honeysuckle*, but it evokes clearly Rossetti's "Blessed Damozel" in imagery of an expanding spatial – and implicitly moral – degree of separation between lovers as they journey upward toward heaven. The octave situates this separation in physical terms from the perspective of a female soul trying desperately to reach the heights of heaven with the wings that she has earned in her earthly existence; unfortunately, her stunted wings, which reflect her flawed life, are inadequate to reach heaven:

> Where eddying shocks of air and whirling light
> Beat all their broken waves to mist, and fall
> About the unseen impenetrable wall
> That girdles heaven round, there strains in flight
> One tempest-baffled soul, whose eager sight
> Would pierce the upper sky, whose pinions small
> Quiver to answer some imagined call,
> But cannot free them from the wind and night. (193)

The imagery of the metaphorical road to heaven in geographical terms implies the connection between earth and heaven that preoccupied the Pre-Raphaelites broadly and Dante Gabriel Rossetti specifically.

In the sestet, however, the speaker is suggestive in casting earthly love as a force powerful enough to impede the lover's entrance into heaven:

> And far away, along the spiral track
> Whereup, having passed their mortal period,
> Flash perfect souls to lose themselves in God,
> One stops and cries for freedom (looking back
> To her whose chaining love forbids him rise)
> With ineffectual flight and darkening eyes.

As the final lines suggest, if we read the parenthetical aside as a descriptor that we can take out of the main poetic syntax, then it is his flight that becomes "ineffectual" and his eyes that lose the light of heaven. It is this element – the power of human love – that links Robinson to Rossetti.

Robinson experimented with the lyrical ballad in *A Handful of Honeysuckle* with some success, and she develops this poetic form in increasingly sophisticated ways in subsequent volumes. The first poem of this second collection, "The Red Clove," is written in the challenging Ottava Rima; however, the poem proper begins with a dedication to Vernon Lee in two Petrarchan octaves in which Robinson situates this unusual tale in the context of her love for and loyalty to Lee in these early days of their friendship. These octaves recount a magical moment that Robinson spent with Lee on the steps of the Uffizi, when Lee told her about Cinthio's 1550 *La Girollée*. The tale is "less beautiful than when I heard it first," says the speaker, in the first octave, implying that it was her experience of Lee's telling the story, not the story itself, that was significant and, in the sestet, she regrets that she has not been able to capture the "magic" of this moment:

> Some magic of the cool and quiet hour
> I thought it then, nor marked the story well.
> For little I dreamed with what continuing power
> Your words upon my inner ear should swell
> In void and distant places, till the flower
> They praised I strove to praise and broke the spell.
> For I have searched my music all in vain
> To find a note that brings your voice again. (82)

In poetry, Robinson expresses her love for Vernon Lee by poeticizing the intimacy of this special moment as she listened transfixed not simply by the tale but by the teller of the tale. The tale itself is a narrative of diverse kinds of love – of the love of a father for his son and of another father for his daughter, and the enduring love of a couple mismatched in terms of age – the twelve-year-old Antonio loves the nineteen-year-old Dafne. However, this poem is particularly contextualized by Robinson's translation of Euripides through Antonio's childlike understanding of love, for "he loved to dream himself Hippolytus / and her white Artemis, the heavenly maid" (87). She is not Artemis and he is not Hippolytus, however, and his illness over the next four years is implicitly linked to his stasis in the emotional context of his love at twelve years, for he has been separated from Dafne for all that time. Dafne's gift of the clove flowers of his childish passion is an agent of revival, and "he wakened from his pain / knowing he loved and was loved again" (89). The trajectory of this impossible love winds and twists its way toward the final scene in which Antonio, his love for Dafne now the "brotherly" love she has requested and thus a form that Hippolytus well understood, returns to find the married Dafne alone and dying from the plague. The symbolic red clove, which was long considered sacred and, during the Middle Ages thought to protect against witchcraft, reappears as she falls dead in his arms and blooms magically when the "lovers" are buried in the same grave. Gosse singles out this poem for particular praise in the *Saturday Review*: "no recent poet, no verse-writer since Mr. Morris, has told a story so fluently, and her manner is entirely different from that of Mr. Morris."[48] Perhaps the subject of a chaste love along the lines of Hippolytus's love for Artemis differentiates Robinson from Morris, for in bringing Lee into the context as the narrative source, Robinson pays tribute to a very similar love that may then have seemed above other earthly forms of love.

History and legend, whether in literary or art form, evoke in Robinson more than anything else an acute awareness not only of the range of circumstances in which love unfolds but also of the relative insignificance of life and, implicitly, love in its place on the larger spectrum of human existence. In her narrative lyrics in particular, she tells the history of a life through detailed delineation of one moment in that history, thereby conveying an essentially tragic trajectory along which so many lives move toward their end. The ekphrastic poem

"Mondzoen," alternatively titled "The Kiss on the Mouth," is inspired by the Dutch painter Pierre Jean van der Ouderaa's *De Mondzoen*, completed at the end of 1878 and exhibited as *La Reconciliation Judiciare* in 1879. Robinson's poetic account of the ancient Antwerp form of restorative justice that brought criminal and victim together is dedicated to the artist and is constructed as a closet drama so as to heighten the dramatic effect of this moment. Traditionally, the victim's family chose a representative to receive a kiss on the mouth from the penitent murderer, signifying a symbolic joining of the families in the important moment of reconciliation. The painting depicts the humbled murderer, dressed only in his shirt and holding a straw, as he advances toward a young girl in black waiting to receive the kiss on behalf of her mother, two younger brothers, and the rest of the family, and the artist well conveys the girl's reluctance to touch the man who has killed her father. In her poetic drama, Robinson focuses on this moment, as the shrinking girl, Agnes, must forgive the murderer, Florent; however, in her grief, she does the unthinkable and refuses to allow the kiss. The twist in Robinson's vision of this moment has to do with the precise nature of the young woman's grief, for the drama is intensified with the revelation that Florent was her lover and remains unrepentant about killing the man who not only banished him but who taunted and ridiculed him for thinking he could love Agnes. In poeticizing Florent's attempt to reason with Agnes that "it was for thee; / And it was best," Robinson complicates the untold story behind the drama that the painting depicts (109). In the poem, the young woman is caught between love for her father and love for Florent, and she is paralyzed, denying the kiss three times. The allusion to Peter's denial of Christ is a significant moment in the poem as it leads others to suggest that she appears dangerously Lutheran and anti-Catholic. Florent's suicide and Agnes's bestowing the kiss in his dying moments reinforces a principal thread of a great deal of Robinson's poetry – the paradox of taking the right action too late and, as the speaker says, when "all's lost" (115). Robinson's willingness to grapple with ethical dilemmas that lead to tragedies such as this – Agnes's terrible regret losing her lover and missing an opportunity to behave with Christian benevolence – foreshadows her continued success in taking her inspiration from sources beyond the inner life that had predominated in *A Handful of Honeysuckle*.

In both "Philumene to Aristides" and "The Gardener of Sinope," for example, Robinson explores this paradox in the context of self-sacrifice, a principle at the heart of Christian faith that is symbolized by Christ himself. "Philumene to Aristides" is based on an Armenian fragment found in 1878, which makes the poem contemporary, both in terms of cultural events and the political relevance of the narrative to nineteenth-century social issues, particularly the restrictions of gender and class. The fragment itself offers the apology of Aristides in order to explain the death of a young boy in his service who takes the man's suffering on himself in order to appease the gods and allow Aristides to live. Aristides, as Judith Perkins points out, "only sees the death of his favorite foster child as a way of mitigating the tragedy in terms of the gods having a plan and his longer life as part of the plan."[49] Robinson, however, gives voice not to the dead boy but to his sister, Philumene, who has now fallen ill and is presumed to be the sacrifice demanded to ensure that Aristides remains healthy. In his dream, Aristides sees Philumene with her body exposed to tell the story of her pain, but it is the young girl compelled to make such a sacrifice who speaks directly. She is a Christ figure who assumes Aristides's "fever" and feels his pain without wanting praise or thanks, not because she thinks of herself in religious terms but because she knows that as a woman, she will not be remembered for this anyway. Yet, there is power in this substitution, she realizes, power that supersedes gender: "But I to all the gods in heaven give praise / That I, a woman, none remembereth, / I, even I, shall turn aside thy death." As she brings her monologue to a close, she becomes increasingly more direct in her silent address to Aristides, underscoring in tight rhyming couplets the tremendous gift she is giving him:

For thou shalt live, triumphant over death;
The sharp, last agony, the catch in the breath,
The ache of starting eyes, the red, blind night,
The fruitless search of hands that grasp at light,
And, worst of all, the horror of what may be,
Thou shalt not know, but I, but I, for thee. (152)

Hence, in language that emphasizes the earthly life that she is leaving behind and in couplets that juxtapose such contrasts as "breath" and "death," she delivers an interior monologue, speaking for herself and never directly to the man for whom she is dying, thereby implicitly retaining control of her position in this terrible drama.

"The Gardener of Sinope" suggests a simpler allegory that takes the shape of Christ's final moments in the garden and his subsequent crucifixion. The legend of St Phocas, known at times as Phocas the Gardener and at other times as Phocas of Sinope, depicts the early follower of Christ whose acts of charity and Christ-like gestures in feeding the poor and sheltering Christians from persecution begin a sequence of events that lead to Phocas's self-sacrifice and make murderers out of the two soldiers who have been sent to kill him but whom he shelters from a stormy night. Phocas's walk in his garden as they sleep, his farewells to his flowers and plants, and his preparation of his own grave echo the footsteps of Christ. The paradox of self-sacrifice is suggested when Phocas reveals his identity to the soldiers and urges them to carry out the murder as they have been ordered. The morality of Phocus's insistence and his willingness to "pardon" the soldiers casts his motives in a questionable light as he again echoes Christ in beseeching God to "save / these men that know not what they do" (124). When the soldiers commit the deed that will send him to Christ, they damn their souls, as the speaker suggests in the final lines of the poem: "One brought back the bloody sword; / Two claimed a murderer's reward" (125). The speaker thus labels them as guilty, but the poem poses an implicit rhetorical question of whose sin is the greater – that of Phocas or that of the murderers? This poem completes a cycle of poetry in which Robinson grapples with religious paradigms that end not in affirmation of faith but in confirmation of the flawed logic she sees at the heart of religious history and practice.

In other poems of this period, "Captain Ortis' Booty," for instance, Robinson separates moral and ethical behaviour from a religious context altogether. She sent a copy of this poem to Symonds 14 October 1879, and it was published in the *Cornhill Magazine* in 1880.[50] This legend was popular at the time, with a version of the story appearing shortly afterwards in *Harper's Young People* 27 June 1882.[51] Without explaining why, Gosse declares that "Captain Ortis' Booty" was "too much in Mr. Browning's manner" in his review, but this cautionary tale is arguably unique in its use of the conventional rhymed couplets and iambic tetrametre lines of the ballad to develop a parable that highlights the value of delayed gratification and astute planning.[52] The incident occurred in 1584–85, when the Spanish were victorious in conquering Antwerp during the Eighty Years' War. Robinson is interested in the victor, Captain Ortis, who, offered a prize of his choosing, asks that he be given the prison for his booty. On receipt, he promptly frees all the prisoners, who were mainly languishing in prison for religious crimes and heresies. Since this is booty, and "each pays a ransom fee," he is rewarded not only monetarily but also with love, admiration, and respect (127). Although some felt that he undermined the value of a potentially good deed by accepting payment from the people, the poetic speaker is clearly supportive: "I praise him, for my part " (129). The question of ethics that the poem poses is complicated by the fact that historically, the city was completely demoralized, and the populace left desperate for food and supplies after such a long siege. Ortis, then, astutely assesses the situation wisely for personal gain, but ultimately, his gain is indeed a humanitarian gesture. Clearly such ethical questions fascinated the young Robinson. Another reinscription of a well-known legend, "The Lake of Charlemain," follows Robert Southey's version "King Charlemain" published in *Poetical Works* in 1798. The historical King Charlemagne was known as a great conqueror and a charismatic leader through his quelling of a rebellion in Aquitaine in 769. However, he was married numerous times and had a number of mistresses, and it is this side of Charlemagne that Robinson situates in terms of the deleterious effect of romance on his kingly responsibility and duty. When he falls in love with a "lowly" plain woman and, in his preoccupied state, ignores his responsibilities, Charlemain's subjects at first find the situation comic – a great king felled by love. Soon, however, there is a tacit agreement among the councillors that an ineffectual king is a problem, and they find themselves acknowledging that "it were well if she were dead" (141). The outcome of this "evil wish" is that she does die and Charlemain, pining for her, dies as well (142). The mystical elements of the legend highlight the intense power of human love – a power that can be used for good but that can just as easily be used for evil.

There are a number of interesting experiments in this volume with poetic forms outside the sonnet and the ballad. "Under the

Trees," written while Robinson was in Rowington in August 1878 and, therefore, on the heels of her *Honeysuckle* success, demonstrates her skill in linking poetic form to theme. In this case, she employs iambic tetrametre quatrains of rhymed couplets to set form against theme, thereby contrasting the speaker's wish for release from a life of stasis even as she knows that this wish is sinful.

> I lay full length near lonely trees
> Heart-full of sighing silences;
> So far as eyes could see all round
> There was no life, no stir, no sound. (160)

The speaker's emotional isolation is enhanced by the "s" sounds in this first stanza, which have the effect of emphasizing the hypnotic and "still" setting that leads the speaker to imagine resting peacefully beneath the ground; however, the imperfect rhymes in the first two stanzas, as the speaker slips into her reverie of what death would be like, become perfect rhymes in the rest of the poem, thereby suggesting not ease but anxiety, and therefore, by the fifth stanza, the speaker realizes that she has a responsibility to resist such a release and to remain invested in her world:

> Ah, no: because, O coward will,
> Thy destined work thou must fulfil,
> Because no soul, be it great or small,
> Can rise alone or lonely fall. (161)

By the seventh and final stanza, the speaker vows to "arise and bear / the burden all men everywhere / have borne and must bear," an echo of the speaker's closing vow in "In La Sua Voluntade È Nostra Pace" but without the directive from God. Technical maturity in lyrics like this one coincided with emotional maturity as Robinson left girlhood behind and began the long process of reconciling her intellectual rejection of formal religion with her understanding that actions must be framed by an understanding of the responsibility and obligation that accompanies the gift of life.

In her "music" poems of this volume, Robinson explores the necessity of remaining committed to the material world through the emotional power of music, as it functions as a transportive medium that brings the speaker to an epiphany similar to that of "In the Organ Loft" of *Honeysuckle*. "Helen in the Wood," which first appeared in the *Cornhill* in 1881, is perhaps less successful in its presentation of a grieving lover whose bereavement is only reinforced by a vision of his lost Helen; however, the thematically and technically complex "During Music," an older poem first published in October 1878 with the title "A Passion of Music," is a haunting poetic experience of the ecstasy of music in which the speaker feels both pain and joy. As Ben Glaser points out, this poem in hendecasyllabic metre is "not a poem that seeks to mimic or describe music, but rather to explore the experience of hearing a music so beautiful that it can 'pierce'," as the speaker says, one's "'hearing with agonized vibrations.'"[53] Diction emphasizes this assault on the senses with words such as "flames," "burning," and "blinding" to describe the intensity of the speaker's experience, which becomes an integration of pain and pleasure:

Lo, some god in the soul rebels at prison,
Stung by furious vain desire for heaven,
Strained through stir of his wings my heart is breaking,
Cease, ah! cease, for behold and pity, Music,
I am dying, unknowing what I die for. (162–3)

The exquisite beauty of the moment is just bearable, whispered through the alliterative "s" sounds as the speaker is transported higher and higher into a realm of consciousness that is as unsettling as it is powerful. By the final stanza, the speaker finds access to the divine through the aesthetic rapture of this moment:

Thou, perpetual element of Beauty,
Thou, whose memory music is, oh hear me;
Flesh, sense, soul of me yearns to Thee and feels Thee;
Now content me with truth and secret meanings
Vast, harmonic, for which we grope in music. (163)

There are a number of compelling ideas in these lines – music as a "perpetual" aesthetic pleasure that is emphasized by the alliterative "m" sounds of the next line and hints at the holy and sacred powers of music that seems to offer the speaker insight into the divine. This insight comes through a progression of the "flesh" first, then the sensual pleasures of sound, and finally from deep into the very "soul." This is a mystical and religious experience for the speaker, both a moment of fantasy and of intuition.

"A Violin Sonata" is even more metrically complex as it follows the movements of the traditional musical sonata, a poetic structure to which Robinson would return in 1922 with her poetic tribute to Albert Roussel, "For Piano and Violin." The movements of "A Violin Sonata" reflect the speaker's shifting moods inspired by music that leads to memories of a lost love, beginning with the Andante, four poetic lines of iambs and anapests that mimic the moderately slow and graceful walking pace of the music:

> What foreign languor in the heat
> And fragrance of this English June
> Brings back the well-known Paris street,
> The voice, the face I lost too soon? (166)

The metre, which suggests that the speaker is slipping slowly into reverie, is complemented by simple alternating rhyming patterns that suggest the speaker's walking patterns as he makes his way along English streets during this process. Sensory details reflect not only the pain of loss but the joy of what once was. This joy is emphasized as the second part, the Scherzo, begins in alternating tetrametre and trimetre lines that replace the stately and even iambic/anapestic tetrametre lines in order to reflect the speaker's excitement and unity with the music in his head:

> I wish I were the violin
> You make your music on;
> For we would quit the city's din
> And find, to make our music in,
> A world for us alone. (168)

The metre and line lengths slow and extend out again in the third section, the Adagio cantabile, as the first stanza introduces the slowest pace in the poem, the moments in which the speaker expresses intense yearning for and desire to return to the past:

Child, do you know all the wonder of your music,
Rising and dying,
Pleading, beseeching, and still the boon refusing?
Mine is the secret it sighs – do you divine it?
Down in your heart are the yearning notes repeated;
Or is all Beauty
Sprung from the meeting of souls, the one perceiving
Splendour the other creates? (169)

The proliferation of "ing" verb forms denotes movement, both within the musical score in the speaker's mind and within memory itself as he brings himself back to a moment of perfection that is evoked through the street player to whom he is listening. By the end of the poem, the speaker has glimpsed in a moment's insight – left unexplained and unspecified – "the source of Beauty" (169).

On the other hand, the musical patterns of the six poetic sections of "On a Reed Pipe" move along a contrasting trajectory as they trace the speaker's loss of rapport with music. The epigraph, "joyous cry of the reed," is given in Greek to emphasize the pastoral influences of the poem, the first section of eight quatrains of which had been published as "Shadow Lovers" in the *University Magazine* in 1880. In evoking the famous passage sung by the Greek chorus in Euripides's *Iphigenia at Aulis* to celebrate the wedding of Peleus and Thetis, the parents of Achilles, the sections that follow are cast in the light of classical tragedy as the speaker searches for poetic inspiration that moves beyond worldly sources. By the end of the poem, the reed player – the poet – achieves access to the divine in earthly terms, ironically realizing that it is the world itself through which he receives his inspiration and, thus, he has not been abandoned by God, as he once feared:

I, from my lowly sombre place,
Look up on high;
The light that flashes from your face
Is sunshine in my sky. (174)

Despite her conviction that she lacked musical ability, Robinson was adept at developing the natural intersections between poetics and musical metrics. Moreover, she suggests in her music poems a form of transcendence that is at times a positive experience and at other times less positive. In each case, however, music leads to an epiphany and an understanding on the speaker's part of the complexity and variety of musical "journeys" into realms beyond the here and now.

Yet, despite such joyful and moving expressions, Robinson could be a morose poet in many ways, as her letters to Symonds suggest and as the type of poetry she would define in later volumes as poems of the "inner life" records. If her music poems are read as records of escape from the "awful brevity" of life, other poems indicate the persistence with which she held on to precisely this perspective on human existence. She was acutely aware of her own past receding into memory and her personal history becoming increasingly intangible and irretrievable. Even a joyous occasion such as Mabel's birthday inspired mournful poetry as the older sister highlights Mabel's loss – and her own loss – of innocence and childhood. Whereas such an occasion is often shaped by celebration of the onset of adulthood and the development of the child into a woman, for Robinson Mabel's coming of age elicited poetic nostalgia and retrospection. We learn a fair bit about the early lives of the Robinson girls in "Two Sisters," a poem of thirteen septet verses in the alternating iambic tetrametre and trimetre lines popular in French Romantic poetry. We learn that Mary was the imaginative child, prone to be unwell, and Mabel the athletic child, generally happy and healthy; Mary was more determined to have her way and Mabel "kinder" (184). These are indeed the traits that Mary and Mabel took with them into adulthood, and they continued in adulthood to be devoted to one another as though, like a magnetic compass, they were attracted and fortified by these contrasts.

> [These verses] mean a love no chance or change
> Can shadow with mistrust,
> No distance weaken or estrange,
> No years decay or rust.
> Love that made childhood sweet and good,
> And growing up to womanhood,
> Hath grown with that and must. (185)

This is one of the poems in Robinson's early work that, in its intimacy, foreshadows the few personal poems in her oeuvre that she would write with Vernon Lee, James Darmesteter, and Èmile Duclaux in mind.

When she thinks of history and historicity in more general terms, Robinson's perspective on the "awful brevity" of life shifts to consideration of esoteric implications of time, passing time, and the past times in which people loved and lived. Even before meeting Vernon Lee, she too was inspired by ruins and monuments, and her first two volumes contain poetry about history and historicity. In June 1878, she mentions in a letter to Symonds the discovery of a beautiful statue in a churchyard hundreds of years ago, and she tells him that this discovery inspired her to write "Before a Bust of Venus."[54] The lyric voice is that of a monk who cannot help but respond in disturbingly manly ways to this representation of female beauty that he has found while digging in a Greek vineyard about 900, for the beautiful bust of Venus not only suggests the disparity between earthly beauty and human finitude, but it also evokes memory of an incident in his youth when his aesthetic response to beauty led him to be sidetracked by a lovely rose just when he was supposed to be retrieving herbs for the monks to use in their meals. Only one monk, aptly named Father Ambrose, understands that the young monk's appreciation of earthly beauty is an oblique but powerful tribute to God. Ambrose realizes that this young man is himself "God's rose," put on earth like the lovely flowers to "light for a moment's space the upward track" of working toward heaven (136). Now an adult, however, without Ambrose there to place his strong feelings into the perspective of his relationship to God, the monk is frightened by the beauty of Venus, which he sees as a dangerous, tangible beauty that threatens his spiritual future. If he loves the finite aesthetic ideal that this object represents, he reasons, he cannot love God, and he will forfeit the infinite life for which he has lived in celibacy. Hoping that "it were enough of Heaven to have kissed" this representation, he is at the same time horrified by the blasphemy that even this simple response to the goddess of love seems to represent (134). Since no one wants to kiss the black Madonna, he thinks, Venus must be the "white devil"; yet, although he tells himself that he will be "satisfied" when he sees God's face, he concludes as ambiguously as he began: "And yet – O Heaven, how beautiful she is!" (135, 138). In this interior monologue, Robinson conveys the natural impulse toward finite beauty that supersedes spiritual love because it is both comprehensible and attainable, and it is a message reinforced by its modernity as it transcends the limitations of historicity.

Gosse describes Robinson's three "London Studies," titled individually "A Square in November," "Outside the Museum," and "After the Storm in March" in his *Saturday Review* as "almost puerile."[55] However, in this trilogy, Robinson conflates memory of a moment with experience of the moment itself, arguably a sophisticated integration that emphasizes the ways in which one's surroundings bring about shifts in mood from one moment to the next. She offers insight into how we might read these poems in a short essay "The Art of Seeing," which was published in *The Magazine of Art* in 1882. In the essay, Robinson juxtaposes actually *seeing* a scene against *remembering* a scene [emphasis mine]. She argues that we need to see things in the context in which they appear at that moment rather than as rigid "material substances, solid and changeless … for, alas, we rarely *see*; we recall, we distinguish; every scene on which we look is a symbol evolving a whole past of incongruous remembrance" [emphasis Robinson's] (462–3). Thus, the speaker of "A Square in November" invites us to *see* the darkness of the scene in its implication of the decay, deterioration, and ugliness that often mark the beginning of the winter season in London:

> Down the street the wind looks black;
> Underfoot the leaves are shed
> Spoiled and dead; overhead
> All the sky is dark with rack. (157)

Synesthesia and personification in the first line aptly convey the speaker's feelings of being enclosed within a space that has no boundaries but that is dark, "spoiled and dead," like the leaves upon which she treads. By the third stanza, however, the trees "groping in the lifeless air" lead the speaker to recall *memories* of the "long-since vanished May" [emphasis mine], a shift from experiencing to remembering that foreshadows the speaker's malaise in the fourth stanza, in which trochaic tetrametre lines and tight rhymes indicate that the speaker has taken from this "scene" impressions through which she can convey her own mood:

> So my life, as bare and blind,
> Towards some beauty unattained,
> Lost or waned, stretches strained
> Helpless aims that never find.

The simile that compares the speaker's "life" with the trees "groping" for breath – implicitly for the scent of spring – suggests the fusion of sights and sounds of wintery London with the speaker's depression and hopelessness that are specifically related to this dark day. The second study, "Outside the Museum," uses alternating iambic tetrametre and dimetre lines to describe the mix of grey and blue colouring as the sky clears:

> A space of luminous tender blue
> But flaked with fire,
> As though the perfect peace there knew
> A pure desire.
> Beneath the fluted columns rise,
> With grey, broad frieze;
> And every dove that coos and flies
> Is grey as these. (158)

The alliterative "perfect peace" brought by the cleansing, refreshing rain and the blue sky in stark relief to the grey of the sky and doves again symbolizes the speaker's mood, this time an emerging contentment consistent with the renewed London cityscape. Similarly, the violence and turbulence of the resettling air in the third study, "After the Storm in March," is conveyed in complex anapestic abab lines in each of three verses, thereby signalling the coming of spring and shifting to a mood more hopeful:

> Heart, keep silence; forebode no more
> Warning and sorrow.
> Who knows, the heavens may hold in store
> Spring for to-morrow. (159)

It is ironic that all three of these "scenes" unfold on the steps of the place where, in 1887, she would meet and fall in love with James Darmesteter, experiencing in those moments a kind of renewal that would change the direction of her life entirely.

The process of transforming "sight" into "insight" into a world of flux that Robinson traces in the three "London Studies" unfolds in an even more sophisticated form in "In Una Selva Oscura." The title is taken from Dante's *Inferno* and is translated as "in a dark jungle." In context of the *Inferno*, the speaker continues, "in the middle of the journey of my life, I found myself in a dark forest, in which I'd wholly lost my way" (Canto 1, 1–3). Robinson conveys this sense of having lost one's way through rhyming patterns that emphasize our reliance on sight as a concrete means of gaining insight or in obtaining information. For example, in the first stanza rhyme brings together words that convey the speaker's dilemma:

> Escape is taken away; alas! I see
> No road to light and life, for all around
> Stretch tyrannous trees whose gnarled boughs endure
> An agony obscure,
> Whose lowering shadows people and confound
> The wood's dim coverture,
>
> And break with mastering arms the flight of Hope.
> Yet on I grope. (177)

In this passage, "endure" and "obscure" suggest a deep plunge into an opaque darkness, and "hope" and "grope" indicate the disparity between the situation and the speaker's ability to rectify it. The first part of the poem indicates the process of pain and suffering that is part of the human condition; however, one finds "hope" even in such dire distress when "the branches part" and one glimpses the light of the moon (177). Inspired, the speaker concludes with a prayer to this symbolic light of the night – the darkness that threatens to engulf her completely:

> Thou, moon, hast heavenly refuge from the clouds,
> And thee no partial shades affright,

But me the darkness shrouds.
Arise, appear and shine upon my dreams.
Ah! give me light!
Flood all my dangers with thy radiant beams,
And drive aside the night. (178)

"In Una Selva Oscura" and "London Studies" are preludes to the sophisticated ways in which Robinson depicts nature as a powerful force as well as a resource. Nature is never to be taken for granted, and in these early poems, nature has the mood-shifting potential to lead the speaker down into a world of darkness and limitations; however, occasionally, as in the hauntingly beautiful expression of pantheism, "Song," the natural world suggests a way out of the darkness. The movement of the dove in "Song" is conveyed by the trochaic first line in each stanza, followed by iambic and anapestic lines that create an effect of the bird soaring:

Oh for the wings of a dove,
To fly far away from my own soul,
Reach and be merged in the vast whole
Heaven of infinite Love!

Oh that I were as the rain
To fall and be lost in the great sea,
One with the waves, till the drowned me
Might not be severed again!

Infinite arms of the air,
Surrounding the stars and without strife
Blending our life with their large life,
Lift me and carry me there! (175)

Reynaldo Hahn set this poem to music in 1904, and indeed the abba rhyming patterns link specific words to create a unified musical effect, such as "dove" and "love" that suggests the Holy Spirit, and "soul" and "whole" that suggests the fusion into the natural world for which the speaker longs.[56] In this, one of her first expressions of pantheism, Robinson mixes metaphors of sky and sea to create a complex conceit that initiates a line of philosophical thought that she would express more clearly and forcefully in later poems.

In several ways, then, the poems of this volume are important indicators of Robinson's principled approach to poetry and poetics and to her sense that meter, rhyme, and other elements of figurative language enable the poet to convey what Robert Browning called "significant moments" in experience. Even simple nature poems such as "Wild Cherry Branches," "Sacrifice," and "A Jonquil" are testaments to her technical development in terms of her ability to reflect the human condition through abstract, philosophical meditation, through history and legend, through art, and through nature. The tight rhyme scheme, with only two rhymes appearing in variation in each stanza of "Wild Cherry Branches," for instance, draws attention to the finitude of the natural world as the branches harvested and placed in a "London room" now look alien to the speaker:

> Lithe sprays of freshness and faint perfume,
> You are strange in a London room;
> Sweet foreigners come to the dull, close city;
> Your flowers are memories, clear in the gloom,
> That sigh with regret and are fragrant with pity. (179)

Visual and olfactory imagery emphasizes the finitude of all living things, as the fading delicate scent and waning physical beauty of the once lovely branches seem now to be an aesthetic mockery. Extending this symbol of transience into a philosophical perspective on human life, the speaker first decides, "the bloom on our living is dead." However, in the next instant, the speaker thinks of her friend and finds a way to transcend the limitations of human life through love, as "in my love for her, all loves blend," and, just as the transience and brevity of the branches in bloom become subservient to the intensity of their beauty, so through love, the speaker comes to understand that "we know what sweetness it is to flower / Let life or death be the fruit" (180, 181).

Robinson was justified in considering the poems of this volume worthy of publication, and some of them are linked thematically to her translation of Euripides. However, these are also tidying up poems that mark the end of Robinson's early perspective on poetry, the role of the poet, and on the aesthetic function of poetry in a Victorian world. They mark her transition to a poet eager to experiment with new forms of poetry altogether and a poet who could now draw on personal experience of the world rather than an abstract "understanding" of it as a teenager in her room. Some of these poems indicate the extent to which she had become accustomed by this time to discussing these philosophical perspectives with Vernon Lee, and after this point, she developed not only a far more sophisticated approach to the techniques of lyric poetry but also a more astute awareness of how she might draw on her wide-ranging knowledge of history, philosophy, mythology, and mysticism to situate the human condition in increasingly complex terms. She would in the next few years leave no stone unturned in her investigation of literary genre, experimenting with socially focused "realism" in poetry, with biography, and with fiction, at times under the tutelage of Lee and at other times in defiance of her.

CHAPTER THREE

Experiments with Fiction, Biography, and Poetic Realism, 1883–85

Robinson's first short story, "Mary Schonewald: A Study in Prophecy," was published in *Fraser's Magazine* in September 1881. This early fiction not only reflects Robinson's interest in the ways in which mysticism, religion, and history intersect, but it also foreshadows her consistent failure in the fiction that she would publish over the next few years. On the other hand, "Mary Schonewald," as Robinson explains, is "a very careful and detailed study" of the historical figure Edward Irving, and in this respect, it anticipates Robinson's biographical writing style as she speculates on the complexity of historicity and as she focuses on how an individual experienced life in order to understand the past and its larger contexts (384). This is a technique that she uses in a great deal of her subsequent poetry as well. The fictional character through which Robinson looks at the influence of this iconic religious zealot is a London shopgirl who reads the *Agamemnon* but skips over the choruses that are not overtly related to the narrative. We can see Robinson's personal history in Mary's name, her nonreligious family background, her interest in Greek classics, and her daydreaming personality. Robinson casts the love that Mary Schonewald feels for Andrew Home, a disciple of Irving and a proponent of prophecy – the belief that God speaks through the voices of the chosen – as a dangerous conflation of religious passion and earthly love that leads to her death. The cautionary message of the story points obliquely to Mary's failure to recognize that Andrew, despite his later protestations, loves his faith rather than her. Therefore, although this story was not particularly distinguished, the fact that it rests as an inauspicious start to several other works of short fiction, including a novel, marks it as an important early indication that Robinson's primary creative talents lay in poetry and nonfiction prose.

Her second short fiction, "Goneril," appeared in *Fraser's Magazine* in July 1882 and was perhaps more successful in that it was published again years later in Scribner's 1902 collection *Tales from Many Sources*. Once again, Robinson treats love philosophically, this time substituting Italy and idiosyncratic "theatre" characters for a religious icon. Moreover, while the focus of "Mary Schonewald" is consistent with Mary Robinson's London life, the focus of "Goneril" reflects her Italian life with Vernon Lee. The seventeen-year-old Goneril, the two elderly ladies with whom she has been left so that she might recover from a bout of malaria while her parents return to India, her youthful cousin to whom she is attracted, and an elderly suitor, Signor Graziano, struggle to further a plot that fails to develop a clear theme. For example, although the two old ladies, Madame Petrucci and Miss Prunty, the colleague and secretary of a recently dead singer, are, despite their association with the theatre, "of the highest respectability," we find out little more about why these details might be significant (87). The implications of the name "Goneril," and its association with betrayal and deceit in *King Lear*, are developed obliquely through Signor Graziano, and there are elements of aestheticism and suggestions of the supremacy of art in the story, but essentially Robinson seems to lose control of the plot, and the tale ends with the sad recognition of an elderly man that his romantic desires are foolish and inappropriate.

Robinson's personal situation was becoming somewhat difficult as her family were less and less inclined to approve of her close friendship with Lee. When Lee came to London to visit in the summer of 1882, things came to a head as George and Frances Robinson made it clear that Lee's influence on their daughter seemed unhealthy to them, and even Mabel found the strident Lee difficult to take at times. After one particularly upsetting confrontation between Lee and Robinson's family that summer, the two women fled to a cottage at Fittleworth in Sussex, where they set up house together and walked about the countryside in a state she would describe to James Darmesteter in September 1888 as ideal: "It was then and there, God knows why – that by some beautiful accident I was perfectly happy. I often think of it. It is mine still and can't be spoiled or taken away."[1] They spent twenty idyllic days at the cottage, from where they wrote letters to Lee's mother to explain why they were not at the Robinson home in London.

These letters to Matilda Paget differ in tone and content and reflect the personalities of the two women – Lee's are strident and resentful, and Robinson's are conciliatory and apologetic. On 22 July, for instance, Lee describes the Robinson family and Frances Robinson in particular to her mother in uniformly cruel and critical terms. "These people seem to be growing quite torpid as a result of their principle of never discussing, of living and let living, of having peace," she complains to her mother. She says that Frances Robinson "is besides one of the stupidest women I have ever met; ideas cannot be got within a mile of her, and this stupidity is at the bottom of her want of sympathy and entirely at the bottom of her treatment of me."[2] Burdett Gardner sees in Lee's letters to her mother attempts to distance Robinson from her family, a goal which she may not have pursued as aggressively as he suggests, but the tone of her letters to her mother at this time certainly suggests her impatience with the Robinson family. "Nourishing by flattery Mary's idea that as a rising young poetess and intellectual she had outgrown her dull middle class family," suggests Gardner, "Lee posed as the champion of enlightenment and intellectuality in its fight with bourgeois stultification."[3] Robinson wrote on 27 July 1882 to Lee's mother to apologize for the way in which the Robinson family had behaved to Lee. Robinson's letters to Matilda Paget clearly situate her family in the wrong, and she felt compelled to reassure Lee's mother that she remained devoted to Lee and Lee to her. "Vernon and I are very, very happy," she writes. "It is such a happiness to be with her. She is so easily contented, so never failingly kind and cheerful." After more apologies, she writes, "It makes me sore at heart to think any of my people have been unjust to her, cruelly unjust."[4] The fact remains that after the Fittleworth escape, Lee did not return to the Robinson household that summer, staying instead with her friend Bella Duffy, who lived in Kensington.

No doubt this incident, as well as Robinson's usual health complaints and the exciting move to Earl's Terrace, all contributed to the repeated delay of Robinson's trip to Florence in the fall of 1882. Lee's mounting frustration at this delay is evident in correspondence in which she points to the needs of her ailing brother, Lee-Hamilton, asking Robinson to reconsider postponing the trip and implying that the Robinson family needed their daughter less than she claimed.[5] In the end, Robinson travelled to Florence and remained there until the move was complete. She writes to Symonds 13 February 1883, "It seems so odd to think that in May I shall be back in London – at home in a house that I have never seen."[6] Lee did not hesitate to take advantage of the friendship on professional levels, however, writing to Robert Browning 6 November 1882, for instance, to remind him that she was "a young woman who had the honour of being brought to you twice by your little friend Mary Robinson" and sending him a copy of her brother's new volume of poetry *The New Medusa*, which Lee-Hamilton had dedicated to Robinson.[7]

In exchanges that concerned Robinson's professional life, the women remained on good terms. Lee did not agree with Robinson's decision to write in prose, but she did offer advice when it was solicited and her assessment of Robinson's abilities in both fiction and biography accorded with critics generally. At this point, Robinson was working in tandem on her first biography, *Emily Brontë*, which brought back her youthful fascination with *Wuthering Heights*, and on her first and only novel, *Arden*, which was written as she read Richardson's *Clarissa*. This two-volume attempt at depicting love and marriage in "edgy" terms falls far short of garnering the interest of the reader in ways that Richardson's more popular and very long novel succeeded. Both the novel and the biography were published in the spring of 1883, and, of course, one of Robinson's earliest readers was Vernon Lee. Lee's assessment of the biography was consistently more positive than that of *Arden*, an assessment with which virtually everyone else agreed. Lee couched her criticism in sympathetic terms, since she too was struggling with *Miss Brown*, which, she says 8 May 1883, "gets hazier every day."[8] Nevertheless, she condemned *Arden* quite unequivocally, writing 22 May 1883 that "the whole fault of it is the unlucky plot" that seems to lead nowhere.[9] Robinson was well aware of the novel's failings, admitting to Gosse 28 April 1883 that she "was very inexperienced and had no idea how the fresco would look when put off the scaffolding." She adds that she was deeply humiliated by the public launch of a work she conceded was "very weak and flabby."[10]

The summer of 1883 offered Robinson and Lee an opportunity to put the stress of all of this behind them and, to the probable dismay of the Robinson family, who Lee visited only now and again that summer, Robinson and Lee again went off on their own, this time travelling in Sussex and Kent.[11] Robinson became understandably more and more upset as time passed and there were no favourable reviews of *Arden*. The kindest review came from Edward Cook, who in the *Athenaeum* casts his comments in light of Robinson's demonstrated abilities with language and the lyrical qualities of her writing. "One is frequently struck by the grace of a metaphor and the aptness of a simile," he notes; however, he then continues, "there is a lack of force in ... delineation of character."[12] In the *Academy*, George Saintsbury implies that Robinson has ventured outside her abilities with this novel. "We cannot honestly say that *Arden* discovers much vocation for novel-writing."[13] Gosse writes in the *Spectator*, the novel "contains hardly anything that can be called an incident, in the sense in which the term is generally employed, and seems to us to suffer considerably from that deficiency."[14]

In person, Gosse accused Robinson of a lack of delicacy in dealing with a baby that does not survive. This perception of indelicacy seems to have been linked to Robinson's failure to develop the character Gerard in light of this incident. Writing to Gosse 28 April 1883, Robinson tries to explain that Gerard is not meant to continue to have feelings for Arden when he finds that she is married; rather, he cannot "resist the temptation to prove to her that she might have done much better. A cad, if you like, and a feeble cad but not immoral or consciously perfidious as you appear to have seen him." She acknowledges to Gosse that her primary character is equally inadequately drawn: "what you say of Arden is right; I found it too hard for me to precision the outline of such a dreary, inert, and yet uncertain character. It is harder to do than one would think. The passionate people come quite natural [*sic*]."[15] Symonds, ever ready to disagree with Gosse in principle, takes the opportunity to do so about Robinson's treatment of this incident. "I do not agree with Gosse as to the indelicacies in this book," writes Symonds to Robinson, "though of course I know the places where he would detect them, & the omission of these could not have enfeebled the whole."[16] However, Symonds then goes on in a gesture of friendship and sympathy to mitigate his own criticism: "I only marvel at any one who can make a story at all. I could as soon fly, I think, as produce anything as excellent as Arden!"

Nevertheless, the truth is that the "uncertainty" that Robinson admitted to Gosse was prophetic, and there was no popular audience for this novel. Character development is uniformly weak, with the titular character misunderstanding her society and the individuals with whom she shares it. As Lee points out in her initial response to the novel 3 May 1883, Robinson "miscalculated her age" in delineating Arden, for she is "too young for her manner of speaking."[17] The bottom line is that Arden is not an interesting woman; she fails first to forge meaningful relationships with her grandfather and Mrs Lawrence, and then she tumbles into marriage to Harry for no discernable reason. Arden's inexplicable reluctance to visit England at the beginning of the novel and her decision at the end to remain in England rather than return to Italy are never reconciled. Robinson misses the opportunity to develop a richer, more complex character through the Italian aspects of Arden's personality, and, of course, in this respect Barrett Browning's *Aurora Leigh* comes to mind as a possible model. In leaving Arden's transnational elements undeveloped, Robinson fails to make the most of the traumatic aspect of a young girl brought up in an Italian cosmopolitan society suddenly transplanted to live as an English country girl. Again drawing on the circumstances of her own life, Robinson integrates into fiction a difficult moment in the Robinson family created by her maternal grandfather's marrying his housekeeper at the house in Warwickshire; however, she fails in this respect as well and does not develop the plot opportunities that a second marriage might offer.[18] Arden's future suggested at the end of the novel is not only anticlimactic but unreasonable in terms of the larger structural frame of Italy and England, and her passive acceptance of circumstances leaves her undistinguished and not the heroine of great fiction.

Other characters in the novel remain representational as well, particularly Gerard, who is throughout a self-centred, financially privileged American travelling with an equally shallow sister and a well-meaning but unworldly mother. William's sister Susie, having befriended Arden and accepted her help in extricating herself from the potentially destructive influence of Fred, fails in the end to grant Arden the understanding and the love that a wiser, more mature woman would have been able to offer. Her petty refusal to commiserate with Arden and her insistence that Arden is directly responsible for William's death do not contribute to the plot or to Arden's maturity. In her letter of 3 May, before she had read the whole novel and come to the conclusion that it was overall a failure, Lee writes to Robinson, "the whole character of Susie seems to me capital," but she adds, "she & Gerard are, as to dialogue, what I like least in the book." Having finished the novel, Lee writes succinctly to Robinson 22 May 1883, "the fault is that in <u>Arden</u> ... Arden doesn't love Gerard, nor Gerard Arden, William dies and Susie doesn't come to grief."[19] Indeed, what little action takes place in the novel is not linked to moral or ethical behaviour. Arden's youthful marriage is not out of place in country society but her complaint to her sister-in-law rings childishly inappropriate and clichéd when she asks, "how could I know, Susie, what it would be like to have some one always there, day and night, no place to call one's own?" (135). Other characters that might have been developed more fully to flesh out the view of this stratified country society disappear – Fred and his family, for instance. Harry himself is a principled, hardworking man, but he is also uneducated and unsophisticated, and there is no indication that Arden is attracted to him. His roughness, awkwardness, and ignorance are at odds with his stepmother and half-sister and with the responsibilities he has in running a large farm estate.

While the plot connection of *Arden* to *Aurora Leigh* stands out, we also find traces of *Wuthering Heights* and Brontë's poem "Death-Scene." The poem might be considered a template for the novel, as Brontë's poetic speaker, in an evening that "gleams / Warm and bright on Arden's lake" holds the dying "Edward" in her arms, depicting poetically the scene of Arden's final sacrifice. Unfortunately, whereas Brontë is able in the brevity of the lyric to focus on a moment of intensely painful human experience, Robinson is unable to sustain this dramatic gesture over a two-volume novel, and, whereas Brontë successfully depicts the power of transcendent love in *Wuthering Heights*, Robinson fails to convince her reader that Sylvia Arden's self-imposed sentence of a lonely graveside vigil is anything other than a sentimental and hollow gesture. Although Robinson was evidently "describing [the] Warwickshire village so familiar to her childhood," as the *Literary World* author notes, she is perhaps unable to imagine anything beyond that comfortable familiarity as she misses the opportunity to incorporate into this peaceful English village some of the foreign elements that might have made the story unusual.[20]

When she had returned to Florence, Lee took the opportunity to phrase her criticism to steer Robinson away from fiction and back to poetry, writing in October 1883: "Darling little Mary, I think I would rather never, never see you again than that you should let the desire for money making turn you, born poet if ever there was one, into the earthworm called a prose writer."[21] As her biography of Brontë predicted, Robinson did indeed have command of prose techniques that brought her success in biography and other forms of nonfiction prose, but on every level, *Arden* reflects her inability to write prose fiction. The dedication to her friend Eleanor Poynter, who had achieved success with *My Little Lady* and who gave Robinson some advice with the manuscript, as well as the numerous exchanges with Lee about *Miss Brown*, did nothing to avert what Robinson considered a personal failure never to be repeated.

Emily Brontë

While *Arden* was a creative struggle from beginning to end, Robinson's second major work of 1883 was clearly a labour of love. Invited to write a biography of Charlotte Brontë for Allen's Eminent Women series, Robinson asked the editor, John Ingram, to allow her to write one of Emily Brontë instead. Years later, she explained to Cunningham Graham that she agreed to Ingram's stipulation that she would earn a fee reduced by £10 from his offer for the biography of Charlotte because "in those days Emily did not command a public." Emily was, she tells Graham, her "patron saint" at that time.[22] In the biography itself, she explains that Brontë "died, between the finishing of labour and the award of praise" (233). Robinson points out that in the eyes of the schoolmaster at Brussels, M. Héger, the intractable and argumentative Emily was "the genius" rather than Charlotte, and Robinson suggests that Charlotte's character Shirley in her novel of that title is based on Emily (80, 162). Robinson awards Emily Brontë the praise that her "patron saint" deserves, balancing her reverence for her subject with astute critical commentary. A "patron saint" in one's early years can have a significant impact on the direction one's life takes, and, in Robinson's case, the satisfying experience of placing Emily Brontë in a context that increased her popularity became an important measure of professional success and a goal that she would pursue in seven subsequent biographies.

In two respects in particular, this intimate and sensitive portrait of Brontë reflects Robinson's varied experiments in genre at the time and foreshadows the poetic elements in her later prose style. First, the biography is poetic in its diction and syntax, often employing metaphor and simile, as well as creating imagined moments in Brontë's life; second, it leans in places toward the genre we term historical fiction rather than formal biography, a technique that she would employ in subsequent historical and biographical attempts to bring back to life people and cultures of the past. For example, in her description of Emily's response to Branwell's final moments of dissipation, she situates Emily at the centre of a household held captive by the degeneration of its prodigal son, describing the scene of his disgrace in language that evokes Brontë's most famous character, Heathcliffe, as well as Anne Brontë's renegade Arthur Huntingdon of *The Tenant of Wildfell Hall*. Robinson writes,

> a strange scene in the quiet parlor of a country vicarage, this anguish of guilty love, these revulsions from shameful ecstasy to shameful despair. Branwell raved on, delirious, agonized; and the blind father listened, sick at heart, maybe self-reproachful; and the gentle sister listened, shuddering, as if she saw hell lying open at her feet. Emily listened too, indignant at the treachery, horrified at the shame; yet with an immense pity in her fierce and loving breast. (119)

This ability to evoke a scene in language that is nuanced to highlight Emily's emotional state belies Sidney Bidell's response when he learned that Robinson had written to Ellen Nussey to indicate her plans to write a "life" of Emily Brontë. "No great woman who ever lived has left so little behind her that can be written about as Emily Brontë," writes Bidell, adding, "what do we know of the inner life of Emily?"[23] Robinson's ability to convey the inner life of her subjects in a way consistent with and contributing to an understanding of their work became a characteristic that she honed during later years in her nonfiction prose, and it consistently earned her praise in critical reviews.

Robinson became the proprietor of how Brontë was perceived well into the twentieth century, and we learn a great deal not only about Brontë but also about Robinson through the activity of biographical writing – the gathering, sorting, discarding, and synthesizing of material necessary for success in the genre. Like an indexer shaping critical response to a text, a biographer establishes the primary focus of the life "text" of the subject and, for a time at least, directs us in our approach to the author and to the author's work. As Robinson herself writes of Brontë, "being dead she persuades us to honor; and not only her works but the memory of her life shall rise up and praise her, who lived without praise so well" (235). To complete this act of consecration, Robinson had at hand an interesting range of research material, since she was able to interview Ellen Nussey and other residents of Haworth who remembered the family well. The result is a biography that includes the archival material unearthed by a capable researcher, the interpretive analysis of an insightful critic, and the anecdotal commentary of those who shared an intimacy with the subject from which the biographer was excluded. Robert Browning developed the word "repristinate" to describe working through the layering of historical documentation and interpretation of this documentation in *The Ring and the Book*, and modern scholars use the term "historicity" to describe the complicated process of reconstruction. Through the parallel literary genre of translation, Robinson had developed some insight into the difficulties of bringing the past to life, and she applies her experience in this respect to the case of the Brontë family who lived a domestic life within the context of what she calls "their father's quaint experiment." This experiment had to do with suppressing emotions, with donning a "mask" from behind which they spoke, and living "restrained, enforcedly quiet, assuming a demure appearance to cloak their passionate little hearts" (26). The result, Robinson maintains, was the "passionate" expression of life in their literature from a very early age.

Robinson's poetic language evokes the air that Emily Brontë breathed, the crushing emotional and physical toll of her brother's dissipation, her father's depression, her intense love for and devotion to her sisters, and the complex aesthetic mind that produced fine poetry and *Wuthering Heights*. In his review for the *Athenaeum* 16 June 1883, Swinburne recognizes Robinson's compassionate depiction of Emily Brontë and contrasts Robinson to Elizabeth Gaskell, whose biography of Charlotte Brontë had been published posthumously in 1857. In order to avoid lawsuits and giving pain to Charlotte's father, her husband, and friends who were still living, Gaskell had to treat materials, particularly letters from Ellen Nussey and others, with more restraint, points out Swinburne, but he also says that Robinson is by nature a better biographer: "The sweet and noble genius of Mrs. Gaskell did not enable her to see far into so strange and sublime a problem; but, after all, the main difference between the biographer of Emily and the biographer of Charlotte is that Miss Robinson has been interested and attracted where Mrs. Gaskell was scared and perplexed."[24] Swinburne disagrees with Robinson's assessment that Branwell significantly influenced Emily's work, but Robinson was delighted to receive such a review from someone she admired, and she wrote to Swinburne 15 June 1883 to thank him profusely for this review.[25] A reviewer for the *St James's Gazette* writes along the same lines 28 August 1883, noting that what "has attracted Miss Robinson to Emily Brontë is not solely, nor even chiefly, her genius as a writer, but her character as a woman," and this affinity, the reviewer suggests, makes Robinson's perspective very different from that of Gaskell.[26] Hence, Robinson's natural creativity and literary interests contribute to her ability to present Branwell's tragedy with sympathy and compassion and, through her nuanced historical "reconstruction" of events, she represents more accurately the increasingly detrimental effect his dissipation had on those who loved him intensely.

As she speculates about Emily's literary response to the family's dysfunctional domestic life, Robinson assumes the informed perspective of an observer, suggesting with assurance, for instance, that "no one in the house ever saw what things Emily wrote in the moments of pause from her pastry-making, in those brief sittings under the currants, in those long and lonely watches from her drunken brother. She did not write to be read, but only to relieve a burdened heart" (129). Speaking as a poet about a poet, Robinson offers examples of the nature of this burden in several of Brontë's poems. For instance, Robinson suggests that when we read "The Philosopher," written in 1845, "what we care for is the surprising energy with which the successive images are projected, the earnest ring of the verse, the imagination which invests all its changes. The man and the philosopher are but the clumsy machinery of the magic-lantern, the more kept out of view the better" (132). "Remembrance" is Brontë's best work in its expression of "defiance and mourning," suggests Robinson, for in this poem Brontë articulates "moods so natural to her that she seems to scarcely need the intervention of words in their confession" (134). Empathy with the emotionally confused Brontë enables Robinson to cast Brontë's poetic genius in terms of her suffering: "It is painful, in reading these early poems, to feel how ruthless and horrible that strong imagination often was, as yet directed on no purposed line" (137). When Robinson identifies Brontë's "creative instinct" as a process that "reveals itself in imagining emotions and not characters" in order to lead us to experience a certain mood along with the poet, she foreshadows the rhetorical process of some of her own poetry, such as "Loss," which would be published in *The New Arcadia* the following year (135). In "Loss," Robinson leads us through the process of grief in ways that subtly comment on the sustained influence of Brontë during the 1880s.

Therefore, Brontë's saintly patronage of Robinson is evident in this biography in the intimacies of an aestheticist expression of ideas. Robinson turns herself into a reader defined both by her analytical powers of reading and by her aesthetic emotional responses to written and oral testimony, and, as this complexly schooled reader, she constructs a study of Brontë that highlights the dead poet's reclusiveness, her extreme reluctance to involve herself socially outside the family, and her morbid premonition of the tragic trajectory of her life and the lives of her siblings. Throughout the biography, Robinson casts Brontë's daily actions and creative works in light of these characteristics, and the result is the first study of Brontë that fleshes out Charlotte's sketch of her sister in her preface to *Wuthering Heights*. The fact that when the biography was published Robinson and Lee had constructed the discourse on the value of poetry and the aesthetic life that is reflected in Lee's "Dialogue on Poetic Morality" situates the biography squarely in what Lee refers to in a letter of October 1883 as Robinson's "pre-Raphaelite days." Indeed, Robinson treats her subject with wishful and wistful regenerative energy, suggesting that through the sensitive eyes of the intuitive writer, Brontë transcends the passage of time and remains acutely pertinent. "Her imagination is narrower, but more intense; she sees less, but what she sees is absolutely present: no writer has described the moors, the wind, the skies, with her passionate fidelity, but this is all of Nature that she describes," writes Robinson (3). This tribute explains Robinson's certainty that Brontë needed to be included in the Eminent Women series, and it initiated Robinson's notable success in a genre that enabled the integration of her intuitive understanding of human nature, the aesthetic perspective of her sensitive poet's soul, and her nuanced understanding of language.

The New Arcadia

The discourse between Lee and Robinson about Robinson's prospects as a prose writer that unfolded during the writing and publishing process of *Arden* and *Emily Brontë* was interspersed with discussions of Robinson's next volume of poetry, *The New Arcadia*. These discussions took place, as usual, in the context of Robinson's repeated complaints to Lee that she was ill, most frequently with neuralgia, and might not be able to travel to Florence. Lee was by now becoming rather impatient with the constant excuses and does not seem to have responded with quite as much seriousness and sympathy as Robinson hoped. Writing 3 October 1883, for instance, Lee softens what must have been harsh comments and has to reassure a worried Robinson, "you must never doubt of me, my dearest, for you know how completely you and your love have become part of the very webb [*sic*] & woof of my life."[27] Lee's old friend Annie Meyer died 18 December 1883 and, although they had ended their relationship about the time that Lee met Robinson, her death now sent Lee into a depression that manifested itself in increased reliance on Robinson. On 22 December 1883, Lee tells Robinson that she met the writer Ouida, whom both she and Robinson knew through Bella Duffy, with whom Lee took refuge during the crisis with the Robinson family. Lee did not like Ouida, complaining to Robinson that "we had hardly shaken hands but she began to cross question me about

Mme. Meyer & whether I had been very intimate with her ... I thought her impertinent & could not help thinking of what she said to you last year about my going in for female adoration."[28] The close of the year is marked by a letter of Christmas Day from Lee to Robinson with the usual references to Robinson's illness, particularly her "delirious nights," and Lee's plea that Robinson "always love" her and that she take care of her own health. However, a few days later, 2 January 1884, Lee again expressed disappointment at not having heard from Robinson and included in this New Year's letter a fresh lock of her hair to replace a previously bestowed lock.

Robinson continued to delay her trip, and ultimately, her mother wrote to Lee to explain that Robinson was too ill to travel to Florence that spring. By March, everyone had settled on the plan that Lee, who was working on *Miss Brown*, would travel to London in June. Lee's letter on 12 May is both conciliatory and condescending, and it perhaps indicates the nature of Robinson's frustration and discomfort in a friendship with so many demands attached to it:

> How much I love you and how much my loving you depends upon your being just what you are, just the particular compound of hairbrained [*sic*] irresponsibility with tremendous sense of duty & obstinacy of determination, just the particular mixture of the person to look up to & of the baby to run after, which satisfies the two halves of your nature ... How do you suppose that I can ask you to live according to my standards? ... I couldn't help laughing at what you said about my wanting to keep you in a harem.[29]

By this point, *The New Arcadia*, dedicated to Lee, was in press and Robinson was busy publishing original poetry in and reviewing for the *Athenaeum*. She and William Sharp continued to oversee the Marston fund, and, by the time Lee came to London in June, Robinson had regained her health and the two attended social events, including on 20 June 1884 a tea party at John Singer Sargent's home in London, where they and Mabel joined Henry James, Walter Pater, and Pater's two sisters Hester and Clara.[30] Now that everyone had apologized to her, Lee once more made the Robinson home her base.

The term "Arcadia" in the title of Robinson's new volume refers to the unspoiled, natural setting of classical legend, as well as to the natural innocence associated with the lost ideal of Eden, a double allusion that provides context for this poetic social commentary. The term also suggests the emerging conventions of dystopia and the spoils of industrialization that were increasingly popular themes in the final decades of the nineteenth century, themes running parallel to and in many ways complementing, the more aestheticist themes of transience and impermanence that unify the Robinson canon. As Emily Harrington points out, "while disconnected from those she writes about by class, she is connected to them by shared feelings of helplessness, which she is able to dramatize in her use of lyric form."[31] Theodore Watts points out in his review of "The New Arcadia" for the *Athenaeum* that Robinson's Arcadia is not "new" but is "as old as the human race itself."[32] Robinson's integration of the poetry of pure aesthetics and the poetry of social and philosophical criticism enables her to study, as Vadillo explains, the "relationship between the enjoyment of the beautiful and the commodification of culture in her study of a dystopian Arcadia."[33] As the prologue makes clear, the speaker directing the overarching narrative of "The New Arcadia" is intent on making the world "look within" to face the truth of social inequity (12).

Robinson's Arcadians are based on real people, she explains in the preface to *Collected Poems* in 1901, people who "lived on a common in Surrey near my garden gate," and yet, again drawing on the material and outer facts of her life for inspiration, she felt she had somehow failed to achieve realism (x). As she confided to Gosse 21 May 1884, the poems "were meant to be very true and real, & somehow they were not at all."[34] In her presentation copy, Lee notes the specific "characters" based on reality, as Robinson had described them to her during the writing process, as well as the dates of composition of several of the poems as noted below.[35] Friends and reviewers alike tended to agree that the effort at realism failed in some of the poetic portraits of the Arcadians, Symonds, for instance, wondering whether "so lurid a piece of cruelty in English life" as she depicts in "The Rothers" could be true or the terrible ending of "Cottar's Girl" possible.[36] Lee at first praised "The Rothers" when Robinson sent her the draft in October 1883: "Whatever I may think of your new forms, Janet Fisher and the Rothers make the New Arcadia your most important work in my eyes, and even supposing it to be mere transition <u>development</u> work, it must have developed in you a power of movement which you did not dream of in your preraphaelite days" [emphasis Lee's].[37] When the poems appeared in print, however, Lee suggested that Robinson "do a realistic Balzac type thing of the Rothers."[38] The reviewer for the *Spectator* describes Robinson as an "esthetic pessimist" like D.G. Rossetti and suggests that "The New Arcadia" evokes Thomson's *The City of Dreadful Night* through poetry that is "elaborate, allusive, obscure, and pitched throughout in a false falsetto."[39] Always sensitive about negative criticism, Robinson moved away from social criticism and did not write anything resembling "The New Arcadia" until her marriage with Émile Duclaux introduced her to another group of country people in the Cantal, and several of these members of the Olmet community appear in *The Return to Nature.*

Perhaps the "false falsetto" that the critic for the *Spectator* hears is the result of a deliberate discord between form and context. Glaser suggests that Robinson's training in classical metre, training in which she learned specifically "the power of irregularity and dissonance," informs much of her work in this period, and arguably in this case discord within the poetic form subtly conveys the failure of democratic and egalitarian principles.[40] To that end, Robinson structures her larger narrative of the whole poem through several different poetic forms that provide a mélange of voices and perspectives from and on the corrupt Arcadian social state. For instance, the prologue, which Lee noted in her copy contains "a licence of elisions and iambic truly running into anapests," is the only poem written in rhyme royal, its uniqueness emphasizing its centrality to the ideas developed through the following poems, just as the epilogue is the only sonnet, singularity of form and the internal argument that is part of the rhetorical process of the Petrarchan sonnet drawing attention to the poet's failure to resolve the overall social problem of Arcadia. As Linda Ely explains, Robinson's intent in the prologue is to make clear that the poems that follow "repudiate the criminal silence of contemporary poetry that consistently and superficially presents a metaphysical illusion or an ideal world, a world that assuages the uncertainties of Victorian life, a world that sells."[41] Unfolding in this frame, the narrative of "The New Arcadia" successfully conveys the impermeable nature of class barriers and the continued social evils that perpetuate the pastoral ideal.

The brief quotation from John Webster's *The Duchess of Malfi*
that provides an epigraph for the whole volume pluralizes "lives,"
singular in the original, to fit the context of the titular poem, and
the line works as a reminder of the terrible moment in Webster's
play when Bosola toys verbally with the Duchess he has come to kill:
"Their lives, a general mist of error." Like Bosola, Robinson implies,
the inhabitants of Arcadia will avenge those who have suffered,
and, as the speaker of the frame fears, their determination to do so
will develop their potential for evil. What is needed, she suggests
through the poetic voice of the prologue and epilogue, is a civilizing
framework that will ensure the disappearance of this horrific Arcadia;
otherwise, the broad social consequences will be catastrophic.

At the end of the poem, then, the speaker implies that in reality
the "garden" is nothing but "wilderness," a lesson that begins in the
metaphorical representation of the garden gate in the first poem,
"The Hand-Bell Ringers," written at Epsom on New Year's Day
1884, a poem in which the speaker recognizes the challenge of truly
understanding those from whom she is separated by the glass window
that keeps the cold winter weather, as well as the handbell ringers,
outside. As her image is superimposed through the window on the
features of those without, she realizes that they are more than a
desultory and miserable group: they are four people with individual
characteristics, and she determines to tell the individual stories of the
inhabitants of Arcadia. Her heart will lead her to an understanding
of these people and their culture, she hopes, but the truncated final
syllable of the first line of the last stanza signalled by "alas" acts
metrically as a warning that crossing social barriers is, as the speaker
concludes, nearly impossible:

> So dark is the night, so dark, alas!
> I look on the world, no doubt;
> Yet I see no less in the window-glass,
> The room within, than the trees and grass,
> And men I would study without. (19)

In this moment, the speaker understands her separation from
the men and the natural world outside. In alternating the iambic
pentametre rhythm typical of the quintain with tetrametre lines,

Robinson creates the illusion of contraction, as if to mimic the speaker's recognition of the shrinking possibility of bridging this class divide.

Individual stories in this society have certain elements in common, and Robinson uses poetic form to depict the ways in which human suffering can be both unique and universal. In "Man and Wife," the Venus and Adonis rhyming patterns conventionally associated with enduring and transcendental love, for instance, comment ironically on an elderly couple so impoverished that they are forced into the workhouse, where they will be separated. The wife points out that "trouble shared" is short-lived and manageable – they could deal with "the shame" and the "workhouse fare" were they to remain whole as husband and wife, but once they have been absorbed into the social organization of the lost bodies and souls in the workhouse, she will exist as "no man's wife or mother" (25). This couple, Lee records in her copy, were actually "two old people, name forgotten, at Epsom," but Robinson wrote the poem itself at Newquay, Cornwall in October 1883, suggesting the profound effect this story had on Robinson as she composed the lyric to tell their story while she was on holiday. "The Rothers," also a Venus and Adonis poem, focuses on the disease-like, radiating selfishness and greed in the Rother family. Lee notes that Robinson was considering the title "The Moor at Fittleworth," and the poem was indeed written in August 1882, during the time she spent there with Lee. Lee's copy is annotated to highlight Robinson's colour imagery. The couplet distinctive of this poetic form concluding each stanza reinforces through rhyme the savagery of the generational evil of Rothers that has been passed down to Florence and Maud, two adult sisters who mistreat the aunt who had been kind to them in their youth and whom they eventually allow to die in misery and degradation. The speaker is a friend of the dead woman, and she concludes her tale vowing to shun the Rother sisters and implicitly calling on others to do the same:

> Forget my friend, forget a crime
> Because the county neighbors fret
> That I'll not meet at dinner-time
> Ingratitude and murder? Nay,
> Touch pitch and be defiled, I say. (66)

It is the couplet at the end that draws attention to this single voice of refusal to accept the Rother sisters as the norm and its elegance as a poetic device implies the social significance of this refusal in the long term.

The didactic strain of the ballad form of "The Scapegoat" also emphasizes the poem's concern with generational patterns, this time of poverty, ignorance, and the moral, sexual, and emotional violation of a young girl, a "scapegoat," upon whom the sins of her drunken father and wild brothers are unleashed until she is transformed from an innocent child desperate for familial love into a hardened, coarse, young woman who satisfies not only their sexual needs but those of the townsmen as well. It is disconcerting to see that Lee identifies the girl as Annie Sutton, who lived in what had become the Robinson family's "tuck-house" in October of 1883, when Robinson wrote the poem. The speaker comes to terms with the fact that the true immorality of this situation is a composite of those responsible, not only the family but also the speaker himself "who gave no sign" that the outrage was taking place (32). Themes of separation and isolation between speakers and the men and women of Arcadia continue in "Men and Monkeys," a ballad in which the balladeer watches those suggested by the alliterative title, a gypsy man, a girl, and a monkey, all who seem at first to the speaker to be less than human in their incapacity to respond aesthetically to their beautiful surroundings. However, the speaker soon realizes that the monkey, with no human responsibilities, responds aesthetically to the brightly coloured ribbons poking out of the girl's bundle and mimics the human-like "rare sweet call of the nightingale" (92). The human pair, on the other hand, are aware only of "the dust that they / raised in their dismal trudging on," for they have had to sacrifice aesthetic pleasure to the instinctive urge for survival (91). An equally dismal lesson is conveyed in the ballad "Church-Going Tim," dated 1882 along with "Men and Monkeys," the speaker this time approaching the difficult relationship between necessity and aestheticism from the opposite direction to point out the dangers of complacency and self-interest that result from blind faith in organized religion. Tim's allegiance to the spiritual life ensures, he thinks, his place in heaven, but in attending church daily, the reality is that he leaves his wife to cope with the consequent poverty and too many sons. Now and again Tim's wife "wished as he was bad," the neighbour-speaker says, as she takes some pleasure in her own "wild" husband and "all those boys" that take up her days (97). The incongruity between Tim's faith and his way of life is suggested through the phrasing of the title, the compound adjective conveying the critical undertones of this poetic voice, who, in expressing her disgust at Tim, represents the position of many women in the social "order" of Arcadia.

Using the quintain form, Robinson explores more carefully the situation of women and children – the very young and the very old – in three poems that highlight the survival of the fittest in this cruel society. The titular character in "Janet Fisher" is a beautiful and "simple" child and is to the community "their one fair thing, their one thing good" (38). Her inability to understand the evil in human beings leads to her death when she is duped by an army deserter into helping him escape; however, the position of their bodies when they are washed ashore suggests to the villagers that she has managed to lead this reprobate to an act of penance in his final moments, and in her simplicity, she becomes a symbol of the capacity for good that transcends their vile existence. "Cottar's Girl," as Symonds complains, does indeed have a terrible ending, but it is not an unrealistic ending because it is linked to the crippling effects of superstition and ignorance, both features of this Arcadian world. The doctor of "Cottar's Girl," placed by education and rank above the misery of Arcadia, is dismayed but not surprised by the fate of a young girl who dies at the hands of her mother, who, suspecting a pregnancy, feeds her daughter lead poisoning in hopes of bringing on a miscarriage and avoiding shame and humiliation.

The third quintain, "The Wise-Woman," also features an educated, middleclass man unable to prevent the seductive power of social approbation from reinforcing cultural behaviours that perpetuate the quagmire of Arcadia, and it demonstrates the complex nature of a society that functions through exclusion. This time the victim is an unappealing old woman who has been persecuted, hunted, had her home smashed, and been "ducked" in the pond as a witch. The college-educated squire's son with "new-fangled knowledge" argues the inclusiveness of Christian belief, even inviting the "witch" to pray with him (83). However, although her response shocks him, by this point in the narrative of Arcadia, it should not shock us: "But horror-stricken, aghast, from his side / The witch broke loose and fled" (83). While he interprets her flight as an expression of fear and the villagers interpret it as an admission of guilt, the woman is simply protecting her position of isolation and social censure because, although she is well aware that she "could never compel / A quart of cream to turn," she enjoys the power of intimidation, the only power that "a woman poor and old" can claim (84, 85). Thus she, like the Cottars, is willing to sacrifice all for the meanest kind of social standing.

"The School Children," the final "study" of Arcadia, deals directly with the relationship between education and social advancement. In rhythmic alternating tetrametre and trimetre lines of the quintain form, the poem begins with the trance-like vision of the sixteenth-century Dutch spiritualist and theologian, David Joris, who provides a context within which the new generation of Arcadia might be nurtured more optimistically. For the moment, academic training keeps the children apart from and above the Arcadian life of poverty and corruption, and the speaker directs her comments to those who suggest that education is wasted on these children and that "too much they know / for their lowlier rank" (103). The argument against this claim is delivered in the form of a parable as the speaker studying Arcadia likens this potential to Joris's vision of ghostly kings, priests, and other figures of authority who, parading through his "twilit painting-room" one evening, are brought to their knees by "playing children – much the same / as we see them here," says the speaker (105). The varied depictions of this problematic society, then, end with the warning that it is the responsibility of the social whole to prepare the children for their leadership.

As the epilogue of the whole poem and the final element of the frame through which Robinson develops her poetic perspective, the concluding Petrarchan sonnet underscores the "shiftless, hopeless, long, brute misery" of the people who have been the subjects of this "study." Ultimately, "I cannot show, / I cannot say the dreadful things I see," admits the speaker (109). Arcadia remains impenetrable and resolute, representative not only of the spoiled Eden of nineteenth century society but also of the ultimate failure of poetry – traditionally linked to the deep and profound expression of emotion – to convey the human condition in all its limitations.

As Harrington suggests, Robinson counters Lee's general position in "The Dialogue on Poetic Morality" "that aesthetic pleasure is democratic, available to all" and suggests instead "that it is in fact the case that the poor do not have the time and energy for the aesthetic."[42] Indeed, in writing "The New Arcadia," Robinson addresses Cyril's complaint in the role that Lee assigns to her in "The Dialogue on Poetic Morality" that it is impossible to write poetry in an evil world.[43] It would seem too that this experiment in social aestheticism, as Ely points out, "reveals her sad determination to keep 'under cover', out of her poetry, her concerns about 'the world full of hunger and sighs.'"[44] On the other hand, also emerging from this depiction of failed ideals is Robinson's conviction that sympathy is possible without the perspective of experience and, while her position as a poet separates her from those whose lives she depicts, it nevertheless enables her to bring her social aestheticism to fruition by providing her readers with a common reservoir of human empathy and understanding from which they can draw to enact social change. Robinson's poetic response to Lee's prose proposition, in its skilled manipulation of metrics and rhyme, is more effective than either Robinson or her friends seem to have realized, for "The New Arcadia" suggests that literature ought to at least try to address human needs beyond living in the aesthetic moment.

The "Other Poems" of *The New Arcadia*

Just as the poems included in the *Hippolytus* volume are for the most part related to the translation in thematic ways, so too the poems in this volume are consistent in subtle ways with the themes of the titular poem and with the fictional conversation that Lee developed out of her interchanges with Robinson on the social value of poetry. Thematically, they might be read as Robinson's rebellious response to Lee and Gosse and even Rossetti, who urged her at various points to move away from the kind of aestheticist poetry that invites intimacy between poet and reader on matters of love, death, and the spiritual life. During conversations specifically related to "The New Arcadia" itself, after all, Lee implicitly urges Robinson to develop her talents along the lines that had until now been successful. As always,

Robinson places first what she considers to be an important poem to focus those that follow, in this case, "Loss," an exploration of grief suggestive of Robinson's debt to Brontë's model, as she says in the biography, "in imagining emotions and not characters" as she traces in this lyrical interior monologue a widower's profound grief at the death of his wife (*Emily Brontë*, 135). Robinson confided to Gosse that this difficult love poem, which is really a poem about the process of mourning, was one of the poems she liked best in the volume.[45] Lee too seems to have found it extraordinary and annotated her copy with "vero," translated as "truthful" or "sincere," to indicate Robinson's mastery at conveying the nuanced stages of grief. The speaker has loved intensely, and he mourns intensely, but he, like Tennyson's "In Memoriam" speaker, is appalled at his fading and failing ability to evoke the physical attributes of his love – her face, her voice, and her touch:

> All of her dead except the Past –
> The finished Past, that cannot grow –
> But that, at least, will always last,
> Mocking, consoling, Life-in-show.
>
> Will that fade too? Seven days ago
> She was alive and by my side,
> And yet I cannot now divide
> The pallid, gasping girl who died
> From her I used to love and know. (114)

This second quatrain is telling – the girl began to "die" in his mind while she was ill, as "used" in the last line indicates. Perhaps, then, there are feelings of guilt lying beneath the speaker's movement from the first phase of shock and denial through anger, resentment, and finally acceptance of the paradox of grief – fading memory dulls the intense and immediate pain of loss, but it also dulls the image of the dead wife in unsettling ways. Later in the poem he says,

> I feel her now as there she lay
> Close in my arms, and still asleep;

Close in my arms, so dear, so dear;
I hold her close, and warm, and near,
Who sleeps where it is cold and deep. (115–16)

However, he admits in the next stanza, "that is my boasted memory; / That, – the impression of a mood," and that "impression" inflects the way he sees the world now to such an extent that, by the end of the poem, he "hate[s]" Florence and the Florentines who surround him but who cannot share his grief (120). Robinson clearly felt strongly about this very nuanced study of grief and about the complex emotions – both comforting and disturbing – that comprise the state of perpetual mourning.

In "Apprehension," which William Sharp included in *Sonnets of this Century* in 1886, Robinson looks at the transient nature of love in more general terms, as this time, the speaker's exquisite joy in being in love is overshadowed by "apprehension" that all human experience, even the joy of love itself, is by definition temporary. This is a technically complicated poem with the first of the three parts consisting of three sixteenth-century Spanish quintillas and the remaining two parts Petrarchan sonnets. Despite the conventions of the quintilla form, these poems depict a landscape that is Romantic rather than pastoral, evoking the setting of "The New Arcadia" and highlighting the paradoxical awe and fear of the Romantic sublime.

And never a change in the great green flat
Till the change of night, my friend.
Oh wide green valley where we two sat,
How I longed that our lives were as peaceful as that,
And seen from end to end! (168)

This final stanza of the first section is spoken in retrospect, the last line suggesting the speaker's naïveté in hoping for a life that would imitate that unchanging, static countryside. In the following two sections, the shift from the quintilla form to the traditional Petrarchan sonnet mockingly emphasizes the speaker's affirmation that although transcendent love is only a "foolish dream ... Yet must I dream" (168, 169). The same theme developed in "Love and

Vision" evokes Robert Browning's "Two in the Campagna" when the speaker declares in the opening line, "my love is more than life to me," and in the following ten verses of "Love and Vision," failure to reconcile different perspectives bodes ill for sustained love (173). While the speaker sees beauty in the wet moors, a "fairyland," she says, that "sparkles, lives, and dances," her companion sees something very different and much less appealing (174). The concluding stanza situates this difference ominously in broader philosophical terms:

> Brown moors and stormy skies that kiss
> At eve in rainy weather
> You saw – but what the heather is
> Saw I, who love the heather. (175)

In conflating the imagery of atmosphere with the imagery of love through the personification achieved with "kiss," the speaker implies that love – in any form – leads to insight into something beyond the human. This is also a gendered statement about the differences in the ways in which men and women view nature and is a reiteration in substance of "A Dialogue" of the *Honeysuckle* volume.

We find a revision of "Church-Going Tim" in the ekphrastic poem "Love Among the Saints," which was inspired by Giotto's painting "Marriage of Saint Francis and Lady Poverty," which is housed in the Basilica of St Francis in Assisi. The painting depicts the patron saint of the poor taking the hand of Poverty in marriage. Poverty is unappealingly dressed in rags and has a rather masculine, harsh face, as she extends her finger for the ring in front of the saints with sober faces "clear and pure" who constitute the wedding guests (138). As the sun moves across the fresco, the images seem to come to life one by one, and the speaker realizes that Saint Agnes and Saint Clare, sisters inspired by St Francis to set up orders of nuns, are not depicted in this painting. Who else is missing, the speaker wonders, and "sees" hovering unseen in the painting, an image of "Love himself in mazed affright" because he has been excluded from the ceremony and is left "starved and naked, wan and thin, / Beautiful in his distress" (139). This poem, writes Henry Charles Beeching, the dean of Norwich, in his review for the *Academy,* is "a beautiful instance of Miss Robinson's imaginative insight and of the simple sweetness of her verse."[46] Indeed, Robinson well expresses here the human need for earthly love rather than the esoteric and spiritual love represented by religious icons, a "phantom Love" that drives us to "madness, and destroys" (141).

> Yet, to all Love must call,
> Only we may choose the voice.
> And whate'er we are or prove,
> Loathe or love,
> Hangs upon that instant's choice. (141)

We cannot live without the warmth and companionship of love in all its weakness, the speaker realizes, and it behooves us to make the right choices in matters of love. Therefore, "Love Among the Saints," like "Church-Going Tim," highlights not only the dangers inherent in undermining the joys to be found in the here and now of earthly life, but also implicitly castigates the subversion of earthly love to abstract religious ideals.

Italian poetic forms in this volume, not only the sonnet but also the rispetto, foreshadow the beautiful and haunting "Tuscan Cypress" of the 1886 collection *An Italian Garden*. Robinson was certainly familiar with Symonds's essay "Poliziano's Italian Poetry," in which he points out that "the rispetti embody no philosophy of love, no chivalrous religion. They are inspired by Aphrodite Pandemos, and the joys of which they speak are carnal."[47] In "Tuscan Olives," this sensual element inflects the analogy Robinson develops between variations in olive genres and variations in love. The overarching narrative of the sequence situates the speaker and lover walking among olive trees in the heat, and moment by moment, the speaker's eyes are riveted not on the beautiful scene but on her companion. The sequence reaches its turning point in the fourth rispetto, when the speaker accepts an olive branch offered to her:

> How hot it was! Across the white-hot wall
> Pale olives stretch towards the blazing street;
> You broke a branch, you never spoke at all,
> But gave it me to fan with in the heat;
> You gave it me without a sign or word,

And yet, my love, I think you knew I heard.
You gave it me without a word or sign:
Under the olives first I called you mine. (126)

The language of intuition and confirmation of love in the last three
lines is suggestive of a great deal of epistolary exchange between
Robinson and Lee in these years, which casts an interesting light
on the remaining three rispetti. The speaker is less optimistic about
the possibility of transcendent love as, located in the same place
several months later, she resists taking an olive branch with her to her
"Northern room," for she knows that realistically it will not survive
there. If the poem does indeed evolve out of one of Robinson's ideal
moments with Lee, this pessimism might be read in context of Amy
Levy's sonnet "To Vernon Lee," which records a walk that Levy took
with Lee, whom she first visited in Florence in 1885.

"Stornello and Strambotti" consists of two eight-line strambotti
and three epigraphic, three-line stornelli placed in opening and
closing positions, as well as between the two strambotti. "Stornello"
in Italian can mean not only a folk song but also and more commonly
"starling," and the bird's strong, forceful, and pithy song is evoked in
the one hemistich line and two hendecasyllabic lines with perfect
rhymes in lines one and three and a slant rhyme in line two:

Flower of the vine!
I scarcely knew or saw how Love began;
So mean a flower brings forth the sweetest wine! (133)

The discourse constructed through the alternating Italian forms that
follow this opening declaration of love is specifically related to the
rhetorical process of each part as well as to the rhetorical process of
the whole poem. In this case, the intervening Tuscan strambotti
of eight iambic hendecasyllabic lines construct a dialogue between
lover and loved one that reveals the inadequacy of the metaphors
introduced in the stornelli to depict the true nature of lasting love.
Watts in his *Athenaeum* review cites technical inaccuracies in metrical
forms and improper employment of syllables in her attempt at this
complex hybridity, elements with which Robinson would have more
success in a poem with the same title in *An Italian Garden.*[48]

Other poems published in this collection overlap with Robinson's prose offerings and her interest in history and mysticism as she worked doggedly on material that would eventually contribute to *The End of the Middle Ages*. "Jützi Schultheiss" perhaps has roots in "Mary Schonewald" in its reflection of Robinson's interest in German mystics. Lee contacted the publisher T.H.S. Escott in 1883 to urge him to "think of making use" of Robinson's "curious paper on German mystics," a project that does not seem to have come to fruition as an independent project.[49] The speaker of this monologue in iambic tetrametre couplets is a medieval mystic who loses her gifts of trance and vision as punishment for a moment of anger when she refuses to intervene and pray to God for forgiveness for some carousing knights who have stormed the convent in which she resides. As a child, the critically ill Jützi was rescued from death and, as thanks, her family pledged her to God as a nun. The tension of the poem is indicated in the second line when Jützi refers to her mystical powers as "the vision and the load," as she describes her Pentecostal insight into the mysteries of God, as well as her attempts to balance the ecstasy associated with that insight with longing for her earthly family (145). The Quietism, or death to the self and empowering resurrection, has come at a price, but Jützi has also developed over the seven years strong feelings of superiority arising out of the gift and the sacrifice she has made, and these feelings ultimately lead to her fall from grace and loss of her powers through her failure to extend Christian forgiveness. The moral of poem, then, is that we humans have a collective responsibility to exhibit human kindness or we risk losing connection to the divine.

This gap between human needs and divine expectations is the theme of "The Conquest of Fairyland," which W.P. Ker describes in his review for the *Contemporary Review* as a "ballad of fairy enchantment" that "is not meant as anything very serious."[50] However, it did receive recognition when it was republished in 1888 in an illustrated children's book, *Young People's New Pictorial Library of Poetry and Prose*, an appropriate venue for this didactic poem with its message that our behaviour on earth has consequences afterwards. On the other hand, "Laus Deo: A.D. 1213" is a more conventional presentation of an ideal afterlife. "Praise God" and the specific date that marks the end of the crusades in the title provide context for this inner monologue that might be called a prayer of reflection and that depicts God as "the common soul of all," who exists both within the speaker and external to the speaker (161). This rather pantheistic God is nonjudgmental and nondirecting, a "chasm" into which the speaker will eventually let go and fall "simply through the dark abyss" (162). Robinson presents God metaphorically, on the one hand as a "mighty womb" where "undreamed deeds are stored" until we, ready to perform those deeds, emerge into the world, and on the other hand as the "tomb" toward which we move (162). In the final few lines of the poem, the speaker is overwhelmed by the enormity of a "God, too far, too strange to bless" her and begs to be released from the stress of living in a state of unknowing:

> Take from me memory, thought and soul,
> Drowned and confounded let me be,
> In Thy surrounding night to roll,
> An atom past my own control,
> In the unconscious sum of Thee. (163)

Delivered in the context of the medieval crusades, the passage suggests the speaker's awareness of the paradox of this time of religious wars – a time of reaffirmation of faith in a loving, forgiving God and a time of brutality and cruelty.

In the final, short poem "Song," Robinson returns to the larger issues of "The New Arcadia," and questions the possibility of expressing human despair poetically. "I have lost my singing-voice," the poet-speaker says in the first of two septets, despite the perfect rhymes of the second stanza that suggest that she has not lost her voice and that belie her claim that her "heyday's gone" (193). This poem reflects correspondence with Lee about poetry and her own capabilities as a poet and reflects similar discussions with Symonds. Robinson was caught in the early 1880s between these two people whose respect she most valued but who had nothing in common but her dependence on them. In fact, during the course of 1884, the difficult relationship between Symonds and Lee became acrimonious. His letters to Robinson are sly in tone, as he casts himself as a well-meaning friend. Writing 28 May 1884, he tells Robinson, "I have got myself into a mess with Miss Paget," but this situation is "owing to my inveterate habit of speaking the truth out crudely whether for good or evil, & her incapacity to acknowledge the least shortcoming in herself."[51] His letters to Lee reveal the same condescension and arrogance, which she, of course, found offensive. He was ambivalent about Lee's work and tended to undermine even the work he actually liked. He reports to Robinson that he "admired the vigour, wealth, originality, penetrative analysis, & exuberant diction" of *Euphorion* but says that "it is a pity that Miss Paget had not studied the prose legend of Faustus instead of taking the metaphor wh [*sic*] she has worked for her title from me."[52] A month later, he could not resist pressing the issue, admitting, "the success of *Euphorion* gives me great satisfaction. It is a very remarkable book, which grows up on my appreciative judgment – though I misdoubt the method." In the same letter he asks Robinson a question that suggests his subconscious interest in the nature of the Lee–Robinson friendship: "Do you know *who* wrote Callirrhoë? Are you in Michael Field's secret? I should like to know. [emphasis Symonds's]"[53] There is some irony in the comment, since Robinson published a signed review of *Callirrhoë* shortly after this exchange, and William Watson commented to Michael Field that such a favourable review "raises one's opinion of the critics."[54]

Robinson generally tried to pretend that the breaches between Symonds and Lee did not exist, and she prevailed upon Symonds in September to help with the promotion in England of Lee-Hamilton's book *Apollo and Marsyas, and other poems*. Whether she asked him to see to finding a potentially positive reviewer is not clear, but he does place quotation marks around his refusal to "arrange" such a thing in his rather pompous reply 9 September 1884, adding that he "so abhor[s] the undignified modern system of arranging beforehand the reviews of books."[55] Ultimately, he reviewed the book himself for the *Academy*, which suggests his motives.[56] A few weeks later, 6 October 1884, he sent Robinson his *Wine, Women, and Song* as a gift to cheer her up after some negative reviews of *The New Arcadia*, but then suggests that problems with her work stem from her being under a not "wholly healthy influence," undoubtedly referring to Vernon Lee.[57] He complains that she is different than she was six years ago and that he would like her to "go & live somewhere away from clever women & clever men for some long while!" He does write three days later to apologize for his "unkind" letter.[58]

By September of 1884, Lee was back in Florence, and, as often happened when they parted, she and Robinson wrote longingly of being together. Lee thanks Robinson 25 September 1884 for a "dear anniversary letter," presumably marking their meeting four years previously, and tells her a few months later that since knowing Mary she has "very rarely suffered from that dreadful ... isolation that seemed to plague me so formerly."[59] During these months, Lee continued to share her increasing distress with the shape that *Miss Brown* was taking – or not taking. When the novel proved to be unsuccessful, Robinson was deeply regretful that she had not taken Lee's fears seriously. She admitted to the unsympathetic Symonds 21 December 1884 that she had failed Lee in not insisting that Lee send the proofs to her:

> I ought to have been more vigilant. And I ought to have kept her from making enemies & from saying things which I know to be unjust but which she, of course, does not know to be so. For after all, I am one of the English & she must have got her idea of it chiefly from me. This is making me most miserable. I feel unwilling to have deluded Vernon & betrayed my dear old friends.

The letter ends with Robinson's testament to Symonds that the one thing she could have done for Vernon Lee was to "understand her and be a sort of shield between her and the world."[60] Colby links Lee's treatment of love in the novel not only to her rejection of aestheticism itself but also to Lee's recognition "in her own life as in Miss Brown's a human need for love and companionship"; however, Colby continues, Lee "felt only revulsion at the thought of sexual intimacy."[61] Robinson surely intuited this tension in Lee during their intimate friendship, and, despite her protests of ignorance to Symonds, also most certainly suspected that much of Lee's struggle in the production of the novel had to do with this tension. Ironically, when Oscar Wilde visited Lee's brother at Casa Paget to express admiration for Lee-Hamilton's work, the meeting between Wilde and Lee was, Robinson confided later to Mary Berenson, "a great success." "Oscar talked like an angel, and they all fell in love with him – even Vernon, who hated him almost as bitterly as he had hated her. He on his part was charmed with her."[62] Perhaps Robinson was reassuring herself more than Berenson with these remarks, but there is no doubt that the failure of *Miss Brown* was painful to both Lee and Robinson, albeit for different reasons.

CHAPTER FOUR

Final Years in London, 1885–88

Sylvaine Marandon describes the years during which Robinson was intimately connected to Vernon Lee and the Paget household in Florence as her "prolonged adolescence," and it does indeed seem to be the case that Robinson had too many parent figures in her life.[1] Lee's tendency to refer to her as "child" hints at the transitional elements of their friendship and explains in part the apocalyptic incident that changed dramatically the direction of their relationship and, ultimately, their lives. Although to many friends, such as Mary Berenson, this "pattern" of Robinson and Lee together for the summers in London and the autumns in Florence "continued unbroken" on the surface until 1887, the friendship in fact began taking on new dimensions in 1885.[2] The impetus for change, therefore, came much earlier from Robinson than her falling in love with James Darmesteter. She was jolted out of her complacency by her very childish and petulant response to what she perceived to be Lee's gravitation toward another woman friend, Alice Callander. There was a positive side to Robinson's misplaced jealousy, however – the beautiful rispetti sequence "Tuscan Cypress," which is included in the 1886 *An Italian Garden*, and that volume led to her meeting James Darmesteter, the man with whom she spent the happiest years of her life. Lee's letter to Robinson on New Year's Day of 1885 reveals fissures in the friendship that had inevitably developed through Robinson's consistent presentation of herself as ill when it most suited her. Anticipating the cancellation of a proposed spring visit due to Robinson's recurring anemia, for instance, Lee writes, "I have been disappointed so often that I scarcely believe in anything now," and she adds, "it is so hard that these disappointments should come always at the eleventh hour."[3] Marandon points out that Robinson's poems written during her time with Lee reflect dissatisfaction and unhappiness on several levels, and "Tuscan Cypress," it seems to me, signals the pinnacle of this malaise and perhaps as well the "falling action" toward what would be the catastrophe of their life drama.[4] In her poetics, Robinson was emerging from this period of "adolescence" with increasing technical ability and maturity of subject, which Darmesteter seems have recognized in the poetry of *An Italian Garden*.

From an early age, Robinson had developed the habit of thinking of herself as "delicate," perhaps because everyone else considered her to be delicate as well, and it is not surprising that she used this "delicate" persona to her advantage for several years. As Mary Ward reminded Lee in mid-February of 1885, although Mary may appear better, she could never be called strong as she caught colds frequently and tired easily.[5] Similarly Vernon Lee confided to Robert Browning a year later, Easter of 1886, "Mary Robinson is staying with us till June. She has been very delicate, but seems to be getting better in this marvelous summer weather, when every day seems made for a holiday."[6] There is no doubt that the Paget household, in particular Lee's neurasthenic brother Eugene, fuelled Robinson's natural tendency to cultivate an image of "delicacy" that she perpetuated despite what turned out to be an ironically long and relatively healthy life. Unfortunately for Lee, these were the years when Robinson was also aware that she was a successful poet, that she had written a biography that Swinburne admired, and that she might cast about for ways in which this delicacy could be used to greater advantage than keeping Lee at a distance when it was convenient. Robinson maintained this persona over the years to come. When in May 1927 Mabel wrote to Lee to cancel a visit to Lee in Italy because of Robinson's lingering illness, she exclaimed to Lee in frustration, "it is difficult to believe that a person who has neither fever nor coated tongue couldn't swallow something if she put her will to do it! However at 70 no one is likely to change and we must wait until things get right again. She never eats enough to keep a cat alive."[7] In 1885, however, Robinson seems to have decided to turn her weak constitution to her advantage, and in later years, she characterizes 1885 as a turning point in her relationship with Lee away from "a long friendship of absolute trust and satisfaction."[8] The poetry of *An Italian Garden* is in many respects, then, poetry that marks an important transition in Robinson's work and in her perspective on life.

An Italian Garden

In his preface to his translation of *An Italian Garden*, James Darmesteter connects Robinson's poetry to her mysticism and to an imagination informed by a meditative and reasoning intelligence. He calls his future wife an "idealist" who shares an imagined spiritual world with her readers; however, he points out that she avoids the vagueness and the emptiness of idealist poetry through "clarity of ideas and the intensity of imagination."[9] These are the qualities in Robinson's three poetry collections published between 1886 and 1893 that establish her as a serious and accomplished poet, and it is notable that her entrance into a new phase of poetic excellence coincides with her release from what Symonds recognized as the aggressive and persistent tutelage of Vernon Lee. This volume is different in structure in that it consists of five sections that are unified through motifs that convey abstract and concrete fragments of an imagined study of love. Like Robert Browning, Robinson adopts the paradoxical stance of the Romantic ironist as she poeticizes the simultaneous joy and despair that inflect moments of insight into the ephemeral and transitional nature of love. Although not everyone agreed that these qualities make good poetry – in her *Athenaeum* review, for instance, Augusta Webster complains that the poetry of *An Italian Garden* does not reflect "the living workaday world of men and women," thereby criticizing what Darmesteter praises – there is much to be said about Robinson's nuancing of form and figurative language in this collection that marks her transformation on professional and personal levels.[10]

Robinson had by now become adept at working within the conventions of the sonnet and other Italian poetic forms, as is evident in her review of Rodolfo's *Strambotti a Sonetti dell' Altissimo* for the *Athenaeum* 28 August 1886, where she writes, "the delicate, romantic, exquisite unreality, so beautifully shot with passion and sentiment" is crucial to the expression of an alternative world experience.[11] She attempts in *An Italian Garden* a similar reconciliation of expansive imaginative insight and tight poetic form, a technique that situates her within the community of late-century women writers whose work had slipped from sight by the middle of the twentieth century. However, it is this same emphasis on poetics that makes the work of Robinson rewarding to those of us who have taken it up again. Hannah Lynch argues in the *Fortnightly Review* in 1902 that after the publication of *An Italian Garden* poetic trends shifted, and Robinson became "submerged" in a "futile wave" of inferior poetry, which meant that she was left behind when "more martial and emphatic singers came and caught the public ear."[12] Lynch no doubt had her finger on the pulse of the contemporary poetic scene, but it is telling, I think, that *An Italian Garden* had a relatively long and international life: Enrico Nencioni's review of *An Italian Garden* for the Italian *Nuova Antologia* in June 1886 was followed in 1888 by Giovenale Sicca's translation into Italian under the title *Poesie*.[13] A version in French published in 1931 containing prints by Jacques Beltrand after illustrations by Maurice Denis indicates the continued popularity and cosmopolitan flavour of *An Italian Garden*, and the volume is perhaps more fruitfully considered as the beginning of what Vadillo identifies as "cosmopolitan aestheticism" in Robinson's later poetry.[14]

The unifying theme of the five sections of *An Italian Garden* is the transitory and tenuous nature of all elements of human existence – love, natural beauty, and, ultimately, life itself. However, the aestheticist development of these themes invites us to reassemble the fragmented sense perceptions of despair into beautiful moments of poetic reflection. These fragmented moments specific to the secrets of the night in "Nocturnes," for instance, lead to the speaker's stages of response to the natural world in the central sections – "A Garland of Flowers," "Tuscan Cypress," and "Songs and Dreams," and then recede into memory in the final section, "Vestigia." This process of poetic contemplation signalled by the titles of each section suggests an integrated way in which we might perceive the beauty of this "garden" of verse. The two epigraphs that focus "Nocturnes" suggest alternative forms of love and desire through Sappho in the first epigraph and through Shelley's androgynous hermaphrodite in "The Witch of Atlas" in the second, and, of course, the nocturne of poetry and music aestheticizes the moods of the night specified by dreams, retrospectives, and private moments. In several poems of each section, as well as in "Tuscan Cypress," the significantly serious break with Vernon Lee is the source of Robinson's inspiration. In the presentation copy of *An Italian Garden* that she sent to Lee she refers to herself in Italian as a lost or cast-off "lamb."[15]

Robinson's admiration of Whistler and his visual representation of perfect musical harmony in his nocturnal paintings is evident in the poems of "Nocturnes," but she draws also on the gothic elements of the Italian "notturno" to suggest the integration of awe and terror that defines the Romantic sublime, thereby conveying through these tropes the paradox of desire that evokes both pain and joy. "Florentine May," for instance, depicts the simultaneity of hope and disappointment through the contrast of spring freshness, purity, and renewal implicit in the title. However, the jarring alliterative description in the first line of the "Night" as "still as the pause after pain" begins a series of transitional moments of release, when experience is transformed into remembrance as the speaker explores the ways in which the dreamy moments of the night ironically become in the penultimate stanza "full of wandering light and of song, / and the blossoming rose" until, in the final stanza, the speaker welcomes night as a lover:

> Night, Angel of Night, hold me and cover me so –
> Open thy wings!
> Ah, bend above and embrace! – till I hear in
> the one bird that sings
> The throb of the musical heart in the dusk,
> and the magical things
> Only the Night can know. (4)

The aural and visual imagery implicit in this "throb" is erotic, as befits the language of seduction; however, this synesthetic integration of the senses – references to the dark night, the birdsong and music, and the sensation of the heart beating – are specifically focused by the allusion to the protective Holy Ghost as the "Angel of the Night." The speaker willingly gives herself over to a space that she has formulated deep in the psyche in which she satisfies implied desire, but desire is fulfilled through a fusion of religious and sexual images that cast love in terms of the mystical ecstasy of saints rather than the earthly love of conventional early Italian poetic forms.

In the nocturnes that follow, these "magical things" are associated with a variety of tangible and intangible moments of experience. The eerily human-like voice of the nightingale penetrates the dark, death-like space of the night in "Invocations" to remind the speaker of the "silence of Death" and the "world of darkness" at the end of life (17). In "The Ideal" the speaker journeys "along the byways of [her] soul" into the inner realms of her being and "Serenade" depicts stars that in their unreachable distance symbolize striving to realize a dream always beyond reach (11,19). "Remembrance: A Sonnet" brings to mind Christina Rossetti's early sonnets as the speaker imagines herself dead and asks that the lover who has abandoned her be plagued by painful memories of "our vanished love and all our vanished ease," echoing the plaintive "Tuscan Cypress" of the third section. The sestet of "Remembrance" specifically evokes Vernon Lee, not only in the context of the private dedication of the copy sent to Lee but also in the phrasing "forgotten tune" of the third line that becomes an entire poem dedicated to Lee in the fourth section, "Songs and Dreams":

Then let my face, pale as a waning moon,
Rise on the dark and be again as dear;
Let my dead voice find its forgotten tune
And strike again as sweetly in her ear,
As when, upon my lips, one far-off June,
Thy name – O Death – she could not brook to hear! (5)

In this passage, the opening simile is developed to suggest the long, permanent "night" when the speaker has died. Just as the speaker has been left with the memory of "one far-off June," when the lover could not bear to consider the speaker's death, so the lover, she implies, will be left with the knowledge that she has contributed to that death. The rest of the Nocturnes investigate specific moments in the night when the speaker – whether looking out of a tent into the void as in "The Pavilion" or emerging out of a dark, unlit city street to find a beautifully lighted church as in "Venetian Nocturne" or watching a guiding light radiate from a lighthouse as in "Calais Beacon" – lives through moments of joy that have to do with the human experience of some form of love but that love always arises out of awareness of the individual as part of a transitional community that hints at unsustainable connections between heaven and earth.

"Fire-Flies" is noteworthy with its sesta rima rhyming patterns that structure web-like, weaving images into a poetic form itself representative of "the web of life, the weft of dreams" (7). The inner light of the fireflies suggests both Promethean insight and Christian faith, which are conflated in the mind of the speaker to indicate the paradox of the human condition: like the beautiful, unique, and irreplaceable patterns formed by the fireflies in the dark, the patterns of our lives shift, reconstitute themselves, and, ultimately, expire. In the canzone "The Feast of St John," the role of human love in these patterns is recast in terms of the tension between innate prenatal grace associated with John the Baptist's feast on 24 June and the celebrations of young love associated with midsummer; consequently, the cleansing and redemptive rituals of baptism are juxtaposed with the sensual and earthy celebrations of the summer solstice. Thus, the poetic perspective emerges out of the transitional philosophical space between Christian aesthetics and ancient fertility rites, as well as in the transitional moments between night and day.

"Nocturnes," then, sets the contemplative tone of the five sections metaphorically posited as a "garden," specifically an "Italian" garden that is both implicitly and explicitly connected to Vernon Lee and that reflects Robinson's familiarity with Florence. The second section of this garden of verse, "A Garland of Flowers," opens with an epigraph from the *Vita Nuova and Canzoniere of Dante Alighieri* that can be translated as "From blooms of little words, my story has danced," which seems an apt signpost for how the second section will contribute to the overarching theme of this garden about flowers that have for centuries been related to love. Charles Waddell Chesnutt writes that Robinson indeed "has taken airy words and spun of them tissues of airy rhyme."[16] This suggestion of blossoming and fruition is born out in poetry that reflects the complex nature of modern love that has moved away from the conventions of pastoral innocence, lushness, and fertility and embraces instead the emotional violence inherent in sexual desire. Therefore, the young girl of "A Foletta," the poem that opens this section, hints at sexual desire in the first stanza, and her name, Rosina, is itself a conflation of the affection implicit in the diminutive form and the sexual passion symbolized by the rose. In placing her hand in the speaker's hand as requested in the first stanzas, Rosina enters into the secret recesses of sexual love:

> O Rosina, Rosinella,
> Give your hand and let us go
> Where, beyond the flowering almonds,
> Scarlet tulips blow.

"Flowering almonds" conventionally symbolize hope and promise, and "scarlet tulips" suggest sexuality. In the second stanza, imagery and allusion hint at the deflowering that will bring the promise to fruition:

> O Rosina, Rosinella,
> Such a thing you could not pray,
> Dared not dream alone at midnight,
> Cry aloud to-day! (23)

As this opening poem suggests, the flowers in this garland hint at the dual nature of love – at love's appeal and at its danger. In "Red May," for instance, the scene depicted in the first stanza is very unlike a traditional May scene:

> Out of the window the trees in the Square
> Are covered with crimson May –
> You, that were all of my love and my care,
> Have broken my heart to-day. (27)

The month of May, usually described in terms of greenery and renewal, signals through the suggestion of blood imagery the speaker's life force ebbing away. Yet, there is also something aesthetically beautiful in this image of the trees outside the speaker's window, making this poem more decadent than purely aestheticist. Sinking into an emotional abyss in the second stanza, the speaker then emerges paradoxically renewed by the experience:

But though I have lost you and though I despair
Till even the past looks grey –
Out of the window the trees in the Square
Are covered with crimson May.

Similarly, in "A Rifiorita," translated as "revival," the speaker moves through physical reminders of love – the "flowers in the wall" and the "flowers on the stone" that remind her of someone who has left her life. She loves "the Past," she says, and, like a Siren abandoned, she sits on a metaphorical "rock" and finds new life in singing of what has gone (24). This poem reflects Robinson's confession to her friend Emmanuel Berl many years later, "like the Sirens love the sea, I love the past."[17] For her, comments Marandon in an apt simile, the past was like a rose without the thorns, and she was perpetually saddened because what is today will soon no longer be tomorrow.[18] In the two quatrains that comprise "Temple Garlands," floral reminders of past love grace the doors to a temple deep in the heart, diction strategically linking the sacred – the "temple" to the profane – the love garland worn by the "soul."

There is a temple in my heart
Where moth or rust can never come,
A temple swept and set apart,
To make my soul a home.

And round about the doors of it
Hang garlands that forever last,
That gathered once are always sweet;
The roses of the Past! (30)

This final image of the soul hiding in a heart and savouring memories of a liaison symbolized by the floral symbols of sexual love is another striking conflation of the sacred and the profane. In her copy, Lee jots down a quick verse that suggests that the poem is "beautiful and fiery" but cautions against "overheating," presumably referring to the sentiments expressed in this lyric. The passage is signed with a reminder of "two in Pistoia," a town near Florence. The rhetorical processes of all three poems, "Red May," "A Rifiorita," and "Temple Garlands," might be summed up by the speaker of "Treasure Song," who reinforces the "delights of dreaming, / so dear, and only seeming" (31).

The rest of the garland poems continue ironic treatment of love, as they pervert the conventional poetic representation of desire in traditional Italian poetry. In "Posies," for example, which Robinson dedicates to F.M.R., most certainly Mabel, the usual floral tribute to young love is transformed into a memorial of love lost as the lilacs and columbine, which symbolize sexual innocence and early love, become "pale" in comparison to the vibrant posy made of crimson peonies given by "a bolder man" than the speaker (25). Similarly, in "Oak and Holly," the symbols of endurance and love in the title are transformed into symbols of degeneracy and failed love as the oak leaves dry up and fall off, seeming to the speaker to "have no life in them to heal a broken heart," while the perennially green holly leaves have "no sap beneath the gloss" to sooth an aching heart (32). Throughout "A Garland of Flowers," the elements of nature's garden that conventionally form the substance of love poetry instead represent painful, unrequited, and lost love, thereby defining the aestheticist moment in terms of the finitude of love. In "Strewings," as the opening stanza demonstrates, these symbols are linked explicitly to death:

Strow poppy buds about my quiet head
And pansies on mine eyes,
And rose-leaves on the lips that were so red
Before they blanched with sighs. (29)

This scene, which reinforces the prevailing and ironic metaphor of a memorial garland that marks not the beginning but the end of finite love, is completed in the next quatrain, when the speaker's tone shifts into a warning: "But do not mock the heart that starved to death / with aught of fresh or sweet."

The generally dark mood of this collection is intensified in the third and central section of *An Italian Garden*, "Tuscan Cypress." The sixteen-sequenced rispetti of "Tuscan Cypress" were "all written in two days of great excitement," Robinson told Symonds, in a fit of jealousy over Vernon Lee's friendship with Alice Callander, the niece of Annie Meyer, with whom Lee had been involved in an intense romantic friendship before meeting Robinson.[19] In the same letter Robinson explains to Symonds that the rispetti sequence emerged out of tumultuous feelings when she had been "ridiculously (though silently) jealous of Mrs. Callander," and, she admits, "the songs are addressed by me, ill and neglected, to Vernon who has already (only in the verses) outgrown her affection. They are the utterances of a jealous dying woman who feels herself forgotten before she is dead." Despite – or perhaps because of – their origin in genuine misery and their morbidity, these are beautiful rispetti sequenced to create a narrative that traces the speaker's state of mind over a brief assessment of the value of love in all its pain and sorrow. In this respect, we see the influence of Baudelaire that Robinson acknowledges directly in the fifth section of *An Italian Garden*. In later years, she would express more often and more fully her appreciation of Baudelaire in both poetry and prose.

Through reference to death implicit in the symbolic cypress tree of the title, with its scent evoking sensations of decay, Robinson conflates the cycles of life and death with corresponding cycles in nature. The two three-line Italian stornelli that preface the sequence juxtapose the sea and the cypress tree as symbols of life and death, thereby suggesting the speaker's growing sense of the finitude of love, and this epigraphic quality appropriately sets the mood for the whole sequence. The speaker hopes that the cypress blooms will enlighten and illuminate love that has faded, thereby providing context for love in the present. In the second stornello, the ebb and flow of the sea suggests the speaker's recurring inclination to view death as a means of escape from the hopelessness of unsustainable desire. Effectively, then, the epigraph establishes the dark mood of the sequence to come. This mood is created as well through uncertainty about the nature of the poetic voice, for, as Symonds notes, the lyrics seem "neither masculine nor feminine." Moreover, he asks her, "What *is* the I? Is it you?" [emphasis Symonds's].[20] Sensing that he has touched on something unanswerable, he closes the letter with his assurance that he doubts that the "I" of the sequence is Robinson, apologizing and blaming fatigue for his raising the issue.

The first rispetto establishes the speaker's isolation and loneliness:

My mother bore me 'neath the streaming moon,
And all the enchanted light is in my soul.

> I have no place amid the happy noon,
> I have no shadow there nor aureole. (35)

Images of death and dying in the cold of night highlight the poetic mood specified in the rhetorical question of the second rispetto: "What good in Love?" (36). Over the next seven rispetti, this bleak tone intensifies in themes of separation, unrequited love, and death that culminate in the seventh rispetto as the speaker shrugs philosophically: "When I am dead and I am quite forgot, / What care I if my spirit lives or dies?" (41). The second quatrain situates this dismissal of spiritual transcendence in the context of earthly passion:

> Ah, no – the heaven of all my heart has been
> To hear your voice and catch the sighs between.
> Ah, no – the better heaven I fain would give,
> But in a cranny of your soul to live. (41)

Vacillating between desire for transcendent love and conviction that human love is by definition finite and limited, the speaker pleads in the eleventh rispetto for "a story, dear, that is not true," certainly not the kind of story that Robinson tried to tell in *The New Arcadia* (45). The remaining rispetti formulate the text of this "story," shaping it into a fantasy that shields the speaker from the pain of lost love. In the twelfth rispetto, the fantasy enables the speaker to suppress memories of love altogether. "Let us forget," the speaker pleads twice in the first stanza – forget having to part and forget having been in love. Love is aestheticized as a form of innocence that the speaker hopes will be sustainable, as like children, the two live – much like Robinson and Lee at Fittleworth – in perfect but unsustainable happiness "without to-morrow, without yesterday" (46). This fantasy is shaped more concretely in the thirteenth rispetto through an alliterative series of invocations to symbols of escape – seas, ships, sails, and the sky – and in the fourteenth rispetto through images of strangulation and suppression as the enduring cypress flower forms a "crown tight round my brows" and a "wreath tight round my breast," says the speaker (48). In the final two rispetti the tone shifts again, and the speaker brings the rhetorical process of the sequence to a full-circled close through images of resistance and resolution that transform unrequited love into the aesthetic embracing of Sorrow as a lifelong companion. In this way, the speaker enters into a new relationship with the beloved, and paralyzing despair is now an enabling awareness of love as a transient feature of human existence. Robinson's inclusion of "Tuscan Cypress" in this "garden" centres the volume in a moment of reality in which she does not long dwell.

The Tuscan rispetto in Italian that serves as an epigraph for the fourth section, "Songs and Dreams," not only provides continuity through form in the overarching theme of the aesthetic value of love but also reaffirms through spring-like birth and winter-like death that acceptance of transience can be transformative and empowering.[21] Although suffering, loss, and despair are prevailing features of the human condition throughout *An Italian Garden*, these features of life tend in the poems of "Songs and Dreams" to be specifically related to the individual experience of love that distinguishes us from one another and that affects how we perceive all aspects of life. In the first poem, "Tuscan May-Day," the speaker, damaged by love and with a heart "mad with sorrow," sits isolated from other young girls who celebrate the anticipation of spring and love. In ancient Greece, the month of May was dedicated to Artemis, the goddess of fecundity well known to Robinson through her translation. This speaker is isolated by her feelings of guilt and her sorrow, both emotions linked to the love that she has not only already experienced but that she has also lost. The final verse sets out her punishment for transgressing in matters of love, for she is no longer entitled to address the *Virgin Mary* [emphasis mine]:

> I sang beside them at the spring,
> And in the weedy furrow;
> But here I feel I dare not sing,
> "Mary, Mary, Mary, Mother Mary,"
> My heart is mad with sorrow! (54)

In the convention of the woman who has transgressed in matters of love and, in this case, implicit consummation of that love, the speaker's sorrow is intensified by her acute awareness that she has sacrificed a great deal for a transient moment of pleasure. It is difficult to avoid reading the autobiographical implications of many poems in this collection, but this particular poem, in its rising panic, seems particularly poignant in the context of Robinson's correspondence with Symonds about her fears that Lee had emotionally left her.

On the other hand, Robinson treats the experience of love more optimistically in "Love Without Wings," in which eight "songs" of varied length, metre, and rhyme imagine love in more abstract terms.[22] The title alludes to Byron's "L'Amitié Est L'Amour Sans Ailes" or "friendship is love without his wings," which the speaker implicitly concedes in the last two verses of the final song:

> Long blessèd days of love and wakening thought,
> All, all are dead;
> Nothing endures we did, nothing we wrought,
> Nothing we said.
>
> But once I dreamed I sat and sang with you
> On Ida hill.
> There, in the echoes of my life, we two
> Are singing still. (58)

Even in the context of what seems to have been an increasingly fragile relationship with Vernon Lee, such dreams bring the speaker a measure of peace through reminiscence of happier days. It may well be that poems such as this arise not from the bitterness of imagined slights but from a deep sense in Robinson that she really was becoming less interested in sustaining the romantic friendship that had become more intense than she had intended it to become.

Just above "A Ballad of Forgotten Tunes" in her copy, Lee noted in pencil, "Written by a person who never felt the pathos of a forgotten tune." Given the dedication of the poem itself to Lee and the situation of their friendship in terms of the problematic historicist act of retrieval, Lee's unkind notation suggests that she was well aware of the crisis that informs "Tuscan Cypress" and that recurs throughout *An Italian Garden*. Perhaps too she was prepared for this poem by "Remembrance" of the first section. At any rate, in this ballad, the "faded notes" of old music and "the soul that dwelt in them" are lost to future generations, the speaker suggests, for ultimately the act of creation and the act of perception occur in separate cultural, social, and political contexts. The ominous repetition after each of

the three stanzas, "dead are the tunes of yesterday," emphasizes the
impossibility of permanence in all human endeavours, including
matters of love and intimacy. That this sentiment is related directly
to Lee is clear in the envoy that follows the three stanzas:

> Vernon, in vain you stoop to con
> the slender faded notes to-day –
> the Soul that dwelt in them is gone:
> *Dead are the tunes of yesterday!* (68)

Given the unifying thread of this poetry collection that is directly
related to the friendship between Robinson and Lee, this poetic
tribute is also a warning, like "Remembrance," that Robinson feels
herself a forgotten tune and a "slender faded note."

Music is the thematic agent in "Semitones" as well. The title
refers to the negligible distance between notes on a keyboard so
that two semitones make a whole tone; however, the three sections
of two quatrains each that make up this poem, are about discord
rather than harmony. In the first section, the speaker suggests that
just as thorns enhance the beauty of the rose, so too does the pain
that comes with love, which has become increasingly problematic
by the first quatrain of the second section:

> Ah, could I clasp thee in mine arms,
> And thou not feel me there,
> Asleep and free from vain alarms,
> Asleep and unaware! (59)

By the final section of the poem, the speaker longs for a physical
proximity that has been lost and gives herself up to the realization
that "they were not happy in the past / it is so bitter to forget." This
is a speaker for whom the nuanced music of love seems in retrospect
to have been lacking and, "like leaves along the tempest driven," she
concludes, they have drifted apart (60). According to Lee's annotation
of this poem, Robinson worked the second section out of a passage
from Stendhal, possibly his novel *Love*, which Stendhal wrote when
he felt fragile and which is often read as an autobiographical story of
his own feelings of having been betrayed in love.[23] Other poems in

this world of "dreams" similarly depict the distance between desire and attainment of that desire, some in religious imagery reminiscent of Robinson's early poetry, such as "Death in the World," "Elysium," and "Lovers," and others, such as "Alternatives" and "Princesses" in more material depictions of lovers at cross purposes. Often these "dreams" emphasize the complexities of sexual desire, failure in love, and regret at having loved and lost, but again and again we see that in diverse ways, the "songs and dreams" of *An Italian Garden* imply the shifting form of the relationship between Mary Robinson and Vernon Lee.

The final section of *An Italian Garden* is focused by the epigraph from Baudelaire's "The Harmony of Evening" from *Les Fleurs du Mal*. Baudelaire's poem is a feat of synesthesia and technical form. In the first quatrain the speaker responds to integrated appeals to the senses, an integration enhanced by the pantoum form in which the second line of the first stanza becomes the first line of the next stanza:

> Now it is nearly time when, quivering on its stem,
> Each flower, like a censer, sprinkles out its scent;
> Sounds and perfumes are mingling in the evening air;
> Waltz of a mournfulness and languid vertigo![24]

In the second quatrain the quivering flower becomes a violin "trembling like a grieving heart" and in the third the heart is metaphorically transformed into a "sad and lovely sky" darkening as the sun, "drowning in its dark, congealing blood," dies out. Robinson takes her epigraph from the first two lines of the fourth and final stanza of "The Harmony of Evening": "A tender heart that hates non-being, vast and black / Assembles every glowing vestige of the past!" The poems of "Vestigia" deal with the human experience of nocturnal intimacy and in this sense close the frame initiated by "Nocturnes." In the first poem, "Rosa Rosarum," the symbolic rose tossed into a well represents passionate, sensual, and transcendent love that the speaker promises will bury "the secret of thy heart" and "the secret of thy life" (77). The illicit nature of the love the two share evokes Baudelaire in the secrecy of this gesture to ensure that "never more the rose shall rise / to shame us." However, the passion hidden forever in the poet's heart that is signalled by "a sudden dawn of red" from deep in the well also suggests the continued influence of this vestigial moment on later experiences of love, and, in the implicitly shameful nature of love that is also thrilling, it suggests the influence of Baudelaire (78).

In "An Oasis," the speaker's soul is represented as a metaphorical "well" in the "desert waste" of love. The irony of the poem's title is indicated by the nonreflective quality of the water in this well, as though in absorbing this tremendous but transient love, the water has lost its reflective powers, and so love remains buried and unrequited:

> The sun shines down, the moon slants over it,
> The stars look in and are reflected not;
> Only your face, unchanged and unforgot,
> Shines through the deeps, till all the waves are lit. (79)

The closing line of the poem suggests infidelity as the speaker admits that things have changed and that "since then you pause by many a greener brink," another allusion, perhaps, to Robinson's misconceived conviction that Lee's feelings for her had changed (80). The conditional phrasing that introduces the water metaphor in the short poem "Torrents" that follows also suggests that love is subject to the temporal realities of life. The first stanza is hopeful:

> I know that if our lives could meet
> Like torrents in a sudden tide,
> Our souls should send their shining sheet
> Of waters far and wide.

However, in the second stanza of this brief poem, this hope is dashed:

> But, ah! my dear, the springs of mine
> Have never yet begun to flow –
> And yours, that were so full and fine,
> Ran dry so long ago! (80)

In these poems, the water metaphor, which is conventionally related to health and vitality, conveys instead failure and hopelessness, and offers insight into the extent to which Robinson was feeling increasingly alienated from Lee. In the two quatrains of "Castello," for instance, the frozen waters of the garden fountain in winter have left the sea god Triton silenced and impotent; however, it is not the wintery scene that the speaker finds sad but the failure of the poetic imagination to evoke the lost beauty of the gardens in this moment of snow and ice. Over and over again, failure in memory, in creative impulse, in poetic genius, and, as is the case here, in imaginative potential give us insight into the emotional stasis of Mary Robinson before James Darmesteter came into her life.

Other natural elements provide the same medium for contemplation of the paradox of human existence more broadly: yearning for assurance that life is a continuum of past, present, and future that is always crippled by the elusive nature of vestiges of memory. This paradox is evident in "A Classic Landscape" as nature extends memory into an archetypal faculty that links the speaker to poets of the past, and leads the speaker to the platonic ideal that, as Marandon notes, we are all only actors in this world.[25] In both "Poplar Leaves" and "Spring Under Cypresses," similar vestiges are triggered by associational sensory appeals directly related to the trees: the poplar is associated with endurance and courage and the cypress with death, mourning, and grief. Pivotal moments in the speaker's awareness of transience and impermanence occur in "Campiello Barbero" [sic, Barbaro] when the past meets the present in a girl's song and in "Music" when the speaker, caught in the transitional space between sleeping and waking, struggles unsuccessfully to recall an exquisite tune that vanishes as consciousness returns. This moment is reshaped in "Song" into the seconds between living and dying to suggest that when only the vestiges of love remain, attempts to recover love are as futile as attempts to breathe in the scent of the rose in the throes of dying.

Hence, the vestiges of memory for this poet-speaker belong not only to the individual but also to the collective memory of humankind, and Robinson is interested in the role of the poet in conveying this collective memory. "Sonnet" situates the speaker on the continuum between life and death, and vivid imagery in the octave conveys the dry, parched quality of the speaker's life restricted to the unfertile strip of land along the edge of the forest. The octave is hauntingly autobiographical when read in tandem with Robinson's confessional letters to Symonds in her youth:

Since childhood have I dragged my life along
The dusty purlieus and approach of Death,
Hoping the years would bring me easier breath,
And turn my painful sighing to a song;
But, ah, the years have done me cruel wrong,
For they have robbed me of that happy faith;
Still in the world of men I move a wraith,
Who to the shadow-world not yet belong. (92)

Reference to the loss of faith that came with maturity in the second quatrain pinpoints a moment in the speaker's life – as it seems to have occurred in Robinson's life – when all chance of reconciling infinite yearning with finite reality appears to have gone forever. The sestet reiterates these dark thoughts, but the concluding lines suggest that the speaker has found a way to conceptualize the relationship between the infinite and the finite outside the parameters of faith, thereby retaining the tenuous, yet determined hope that keeps the abyss at bay: "But all the skein, I do beseech you, break, / And spin a stronger thread more perfectly" (92). This theme is developed from another perspective in "Art and Life" through the intricate relationship between the aesthetic representation of beauty in still life painting and the natural beauty that art aims to represent. The French term for "still life," "nature morte," conveys this theme more clearly than the English term, perhaps, for as the speaker realizes, in picking living blooms to transform them into static representations, she has not only denigrated the beauty of spring but has also forfeited the harvest fruit. Hence, in satisfying her desire for infinite pleasure, she has compromised pleasure in finite terms.

For inclusion in *An Italian Garden*, Robinson reinscribed poetically her 1882 obituary article on Rossetti as "In Memoriam: Dante Gabriel Rossetti." This relatively long lyrical elegy in the form of a musical Italian madrigal pays tribute to the poet and artist whose ekphrastic work explores transdisciplinary representations of love. Robinson links Rossetti through his May birth to the Virgin Mary, as well as to conventional representations of rebirth and renewal in the natural world, and through his Easter death she links him to the Resurrection and implies the possibility of a transcendent life after death. The songbirds that fill the air with joyful tunes in the first

stanza underscore the unnatural silence that seems to have fallen
on the earth with Rossetti's death:

> The swallows sweep with darting wings
> At last and larks arise,
> For spring is here and only waits in vain
> One sweeter note for which we all are fain
> That sounds in Paradise. (93)

In situating this moment of transcendence as Rossetti's escape
from a difficult and unhappy life, the speaker urges Rossetti's soul-
companions to rejoice now that he is among them and Rossetti
himself to participate in singing with the "eternal lyre" for which he
seems to have been destined. The poem concludes with a striking
image of Rossetti moving upwards: "with unrelenting wings / thou
fleddest past us towards eternal things / as swallows fly to summers
never seen" (94, 95).

The two sestinas that conclude *An Italian Garden* finalize the
aestheticization of the transient process of life in a twelfth-century
poetic form that complex word patterns make challenging to construct: the same set of six words end each line but appear in different
lines in each of the six stanzas of six lines each; the closing tercet
makes a total of thirty-nine lines. The overall effect of this form is to
emphasize containment and restriction; in this respect, the sestina is
appropriate for the aestheticist themes of isolation, impermanence,
and death. In "Personality," the poet figure of "Sonnet" banished
to the "purlieus" reemerges, but now the abstract human quality
denoted in the title is allegorized as high garden walls between
which our souls progress separated from one another with nothing
but emptiness stretching before and behind. Although we may yearn
to break through the walls in pursuit of love, we remain imprisoned
within our own "walled" personalities, "for ever, irremediably alone."
The release of tension at the end of the poem is consistent with the
larger themes of "Vestigia":

> Ah, hope of every heart, there *is* an end!
> An end when each shall be no more alone,
> But either dead, or strong enough to break

This prisoning self and find that larger Soul
(Neither of thee nor me) enthroned in front
Of Time, beyond the world's remotest walls! (98–9)

These pantheistic images of absorption by a spiritual presence are not
new to this 1886 volume, but in this and the final sestina "Pulvis et
Umbra," Robinson emphasizes the solitary nature of human life. The
titular allusion to Horace's "dust and shadow" explicitly highlights
this speaker's experience of life in these terms:

Along the crowded streets I walk and think
How I, a shadow, pace among the shades,
For I and all men seem to me unreal. (100)

Death is the only certainty for this speaker in a platonic world of
shades and shadows: "Shades, like the prisoning self that bounds
them all, / Shades, like the transient world, and as unreal" (100). Even
death, certain as it is to mark the end of life, she thinks, "may be a
passage from the shades" or it "may be a step beyond the Unreal /
Towards the Thought that answers all I think" (101, 102). The sestina
form reinforces the fragmentary nature of human insight into the
infinite, as well as the transient nature of the human condition.
Despite the ambivalence of the reviewer for the *Spectator*, who writes
that although the poems in the volume "are full of elegance, and even
tenderness" they lack "substance," Robinson's story of transient love
reflects the strong human yearning for endurance in a world defined
by impermanence, and it reflects, I suggest, Robinson's specific feelings of impermanence related to Vernon Lee.[26]

Despite the personal context of its production, *An Italian Garden*
aestheticizes the isolation inherent in the individual inner life through
an intimate expression of androgynous desire that transcends gender,
time, and place. Robinson depends on lyrical Italian forms, with
their rich heritage as love poetry, to shift her perspective from the
aestheticist socialism of *The New Arcadia* to the aestheticist individualism of *An Italian Garden* in order to write about love marked by
unrequited desire and failed passion – love dissociated from gender
restrictions and indeed from sexual desire. She poeticizes Pater's
anxiety related to our "sense of the splendour of our experience
and of its awful brevity."[27] If, as Marandon suggests, Robinson did

not write about love when she was in love, then it appears that her relationship with Vernon Lee had already been reshaped when she began to put this volume together. *An Italian Garden* seems to reflect in essence Robinson's own trajectory of love as she imagined it, a trajectory defined by the ironic beauty of transience, impermanence, and instability that characterize love within the individual heart.

Prose Writings 1886–89

During the summer and into the fall of 1886, Robinson was busy working on two significant prose works, *Margaret of Angoulême, Queen of Navarre*, her second biography for Allen's *Eminent Women Series* edited by John Ingram, and *The End of the Middle Ages; Essays & Questions in History* published by Fisher Unwin in 1889. *Margaret of Angoulême* was her first major publication in French, and it was her friend Arthur Machen who translated the book into English in 1887. She wrote the introduction for the English version and reciprocated Machen's favour with an introduction for his translation of the *Heptameron*, a collection of seventy-two short stories that Margaret wrote while she was Queen and that was published posthumously in 1558. Machen's work is modeled on Boccaccio's *Decameron*, with the goal being one hundred stories over ten days, but Margaret died before completing the project. Machen's edition is beautifully bound and decorated as a coffee table book, and the material for the introduction comes, of course, from Robinson's French biography. In this preface for Machen, Robinson highlights Margaret's morbidity and fear of death, but she does so in an informal style, reminding her "gentle reader" to remember that the French Marguerite's world informs her presentation of the "Heptameron," and this is "a world full of good humour and well-being, of life and wealth and stirring impulse, of signs of prosperity and vigour" (34, 48). Robinson editorializes at times, revealing her ongoing interest in death: "To die, to die. We all do it. And what is it to die? To drop into the abyss of nonexistence: so says the natural man. To escape from a world of shows in *Whatever is:* so speaks the philosophical thought. To return to God: so hopes the soul of faith" [emphasis Robinson's] (51). She was approaching thirty as she wrote these words, and she would spend the rest of her life trying to decide which of these three options she might adopt as her own characterization of death and dying.

The biography itself is a detailed account of the life of Margaret of Angoulême, of Valois, and of France, Queen of Navarre, Duchess of Alençon and Berry. Robinson focuses on the historical events rather than the literary events of Margaret's life. "Her mercy and magnanimity were the saving of a nation," she writes, indicating the enormous respect she felt for this political figure, and "for this, and not for her novels or her poems, she will be remembered" (316). Using archival material, letters, and published accounts, Robinson reconstructs the life of Margaret, the sister of King Francis, who reigned from 1515–47, tracing the profound family feelings that left Francis and Margaret closer to each other than they were to their respective spouses. Not surprisingly, Margaret's importance to modern France lies for Robinson in her contribution to education, for she "inspired the College of France; it was she who protected and guaranteed the Renaissance in France from the ignorant rage of the Sorbonne." Hence, Robinson tells the story of Margaret's life in the context of her influence and "inspiring spirit," both qualities that reflect Robinson's approach as well to biographical writing (6).

This literary portrait of Margaret, then, is gendered as Robinson creates a sympathetic portrait of a woman with a clear sense of duty and admirable perseverance in furthering the causes of an unappealing king during a time of political turmoil. As the biography makes clear, Margaret is a compelling example of the difficulty of living as a European royal woman, a topic that Robinson would explore in future prose and poetry. As she had done when writing Emily Brontë's life and would do in her preface to Machen's book, Robinson evokes sympathy for her subject through her narrative style, which is peppered with interjections such as "I think" and couched in phrasing that highlights the human fallibility behind all historical events. This account of "the busiest woman in France" concludes enigmatically but perceptively, as she suggests that Margaret's death in 1539 was a good thing, for "she had no place in the new order of things" (314). This biography signals a shift in Robinson's biographical writing in that all of her future subjects are French, and the books were written first in French for a French readership and translated into English later. Margaret would also be her last female subject.

Robinson's biographies reflect her care in working with both print and manuscript sources, but she was limited for the most part to what was available to her in Paris, and, while they appealed to a popular readership, only *Emily Brontë* seems to have endured in scholarly circles. By and large, she remains known best for her poetry.

In October 1886, Mary and Mabel visited Symonds in Davos, and she was already assembling articles to make up *The End of the Middle Ages; Essays & Questions in History*, which she dedicated to Symonds. She and Symonds discussed the project at length during this visit, and their shared perspective on history as it informs contemporary life is reflected in the diverse subjects of this text, she explains in the preface, as she credits Symonds with inspiring her to bring the past to life and to evoke not only historical details but also the cultural context in which people lived. Perhaps prompted by the dedication, the critic for the *Cambridge Review* notes, "her brilliant descriptive style is apt to run into rhapsody, though not so dangerously as the style of her 'master' J.A. Symonds, occasionally does in his great work."[28] The hybrid nature of this book, with the two seemingly unrelated threads of mysticism and history, led to a bifurcated critical history as well. While the *Cambridge Review* finds the hybridity problematic, the reviewer for the *Spectator* approves of the historical and the mystical content.[29] "The Attraction of the Abyss" is deemed in the *Historical Review* to be the "most incoherent of her sketches" and in the *Cambridge Review* to have failed to situate mysticism in the Buddhist movement. One essay in particular, "The Ladies of Milan," subtitled "Cherchez la Femme," earned specific criticism for including personal reminiscences of Robinson's own travels, leading the reviewer for the *Cambridge Review* to write that the chapter "reads grotesquely" and that poetic language makes passages "not only incongruous, but in bad taste."[30] The reviewer for *The Art Journal* concurs that Robinson's account of her travel to the tomb of Beatrice is "too personal" and suggests that her "sympathy has outstepped her judgment."[31] Even Robinson's mother worried about the eclectic nature of a book that brought together two antithetical genres under one title, and she writes to Mabel 16 June 1888, "I fear Mary's book is not a very deep & serious one. But I am afraid it has really done her no good publishing it. I hope she will be very careful before she publishes anything more or she will get a Gossian reputation."[32] Frances perhaps refers here to Gosse's critical writings, which at times suggest an authority and formal education that he did not have. Robinson herself admits in the preface that this book is a collection of fragments rather than a coherent whole, and as such, it has little chance of enduring (iii). Nevertheless, although the essays comprising *The End of the Middle Ages* are varied in style and content, the first three chapters on mysticism and the following seven on history are artfully arranged in thematic modules to reflect the complex integration of Catholicism, monarchy and government, and domestic life during the middle ages. Robinson explains that she views historical timelines as fluid, and that history as a discipline is "too complex to be accurately fixed in words" (v).

Robinson followed the same pattern in publishing her prose as she did in publishing her poetry, republishing articles that had already appeared in English journals: from the *Fortnightly Review* she culled "The Convent of Helfta" (November 1886), "Valentine Visconti" (March 1887), and "The Flight of Piero De Medici" (October 1887); from *Time: Monthly Magazine of Current Topics in Literature and Art* she took "The Beguines and the Weaving Brothers" (January 1885); and from *The English Illustrated Magazine* she republished "The Malatestas of Rimini" (November 1884). "The French in Italy and Their Imperial Project" was originally written as a preface to a book project titled *The History of the French in Italy* that Robison did not complete, and the essay was published on its own in the *Quarterly Review* the year following its appearance in *The End of the Middle Ages*. The original publication dates trace Robinson's preoccupation with medieval women's lives and with the paradox of convent life specifically, for in the convent women enjoyed a certain amount of female autonomy on the one hand but found themselves bound by religious restrictions on the other. These are articles concerned with the political power of the Catholic Church in Italy and with the intricacy of Italian/French relationships in medieval history; however, they are also concerned with human fallibility in the complex integration of gendered and religious "political" arenas.

During the late 1880s, Robinson was writing reviews that foreshadow her extended time as a reviewer for the *Times Literary Supplement*. In "The Novelists of Naples" for the *National Review* in July 1886, she highlights three Italian authors, Matilde Serao, Gabriele

D'Annunzio, who became a friend and promoter of Robinson's work in Italy, and Verga, who had risen quickly and recently to transform Naples into a cultural literary centre of Italy. These "realists who have, for all their pessimism, the gaiety, the frank out-looking and objective mood, the passion and vivacity and lightness of the south" are comparable to Zola in their ability to write impressionistically, she argues.[33] She was invited in March 1887 to participate in an author's conference in London. She tells Lee 13 March "the council paid me the flattering compliment of selecting me above all people as the Representative Lady Author," and, in "a fit of mingled vanity and vengeance" for Mabel's success with her own career in fiction, she says, she put her nervousness aside and agreed to speak. "The only comfort is that nearly all the men were just as nervous," including Monk Lewis, who, Robinson reports, "gulped down a few sentences before a crowded audience."[34]

It may be that her return to fiction with a short story in December 1886 for a collection of tales for Unwin's *Christmas Annual* for 1887 contributed to her anxiety, for despite the reissue of this volume the following year in the United States as *The Witching Time: Tales for the Year's End*, this tale is not particularly distinguished and evokes some of the reviews of *Arden* in that characters are not clearly delineated, and they act on motives not explained. The forty-year-old titular bachelor hero "Vincent Hadding" seems to pursue the sixteen-year-old Marian Bassett for reasons that remain unclear even to him, and the unexpectedly dark ending casts this as a cautionary tale that highlights the disturbing nature of this pursuit. The young girl's early attraction to the older Vincent takes the form of a schoolgirl crush – a desire to be friends with an older mentor type that is eerily reminiscent of Robinson's own friendship with Symonds. In other ways as well, the story seems to have its roots in earlier times in Robinson's life. The narrator, for instance, is reminiscent of the narrator of *Arden* in a tendency to make immature narrative asides, such as "I always preferred" one character over another without explaining why. Perhaps too this story has origins in some of Robinson's correspondence with Lee about *Miss Brown*, since Vincent Harding and Walter Hamlin have more in common than the ring of their names. They are fascinated by the idea of transposing fiction into reality and Vincent's unhappiness at the end is the consequence of arrogance and not wanting to face the fact of his aging, both themes that echo Robinson's 1881 "Goneril" as well.

During 1887 and 1888, Robinson was quite eclectic, writing and assembling prose essays and fiction, as well as reviewing for the *Athenaeum* and, of course, writing poetry for her next collection, the 1888 *Songs, Ballads, and a Garden Play*. Her reviews for the *Athenaeum* in the spring of 1887 were directly related to the Italian poetic forms in which she had worked in *An Italian Garden* and that reoccur in *Songs, Ballads*. She reviewed *Folk Songs of Italy* by Helen Busk 9 April, *Costanza* by G. Pierantoni Mancini 21 May, *Spanish and Italian Folk Songs* by Alma Strettell 30 July. In February 1888 she reviewed *Modern Italian Poets* by William Howells. She was busy, yet, she would admit later, she was profoundly unhappy and feeling increasingly alienated from family and friends. Eugene Lee-Hamilton may have influenced her in this tendency toward depression, for she wrote her poem "In Affliction," later to be named "Neurasthenia," at this time, and she gives the poem context in her obituary article for *Country Magazine* just after Lee-Hamilton's death in 1907.

In retrospect, then, Robinson's frequent illnesses – some imagined and others more minor than she might have admitted – as well as her physical lethargy and self-absorption in matters of health, may have seemed to her to parallel the more extreme paralysis of Lee-Hamilton, with whom she had always been on very good terms. Lee-Hamilton greatly admired her and her poetry, and he dedicated his own poetry collection *The New Medusa* to her in 1882. "You have a Shelley-like splendor of imagery, which God ought to have given to me but didn't," he writes to her 16 December 1883, and he says that he has memorized some of the poems of *A Handful of Honeysuckle* and that he "thinks of [her] a great deal."[35] By 1907, she was able to write sympathetically of his suffering, but she also conveys some ironic understanding of what his sister felt was a determination not to get well. That he did indeed experience signs of recovery before the publication of *Sonnets of the Wingless Hours* in 1894, a sequence in which he links his poetic insight to his illness, was little known by those outside the family circle, and many were surprised at his complete recovery once his mother had died. That he subsequently married and fathered a child supports Lee's view, as do medical records that indicate that Lee-Hamilton's recovery was related to the tendency toward autosuggestion that may have been a "cause" of the disease itself.[36] Neurasthenia was a complex, little understood collection of diseases and Robinson was compassionate and empathetic by nature, writing to Gosse in 1887, for instance, to justify her fondness for William Sharp, who Gosse did not like. She makes an interesting generalization in this letter about the people with whom she and Mabel were close friends. "All our best friends are rather unjust, quick, and sensitive people," she writes. She also commiserates with Gosse, who was suffering from what she calls in the letter "hyperaesthesia [sic]," which was an element of Lee-Hamilton's neurasthenia, and she goes on to say, "I know very well what it is to get into that state and how slowly rest and quiet lead one out of it."[37]

In the spring of 1887, Robinson again postponed a visit to Florence, citing her mother's ill health as well as her own, and this was the postponement that kept her in London to meet James Darmesteter that summer. Lee was clearly becoming tired of these delays and perhaps conscious that there was a core part of Robinson that she would never control. The tone of her response to the postponement 12 April 1887 is subtly manipulative, as she says that "every baby" would know that Robinson was working too hard and that she is "awfully, awfully sorry to know you so weak and ailing, and that pain in the nape of the neck sounds dreadful."[38] She apologizes 25 April 1887, for not writing more often, partly because she has "been fearfully busy and still more because I don't want to hurry you into writing to me." She goes on to say, "but I want you to know that I constantly think of you (along with faint anxiety of heart) and that I love you dearly, *my dear little child*" [emphasis mine].[39]

When Lee went to London as usual in June 1887, she once again stayed off and on in the Robinson house when George and Frances were away in the country, but letters to her mother are filled with the usual vitriol. She tells Matilda Paget 24 June 1887, "the Robinson parents have come up to town, which means that on the very rare occasions when I can lunch or dine at that house I sit silent among a flow of wholly boring gobble," and she says that she sees little of Robinson, who works all morning and, if Lee interrupts this work, Robinson insists on making it up in the evening, "which is very hard for her. So I stay in my lodgings to read or write until it's time to go for lunch somewhere."[40] On 2 July 1887, Lee tells her mother

that she is at the Robinson country home in Epsom getting ready
for "a fearful party at the Rossetti's" and on 8 July explains to her
mother that she had stamped the envelop incorrectly because "the
Robinson girls were tearing at me to come to the Rossetti's and I
didn't know what I was doing."[41]

Clearly uncomfortable with the Robinson family, Lee had plans
to travel to Scotland to meet Kit Anstruther-Thomson, "with whom
I am expected to make great friends," she tells her mother 24 July,
and she was able to report to her mother 25 August, that "with the
exception of Mary, I have never been drawn so much to anyone, nor
felt so much confidence in anyone," adding that Kit reminds her as
well of Annie Meyer.[42] References to the two most important women
in her personal life to date with respect to Anstruther-Thomson
are highly suggestive that the Robinson–Lee friendship was about
to take a different course with the appearance of the woman who,
as Diana Maltz says, "coined the phrase 'delicate brains' as a code
word for lesbianism, implying that a sharpened aesthetic sensibility originated in one's sexual orientation."[43] The door widened for
Anstruther-Thomson when Robinson postponed joining Lee back in
Florence, for in August, she fell in love with James Darmesteter and
by September, she had announced her engagement to him. Lee was
horrified and terribly offended, ironically finding herself in agreement
with the Robinson family for the first time in years.

Mary James Darmesteter

James Darmesteter's request that he be permitted to translate *An
Italian Garden* into French initiated a period that Robinson always
considered one of perfect happiness. Darmesteter was thirty-eight,
eight years Mary's senior, a professor of language and literature at the
Collège de France, with a doctorate in letters awarded in 1877 and a
reputation as the foremost scholar of ancient Persia in Europe. In 1893
he would publish a French translation of the most sacred of Persian
religious books, the *Zend Avesta*. He was also a student of English
literature, a translator of Shakespeare and Robert Browning, and
an author of essays on the romantic poets and on George Eliot.
During their third meeting at the British Library, Robinson asked

Darmesteter to marry her. His bodily deformation that was sadly prophetic of other problems led him to demur at first, but on hearing from Robinson that she too was happy with a nontraditional, platonic marriage, he agreed to marry her.

Unfortunately, Robinson's family and close friends, including Lee, saw only that he was Jewish, that he was dwarfed and crippled by a childhood spinal disease, and that he came from a poor family. Darmesteter was very short and probably did suffer from dwarfism and its inherent problems, and he was also a hunchback; however, when Robinson's family and Lee pointed all this out to Robinson she was not only hurt and defiant but also shocked that those she loved could view him with disgust. When her mother cried, "Mary, how can you? How can you love him? He's a Jew! He's almost a dwarf," Robinson replied, "When I look at him, I don't see it."[44] Lee's letters to her mother express the same sentiments as Frances Robinson, compounded by her outrage at the suddenness of Robinson's news and the terse manner in which Robinson conveyed it to Lee. The note that Robinson sent Lee is indeed brief, perhaps because there was not a great deal that she felt she had to say and perhaps because she knew that whatever she said, Lee would take it badly. The fact that this was to be a platonic arrangement and that the "delicate" Robinson would not face childbearing seems to have been of little comfort to Lee, who writes to her mother, "if she be saved from risking her life (for she isn't fit to have children) from producing abortions fit for Paret's strychnine, the matter becomes, in my mind unnatural and sickening."[45] She casts the impending marriage in terms of Robinson's chance at "moral dignity" and suggests that there is something to be said for her finding "a man willing to consent to such an anomaly."[46] Eugene was equally appalled, also calling a platonic relationship "unnatural."[47] The only thing more "sickening" to Lee and her brother at this point seems to have been Robinson's decision to accompany Lee to Italy as usual that fall, travelling first to see James in Paris and then joining Lee before James followed as well, which is indeed the way events unfolded.

Throughout September 1887, when Robinson and James were planning how he should approach George Robinson to ask formally for Robinson's hand in marriage, Lee kept her mother abreast of how isolated Robinson had become, with none of her friends offering congratulations. Arthur Symons nastily suggested that Darmesteter orchestrated the whole affair. "By the way, do you know if it is true that A. Mary F. is going to marry Darmesteter," he asks James Dykes Campbell. "I hear so. So <u>that</u> is why he showed so much enthusiasm in the translation of her poems!"[48] It was a very difficult time for Robinson, as she indicates to William Michael Rossetti 13 June 1888 in response to his good wishes about her upcoming marriage that August: "For a long time I did not think I could ever be happy again even with James, but now I feel sure that together we shall be most content and that in time our friends will let themselves be persuaded" that the marriage is right for them.[49] Certainly her letters to and from James in September 1887 reveal her distress and fear – distress at the violent reaction of friends and family to James and fear that James would give up and lose the desire to proceed in the face of such opposition. Ultimately, George and Frances Robinson extracted the promise that the couple would wait for one year before marrying, and they did wait for exactly one year, marrying 23 August 1888, which was the one-year anniversary of their decision to marry. During that year of waiting, there was among family and friends a general softening of feelings toward Darmesteter, but the sense that a young, beautiful, talented woman was throwing herself away on what Lee terms "almost paternal affection" remained in the hearts and minds of those she loved.[50]

To Vernon Lee, this liaison continued to be nothing less than a "horror" and a most "unnatural" union. Wild with grief, she blamed Robinson's mother for having the bronchitis that had kept Robinson in London longer than usual so that she was at the British Library that August when she should have been in Florence. The fact that Robinson's visit in late September would include James was particularly galling both to Lee and to Lee-Hamilton. Lee wrote to her mother 24 September "in order again to beg and implore Eugene to restrain himself with her, and with Darmesteter, for the latter is coming almost immediately to Florence." She complains, "it will be a bore, of course, having him perpetually about," but she was still preoccupied with making Robinson see that marriage was a mistake. Lee's strategy was to claim that she was actually helping the couple: "I think it is our duty, at least to enable them to see as much of each other as possible <u>before</u>; not in hopes of their breaking off (Mary is in such a state that to do so wd I really think, kill her) but in order that the inevitable friction due to ignorance of one another may be diminished."[51]

However, while she had Robinson beside her in Florence that September, Lee succeeded in unsettling her to such an extent that she consulted James and then read his letter of reply aloud to Lee. In the letter, James assures Robinson of his happiness with their plans and confirms, Lee reported to her mother 29 September 1887, that he knew he should not have children, that he had never wanted children, and that "he proposed to Mary because, considering her health, he thought she might be willing to accept the condition under which alone he would get married." The discrepancy between this account of the proposal and Robinson's earlier account begs the question of whether she was editing the letter as she read it or whether Lee was editing it for her mother, but in the end, James remained steadfast that although he agreed to wait the engagement out for one year, he would not accept money from Robinson's father. Lee had to acknowledge to her mother, "he is so strange, yet so extraordinarily good and kind that, considering Mary's peculiar physical condition, it is most possible all may come right."[52] There is no correspondence to suggest what Lee might have meant with this description of Robinson's physique other than a reference to her general "delicacy."

It did indeed "come right," as the few letters that remain between Robinson and James Darmesteter during this period indi-cate. Robinson fell in love swiftly, and as early as 1 September she was addressing James as "My Dearest Love," asking him parenthetically, "is this wrong?" She points out, "I often call Miss Paget my dearest love, and she is a friend" [emphasis Robinson's]. She warns him that "they will try and induce you to give me up ... to be my friend and never anything more. Do not abandon me, my Soul."[53] In the same letter, she is not without humour as she self-consciously situates herself in highly dramatic terms, writing, "I am not good enough for you, but love me a little and I will love you always. Seriously. I would gladly die to make you happy, though I should, on the whole, prefer to live to make you happy." The following day, she writes, "If you love her [Lee] you will make me the happiest woman alive. And indeed, if you love me, you must love her, so much of her is me. Seven years of the most intimate & loving & profound companionship leave an indelible imprint for good or evil. And in this case, I really think that each of us is better for the other." She prevails on James to see her father the next day to ask for her hand in marriage and she seems to predict the outcome, complaining, "And yet we want so little. Only ask for a regular engagement, that I may wear your ring, see you every day, go out with you, look upon you in time as my natural protector," but she acknowledges that they will have to wait "to be so open about it."[54] She writes the next day, "what a good, beautiful happy life it would be, to sit always at your feet with my head upon your knees, learning the wonderful things you can teach me. I have always felt so 'out of it' in Life. There never seemed any future made just for me."[55]

It is difficult to see this need for reassurance and protection as other than her transference of romantic love from Lee to Darmesteter, and it was precisely the kind of love that suited James as well as it had suited Lee. His response to the desperate letters of early September was simply "croyez-en-moi," as though he sensed that it was more helpful not to be caught up in the dramatic expression Robinson had developed in her letters to Lee. Writing on 13 September, she presses him for more: "do you love me? Do you really love me? If it is true, say it sometimes," and she admits 16 September that Mabel and Vernon complain about her in similar fashion: "we tell you everything, you listen, and tell us nothing." In the same letter, she expresses her delight that she is indeed marrying a Jew because she "used to dislike Jews so much I could not bear to know them, and I was always very honestly ashamed of this prejudice which however I could not conquer."[56] Finally, to round out this first month of their engagement, she and James entered into the more practical activity of redesigning and redecorating what would be their flat in Paris on Rue Bara, and, in one letter in particular dated 4 October, she sends floor plan sketches that clearly show the nature of their marriage, for she is worried that in "taking the large bedroom & the dressing room I am leaving you no room at all."[57] She was deeply happy and by January 1888 was able to tell James that her mother seemed to be reconciled to their union.[58] She had responded to Oscar Wilde's request for something to publish in *Woman's World* and had sent him the sonnet "La Californie," which would soon appear in her next volume of poetry, telling James that the £10 she received would go toward table linens for their flat in Paris.[59]

The summer of the wedding began with a visit to Worthing in June of 1888 to stay with William Michael Rossetti's wife Lucy and children. Lucy Rossetti and her daughter Olive were ill, and James was ill in Paris with symptoms of the persistent cough that seemed to be with him routinely.[60] Writing to him from Worthing, Robinson reminisces about the time she spent with Lee in the gamekeeper's cottage, when they "were just alone in the world, she and I" and remembering again her happiness.[61] Vestiges of her tendency to present herself to Lee in childlike terms are suggested in some of these exchanges with James. "I so hope you will like the things your little girl has bought," she writes to Darmesteter 24 June.[62]

For Lee, this continued to be an extremely difficult time, and while Robinson was in Worthing, Lee's mother asked Robinson not to pursue Lee as a friend. Robinson did not write directly to Matilda Paget but wrote instead to Eugene from Worthing on 15 June 1888, asking him to give his mother her love "and assure her I will seek no interview with Vernon." She continues, however, "I will neither seek nor avoid. I can not mind a dear dear friend with whom I have no quarrel. I will only consider she is not in town."[63] However, once she had returned to London, she did indeed write Lee from Earl's Terrace on 4 August, addressing her as "My belove'd Vernon" and explaining that she had not tried to contact her while she was in London for fear of upsetting her. She also says that she is grateful to Kit Anstruther-Thomson "for her love and care of you" and expresses her regret that she has "vanished like a ghost" out of Lee's life."[64] After her marriage, when she was comfortably settled in Paris, Robinson continued to attempt to win back some measure of Lee's affection, reminding her of the "whole years of a perfect companionship" and prevailing upon Lee to wish her happiness with James. She hopes for a response, she tells Lee, and adds, "in case you should ever wish to see me again, to feel my arms around your neck – or to talk to me of your plans and adventures – darling my address will be Rue Bara."[65] Lee, meanwhile, began the process of recovery with Kit, establishing a relationship right away that blossomed and was commemorated by a rose that Lee saved in an envelope marked "neue Liebe, neues Leben," or "new love, new life."[66] Her attitude toward Mary shifted from hurt to vindication, and in late 1889, Mabel had to write to Lee to tell her that Lee's gossip about Mary had reached them and that she should stop spreading stories.[67]

Lee's old friend Marie Spartali Stillman wrote 30 September 1890 to ask Lee to make amends with Robinson.[68] In October 1890, Lee was still avoiding Robinson, telling Kit 24 October 1890, "I wrote two letters to Mary begging her to cease writing to me as it puts me into a disagreeable position. But she goes on writing as if I had never said anything. She is very long suffering."[69]

Songs, Ballads, and a Garden Play

Songs, Ballads, and a Garden Play marks an important milestone in Robinson's life, for its publication in 1888 coincided with her marriage to James and her departure from England. It was the last of her "youthful" volumes and is thematically a coming-of-age work as well, anticipating in significant ways the more sophisticated aestheticist poetry of *Retrospect*. Robinson's shift in poetic perspective is reflected in three important features of *Songs, Ballads* that provide context for its contents: an image of the imposing Albrecht Dürer painting, "Melancholia," which prefaces the poems and typifies the mood and subject matter of the whole volume; Robinson's "apology" in the form of her dedication to Mabel; and the division of the volume into three groups – "Songs of the Inner Life," "Spring Songs," and "Romantic Ballads" – followed by the verse drama "Our Lady of the Broken Heart." Each of these elements directs our reading not only of the various sections but also of the whole volume.

The haunting engraving "Melancholia," often regarded as Dürer's abstract self-portrait, was completed in 1524 and shows Melancholia surrounded by instruments and objects that are related to the temperament indicated by her name. In its time, this representation was understood philosophically in the context of Renaissance notions of artistic "genius," rather than in the classical sense of a tutelary spirit; that is, the imagination, suggests Dürer, dominates in artists, while reason takes precedence in scholars and the spirit in theologians. In choosing this image as the unifying frontispiece for the volume, Robinson highlights the paradoxical beauty and horror of the late nineteenth-century aestheticist vision that was by 1888 nudging her and other poets in her circle toward a decadent philosophical perspective. In the painting, Melancholia sits next to the spirit, Genius, looking as glum and unmotivated as she. The objects around Melancholia emphasize her paralysis: the hourglass with time running out, the empty scale, her keys and money bag hanging loosely from her belt to indicate her wealth that offers no comfort. The tools needed to build and maintain the modern world lie unused at her feet, and geometrical shapes, particularly the rhombohedrum, with its image of a human skull, underscore her inability to function. The bat, a symbol of darkness, flies near the banner that bears her name. She has so much available, it seems, but she remains inert, turned away from the light, and unable to do anything but hold her head in despair.

Robinson's direct response to the painting is the Petrarchan sonnet titled "Melancholia," which emphasizes in the octave the length of time spent on attempting to integrate a deistic being into human existence, and the speaker implies the deceitful nature of such labour:

> So many years I toiled like Caliban
> To fetch the stones and earth to build my fane;
> So many years I thought before the brain
> Reluctant would divulge the final plan.
>
> Years upon years to forge the invented tools
> Novel, as all my temple should be new;
> Years upon years to fashion and to hew
> The stones that should astound a world of fools. (34)

Through repetition of "years upon years" and through the diction of the final line that situates this labour not as a labour of love for God but a labour meant to perpetuate the faith of "fools" in God, Robinson conveys the frustration and resentment that has left Melancholia in a state of stasis. The first line of the sestet begins with two important questions and Melancholia's reluctant answer: "Now shall I build? *Cui bono*" – lo, the salt / has lost its savour and I have no will." Hence, she sits "among the ruins of the thing undone," paralyzed by her sense that the workings of the world have nothing to do with her because she has seen through the sham of human faith and, at the same time, is devastated by, as "cui bono" is translated, the fact that she can only ask "for whose benefit – for what." Although this collection of poetry develops themes that go beyond disappointment and Baudelairean ennui, its connection to the painting that provides a visual context for the poetry that follows highlights Robinson's aestheticist focus.

In the dedication to Mabel, Robinson situates the complexity of literary achievement in terms of contrasts of a more general nature – the novelist and the poet, realism and fantasy, subjectivity and objectivity, imagination and reality – that provide a framework for the "apology" for the genre of poetry. In reminiscing about Mabel's preference for fiction and her begrudging agreement to at least read poetry, Robinson now hopes that Mabel, whose first novel *Mr. Butler's Ward* was published in 1885, will enjoy this volume of poetry for its narrative qualities. Although the majority of the poems in the volume are lyrical in form, there are a number of poems, both narrative and lyrical, whose subjects "are founded on fact" and might appeal to a "Realist" like Mabel, Robinson suggests (5). Her argument that she has "only" produced verse in which the connections and distinctions between reality and fantasy are tenuous implies an uncharacteristic undermining of poetry on Robinson's part, but it also reflects her own decision to produce prose works that provided more immediate financial rewards and perhaps suggests some rebellion on her part at Lee's disapproval in 1883 of her forays into genres other than poetry. In the last paragraph, Robinson reveals the origins of the closing verse drama, constructed in the "sunny Epsom garden" where Robinson was walking with Lee and Mabel (6). This dedication was written on her birthday in February 1888, when she was anticipating that her life was going to change in a few months with her marriage to James.

Although some poems were published in advance of the collection itself, Robinson wrote the majority of the poems in this volume during the year of her engagement, and true to her tendency to avoid poeticizing love when she was actually in love, the majority of these poems treat love obliquely. Indirectly, however, her increased awareness of passing time, of the brevity of life, and of the inevitability of death might well have resulted from that difficult year as she described her own "melancholy" to William Michael Rossetti. All of the "inner life" poems touch on one aspect of what modern poets would term the human condition: the state of existing with no sense of why we exist. In his preface to *Poèsies*, Darmesteter comments on Robinson's poetic soul informed by a perspective that is both meditative and scientific, and he suggests that all of her poetry reflects her craving to understand the world through political history, religious beliefs, and literature.[70] We see this intricate integration of knowledge and intuition emerging in these "songs of the inner life."

A striking feature of this collection is the number of Shakespearean sonnets, a deviation from the Petrarchan form that Robinson had privileged to date. She uses this form, with its ironic couplet that completes an expanding rhetorical process over three quatrains, to highlight the ways in which poetry and history engage in the philosophical context of transience and impermanence. This preoccupation in her "inner life" with historicity and the obligation of the poet is the theme of "Writing History," a Shakespearean sonnet in which the speaker suggests that poetry should be used to ensure that the dead do not disappear permanently. She analogizes poetic activity to the historian's act of stooping in a churchyard by the sea "to clear the graves of their encumbering sands" in order to reveal the names and tributes inscribed on lonely tombstones (31). "Etruscan Tombs" is a sequence of four Shakespearean sonnets that delivers the same message through the unique funeral urns of the ancient Etruscans, who were defeated by the Romans around 200 BC in the region now known as Tuscany. The three quatrains describe these physical reminders of the lost civilization of Etruria as individualized urns primarily shaped as heads but some with arms extended as though reaching out from the next world:

> To think the face we love shall ever die,
> And be the indifferent earth, and know us not!
> To think that one of us shall live to cry
> On one long buried in a distant spot!
>
> O wise Etruscans, faded in the night
> Yourselves, with scarce a rose-leaf on your trace,
> You kept the ashes of the dead in sight,
> And shaped the vase to seem the vanished face. (13)

In these first two quatrains of the first sonnet, the speaker views the urns like the tombstones of "Writing History," markers representing not only the bodies that once lived and loved but also the human form itself. The Etruscans were clever in recognizing the paradox of memorials, for they are both tributes to the joy of human existence and records of human misery and despair. By the end of the third sonnet, however, the speaker is forced to acknowledge an even more complex aspect of this paradox conveyed in the concluding couplet:

A carven slab recalls his name and deeds,
Writ in a language no man living reads. (15)

Acts of commemoration are always reminders of the transience and impermanence that define the human condition, but they are also reminders of the complexity of historicity and of the larger effects of the passage of time. These effects are suggested in the speaker's recognition of the irony of the fact that symbols remain etched on stone but collective human memory has failed to retain the key to understanding the symbols.

When she is concerned with love in this volume, Robinson tends to reflect elements that move beyond ordinary experience and reflect her premise in the introduction that "the only real things, you know, are the things that never happen" (6). Love exists here in the context of bravery, courage, and loyalty. In "Arnold Von Winkelried," for instance, she blends history and fantasy to suggest that the self-sacrifice of the titular legendary Swiss soldier in throwing himself on the spears of the advancing enemy in the Battle of Sempach in 1836 might serve as an exemplar for intimate forms of love. She sent this sonnet to James with the title "Inaction" crossed out and replaced with "Devotion," neither which appears as the title of the published sonnet.[71] In changing the title for publication, she highlights the man rather than the more abstract perils of inaction and the joys of devotion, clearly her original intention. A statue commemorating this military moment was erected on the battlefield in 1886, which may have inspired this Petrarchan sonnet, and it is difficult not to see the notion of self-sacrifice prominent in her mind in September 1887 when she and James gave in to her parents' request that they wait for a year before marrying. In fact, the sonnet itself moves in a trajectory to suggest a link to her own situation through the uncaring, voyeur-like God of the octave and the extreme, hyperbolic sacrifice of its last line:

The great things that I love I cannot do,
The little things I do I cannot love!
Far from the goal I wander, and above
The voice is mute of Him I never knew.

Nothing is sweet, I find, and nothing true,
And none of all my dreams is dear enough –
And only one is worth the dreaming of;
If I could give my life and die for you! (19)

This octave is consistent with the letters she was writing James in early September 1887, when she expresses her love for him in such inflated terms, offering to die for him. In this poem, however, her speaker's pessimism about the prospect of grand action and achievement in life is situated in the specific context of Winkelried's sacrifice in the first tercet of the sestet:

O easy death, surrounded with alarms,
Blue ranks of serried spears that swerve and start
Where heroes clench their eyes and catch their breath! (19)

The image of Winkelried's self-sacrifice as a pure and ideal act of courage belongs to the world of war, the speaker realizes, but it serves as a model for the kind of courage she longs to have to summon in order to show her love for someone real, for someone who, like she, lives outside the realm of grand action and epic passions – for James:

To clasp a score of lances in my arms
And from your front to turn them in my heart
And die, and do you service in my death! (19)

In the letter to James that accompanied this poem, Robinson writes, "I love you better than I love my image of you, and am willing to shatter it if necessary in order to get at the real you. But then I think I do understand the real you and worship you."

Love between men and women takes different shapes in other inner life poems, but Robinson consistently idealizes love in Pre-Raphaelite terms that reinforces the primacy of earthly love. In the

Shakespearean sonnet "Adam and Eve," for instance, she casts the expulsion from the garden not in terms of a paradise lost but in terms of Adam's gain of Eve's love. In loving each other, Adam and Eve "saw / the light they missed in Heaven," the speaker suggests, and although Eve brought him a "dowry" of "death and shame," Adam's "dream and she were still the same" (17). Robinson seems to respond to Christina Rossetti's philosophical reference to the same scene in her Petrarchan sonnet sequence "Later Life," published in *A Pageant and other poems* in 1881: "When Adam and when Eve left Paradise / Did they love on and cling together still, / Forgiving one another all that ill / The twain had wrought on such a different wise?"[72] The two Shakespearean sonnets that make up "God in a Heart" situate love in a religious context as well. In this case, the speaker enters into a long-abandoned temple that at first seems to be a welcoming remnant of the past but is ultimately only the abandoned "altar of the unprayed-to God" and now the home of a "blind, crawling, chill, discoloured, and impure" natural life. However, in the second sonnet, the speaker's light that has revealed God's absence becomes instead the "Light of God" shining in the "heart of man," and this time the couplet completes the larger conceit of the sequenced sonnets as the "revealing Light," signalled through capitalization, becomes the knowledge that the body is a "mortal Temple" that houses the "transient soul" (29). Therefore, the overarching narrative of this two-sonnet sequence constructs the human body as the temple of the soul that, like a temple built in which to worship God, must be protected and kept beautiful.

In two short poems, "The Wall" and "The Idea," Robinson intellectualizes this "blind desire" for religious certainty, and in each case, the "Eternal Mind," as she terms it, points to the pantheistic absorption by a universal entity once human life is over. In "Tuberoses," however, the speaker is less dismissive of the quest to understand the esoteric questions of "why" we are here and deals more explicitly with the thorny issue of human yearning for transcendent love in a finite and limited world. The three Shakespearean sonnets that comprise "Tuberoses" draw on the duality of this flower to highlight the finite nature of human life and human love. The perfume of the tuberose is historically associated with the dangers of sexual attraction and, like many other members of the rose family, with funerals as well.

In this case, the rose has been bestowed by a lover who has left and, the speaker suggests in the first quatrain, "It could not live when you were gone away" (22). In the second quatrain, the speaker more specifically conflates sexual love and death:

> And all the fragrance of the dying flower
> Is grown too faint and poisoned at the source,
> Like passion that survives a guilty hour,
> To find its sweetness heavy with remorse.

The question of the sestet is what to do with "things that perish, / Memory, roses, love we feel and cherish?" The second sonnet extends the initial analogy through the flower that "grows and grows" until "at length it blooms itself to death." Indeed, the speaker begins the second quatrain with the acknowledgment that "everything dies that lives," and, by extension, all of living is a process of dying. The resolution of this dilemma is a Shakespearean resolution – a "song," such as this poetic tribute, contains "a dream" and "a thought" that cannot die. In the third sonnet, the speaker suggests that transience as a quality of earthly existence is what keeps us moving forward, and her advice in the couplet is to "forswear to-day" and "take to-morrow" instead, for only then can we situate our goals in a meaningful context, as an "eternal Thought" that we cannot understand. Robinson's preoccupation in her poetry with the "Eternal Mind" and "eternal Thought" suggests her continued struggle to conceptualize some sort of universal and inclusive entity within which she might invest her own inner life.

Virtually all of the inner life poems, then, deal with the contemplative moments related to the same paradox that intrigued Robert Browning: reconciling infinite desire with human finitude. The title of the Petrarchan sonnet "The Departure" suggests leaving in order to arrive somewhere else, and through the conventional contrasts of waking and sleeping, of day and night, and of living and dying, the speaker thinks about leaving this world for the next:

> The night wears on, the lawns are grey with dew,
> The Easter of the dawn will soon be here:
> And I must leave the happy world I knew,
> And front the Heaven I worship and I fear. (18)

The religious allusions in this first quatrain evoke the Day of Judgment, and in the second quatrain, a reference to Enoch, Adam's descendent and the great grandfather of Noah, who was taken suddenly by God, emphasizes the speaker's loneliness as she hints that each of us, like Enoch, enters into "the wilderness alone" as we move along the living/dying continuum. On the other hand, the speaker of "Love in the World," walking with a lover through over-ripe olive groves, sees "in all the flowers, in all the leaves ... a tender hint of vanished bliss" (25). She suggests that rather than "departing" this world for the next, we exist in this world in a spiritual form, and she senses all around her the spiritual presence of those who had previously inhabited that space. One day, she and her lover will be spirits themselves, and they will "breathe in this Elysian wood" for others walking as they are now, she concludes. The substitution of "Elysian" for the biblical contexts of "The Departure" underscores Robinson's hope for transcendence, both within and outside a Christian context.

Several poems in this collection continue threads begun in the nocturnes of *An Italian Garden*, but the tone of Robinson's night poetry of 1888 is subtly more sensual and more erotic. The expanse of darkness, in "Night," says the speaker, "seems to lay on my forehead / the touch of an infinite love" (20). Night is personified as a lover that "never / will understand" the speaker's desire, and the three quatrains end in an image of the speaker alone in the dark, with her "wintery face of despair." The imagery of the poem that follows, "Spanish Stars," is even more threatening as "white and pale" stars "coil on coil" like a "serpent's Argus-Eyes" and they are "venomous and full of bale" (21). Robinson refers to this poem in her dedication to Mabel as an example of the blend of realism and imagination for which she strives in her poetry. The fact that these stars shine in "tragic skies" provides context for the unidentified "picture" that forms the subtitle – one of the many images of Argus and, as she tells Mabel, an allusion to Shahied the Bactrian who lived and died under the same stars in the ancient world. These stars reflect the violence of that world:

> They throb and pulse in all the night,
> Like Life that pulses in a wound,
> Until the unhappy earth has swoon'd
> In aching languor out of sight. (21)

Diction turns the night sky into a dangerous monster that becomes, in the sestet, the "Serpent of the Soul" that spreads poison and creates divisiveness within. Hence, the speaker, like the speaker of "Night," is left in a state of stasis: "who cannot love the thing I clasp, / nor ever clasp the thing I love," a rephrasing of the "Winkelried" poem originally titled "Inaction" for James.

In contrast, the "The Stars," dedicated to James, is a moving sestina, with the key sestina repetitions, "years," "beyond," "abyss," "world," and "air" conveying the despair, isolation, and stasis of the speaker who sees only the unreachable, the unattainable, and the unsustainable in the night skies, much as James seemed to Mary as he hovered on the periphery of her life, banished to Paris while she remained in London during the long year of waiting to marry. In repeating "years" as the transition from the first stanza to the second, for instance, the speaker emphasizes the larger timeline that links humankind to a creationist God, and the reappearance of "abyss" situates the human experience in terms of trying to comprehend the greater implications of the sky filled with stars:

> Pale stars, whose light down the unplumbed abyss
> Falls, ere it reach us, through a thousand years.
>
> There was a God in the unwritten years
> Who lit the flaming order of the stars:
> Let there be Light! He said, and lo! the abyss
> Grew live and tremulous with rustling air,
> Grew bright with stars and moons and each a world
> Shining, a light to other worlds beyond. (37–8)

Robinson adds a footnote to link this poem to "Darwinism" and "Melancholia" to indicate that they had appeared in Darmesteter's translation of Robinson's poetry. All three poems focus on the threat of the abyss in some form, subtly evoking one of Baudelaire's most important tropes. In the second and third stanzas of "The Stars," God has disappeared and left the abyss to form itself. The solemn iambic pentametre lines reinforce the speaker's sense of moving in place rather than moving forward, and the harsh sounding, unrhymed lines convey the speaker's unease. The keywords "abyss" and "world" in the fourth stanza reinforce the distance between the stars and the earth:

O stars that dance indifferent in the Abyss,
Our Earth may seem as bright to you beyond;
Yourselves, to them that breathe your delicate air,
As desolate; Life in the Lunar years
As long: and the straight rivers of the stars
And primal snows divide as drear a world. (38)

In setting the metre of the line in contrast to the syntax of the poetic
sentence in lines 3, 4, and 5, Robinson creates the effect of jarring and
disjointed rhythms appropriate for the point to which she arrives
in the fifth stanza that Christ's sacrifice has been in vain. The sixth
stanza points toward the envoy, which, using all the keywords in
accordance with the sestina form confirms the speaker's conviction
that there is no reason to hope for a second coming of the saviour
and no judgment day to put an end to despair:

For Light, the stars; – for breath, the realms of air:
For Hope, beyond this dark and suffering world,
Nought in the Abyss, nor ought in the endless years. (39)

Baudelaire's presence in Robinson's inner life poems through the
concept of the abyss gives some context to her personal expressions
of despair to William Michael Rossetti, for in both "Darwinism"
and "Honour" this trope signals the speaker's sense of falling into a
void. In the six quatrains in iambic tetrametre and alternating rhyme
of "Darwinism," the speaker is uneasily aware that if we have not
evolved as far as possible, we are simply part of an ongoing process.
The first stanza sets the tone of the whole poem in this respect with
the "vague unconscious long unrest" that lurks within the land that
holds evidence in its fossil development to suggest that we are an
insignificant part of something larger and ongoing (40). The speaker
sums up the process to date over the next stanzas as the apple flower
that eventually blooms leads to the fruit that feeds the "unquiet ape"
and then the "brute became the man" during the course of evolution.
The ellipses in the last stanza that separate this development from
immediate history underscore the speaker's fear:

Long since ... And now the same unrest
Goads to the same invisible goal,

Till some new gift, undreamed, unguessed
End the new travail of the soul. (41)

In the opening quatrain of "Honour," the speaker's inner turmoil is initiated by the "one star" whose light "streams fitfully across the windy heath," an image that suggests similar insecurities linked to nature in turmoil. This faint guiding light proves to be unequal to the intensity of the storm, evoking metaphorically the tempest that continues to rage within the speaker. The star becomes threatening and dangerous as it beckons the speaker to follow it "over the cliff's edge" to the sea below. The conclusion of the poem is ominous as the speaker asserts,

Yet shine again, O white Divinity,
And wheresoe'er thou leadest I will go –
What, down? Over the cliff's edge?
Forth and down?

There shines the path I follow! yet I know
The infamous blind creatures of the sea
Swim dimly with wide faces where I drown. (27)

The fact that "edge" is the only word with no rhyming partner in the poem emphasizes the betrayal of what seems to be a promise of a spiritual life but that results only in oblivion.

One of the more interesting depictions of the abyss in this volume is the Shakespearean sonnet "In Affliction," retitled for *Collected Poems* in 1901 as "Neurasthenia." In this poem, the abyss takes the form of physical and psychological illness, specifically evoking Eugene Lee-Hamilton and his long-term neurasthenic paralysis. In its original context here in *Songs, Ballads* and with its original title, "In Affliction" conveys the inner life of a maudlin and self-absorbed poet, who feels alienated and isolated from the "happier people of the house" (33). Lee-Hamilton described his condition to Robinson as lying "on the shelf, in silence, alone, unable to bear the sound of a voice, the sight of the day, the smallest movement" but with no hope of recovery; therefore, accepting his fate, he became, as he put it, "intelligent" ("Casa Paget," 936). Robinson's speaker imagines herself viewing life from a similar perspective:

I watch the happier people of the house
Come in and out and talk and go their ways;
I sit and gaze at them; I cannot rouse
My heavy mind to share their busy days.

I watch them glide like skaters on a stream
Across the brilliant surface of the world;
But I am underneath; they do not dream
How deep below the eddying flood is whirl'd.

The last line hints of a vision unique to the speaker, much as Lee-Hamilton's perspective on life from the confines of his "wheeled bed." Robinson's imagery recalls Lee-Hamilton as the avid ice skater before illness left him paralyzed and prone, convinced that his paralysis was linked to intellectual and creative fatigue. Compensation for his terrible suffering, he reasoned, was a superior understanding of life and heightened creative powers. Robinson's speaker continues in the next quatrain to imagine swimming ineffectually beneath the ice against the tide in fear of the "abysmal wave" that threatens to sink her forever. This is the imagery of depression – of, as Linda Hughes notes, "entrapment, disorientation, and dysphoria"; however, there is also a way out of this mental mire suggested in a very specific image of rescue by a "mightier arm [that] could reach and save" the speaker, much as James Darmesteter seems to have "rescued" Robinson from a life that was becoming increasingly disappointing.[73]

Vacillating between hope and despair, these inner life poems underscore the pain associated with the unanswerable "why" of the human condition. Although this perspective on the question is more often than not dispiriting, there are times when the speaker expresses what we might call a qualified optimism, as in the ekphrastic poem "Hope," which was inspired by George Frederic Watts's painting first displayed at the Grosvenor Gallery in 1886. In tones of pale green, grey, and brown, the painting depicts a blindfolded Hope sitting atop the globe and holding a lyre with only one string remaining. Within the Petrarchan sonnet convention, Robinson presents Hope in terms true to her name, "clothed-upon with soft humility" and "patient." The particular "hope" she offers has to do with the only sight that the blindfolded Hope might have – insight. This is precisely the type of sight that inspires the speaker to look "beyond the broken instrument / The Flame, the Music, undisturbed afar," but what she might see is, true to the ambiguity of Watts's painting, left unspoken (30).

"A Reflection" and "The Alembric" can be read as partner poems about poetic inspiration and the kind of dissatisfaction with herself that plagued Robinson in the lead up to her marriage. The nostalgic speaker of "A Reflection" mourns the passing of youthful optimism, when she was able to mount "the stair of Heaven," an echo, perhaps, of Robinson's once calling Symonds her "ladder to heaven" – the heaven of fulfillment as a poet. The speaker realizes in the sestet of this Petrarchan sonnet that poetic inspiration from outside sources – the "dew of lilies," the scanty wine of Amphoras, and the "blood that flows from trivial scars" – has led to banal and trivial poetry that has little to do with the speaker herself (26). Reduced to writing now in the "bitter ink of mine own heart," the speaker feels that she has little to offer in poetry that "reflects" nothing meaningful and lasting. Similarly, the titular vessel of distillation of "The Alembric" contains the speaker's youth, innocence, and purity that remain untainted by experience. She hopes that corrupting influences might be distilled out and, moreover, that through the fiery process of distillation the unencumbered soul might glimpse "the eternal gold of Truth." In the second quatrain, the speaker realizes that in looking back on youth as the ideal, she has made a grave mistake with respect to her future:

Therefore the future is an empty name,
And life to me a dream that will not last,
And all my care is only for the Past,
Veiled with the veil of no man's ruth or shame. (32)

In the final verse, the speaker concludes that the future is important to her only in terms of her death. "Death," she says, "hast the secret Life withholds," and after death, she intuits, her vision may clear and the eternal question – the "eternal How and Why" – may be answered.

The poem that concludes the list of "inner life" poems, "Antiphon to the Holy Spirit," Robinson explains in a footnote, alludes to Ernest Renan's imagined scene of "the men and women of the earth as they are singing a continual Antiphon to the Unknown God" (42). An antiphon, or a short verse that normally concludes a longer prayer service, becomes in Robinson's hands an extended dialogue, not between God and his people but a gendered discourse between men and women. As in her other gendered discourse poems, the men are practical-voiced and, in this case, preoccupied with efforts to make the mystery of God concrete and knowable. In their first verse, the men speak with determination, vowing to persevere in faith despite the fact that they "may not clasp" him, explaining in their second verse the more general sense of evidence of God in the world (42). The women, in contrast, affirm in their first verse that God is "within" the self, and in their second verse, the fourth stanza of the poem, they construct God as both pantheistic and, through allusion to the Holy Spirit, Christian:

> Thou art the ripening of the fallows,
> The swelling of the buds in rain;
> Thou art the joy of birth that hallows
> The rending of the flesh in twain;
> O Life, O Love, how undivided
> Thou broodest o'er this world of Thine,
> Obscure and strange, yet surely guided
> To reach a distant end divine! (43)

The men bring the dialogue to a conclusion in the fifth stanza, again skirting the issue of absolutes but settling on the idea that, as Renan believed, we know God through what he is *not* rather than through what he *is*. Male and female voices in unison conclude this antiphon with the sense that they must find ways on earth to serve and praise this silent presence.

The seven poems gathered under the title "Spring Songs" are thematically consistent with the unease that Robinson conveys in her inner life poems, and the epigraph from Wordsworth's "To the Cuckoo" from his 1807 *Poems in Two Volumes* that focuses this section establishes a thread of illusion and ambiguity that runs through the poems. Wordsworth's speaker hears the bird but cannot see it, and this "invisible thing, / A voice, a mystery," he says, is a harbinger of spring but also a reminder that, as the lines that Robinson takes for her epigraph specifically suggest, "the earth we pace / again appears to be / an unsubstantial faery place" (45). For Wordsworth, it is the memory of the song and the poet's power to evoke the cuckoo that conveys joy in nature; for Robinson, the transient and temporary qualities of the natural world undermine the speaker's attempts to find joy in that world. In "La Belle Au Bois Dormant," for instance, a poem thematically linked to "Love in the World," Robinson reinscribes Wordsworth's cuckoo as a mysterious sound that seems to the speaker to come from a horn from long ago and that evokes a synesthetic experience as the speaker imagines the medieval life the forest once supported. In this forest "sleeps the knight and sleeps the steed / under him," the speaker imagines, able to almost "hear" the elusive horn sound that seems a vestige of the past and that sounds just out of the range of human activity (47). The traditional abbaba rhyme scheme of the medieval Spanish sextilla, each sestet followed by a quatrain in alternate rhymes, mimics the echo of the knights and ladies who once lived and loved there and whose spirits have become the inner life of the forest. At the end of the poem, vestiges of the past compete with the increasingly intrusive sound of a horn entering into the speaker's consciousness in the present.

> Till beneath the flowering tree,
> Novel music in her ears,
> Lo, asleep a thousand years,
> It is She!
> Blow thy clarion, Spring; She hears!
> She is free!
> Break, O bower above her,
> Briar and thorn divide.
> Hark, the Eternal Lover
> Calls the Enchanted Bride! (49)

The long-dead medieval lady the speaker imagines is personified as spring, and the love story from long ago becomes now part of the speaker's awareness of her own place on the continuum of life.

The poems that follow reinforce the paradox that while time is always passing, it passes in circular, repetitive patterns through the cycles of renewal in nature. In the simply titled "Spring," the season of promise is personified as a "tender maiden / like a girl who greets her lover," but as she rushes forward, she signals not only the fruition of love in summer but also the inevitable rush toward December and death (50). The speaker of "Going South" likens herself to a "little grey swallow" leaving "the sheer white cliffs" as she departs from southern England to find poetic inspiration away from her wintery home (52). Ironically, however, she finds that once she is away from home, she is also away from the inspiration of the natural world with which she is familiar and to which her creative powers are linked. Similarly, in "Promise," the anticipatory moments of spring that precede its fruition are connected to poetic genius, as the "armour-blue aloes" that precede the olives remind the speaker that she too awaits fruition when her own poem will "flower" (53). These are all poems that evoke Robert Browning's paradox that anticipation points to fruition and fruition points to deterioration, a central trope that emerges out of the cycles of nature.

Both "La Californie," published in *Woman's World* in December 1887, and that would purchase table linens for the home Robinson would share with James, and "An Orchard at Avignon," published in the *Athenaeum* in October 1886, are sombre and perhaps more mature reminders of human transience. The former has been read in the context of the American state California, but La Californie is also an area on the Riviera just outside Nice.[74] Today this area is known as St Augustin and is the location of the Nice airport, which lies just at the western tip of the famous Promenade des Anglais. However, at the time of Robinson's poem, the land was, of course, undeveloped. Hence, the speaker says that it is "an arid place, I would not call it fair" (55). The poem is dedicated to E.S., possibly Emily Sargent, with whom Robinson did travel to the south of France. After the three stanzas with Petrarchan rhyme schemes that highlight the dry, marshy, and stark land, broken only by "straggling Cyprus" and "Indian reeds" that allow glimpses of the blue sea, the speaker offers her direct address to E.S. in the last line: "And yet, my Dear, we were so happy there." "An Orchard at Avignon" also reflects the visits that Robinson had already made to France before her marriage, when she became familiar with the landscape of southern France that she would ultimately come to know intimately. The speaker asks us to imagine the stark whiteness of the lime hills leading down to the Rhône and the orchard juxtaposed with the sterility of the hills. This is an orchard of almond plants that thrive in the arid conditions, thereby not only lending beauty to the land but also acting as a reminder of the diversity of life on earth. For the speaker, this reminder makes the orchard "a place of secret peace"; however, this peace is transitory and although "it fills the amazed heart," it "never comes again" (57). For a woman deeply in love and on the cusp of a new life with James Darmesteter in Paris, the poems of the inner life and the spring poems of *Songs, Ballads* may seem strangely dark and foreboding. However, as 1888 unfolded and Robinson and Darmesteter rushed toward August, Robinson was able to put the period she described to William Michael Rossetti as one of the most difficult in her life behind her. Notably absent in these poems are Vernon Lee and Italy.

In the third set of poems, which are listed under the title "Romantic Ballads," Robinson integrates her considerable background in history, the classics, and mythology into the romance ballad, thereby poeticizing aspects of humanity from a perspective simultaneously contemporary and archetypal. The proliferation of the ballad in English at this time attests to the modernity of Robinson's poetry, which, as H.F. Wilson, reviewing for the *Athenaeum* points out, reinforces the relevancy of the ballad to the present precisely because it draws on the past.[75] As James notes in *Poésies*, Robinson's perspective reflects not only her intellectual interest in medieval history but also her more esoteric interest in female mysticism.[76] These ballads "have grace, movement, passion, and strength," writes the reviewer for the *Spectator*.[77] This reviewer goes on to say that "there is a touch, and more than a touch, of real genius in at least six out of seven of the romantic ballads." The ballad that does not make this reviewer's list is "Sir Hugh and the Swans," which is dated 2 February 1888. Indeed, there is not a great deal to commend this blend of history and fantasy developed out of the failed attempt to rescue a political prisoner, Maximilian of Austria. However, the concurrency of *The End of the Middle Ages* with the ballads of *Songs, Ballads* is an important point of intersection between genres and an indication of Robinson's ability to integrate history, mysticism, and the supernatural into poetic studies of human nature. The *Spectator* reviewer notes that Robinson captures "the goodness, the wisdom, the wildness, the wickedness, the worst and the best of that wonderful time. We meet with devoted saints and desperate sinners."[78]

"The Tower of St Maur," writes the same reviewer, demonstrates Robinson's "power of painting what is eerie without overdoing it, without laying too much emphasis on the effective points." This is a disturbing poem which, as Robinson reminds Mabel in the dedication, comes out of "documents" that she accessed to demonstrate the ways in which the ethics of love and duty can conflict in catastrophic ways. In this case, the conflicting elements are a father's duty to protect his young son and his duty as lord to protect those dependent on him. Robinson indicates in the preface that Mabel particularly admired this poem for its realist qualities in contrast to what she as a novelist thought of as the allegorical and representational nuances of poetry. However, in drawing on the elements of magic and fantasy that legend tends to incorporate, Robinson achieves in "The Tower of St Maur" a different kind of realism than Mabel probably had in mind. In this case, a gypsy with the power, she tells St Maur, to cast a spell that will enable him to keep his family safe from their enemy, Lord Armour, will only help him if he consents to bury his youngest "christened child / alive into the wall" he is building to protect the town. In great detail, the ballad traces St Maur's refusal, the magical rise of waters to destroy the barrier, and his ultimate concession to the gypsy's request. As his son is bricked in "St Maur stares out of his bloodshot eyes, / Like one that's well nigh mad," and in the following verses the cries of the child are depicted graphically enough to convey what must have been agonizing moments for the father:

"O father, father, lift me out!
The stones reach over my eyes,
And I cannot see you now, father,
So swift the walls uprise."

"O father, lift me out, father!
I cannot breathe at all,
For the stones reach up beyond my head,
And its dark down i' the wall." (73–4)

The iambic tetrametre lines of the ballad metrically emphasize the horror of this moment precisely because the lilting metrics seem so inappropriate to convey the child's cries. The repetition in these stanzas of "father" emphasizes too the magnitude of St Maur's betrayal of his son's trust in him and the boy's innocent conviction until the very end that his father will rescue him. However, as earlier references to God and Christ foreshadow, St Maur at this moment is like God the Father, who also sacrificed his son for the good of many. As the gypsy points out in the last stanza, sometimes doing the right thing comes at great personal cost:

> "Your wife will mourn him a year, St Maur,
> You'll mourn him all your life,
> For you've lost the bonniest thing you had,
> Better than bairns or wife." (75)

Ultimately, he has lost his self-respect, for he has betrayed his young child's unwavering trust in his father, and the ambiguity of this final verse, dated 8 February 1888 during the year of waiting to marry James and just before her thirty-first birthday, indicates, perhaps, the conflict between desire and duty and the constraints of self-sacrifice that feature prominently in Robinson's epistolary exchanges with James.

Only four days after she finished "The Tower of St Maur, Robinson wrote a second ballad about sacrifice in a Christian context. "The King of Hungary's Daughter" is drawn on the Christian parable that concerns the historical mystic Elizabeth (1207–1231). Elizabeth was canonized by Pope Gregory IX for her philanthropic work with the poor and the diseased. Written in couplets, this tale of the young woman who takes in a beggar pointedly named Lazarus and puts him to rest in her bed is an allegory: when her father pulls back the bedcovers he finds that the beggar has taken the form of the crucified Christ, thereby highlighting Elizabeth's recognition of Christ in all suffering beings. In contrast, "Rudel and the Lady of Tripoli" is a quest narrative about the historical figure Jaufre Rudel, a troubadour who is said to have followed Eleanor of Aquitaine on a crusade from which he never returned. To Robinson, Rudel's extreme loyalty is not only obsessive but also perverse; it is devotion to the abstract ideal of chivalric beauty, and, after a life of chasing this beauty only to find his object old, decrepit, and dying, Rudel seems to represent the problem with devotion to a transient ideal.

Robinson's reference to Joan of Arc in the dedication points to "A Ballad of Orleans," which is dated 1886 and is, therefore, one of the earlier ballads in this volume. The historical context for the poem is the important shift in the Hundred Years War between England and France that unfolds in four verses in iambic tetrametre lines to describe the bloody battle. In this case, mysticism, legend, and history are integrated into the tightly woven narrative that highlights the French victory. However, in a more fully developed historical romance ballad, "The Duke of Gueldres' Wedding," dated 27 April 1887, Robinson not only highlights the wedding on 5 May 1405 of Mary Harcourt, the cousin of the King of France, and the Flemish Duke Reinald of Gueldres but also offers insight into the human aspect of political unions. It was widely assumed that Mary Harcourt would marry the Duke of Limburg, thereby reinforcing an internal alliance. However, the marriage to Gueldres shifted the alliance to that between France and Flanders, thereby making a friend of someone who could have become an enemy. In her ballad, Robinson highlights Mary's trepidation as she awaits her fate, for like all women of her time and class, she had no say in the shape her future would take. We come to understand Mary's personal anxiety as the King of France uses her to decide "who shall be the peer of France / Her lily hand to win" (77). In verses that parallel the king's deliberation as he makes his decision about Mary's future, Mary struggles to come to terms with the consequences of that decision for her and the practical effects of it on her life:

"O shall I leave my own country,
And shall I leave my kin?
O strange will be the Flemish streets
My feet shall wander in!"
...
"O shall I marry a Flemish knight,
And learn a Flemish tongue?
Would I had died an hour ago,
When I was blithe and young?" (79)

The fact that historically this tale had a happy ending in that Mary found herself falling in love with the husband to whom she was handed over suits the fast-moving narrative of the ballad form. However, in this and her other ballads, it is Robinson's depiction of the inner life of historical figures that gives her poetry currency and "affect."

Finally, in the "The Dead Mother," dated 5 July 1886, Robinson demonstrates the inextricable links between mysticism and history in medieval French literature. Roland, who is depicted ubiquitously in medieval legends throughout Italy, Spain, and France, appears in French history as an eighth-century French military man charged with protecting Breton from invaders, and Robinson sets her ballad during his return from a quest in Palestine and Syria. Despite his success on foreign soils, Roland is in despair upon learning that he has arrived home too late to see his mother alive. His journey homeward over a stark, wintery landscape provides ample foreshadowing of his disappointment in the first stanza:

> Lord Roland on his roan horse
> Is riding far and fast,
> Though white the eddying snow is driven
> Along the northern blast. (102)

The frozen, wintry landscape seems in harmony with the news that awaits him at home – his mother has been dead for a month. The thrust of the ballad shifts at this point as Roland, instead of regretting his delay in getting home, invests instead in fervently wishing for her return "but for an hour" so that he can assuage his disappointment. Maternal love is transcendent in nature, the balladeer implies, and, although "it's a long, long road from Heaven to Earth" and this "long road from the heart of the grave" is difficult, the mother makes the journey back to fulfil Roland's selfish and unnatural request (105). However, what might conventionally have been a tale of a mother's sacrifice and a son's joy takes a very different turn in Robinson's hands as she allows the mother to speak:

> And something stirs in the firelight,
> Drifting nigher and nigher –
> My hands are blue, says the pale voice,
> I'll warm them at the fire. (105)

She is distressed and resentful at what she has been asked to do, and her first concern is for herself and not for the son who let her die alone.

> "My limbs are faint," sighs the weary voice,
> "My feet are bruised and torn –
> It's long I've seen no linen sheets,
> I'll rest me here till mourn."
>
> There's a pale shape in the chamber now,
> And shadowy feet that move,
> The fire goes out in a sullen ash,
> Like the angry end of love – (106)

The simile in the last two lines suggests that the mother well understands her son's motives, his failure to fulfil his filial responsibilites, and his privileging of duty to his country; Roland's conflict is thus similar to that of St Maur. His horror as he realizes that he has forfeited his mother's love precipitates his own death, and the "look of dread" left on his face after death implies awareness of what he has lost, very much like St Maur's realization that he has lost the most valuable thing he had – his son's love and trust (106). In structuring the ballads of this section through an integration of mysticism and the supernatural with real world concerns, Robinson investigates the inner lives of those we often think of collectively and generically rather than as individuals, and she highlights the often-conflicting demands of love, loyalty, and duty.

"Our Lady of the Broken Heart"

"Our Lady of the Broken Heart" is Robinson's only lyrical drama. Its subtitle "A Garden Play" suggests not only pastoral innocence but also the unsustainable ideal of Eden. Moreover, this play unfolds in an "Italian Garden," thereby evoking some of the themes of the transience of life, of the complexity and uncertainty often associated with love, and of our quest for knowledge about the afterlife. In setting the play in the "seventeenth century, or any time," Robinson makes oblique reference on the one hand to the tension, unrest, and transitional anxieties of the seventeenth century metaphysical poets, who experimented with developing poetic forms to express increasingly liberal ideas about love, and on the other hand to "any time" and our time, expanding the theme of love into a timeless abstraction (115). Finally, in reminding Mabel in the preface that this play originated during a walk with Mabel and Vernon Lee in the summer of 1886 in a very real garden, the garden at the family home in Epsom, she hints at why the play remains essentially unfinished as she makes the cryptic remark that seems in retrospect to comment on the whole volume: "the only real things, you know, are the things that never happen." "Things" did happen with James Darmesteter, and, anticipating her marriage as she wrote the dedication on her thirty-first birthday, 27 February 1888, she makes clear that she would not develop the play further: "it will always seem to me that the Play belongs to you and Vernon and to the Epsom Garden" (6).

Therefore, although act 1 heads up the first scene, implying that act 2 will follow, there is in fact only one act made up of four scenes in this work, and the physical space in which the action unfolds consists of four small "closets," each inviting the reader to shape it imaginatively: an Italian garden, a terrace, an arbour, and an ilex-grove with a shrine. This contained and compartmentalized set represents the limited "stages" in which the complexities of human love take place. This is a simple tale of youthful promises that alter with maturity, a tale of unrequited love and of falling in love. There is an air of unfinished business in the conclusion with Hesperia's rather odd impersonation of Our Lady of the Broken Heart, and it is indeed tempting to see an unsuspecting Vernon Lee brought to life as Hesperia forced to step aside for Julian's new love, Bellamy. Furthermore, the epigraph, which is the first stanza of the Clod's song in William Blake's "The Clod and the Pebble," suggests the thematic prominence of selflessness in unrequited love, which is the end toward which the plot moves. Like Blake's Clod, Hesperia and Hilarion are self-sacrificing and altruistic, ultimately finding some self-satisfaction in rising above the "pebbles," Julian and Bellamy. In its unfinished state, the play suggests that, just as Blake depicts both kinds of love as problematic, selfless love and self-sacrifice lead to some measure of happiness different from but equal to carnal unions like that of Julian and Bellamy.

Characterization was as difficult for Robinson in drama as in fiction it seems. Ironically named after the evening star, which shines most beautifully and brightly just before morning to signal the end of the night, Hesperia also represents Italy itself, called so by the Greeks because the evening star was thought to rise and set in Italy. However, the evening star is also known as Venus, the Roman goddess of love, and so Hesperia becomes ironically associated in the play with the suppression of female desire. Her practical reasons for engaging herself to Julian foreshadow the collapse of desire on his part and his attraction to the sensual and earthy Bellamy, who contrasts the "hateful ghost" of "cold, pale beauty" to whom he is engaged (128). In her assumption that Julian is playing his love song on his mandolin to her in the third scene, Hesperia is influenced by reading Aristophanes to her father, ironically evoking in this moment the scene in *The Frogs* when Iacchus dances seductively and wildly; however, she promises her father in the same moment that she will never leave him.

Bellamy, on the other hand, is capable of the kind of warm, organic love that Julian craves, for she is an "April-minded" girl, as her brother says, suggestive of spring, fantasy, and youth (115). She will be Julian's "moon," she says, unless she is "too little" for such a task, and then she will aspire to be "the small evening star," reinforcing the inadequacy of Hesperia (122). Bellamy feels little loyalty to her brother Hilarion, who, a practical figure like the secret object of his desire, Hesperia, is a substitute father to her, and she disintegrates into hysterical crying at the shrine of "Our Lady" as she prays for divine interception to change Hilarion's mind about taking her away from Julian. There is some irony in the fact that it is the religious aesthete Hesperia in the guise of the Virgin Mary who calms Bellamy and concludes the play in a symbolic marriage, as she gives to Bellamy the ring that Julian once gave her. Although the idea for the play originated in the Epsom garden before she met James, Robinson seems to have set in print during the year of waiting to marry James a metaphoric representation of her transfer of affection from Vernon Lee to James Darmesteter in a marriage that was also, it seems, highly symbolic.

CHAPTER FIVE

Mary James Darmesteter, 1889–99

Robinson's love for James Darmesteter intensified and matured after her marriage, and the concerns of her friends, as well as her own reservations about her ability to make him happy, were put to rest. As she told Emily Sargent, "all our fears were for nothing. I <u>adore</u> my husband and see no reason why we should not go on being endlessly happy and peaceful."[1] The only disturbing aspect of her marriage was James's increasingly poor health. His cough worsened and Robinson exhausted herself caring for him. She remained very close to Mabel, who was prolific during the 1880s and early 1890s, publishing reviews of books about Ireland in the *Athenaeum,* and six novels, as well as an Irish history, between 1885 and 1895. Mabel's literary pseudonym was W.S. Gregg, and the fiction tended toward, as Marysa Demoor writes, "the naturalistic tradition, presenting grim pictures of Irish characters who are bogged down by their fate."[2] Mabel retained the athletic skills that Robinson poeticized in "Two Sisters" and was a cyclist as well as an excellent horsewoman: she is recorded in the *Islington Times* as taking a third place in show in 1889.[3] Mabel maintained friendships with Gosse and others in her sister's London circle; Robinson, meanwhile, received old English friends in her increasingly popular Paris salons. Havelock Ellis took Arthur Symons to what he calls the "more distinguished salon of Madame Darmesteter," where they met Taine, for instance, in 1890.[4] However, her relationship with Vernon Lee remained strained.

A few months after her marriage, Robinson had the unhappy task of writing an obituary article for James's brother Arsène Darmesteter, which was published in the *Athenaeum* 24 November 1888. She wrote reviews for the *Athenaeum* and for the *English Historical Review,* and

she remained the "London Correspondent" for the *Glasgow Herald*.
She published a historical essay, "Captain Antonio Rincon: A Study
in the Sixteenth Century," in *Macmillan's Magazine* in September
1889. This article of intrigue and political secrecy fleshes out a section
of *Margaret of Angoulême*, focusing on King Francis's reliance on
Rincon to persuade King Henry the Eighth to join forces with
France by entering into an anti-imperial league with Hungary to
oppose the Pope and the German princes. The Pope would then move
to Avignon and the Catholics of France and Italy could be united.
Robinson's scholarship rests on documents in the national library
in Paris, and, as is the case in general in her historical writing, the
historical details are meticulously provided and creatively woven into
a tale that makes an interesting supplement to her previous work.
Robinson, then, plunged into her new life in France with gusto,
both in terms of her own work, her work with and for James, and
their fulfilling social life together. To William Michael Rossetti she
writes 26 November 1889, that she was pleased to receive a letter
from his young daughter Olive, and, she adds in an echo of what
she had said of Margaret of Anglouême, "If I were not the busiest
woman in France I would have answered it long ago. But every letter
has to be fitted into the mosaic of my busy hours and so too many
don't get fitted.[5] Robinson's relationship with Olive Rossetti and
with Olive's parents and famous maternal grandfather Ford Madox
Brown was longstanding. At the death of his father-in-law, in 1893,
she reminisces to William Michael Rossetti about the "loveable old
gentleman," continuing, "I remember how fond we two girls were
of him when we were girls of Olive's age; and how we admired him,
not only for his talents but for his great goodness.[6]

Lee and Robinson published companion articles clearly conceived and written before the disruption to their friendship in the
Contemporary Review in 1889, Lee's titled "Christmas Legends: A
Nativity by Fra Filippo Lippi" and Robinson's "Christmas Legend:
The Kings." These articles use humour and wit to debate the significance of the story of the birth of Christ. Lee's narrator, Robert
Browning's painter-monk, Fra Lippo Lippi, who wanted his art to
reflect reality but as a monk was conscious of the church's expectation
that his art would reflect the soul instead, tells the tale of the poor
man who gives shelter in his barn to Mary and Joseph. The main

characters of the story suggest its contemporaneity with Robinson's garden play – Hilarion, the poor, saintly servant who acts as an intermediary between the angels and the earthly contingent awaiting the birth, Hieronymous and Magdalen, "a princess and a courtesan," who is the most beautiful woman on earth and seeks someone more beautiful than she. In the end, these characters, dissatisfied with perfection, remain unhappy and unfulfilled, in contrast to Mary, a poor, simple woman, who has given birth in the shelter of the woods and produces the perfect gift for humanity.

The subtitle of Robinson's contribution, "A Medley in Prose and Verse," links the framing prose narrative to an internal ballad, "The Three Kings," which appears also as Benozzo Gozzoli's "Procession of the Magi" and serves as the frontis piece image for Robinson's next volume of poetry, *Retrospect*. Like Lee, Robinson emphasizes the human qualities of those involved in the Christmas story, using the ballad of the three magi, Balthazzar, Melchior, and Caspar, to focus on their conversation en route about the king they have left behind and the king they hope to find. Balthazzar hopes for a king who is like the star guiding them, a king above and aloft from the world; Melchior would choose a "soul alive" in the form of a "sinless child / laid in a manger-stall"; Caspar simply wants the Son of God. The poetic narrative is familiar: following Balthazzar's star, they find themselves viewing Melchior's baby, who is, of course, Caspar's Son of God, lying in a manger.

The satirical framing "story" of Robinson's poem is linked to Lee's narrative through the primary characters, Vera and Stella, who argue about the best way to interpret the Christmas story and look to their elder, the Mage, or the wise one, for guidance. The artist, Vera, as her name suggests, considers the story to be truthful, and she maintains her lifelong faith in it; Stella, as her name suggests, is the light that guides Vera in her interpretation of reality. Of course, the two young women of this story are also very much like Mabel (the artist and more pragmatic sister) and Mary (the poet and idealist), and Vera's suggestion that "only religious people should write about religious subjects" is suggestive as well (857). "Vera says nothing and believes," says the Mage suggestively in the voice of Vernon Lee. "Stella waxes enthusiastic over her Three Kings, and hasn't the faintest belief in their existence" (849). What follows is a long history lesson on the biblical context of the nativity, which ends with emphasis on the ambiguous nature of the Christian myth and the implication that the only "truth" to be found lies in the representative function of the dolls of the traditional *crèche*.

During the summer of 1889, Robinson and Lee were in England at the same time, but since Lee was avoiding all contact at this point, they did not meet. An undated 1889 letter from Robinson invites Lee to visit her at Rue Bara to have tea and dinner, without "fatted celebrities," although it would be her afternoon salon. Lee could come for that and stay for dinner, Robinson suggests, "and perhaps for the first few minutes you would rather we were not alone. I will ask no one to dinner: after dinner James has to work at the Zend Avesta: you can lie on the divan and talk lazily to me."[7] That letters like this remained irritating to Lee, who refused to even answer them, indicates the serious nature of this breach once Robinson and James Darmesteter had married. Meanwhile, Frances Robinson worried about the drain on her daughter's health as she looked after her ailing husband. She needs "nourishment, moderate exercise & care," she writes to Mabel 23 May 1891. As much as she was slowly coming to know and love James, Frances was still bringing up the marriage crisis as late as 10 March 1892, writing to Mabel about a friend's son, who was causing his parents some anguish in his choice of a wife: "It requires a great deal of love Magdie dear, to make up for such sorrow as Mary caused us by her marriage!!"[8]

Robinson herself worried not only about James's health but also about her eyesight, which had always been less than it should have been and that, as she aged, became increasingly worse. She writes to Lee 9 December 1892 from the apartment that she and James now occupied on B. De Latour-Maubourg, for instance, to express her regret that Lee was in Paris and did not have this address – she seems not to have sent the new address to Lee, perhaps because she was by now certain that Lee would not reply – but also to excuse her lapse with reference to trouble with her eyes. "The oculist says it is really my circulation and not my eyes that are to blame, but it comes to much the same as I am obliged to rest after every ten minutes reading or writing, and to spend a great deal of my time lying flat," she says. She also tells Lee that although she had been very happy in her visits to Italy over the years, she had worried constantly about not being at home in London, but now, "the comfort of being married" gave her freedom from such worry.[9] It is difficult to see how she expected Lee to respond to such messages.

Lyrics Selected from the Works

In 1891, Robinson gathered poetry from pervious collections, as well as from the *Living Age*, the *Athenaeum*, and the *Critic*, for the Fisher Unwin Cameo series. Organized under three headings – Music, Rosa Rosarum, and Stars – this eclectic group of poems is unified by the usual themes that reflect Robinson's preoccupation with transience and her increasingly astute use of poetics to develop these themes. The "bubbling" metrics, alliteration, and repetitive refrain of the last three words of each stanza of "The Springs of Fontana," published in the *Athenaeum* in 1890, for instance, suggest the circularity and continuity of the movement of the water:

> The springs of Fontana well high on the mountain,
> Out of the rock of the granite they pour
> Twenty or more;
> Ripple and runnel and freshet and fountain
> Well, happy tears, from the heart of the mountain
> Up at Fontana. (38)

The plethora and diversity of the energetic springs well convey the speaker's joy in this particular "Music" poem. Another *Athenaeum* poem of 1890, "Twilight," placed under "Stars," is consistent with poetry she was writing for *Songs, Ballads*, particularly "Stars," dedicated to James. "Twilight" is dated 1889 and depicts an abstract experience of time and place in a metaphoric representation of the interstices of day moving into night and a young life moving into the "granaries of Age." Robinson writes with self-conscious awareness of her own entry into a new life in Paris, and, as the details of the first stanza suggest, she seemed to be gathering her memories of her youth in the country she had just left:

When I was young the twilight seemed too long.
How often on the western window seat
I leaned my book against the misty pane
And spelled the last enchanting lines again,
The while my mother hummed an ancient song,
Or sighed a little and said: "The hour is sweet!"
When I, rebellious, clamoured for the light. (131)

In the second stanza, the speaker is a mellower, older woman who now can understand her mother's contentment at the hour of twilight, and who now "love[s] the soft approach of night" when she might dream and let her mind "wander" imaginatively through "undying memories." However, the cost of this change in perspective is an underlying awareness of transience, for "all too fleet the hours of twilight seem; / And thus I know that I am growing old" (131). In the paradox of transience depicted here, Robinson points toward what would be the unifying theme of her next collection of new poetry, *Retrospect*.

Robinson's preoccupation with the brevity of life in other previously uncollected poems in *Lyrics Selected* reflects her ongoing concern in this respect but also the fact that now that she was married to James and happier than she seems to have ever been, she was more intensely aware of the need to celebrate every day. The poetry written during her short marriage is all the more poignant and ironic in view of how brief his life was to be and how transient their happiness together. In "Epilogue," the allegorical "cup of life" contains "the love of women, minds of men," and the speaker urges us to "take the cup" but warns us not to "break it" (139). Similarly, in "Pallor," which the reviewer for the *Critic* suggests is indicative of the excellence of the whole volume, white symbols of purity – lilies and angels – are also reminders of death and the absence of life, just as white is the absence of colour.[10] In "The Dead Friend," which is dated 1890, the speaker recalls having the luxury of being able to forget a friend from time to time, but now that the friend has died and become "this tragic friend of After," the speaker must live with the friend always in her thoughts (98).

The final uncollected poem, "The Mushrooms of the Mine," is an 1890 poem that celebrates a Swedish phenomenon of note – the growth of wild mushrooms in iron ore mines in the far north of the country. In each stanza, embedded anapests suggest the depth and distance from the surface that keeps the mines in perpetual darkness and that contrasts the beautiful setting above ground. Yet, it is deep down in the mine that one discovers the natural treasures of the mushrooms, the "flowers in the mine," as the speaker calls them, for "these are the stars of the miners" as they navigate their way up and out (127). The last stanza conveys the speaker's wonder at these beautiful and functional growths that only those working in the mine have the opportunity to know:

> Mushrooms of the mine – no more – that the sun never visits,
> Born of the ooze and the damp, bred in the slime and the cold,
> Scentless and petalless blossoms, made without pleasure
>   and hidden:
> See, how they shed in the darkness the light they shall never
>   behold! (128)

The word "blossoms" contrasts starkly with other diction to emphasize the special aesthetic value of these natural phenomena. Selected lyrics are always an interesting record of the work that the poet feels most representative of his or her best work, and this volume of lyric verse suggests that even her happy personal circumstances had not altered Robinson's aestheticist anxiety about the fleeting and fractured moments that define human life. In fact, her worry about the brevity of life seems to have intensified with her happiness in her marriage, which is ironic, but given concerns about James's health, also logical.

Travels with James and Travel Journalism

It may be that this sense of temporariness fuelled Robinson's ability in life to close doors behind her and move forward into new circumstances that always surprised her family and close friends. Although she maintained her English accent, her French was fluent and her cultural affinity with France complete. She reviewed two histories in French for the *Athenaeum* in July 1889, Monod's *Bibliographie de l'Histoire de France* and Perrens's *Histoire de Florence*. In the happiest days of her marriage, she and James travelled quite extensively in France, and she wrote engaging letters home describing the country-side and expressing her love for France and all things French. Her father, hoping to keep some of her attention on England, suggested that she share these trips with English readers of "the *Contemporary* or some other English magazine," adding, "it would certainly be very interesting to a great many who want a green field to wander in."[11] George Robinson had in mind that she would eventually write English histories as well, but she pointed out to him that she would not be in England long enough to carry out such research. Robinson did take her father's advice in developing a new form of writing in which she became quite successful, however, fleshing out her travel experiences with commentary that reflects her growing familiarity with French history and culture and producing what might be described as travel journalism. She signed herself Mary James Darmesteter as she created a persona for this extended "auto-biographical project," as Carl Thompson terms travel writing, which she could share with English readers.[12] As she remarks in a long review article in 1898 of John Bodley's two-volume study, *France*, "we change something of our personality in changing our country" (63).

Robinson had already published historical articles in English journals, such as "The French in Italy," which appeared unsigned in the *Quarterly Review* and "Workmen of Paris in 1390 and in 1890" in the *Fortnightly Review*, both in 1890, as well as "Rural Life in France in the Fourteenth Century" in the same year. Subsequent articles, how-ever, differ in tone and style from these earlier histories and strive for an intimacy with her readers more appropriate for the genre of travel writing. In "Private Life in France in the Fourteenth Century" for the *Fortnightly* in 1892, for instance, she calls upon readers to "imagine a long low hall opening on the street by two wide arches, not unlike the arcaded streets of Lombardy or Savoy," thereby taking them on an armchair journey through reference to familiar English places, and she establishes a rapport with English readers through people familiar to them as well, such as Matthew Arnold, Mrs Beeton, and Robin Hood. Treating readers to a seductive, virtual tour in "Impressions of Provence," she describes the journey south by train in prose that evokes the transformation in terrain and climate, situating herself and

James in the first sentence with a jointly formed "first impression" that personalizes all the other "firsts" in the article and that invites the English reader into the train carriage with them. The article is filled with descriptive appeals to sight, sound, and taste, with similes and metaphors constructed to make comparisons meaningful to her readers, and in describing the towns through which the train moves, Robinson creates a panoramic "impression" of Provence – a beautiful painting in words. Similarly, in the *Contemporary Review* in 1893, "The Medieval Country-House" takes readers on a virtual walking tour outside and inside the grand houses and castles that dot the landscape where Froissart once roamed, and "Spring in the Woods of Valois" recounts Robinson's experience with James in a beautiful Gaulish forest; however, she tells her readers, "I can remember older trees in Warwickshire" (198). Writing a decade later, Robinson's contemporary, Hannah Lynch, recalls reading "Spring in the Woods of Valois" alone in her room in London and feeling it "grievous to lift [her] eyes" away from the beauty of France to look at her "little city chamber."[13] Indeed, in this article Robinson links the beauty of contemporary Chantilly to an abstract concept of beauty that exists outside the specifics of time and place, hinting that readers could expect to enjoy this aesthetic experience for themselves should they visit. The informality of the rhetorical question that ends the article is also inclusive, as she asks, "where shall we go to-day?" "Let us set out again for the Vieux Moulin!" Her enthusiasm implicitly invites readers to agree (208). In this first set of travel articles – the second set would appear during her second marriage – Robinson draws on her facility with figurative language to create prose that is not only vibrant but also informative and reflects the ease with which, as an expatriate, she could communicate to English readers her Anglo-French perspective on French culture.

Marguerites du Temps Passé

Robinson's ongoing mystics project of the 1880s surfaced in certain ways in her poetry, particularly when she was dealing with matters of religion and philosophy in the narrative poems of *Songs, Ballads*, and, of course, it played a substantive role in the *End of the*

Middle Ages in 1889. To bring this project to completion in 1891, she published an unusual collection of tales in French into which she integrated her studies of mysticism and the supernatural with historical events. She dedicated these "Marguerites trouvées entre les feuillets de vieux livres" to James, who had already introduced Robinson to French readers with his well-received translation of her poems. *Marguerites du Temps Passé* received positive notice as well, the *Revue bleue* praising Robinson's ability to convey medieval and Renaissance literature in modern French and noting her astute selection of tales that are interesting and characteristic of the time and place of their creation.[14] She was clearly able to return to the past with the same blend of intuitive and factual knowledge that she had demonstrated in her poetry and in her biographical writing. Robinson offers no explanation for the title, but she perhaps makes reference to the medieval mystic Marguerite Porete, a Beguine who was burned at the stake for heresy in 1310. Porete is best known for *The Mirror of Simple Souls*, a book of Christian mysticism that extols the freedom of thinking in ways independent of conventional church values. Traditionally, mystics have been primarily women, and in Porete's day, the integration of feminism and spirituality that characterizes the mystic unsettled church leaders. In 1898, Robinson's friend May Tomlinson translated the book into English, and it was published with the title *A Medieval Garland*. The difference in meaning between the French and the English titles perhaps shifts the focus of the work somewhat, with the literary meaning of "garland" suggesting a miscellany of short fictions.

The 1891 French edition was meant for an audience who had by and large not read *The End of the Middle Ages*. This was the first opportunity that Robinson had to highlight in French the importance of the past on how we understand the present, a principle prominent in the poems of her next collection, *Retrospect*. English critics who read the original *Marguerites* were impressed, the *Spectator* praising Robinson's ability to produce "a series of detached, though … homogeneous essays in fiction" that are written with "simple grace and ease."[15] Frank Marzials comments in his review for *The Academy and Literature* that "in their sadness too there is something sweet" in these stories.[16] The unique element of this text is its narrative structure, for each story is told to a specific listener who can be identified and who is sometimes a contemporary of Robinson. This technique highlights the allegorical nature of this collection and situates the stories as legend – part history and part fantasy. The opening "conversion" tale, "The Story of Antonio," for instance, is told to "the Blessèd Saint Francis," the Assisi monk who founded the order of "the Glorious Poor of God," but the second story, "Alipz," is told to M. Douet D'Arcq, who was the director of the historical National Archives and who died in 1883. His special interest was the situation of women in the medieval period, and he edited a collection of stories on the topic. "Philip the Cat" as told to M. Siméon Luce is set in Cherbourg, July 1429, at the time of the French rebellion against England, when Joan of Arc entered history. Luce, who died in December 1892, was someone Robinson knew well as a writer and friend. Their literary interests intersected in his 1886 *Jeanne D'Arc Á Daumery*, his 1890 *La France pendent la Guerre de Cent Ans*, and his eight volumes of Froissart's *Chronicles*, published between 1869 and 1888. "Philip the Cat" is a tale of political intrigue that recounts the bravery and courage of those actively resisting the British takeover of France. These are legends well known by both English and French readers, and the connections made through the literary auditors to the present suggest the fluid nature of human history.

One tale in particular, "The Ballads of the Dauphine," had been on Robinson's mind for some time, as she indicates in a letter to her father 5 November 1890. The tale reminds her, she tells him, of when she used to "write Mabel Birthday Odes in old French," and indeed she did publish this story in the *Revue bleue* in May 1891, with the subtitle "Marguerite of Scotland."[17] In *Marguerites* the tale is told to Charles Pinot Duclos, a French historian and author known for his scholarship on Louis XI, and the tale itself focuses on the Dauphine's circle of well-known female poets, highlighting the unhappy situation of the medieval wife. "The Countess of Dammartin," a tale that has to do with class and gender, has two listeners, M. Cimber and M. D'Anjou. The latter edited the *Archives Curieuses de l'Histoire de France* in 1838 and, along with Cimber, published an article on Louis II in *Revue des Deux Mondes* in 1836. Robinson offers a thoughtful portrait of a woman abandoned, who in turn abandons the peasant who helped her in order to return happily to the husband and king who had left her without a thought. Years later, in 1915, Robinson published another version of this story as a poem titled "Poor Nelly" in *The Country Life Anthology of Verse*. In the figurative language of poetry, the young woman this time recognizes the Christ-like symbol of the shepherd and wishes that her "little son / Grow such an one as" he (93).

The story of the "Marguerite" named in the title "The Wife of Ludovic the Moor" is told to Messer Marin Sanudo, whose private diary is a compilation of documents and anecdotes that during his lifetime earned him the reputation of being a gossip. In this case, Robinson focuses on a moment in the larger version of this tale in *The End of the Middle Ages* in the chapter "The Ladies of Milan."[18] However, drawing on the chronicles of the historian Philippe de Vigneulles Metz (1471–1527) in "The True Story of White-Rose and the Fair Sibyl," she more successfully highlights the significance of individual acts – this time the affair of Sybil, the beautiful wife of Maitre Nicolas, and White-Rose – that have broader social and political consequences. In "Madame de la Roche," told to M. L'abbé Pierre de Bourdeilles (1540–1614), another French historian and biographer, the Duchess Renée, unhappily married to the Duke of Ferrara, ends like so many other medieval women, abandoned and forgotten. One can see in these stories, Robinson's interest in women in history as she tells of women who choose unwisely in love, women in difficult political marriages, women whose love is unrequited, and women suicides.

"The Brou-en-Bresse Architect of Brou," told to Rev. Father Rousselet, the last priest of the church at Brou and the man who authored its history, ends with modern comments on ambition and on marriage. However, it is the final story, "La Giroflée," which is a prose version of the poem "The Red Clove" of the *Hippolytus* volume, that evokes an interesting comparison with Robinson's poetic past. This story is told in Ferrara in 1573 to the Italian poet Giambittista Giraldi Cinthio, the original author of the tale, and, as she had done poetically, Robinson takes the opportunity to highlight the nature of the relationship between Antonio and Daphne. "In his solitary hours [Antonio] liked to dream that he was the young Hippolytus, and she Artemis the White," the narrator says (234). Other elements of the *Hippolytus* poem are fleshed out in the narrative, such as Christofano's jealousy of the lost hours with his son once the boy, at sixteen years of age, falls into a strange languor brought on by a Hippolytus-like desire for "Artemis" and becomes perilously ill. The moment of epiphany occurs in the prose narrative when "for at least one hour in their lives, they tasted absolute happiness," and it occurs in the poem when the lovers experience "the sudden freedom from the solitude of separate souls"; arguably, both versions signal through diction that the lovers have consummated their love. The narrative, like the poem, ends in Daphne's death, Antonio's placing of the clove flower in her coffin, and, when he is buried with her years later and the coffin opened to receive him, there remains "a little dust, and a clove carnation fresh and sweet" (255). In subtle ways, these Marguerites that blend history and myth, as well as mysticism and the supernatural, function as an apt sequel to *The End of the Middle Ages*. In the first years of her marriage, then, Robinson was professionally very busy, concerned not only with bringing works that she had begun in her English life to fruition, but also with experimenting with different prose genres, as well as with different poetic genres, and with cultivating a French readership.

Retrospect and other poems

Robinson had not, however, forgotten her English readers nor had she lost her identity as an English poet. In the spring of 1893, she published again in Fisher Unwin's Cameo Series, this time a collection of new poetry, *Retrospect and other poems*. She sent Vernon Lee an inscribed copy 13 May 1893.[19] The reviewer for the *Saturday Review* writes in praise, "this little book contains some of the most exquisite and, let us add, least self-conscious lyrics that the writer has produced."[20] Reviewers for the *Bookman* and for the *Dial* are equally enthusiastic, the latter praising the poetic depiction of "a life varied in experience, both objective and subjective, of a mind that has borne the full stress of modern thought, and of a heart that, unchanged by new appeals, still recurs to the familiar themes endeared by early association." The reviewer continues to describe this collection as "lyrics with a touch of melancholy, ballads of terse dramatic force, and sonnets of the life of culture and intellectual preoccupation."[21] William Watson in the *Academy* is extremely positive in every respect, citing Robinson's "emotional sincerity and spontaneity" as a feature of excellence throughout.[22] In its emphasis on the relationship between past and present, the title of *Retrospect* underscores that this collection of verse is a continuation of Robinson's central preoccupation with viewing the present through the reflective lens of the past and with the issues of transience and impermanence that not only define the human condition but for Robinson place particular emphasis on how one should live in the present. Robinson was living her present happily married, and it is no accident, perhaps, that she treats the relationship between past and present differently in this collection than she had previously. Specifically, although she was still writing prose that relies on historical accuracy in the collective memories she culls from documents and archives, she produces in *Retrospect* lyric poems of contemplation and reflection that invite us to enter into a philosophical discourse on how one's personal experience of the past might be shared in order to suggest a collective way of looking toward the future. It may be this unifying thread of the volume that appealed to English reviewers anxious to reclaim the British poet who was now living in Paris as Madame Mary James Darmesteter.

The titular poem "Retrospect" consists of Shairi or Rustavelian Quatrains, a medieval form named after the Georgian poet Rustaveli and having the same rhyme for each of the four lines of each stanza. This poetic form conventionally emphasizes high ideals, historically the ideals of the Georgian nation, but in this case the lofty ideals are personal and have to do with the poet's contemplative perspective on her past and the present. The poetic voice of this autobiographical poem is reflective as she sits by her Paris fireside and moves in her mind through the scenes of Robinson's youth at her grandfather's cottage in Warwickshire. Therefore, the overall tone of the poem is nostalgic, but this is also on another level a poem about the limitations of memory and its associational aspects. The speaker begins,

> Here beside my Paris fire, I sit alone and ponder
> All my life of long ago that lies so far asunder;
> "Here, how came I thence?" I say, and greater grows the wonder
> As I recall the farms and fields and placid hamlets yonder. (3)

Poetic form is crucial here to creating the intensity of the *act* of remembering, as in this opening stanza the single-rhyme pattern evokes the speaker's mood – a mixture of nostalgia for the past and relief at having escaped the past. The word "asunder" in particular suggests a leaving by the wayside or an abandoning of a life. Robinson's family never really understood how she could be happy away from familiar English haunts and family, and, although she was indeed deeply happy during the production of the poetry of *Retrospect*, she was clearly sensitive to the fissures in so many relationships brought about by her love for James.

In this poem filled with visual imagery derived from memory, Robinson and her poetic speaker are conflated in their creation of a detailed word "picture" of the country house in Warwickshire that had been the scene of youthful joy and happiness. The descriptors are eclectic and specifically English in the second stanza as the speaker addresses the reader directly to bring us into the scene in her mind:

> … See, the meadow-sweet is white against the watercourses,
> Marshy lands are kingcup-gay and bright with streams
>   and sources,
> Dew-bespangled shines the hill where half-abloom the
>   gorse is;
> And all the northern fallows steam beneath the ploughing
>   horses. (3)

Although the single rhyming patterns result in the awkward word choice of "the gorse is," these two-syllable repeated end-rhymes are lilting, melodious, and most important, suggest an organic movement and fertility. Diction in this and the stanzas following highlight Englishness and take the speaker, implicitly Robinson herself, on an imaginative journey back to the specific place where the speaker formed her happiest memories – Warwickshire. "Kingcup-gay," for instance, is the English term for the marsh marigold, and the speaker remembers the "red-brick-chimneyed house" where she sat by other fires, the fields, a particular bush that "a thousand / thousand pities" has been clipped, the "land of milk and honey," and her grandfather who "smiled his Nunc Dimittis" (3–4). The strange use of "smiled" to replace the sound of the music that is associated with the evening

Vespers and that evokes Simeon's joy when he saw the baby Jesus, as promised, bespeaks the power of these memories. At the end of the poem, the speaker casts this power in terms of her ability as poet to evoke these scenes and the mood associated with them, and it is place rather than people that inspire her to recreate the mood of the past. In the final stanza, she addresses Warwickshire itself:

Patience, for I keep at heart your pure and perfect seeming,
can see you wide awake as clearly as in dreaming,
Softer, with an inner light, and dearer, to my deeming,
Than when beside your brooks at noon I watched the sallows
    gleaming! (5)

By deliberately leaving the first word of the second line uncapitalized, Robinson conveys the expansive and profound nature of her ability to evoke images of the place, suggesting both the power of place and the power of the poet. As Vadillo suggests, for this speaker, these are "recollections helping to illuminate her current life."[23] While the poems that follow "Retrospect" continue the process that Vadillo describes in terms of looking backward in order to know how to look forward, they also highlight the ability of the human mind to idealize and reinvent the past and the creative powers of the poet to articulate this revisionist view. As had become her custom, Robinson organizes this collection generically, offering lyrical articulations of this view first and then ten "Ballads and Legends" that highlight the contemporaneity of medieval perspectives on modern life.

The extended meaning of "retrospect" is particularly important to our understanding of the ways in which Robinson brings her skills in lyric poetry to new heights in this volume. When one looks retrospectively, one looks from a position changed through experience and, therefore, understands the past not only in terms of remembering but also in terms of realizing something new about the past with each passing year. There is a freshness and vitality about the poems in this volume, as well as technical sophistication, that suggest Robinson changed her perspective on the implications of transience and finitude as she found herself nearing middle age and happier than she had ever been before. She was thirty-six years old when *Retrospect* was published, married to James, and had been out of her parents' house for more than four years. In the poems of *Retrospect*, the speakers are more conciliatory about and less panicked by the aging process, and although some of these poems are nostalgic in tone, they are not as morose or as self-absorbed as some of the poetry she wrote in her London days. A good example of her subtle development in this respect is the poem "Souvenir," which was first published in *Living Age* with the title "Recollection." The term "recollection" has a dual sense, suggesting both a deliberate recalling of events of the past and the tranquility of mind that is tied to religious contemplation. "Souvenir," on the other hand, conflates the French denotative meaning of memory with the concept of keepsake or memento, thereby focusing the poem more specifically as an expression of pleasure. The octave, for example, subtly conveys the speaker's simultaneous tendency to idealize youth and her acceptance of her passing from youth into a more complex state.

> Even as a garden full of branch and blooth
> Seen in a looking-glass and so more fair
> With boughs suspended in a magic air
> More spacious and more radiant than the truth;
>
> So I remember thee, my happy Youth,
> And smile to look upon the days that were,
> As they had never told of doubt or care,
> As I had never wept for grief or ruth. (11)

The simile suggested in this octave hints at the speaker's wry awareness that her youthful perspective on life had been as warped and distorted as the image of the garden projected through the mirror of the first stanza. Language such as "blooth" and "ruth" is old-fashioned, awkward, and hyperbolic, but it gives this Petrarchan sonnet a playful tone, as the speaker remembers fondly and with humour the idealist she once was:

> So, were our spirits destined to endure, –
> So, were the After-life a promise sure
> And not the mocking mirage of our dearth!

This is the mature poet speaking in conditionals that indicate her certainty that of course such a youthful perspective cannot be sustained. In addition to giving the poem a new title, Robinson made a significant change in the last line of this poem when she republished it in *Retrospect*, a change that makes the responsive sestet a more forceful rejection of the idealization of youth in the octave.

> Through all eternity might Heaven appear
> The still, the vast, the radiant souvenir
> Of one unchanging moment known on Earth.

Whereas the wording in the final line in "Recollection" is "one transfigured moment," suggesting the loss of this moment, the final line in "Souvenir" works with the title to suggest that through memory we retain the pleasure of a time when we thought that such ideals were possible.

In other poems that deal with the transience and impermanence that characterize life, we have the same sense that the poetic speaker views her past as contributing to the person she has become rather than expressing regret that the past recedes each day. In "Spring and Autumn," for instance, the speaker suggests a revision to the ways in which we view the seasons: the fading out and dying off associated with autumn, she says, gently introduces the concept of aging and decay to the young; on the other hand, spring is "the consolation of the old" because it reflects "the image of their youth in everything." Once again, pleasure comes through memory even though the "harvest is not for their gathering" (12). In other lyrics, themes related to aging – death and religious faith – suggest that Robinson had found ways to reconcile her youthful longing for religious certainty with the intellectual agnosticism that she suggested to Symonds in 1879 had blighted her young life at times and that left her feeling "hurt, unhappy, even wicked at renouncing" the Anglican Church.[24] Evidence of her persistence in coming to terms with transience is suggested in this volume with recurring images in different contexts. For instance, in "The Vision" the speaker begins with a description of a difficult world from which she is able to escape in fragmented moments:

Sometimes when I sit musing all alone
The sick diversity of human things,
Into my soul, I know not how, there springs
The Vision of a world unlike our own. (13)

This opening octave is reminiscent of "Retrospect" in situating the
speaker as looking inward; however, in the next quatrain she focuses
not on a specific memory but on the experience of memory itself.
Robinson's allusions like this to her own work have the effect of
suggesting the struggle of the creative process, for in the sestet, there
is another reworking of a now familiar image – the distorted garden
of "Souvenir" is reinscribed here to further the implications of "sick"
in the second line of the octave:

Yet, as a passing mirror in the street
Flashes a glimpse of gardens out of range
Through some poor sick-room open to the heat;
So in our world of doubt, and death, and change,
The vision of Eternity is sweet,
The vision of Eternity is strange! (13)

Diction and repetition in the last two lines of the sonnet complete
the central simile that compares moments of imaginative insight once
again to the distortion caused by fragmented mirror imagery. This
"vision" is not memory, nor is it an insight in any intellectual sense.
The parallel structure formed by the alliterative "sweet" and "strange"
conveys the speaker's ambiguity and her failure to reach certitude
through her "musing." Yet, there is a sense as well of the speaker's
satisfaction in the "sweet" and "strange" vision of "Eternity" that she
has experienced and the sense that she no longer craves the kind of
certitude about eternity that she has expressed in her early lyrics.

When she turns outward from these inner life moments and once
again looks to nature for inspiration, however, Robinson's imagery
tends to suggest inner turmoil rather than peace. For instance, the
complicated rhyme scheme of "The Frozen River" conveys restriction
and enclosure in this metaphorical presentation of Baudelaire's abyss
that lies temptingly close in specific moments of despair. In the first

two stanzas, the speaker's mood reflects the implications of a moving river beneath the ice that suggests "a sudden desolation, empty, lone, / and silent with a silence of its own" (6). This void beneath the ice becomes in the speaker's mind dangerously alluring: "the crust is thin; / One step – and lo, the Abyss would draw him in" (6). This is a moment of intense preoccupation as the speaker grapples with an impulsive movement toward the "Abyss."

> Athwart the happiest lives of every day
> Beside the Lovers' Walk, the household mart,
> Think ye there lies no silent road apart?
> No mute and frozen Chasm of the heart? (7)

Similarly, in "Fair Ghosts," a quintilla with the five line stanzas of this sixteenth century form constructed in octosyllabic lines of abbab, the speaker counsels her heart to take "courage" in the "vision of the spring" during the autumn months in the first stanza and the seasonal reference becomes metaphorical in the second stanza as the speaker, once again threading the lyrics of *Retrospect* together through language, calls for courage as "vision" replaces memory "when the oncoming years dispel the magic of our morning" (8). Reference to Robinson's complaint to Lee a few years before as having "vanished like a ghost" out of Lee's life is perhaps implicit in the "ghosts of our regret" of this speaker.[25] The speaker concludes rather defiantly determined to shake off these morose feelings:

> The skies I watch are Spring's,
> Lovelier still and haloed with the soft poetic glory,
> Of all remembered things! (9)

In *Retrospect*, as in each of her previous poetry collections, Robinson's approach to religion tends to rest in the Judeo-Christian tradition and tends also to reflect her interest in history rather than theology. The poetry about religious concerns in this volume particularly reflects her discussions with James and with Renan that led her to view Christ not as an intermediary to whom she could pray but as an admirable man and scholar himself. In "The Gospel according to St Peter," for instance, the speaker poses a question with both practical and philosophical implications: what if the earthly remains of Christ were one day discovered? This discovery, of course, would mean that Christ did not rise bodily into heaven after all. The speaker suggests that although such a discovery would be problematic for theologians, Christ has nevertheless had a positive influence on human ethics. Robinson's friendships in the early 1890s with Taine and Renan, as well as her work with James Darmesteter on his orientalist studies, including the *Zend Avista*, certainly broadened her perspective on these matters and are reflected in two memorial poems, "Veritatem Dilexi" and "Le Roc-du-Chère." She wrote "Veritatem Dilexi" for Ernest Renan one day after his death on 2 October 1892 and "Le Roc-du-Chère," for Hippolyte Taine, who died 5 March 1893.[26] "Veritatem Dilexi" begins its tribute with the Latin title that translates "I delight in the Truth," which, at Renan's request, is the epitaph on his tomb and represents his lifelong dedication to seeking Christian truth through the higher criticism of the Bible. James Darmesteter ends his September 1893 essay on Renan with reference to Robinson's poem, reinforcing Renan's reconciliation of science with a greater, ideal God. "Veritatem Dilexi" emphasizes Renan's commitment not to one particular religious perspective but to truth itself. Christianity, Pascal, Plato, all suggest various ways in which we conceptualize truth, but Renan, says Robinson, loved "no One truth … but the Whole," and he came to that Whole not through the suspension of disbelief but through science, which is the position that Robinson herself takes in "The Gospel According to St Peter" (15). The title "Le Roc-du-Chère" refers to the scenic cliffs that overlook Lake Annecy in southern France, the burial place of Taine, whose development of the philosophical perspectives of naturalism and historicist criticism influenced French and English literature. The poem evokes not only the tomb itself resting "high on the heathery hill-brow o'er the lake" but also the spiritual presence represented by the tomb and Robinson's continued respect for a man who had become a close, although at times irascible and difficult, friend (16). Her poetic speaker notes the "passionate and loyal Spirit of Life" that Taine had been and suggests that in death, his "large and grand and simple soul" is perfectly aligned with nature. In later years, she would write essays about both Taine and Renan, and, in the case of Renan, a full biography.

During this period, Robinson seems to have become the image of herself that she described to James in the early days of their courtship. She was metaphorically resting at his knee, a pupil intent on soaking up as much knowledge as she could. By 1892, Darmesteter had published extensively on Zoroastrianism and was hailed as the western world's most erudite scholar of Iranian studies. Robinson's poetry in *Retrospect* indicates the interest she took in James's work, as well as her interest in religious history more broadly, and her poetry echoes the explorations of the intersections of eastern and western religious history that occupied James, Renan, and Taine. James is implicitly present in the two Petrarchan sonnets that comprise "Vishtaspa" as the speaker traces the Persian king's conversion to Zoroastrianism around 750 BC. Vishtaspa's boredom with his life as ruler is clear in the sestet of the first sonnet:

Therefore who knows the limit of his power
Disdains the trivial baubles of an hour,
And plunges where the seas of silence roll. (17)

Vishtaspa's ennui in these moments foreshadows his suicidal thoughts in the octave of the second sonnet, contributing to the building tension that is released in the sestet when Zoroaster appears. This tension is dissipated as Vishtaspa intuits the presence of a superior entity that leads to his own "sudden peace of heart":

Lo, at his side, unguessed, Zoroaster trod.
– O sudden peace of heart, O deep delight
Of souls outgrown religion's earlier rite,
Yet spent and thirsting for the springs of God,
When the undreamed-of Prophet deigns appear! (18)

The concluding line specifies the relief that the historical Vishtaspa felt, not because he had certainty of God, but because faith and anticipation resolved his boredom and he "reigned in rapture many a year." Vishtaspa was similar to the apostles of Christ, spending his life in a pattern of devotion and spreading the word. A companion poem, "Zeno," on the other hand, offers a different model for making the abstract concepts of truth and duty part of daily life. The Greek philosopher Zeno, who lived 490–30 BC, preceded Socrates and was one of the subjects of Plato's *Parmenides*. Aristotle credited Zeno with founding the dialectic, and through this form of logical discourse, Zeno comes to the conclusion at the end of this sonnet that duty to the self is the ideal goal of human existence.

This discourse on the integration of religious tenets into the practicalities of life continues in "Philo Judaeus" and "Irenaeus contra Gnosticos," both which highlight historical figures who, like Vishtaspa and Zeno, can be connected to James Darmesteter's work on the historical roots of the merging of Eastern and Western religious and philosophical ideas. James's contribution to the scholarly community in this respect is set out clearly in his 1880 article for Max Muller's *Sacred Books of the East*:

> Nowhere in the Avesta is the effort of any man felt who,
> standing against the belief of his people, enforces upon them
> a new creed, by the ascendancy of his genius, and turns the
> stream of their thoughts from the bed wherein it had flowed
> for centuries. There was no religious revolution: there was only
> a long and slow movement which led, by insensible degrees, the
> vague and unconscious dualism of the Indo-Iranian religion
> onwards to the sharply defined dualism of the Magi.[27]

Philo Judaeus, also known as Philo of Alexandria, who lived from about 25 BC to 50 AD, was a Hellenistic Jew and, therefore, contributed to but was not solely responsible for the merging of Greek philosophy and Judaism. Robinson's speaker is perplexed by the sense that Philo was thought to have influenced the course of religious history when he kept himself distanced from the strife of human life, and we see in the sestet of this Petrarchan sonnet a reinscription of James's introductory remarks above:

> How should he frame the spirit's world anew?
> Answer me, Philo, meek and studious Jew,
> Who winged the Six Archangels of the Mage;
> And, all unconscious of the marvel done,
> Whispered his loftiest secret to St John,
> And left in East and West another age. (20)

This reconciliation of Hellenism and Judaism led to the development of modern Christianity that is the foundation of James's work, but to provide balance, perhaps, Robinson follows with a second poem that reflects her own studies of mysticism, "Irenaeus contra Gnosticos." St Irenaeus, who wrote *Adversus Haereses* (Against Heresies) in about 202 AD, attacked the Gnostic position that the "demiurge" rather than God organized the universe. Robinson's speaker is angry at the two Gnostic prophets, Carpocrates of Alexandria and Marcion of Pontus. She is dismissive of their rejection of God, calling their writings a "babble of magic like a village wife" (21). The vitriolic tone, however, betrays the speaker as it implies uncertainty that conventional Christianity can weather this assault, for ultimately, it seems that all we have are the platitudes of conventional faith. The final tercet is ironic, for the reality, says the speaker, is that Christian teachings, were they to be truthful, could only reflect

How, from a gulf of Sin, in poisoned fumes
The Soul of Man exhales, expires, consumes,
And mocks the God above him blind and mad!

It is appropriate that all of these discussions on religious practice are Petrarchan sonnets, a poetic form that enables argumentation in its rhetorical process and that has a long historical association with religious themes and with varied manifestations of love.

This emphasis on the ways in which "faith" is too often linked to coercion in matters of religion is clear in other lyrical forms as well. "Taking Possession" is an allegory of an Arabian Sheikh who, finding a good piece of land in the desert, does not stop to fence it in but simply moves his animals and goods onto the land and takes possession of it. The speaker analogizes this land claim to people establishing rights to certain forms of worship and suggests that we have the right to settle ourselves wherever we like with respect to God. We see a similar thread of diversity and inclusiveness in a poem of three octaves toward the end of the collection, "Oriental Jealousy," which Robinson dedicates to Sheikh Mohammed of Tehran. She refers most probably here to Muḥammad 'Abduh (1849–1905) who argued that the Koran needed to be read with reason and intelligence and not simply followed literally. He lived in exile in Paris from 1884 until 1888 and was a world traveller and orator and most likely knew James Darmesteter, since he attended meetings with philosophers from many religions and Darmesteter had been honorary secretary of the Société Asiatique since 1882. The "secret of my heart" to which the speaker refers in the first stanza is focused by the poem's title and the dedication, and it emerges enigmatically in a tale of a gardener who suffers terribly as his glorious – but transient – flowers, which he has hoarded and resented others seeing, die off (51). These "fruits / no stranger's eye should look upon" are gendered as female in the context of oriental jealousy when the desired balance of yin, the female, and yang, the male, is distorted and upset by such undesirable and negative thoughts (52). This is a subtle and sophisticated argument on Robinson's part that ends on a chiding note as the "secret" is revealed to be the gardener's selfishness. Singing nightingales warn the gardener that no good will come from this battle raging within his conscience: "Tear up, O Gardener, branch and roots, / the flower's a mock, the perfume's gone!" (52). A more autobiographical perspective on the need for generosity and shared beauty unfolds in the narrative poem "The Children's Angel," which outlines an incident that may have occurred during a visit with James to Clermont, now Clermont-Ferrand, in the Auvergne region. This verse in alternating rhymes tells the story of the couple's climb up through the dark and winding streets of the old town to a small vendor's stall with what from a distance seemed to be a perfect angel head that was once part of a church statue. When they get closer and can see the angel more clearly, she is worn and marked, for she has given much pleasure to the young children of the village, who, in kissing her daily, have left her mouth damaged. The lesson, of course, is driven home when the speaker and her spouse decide to leave the statue with the disappointed merchant, not because they resent paying for something damaged, but because, they say in the final stanza,

> "What, did you think us basest of the earth?
> That we, grown old, and heartsick with the truth,
> Should rob the little children of their mirth,
> And take the children's Angel from their youth." (38)

This is yet another version of the prominent thread of the *Retrospect* collection that focuses on memories of the past, when youth and innocence shelter one from the harsh disappointments of, in this case, religious uncertainty. The children's simple gesture of love is ironically consistent with the Christian ideals that the statue represents to them, but the "heartsick" couple in this poem are no longer able to summon up those ideals and realize that they have no right to the statue that represents them.

Therefore, the pattern that emerges in *Retrospect* is Robinson's altered perspective on life as a series of transitions that are no longer connected to an abstract ideal, such as attaining transcendence of some sort, but are instead linked to history and the ways in which she was experiencing the past and the present with James. She had made two significant transitions, first in her marriage and then in leaving England, but she was also making her way through her thirties and could see her own life in terms of edging closer to what she could expect to be its midpoint. In the two quatrains of "The Present Age," she treats life as transition in a layered and complex manner in precisely this respect:

> We stand upon a bridge between two stars.
> And one is half engulféd in the Abyss;
> While unarisen still the other is,
> Hidden behind the Orient's cloudy bars.
>
> We tread indeed a perilous path by night!
> Yet we who walk in darkness unaghast
> Prepare the future and redeem the past,
> That after us the Morning-star be bright. (23)

Beginning with the implications of stars that are conventional representations of light and insight into the heavens, the speaker suggests that we come up abruptly against "the Abyss," a word evocative first of Pascal in his *Pensées* and then of Baudelaire, and his *Fleur du Mal* poem "Le Gouffre" or "The Abyss," which begins "Pascal had his abyss always at his side." The line refers to an incident in Pascal's life in 1864, when a bolting horse left him dangling in a carriage on one of the bridges over the Seine. Baudelaire refers to

Pascal's posttraumatic sense that his left side – the side closest to the water – was perpetually held over an abyss and ready to fall in. Robinson was fascinated with Pascal her whole life, finally writing a biography of him in 1927. In this poem, she situates her speaker to depict the terrible moment when a tumble into the abyss seemed to Pascal as likely as a rescue. In this context, the light emanating from the stars on either side is obscured, one half hidden in the abyss and the other not yet arisen out of it. In the second quatrain, then, the speaker develops the analogy that both Pascal and Baudelaire suggest – it takes tremendous courage to proceed through life in this darkness, but it is the only way in which we *can* proceed so that the brightest of these stars, the Morning-star, occluded as it prepares to arise in the Orient or the east, will bring with it a new day and, as the Morning-star specifically represents, new hope. This poem is one of several that follow in which Robinson thinks seriously about hope and the unanticipated "abyss" into which hope can unfortunately lead us.

Pascal's paradox reflects Baudelaire's sense that all human actions have a positive side and a negative side – they are influential in paradoxical ways. Robinson depicts a similar duality poetically in the Petrarchan sonnet "Liberty," possibly inspired by Eugène Delacroix, Baudelaire's favourite painter. Delacroix's "Liberty Leading the People," which came out of a period in storage to rest in the Louvre in 1874, situates Liberty in her transition to Marianne, the symbol of France. The painting depicts Liberty as the brutal spirit of the 1830 revolution stepping over and on the bodies of those she has vanquished. Robinson might also have been thinking of Frédéric Auguste Bartholdi's Statue of Liberty, which was completed and formally presented to the Americans in Paris 4 July 1884. The poem outlines the dangers inherent in unrestricted and unrestrained acts carried out in the name of "Liberty, fiery Goddess, dangerous Saint" (24). Similarly, the personified France in "The Disguised Princess" is a reminder of France's obligation to her people, an obligation which, the parenthetical reference to "France 1893" as a subtitle implies, she has not always kept. In the octave, the speaker implies that she has taken in strange bedfellows, perhaps in the form of the Franco–Prussian alliance and the visit of the Russian navy to Toulon in the south of France that year. The sestet is a plea for the Princess to be what she is in the eyes of the speaker, the "Elect of Heaven, a Queen / and strong" (25). Both "Soldiers Passing" and "A French Lily" are other patriotic poems that highlight Robinson's increasing interest in having her British readership understand that France has concerns not unlike those in England, the former highlighting France's military exploits and the country's enduring patriotism aroused by the inspirational power of soldiers on parade and the latter comparing and contrasting the flowers that represent England and France, the rose and the fleur-de-lis.

Therefore, on several levels *Retrospect* deals with the emotional investment in contemplation of the past, at times in concrete terms, as in "The Widow," who lives isolated in her grief and at other times in more abstract terms, as in "The Barrier," which develops the idea of loss symbolically through the speaker's younger self in a dream approaching a garden gate that disappears the closer she gets to it, thereby reminding the older speaker that she cannot reenter the world enclosed by the wall of memory. However, in "A Controversy," which Robinson sent to Lee in 1893, she voices her symbolic "widowhood" with Lee, who was still essentially absent from her life. The undated letter to Lee accompanying the poem mentions the publication of two works by their mutual friend Anatole Leroz-Beaulieu, *La Papauté, le socialisme at la démocracie* in 1892 and *Les Juifs et l'Antisémitisme; Israël chez les Nations* in 1893, thereby indicating a time frame for the composition of "A Controversy."[28] The opening allusion to Blake's *Marriage* and to the popular story of Ezra's dispute with the angel come to take his soul implicitly questions the wisdom of arguing about what cannot be disputed:

> Let us no more dispute of Heaven and Hell!
> How should we know what none hath ever seen?
> We'll watch instead the same sweet miracle
> That every April works in wood and green ...
> The apples in our orchard are a bower
> Of budding bright-green leaf and pearly flower,
> No two alike of all the myriad blossom!
> Some faintly-flushing as a maiden's bosom,
> Some pursed in hardy pinkness, some as pale
> As stars that glitter o'er the twilit vale. (39)

"A Controversy" sets out that what we know about the "miracle" of spring is what our senses tell us. Therefore, since we cannot see heaven and hell, we should place our faith in what we can indeed see. The shift to couplets after two sets of alternating rhymes conveys the heightening intensity of the speaker's argument; however, although the couplets continue to build this tension in the second stanza, the conditional with which it begins points to the analogy that the speaker is making to clarify the larger theme of diversity that perhaps expresses Robinson's growing frustration with Lee and her deep sadness at the loss of the friendship:

> If sometimes from His balcony on high,
> The Lord of all the stars, with musing eye,
> Look down upon this orchard of our world,
> Methinks he marks as blossom dewy-pearled
> Sprung from the branches of the self-same tree,
> Our varying faiths – and all the creeds there be! – (40)

Religious diction – "His" and "Lord" – implies the speaker's democratic view of religion as she uses specifically Christian terms to make her point that in matters of faith, as in all matters, there is no point in arguing about what we must take on trust. The final lines begin with a couplet and then move out into an alternating rhyme pattern, thereby suggesting a break in tension and resolution of the controversy:

> Indifferently radiant, chiefly dear
> For that ripe harvest of the later year
> Which promises a winter-wealth of mead
> To fill the goblet up and brim the bowl: –
> His wine of generous thought and ample deed
> Sprung from the perfect blossom of the soul. (40)

In actuality, Lee and Robinson do not, before 1893, at least, seem to have settled "the controversy" that began with Robinson's announcement of her intent to marry James. Unfortunately, Lee never came to appreciate James Darmesteter as she came to appreciate Émile Duclaux, which no doubt hindered Robinson's attempts to end "the controversy."

In the lyrical poems of *Retrospect*, then, Robinson is indeed "retrospective" in her presentation of herself as a culmination of her past and her present, as an English "transplant," and as a woman who considers herself successfully integrated into French society and culture in subtle ways that went beyond her immediate love for James. She had adopted James's friends, not only Renan and Taine, as well as Taine's daughter Geneviève, but also Gaston Paris, to whom she dedicates "The Sonnet." Paris had considerable expertise in Medieval French literature, and Robinson highlights this aspect of Paris's work as she shows her own familiarity with medieval language in this Petrarchan sonnet, using ancient English and French diction to suggest the Anglo-French context in which she was living:

Sonnet, a thousand years ago to-day
Thou wast indeed the wild instinctive song
That women chaunted for the Feast of May!
But now, O solemn mirror of the mind,
Now it is I am weak, and thou art strong,
Keep me a coign of clearness and be kind! (47)

Diction such as "chaunted" and "coign," the latter word placed in the final line of the poem to convey the speaker's hope for clarity in perspective, imply not only her admiration for the women of medieval times but also her fear that in contrast to them, she spins her poetic yarns roughly and inelegantly. Her poetic speakers feel at times lost, as, for example, the speaker of "Selva Oscura," the title of which evokes the woods in which Dante finds himself at the beginning of the Inferno. At other times, her speakers are more hopeful about poeticizing truth, such as the speakers of "The Sibyl" and "Ephphatha." The title of the latter means literally "be opened," the words that Christ uttered when he cured a deaf and dumb man. The context of this poem is the poet's wish for the ability to sing the praises of spring as effectively as the nightingale.

The closing lyric of *Retrospect*, "Song," acts as a transitional poem to the ballads while developing the unifying themes of this collection, themes that vacillate between hope and despair:

A Heart as deep as the sea,
A heart as vast as the sky,
Thou shouldest have given to me,
O spirit, since I must die!

For how shall I feel and attain
The joy and the fear and the strife,
The hope of the world and the pain
In the few short years of a life? (54)

In these two short verses in iambic tetrametre Robinson returns to the question central to Robert Browning's poetry concerning the relationship between finite capacity and infinite aspiration. In choosing this lyric as the final expression of lyrical retrospection, Robinson also returns to the threads that unify all of her retrospective themes – the human history of coming to terms with life that ends, with death that remains an enigma, and the power of poetry to convey the irony of, as Baudelaire reminds us in "Ill Fortune," "Time is fleeting, and Art is so long!"

The successful ballads of *Songs, Ballads* in 1888 laid the groundwork for Robinson's intellectual engagement with history, legend, and mysticism as this engagement is framed now through retrospective activity. The reviewer for the *Bookman* writes, "Madame Darmesteter has an exceptionally happy ballad knack and her historical studies have suggested picturesque and not too hackneyed episodes."[29] Most of these ballads were written and first published in 1889, concurrently with *The End of the Middle Ages*, and they demonstrate Robinson's increasing adeptness at integrating historical prose material into her poetic ballads. For example, first published in the *Athenaeum* 16 November 1889, "The Death of the Count of Armaniac" originates in one of Froissart's tales, and Robinson was at this time involved in two significant projects on Froissart, an essay for the *Revue de Paris* and a biography, both of which would be published the following year. Armaniac's sister, Beatrice, married Carlo Visconti, and an oblique reference to Beatrice in the first stanza links the events of the poem as well to Robinson's article "Valentine Visconti," which she had integrated into *The End of the Middle Ages*:

"There's nothing in the world so dear
To a true knight," he cried,
"As his own sister's honour!
Now God be on our side!" (57)

The context for the story is the Armagnac–Burgundian civil war,
which the Armagnac faction lost 12 June 1418, with Bernard Armaniac
falling early in the day. Robinson's ballad is a song about this legendary death that occurred not on the battlefield itself but beside a
cool stream. This is a tale of poor choices in general and a failure in
leadership specifically. "Why rode ye forth at noon?" the speaker asks,
foreshadowing what turns out to be a catastrophe as the ballad traces
the story of a distraught Armaniac, heat-stricken and desperate,
deserting his troops and, on finding a stream, drinking so deeply that
he goes into a state of physiological shock. In his version of the story,
Froissart explains this phenomenon as a freezing of the blood upon
consumption of cold water, and, as the balladeer's repeated "Armaniac,
O Armaniac" highlights, it is an ignoble way to die. "Thy name is
made a mock," the speaker ends, and "we must pine in Lombardy /
for many and many a day" (59). This opening ballad, in its realistic
treatment of the limitations of human nature, is aptly positioned to
introduce the themes of the ballads of *Retrospect* that resonate with
modern readers. In dealing with the ethics of leadership and the
harsh reality of war in human history, moreover, it foreshadows some
of Robinson's poetry of the First World War that would appear in
the 1922 *Images and Meditations* and that would, in its defence of the
noble goals often associated with battle, bring Robinson back into
conflict with the pacifist Vernon Lee.

In ballads that deal specifically with Christian ideals, Robinson
points to the disparity between religious precepts and human
understanding of the logic of these principles of faith. "Sir Eldric,"
first published in the *Independent* 26 December 1889, highlights
through the tale of an old knight hunting for "heathen" in the name of
Christ the hypocrisy of those who embrace religious tenants blindly
and absolutely. This knight is riding literally and metaphorically in
the dark, as he defines Christian behaviour solely in terms of singing
"litanies" to an abstract entity. Only when he and his non-Christian
attacker mortally wound each other does he gain insight into the

"plight" of the non-Christian, and, at the moment of death, dips his fingers into his own chest to use his blood to baptize the foe. His reward for this Christian gesture of salvation is a glimpse into the infinite as the dawn sun breaks through, and he sees that "at his side, *Himself*, lay dead" (66). The parallels between this poem and "The King of Hungary's Daughter" of *Songs, Ballads* are clear, and, of course, the inclusion in *Retrospect* of "The Three Kings," originally published in the *Contemporary Review* story of 1889, also highlights Robinson's continued preoccupation with varied threads of mysticism in these years.

In both "The Slumber of King Solomon" and "The Death of Prester John," the titular figures suggest the mystical rather than practical grounds for faith. The biblical Solomon was famous for erecting magnificent buildings with, it was said, the help of angels who magically placed large heavy stones one upon the other. In situating Solomon in the sleep of "eternal night," guarded and pro-tected by thirty horsemen on either side of the house and by the four archangels at the four corners of his bed, the balladeer implies that Solomon was well loved and assured of heaven (75). However, the historical Solomon sinned in taking many wives and concubines and in establishing idolatry, among other sins. Perhaps, then, there is some irony in the speaker's wish for Solomon that he "sleep well, sleep well" when the biblical punishment for his sins was God's reduction of Israel to two tribes from twelve and the legacy of a divided Israel in the years following his death (75). A partner poem, "The Death of Prester John" focuses on the dying moments of the legendary figure about which many stories have circulated over the centuries but whose remains have never been found and whose existence has never been established. Robinson's subtitle, a chapter from "Yasht," is taken directly from the work of James Darmesteter – his translation of *Sacred Books of the East*. Indeed, the legendary Prester John travelled though China and India, leaving his mark on those countries as he spread Christian principles and teachings throughout the East. In focusing on John's uncertainty in these dying moments, on his need to know "where is the soul of the man who is dead," Robinson emphasizes the familiar fear of death that affects even those who live in a state of faith (76). The priests to whom he speaks in these last moments give Prester John the details he wants to hear – they are the details of a ritual in paradise that can never be certified as true, just as paradise itself can never be certified as existing. As the priest warns at the end of the poem, it is ultimately not appropriate to ask questions about the soul after death, for all we need to know is that "the will of God is best" (79). The platitude rings as false comfort after such intellectual wrestling and reinforces Robinson's conviction that agnosticism, while failing to offer the spiritual comfort she craved, was the only reasonable stance to take.

The conventional subjects of the ballad, of course, tend to highlight the epic moments in human life – war and death. However, the ballad is also well suited to the complicated narrative of love paired with betrayal. Calling to mind Victor Alfieri's 1774 "Rosamund," for instance, Robinson's "Rosamunda" takes a particularly modern look at the gendered plight of women in such a context. This medieval legend of murder, adultery, and betrayal is presented through discourse rather than through a single balladeer, and it highlights the final moments in Rosamunda's life when her controlling husband and equally controlling lover victimize her. Once the lover decides that Rosamunda's husband should die, he also decides in the third stanza that the fearful and reluctant Rosamunda will carry out the deed:

"Within thy mother's garden
An asp is in the vine:
Go, bray it in a mortar
And put it in his wine." (60)

The three asterisks that follow this third stanza not only denote passing time but also eliminate any discussion of the matter and imply that Rosamunda has gone to obey her lover. The mystery of Rosamunda's faithfulness and obedience without indicating her love for her "lover" is sustained until the reason for her meekness is revealed at the end of the poem. When Rosamunda's husband realizes that "the good red wine is troubled" his response increases the risk for Rosamunda:

– "Come hither, Rosamunda,
Come here and drink the first!"

– "Alas, how shall I drink it
That never drank of wine?"
– "Thou'lt drink it, Rosamunda
By this drawn sword of mine!" (61)

Robinson conveys just how dire the situation is for Rosamunda by allowing her to speak to both lover and husband only in response to what they say. In the end, Rosamunda is completely trapped, for it is revealed that her lover is "the King o' France," and so she is caught between the two men to whom she owes absolute obedience. "A dead woman am I," she concludes before she drinks. Now her reticence with her "lover" at the beginning of the poem is explained and the ballad becomes a sad tale of a young woman trapped by gender and class.

For "Captain Gold and French Janet," Robinson consulted archival documents, the four letters of William Gold to Ludovico Gonzaga, the Lord of Mantua, that are held in the Mantuan archives. This is another gendered tale, this time of a woman kidnapped from her husband by a man determined to make her his. Janet fares better than Rosamunda, for the focus in this sophisticated ballad is Captain Gold, the kidnapper, who admits stealing Janet from her husband Savoy. However, Captain Gold sinks lower and lower into an ethical abyss when Janet escapes, and he tries to retrieve what he feels has been taken from him but that was never his to claim as his own. Robinson follows the pattern of the letters in the archives and depicts Gold's repeated and increasingly intense requests until, derelict in and distracted from carrying out his duties, he dies. In "Captain Gold" and in a second ballad about the ethics of love, "The Widower of Haiderabad," Robinson's tales are cautionary, gendered tales about abuse of power. In "The Widower," a man who married a young child allows his mother to drive her to suicide, and, in consequence, he lives in terror that she will rise from her grave at night to haunt him and his family.

Yet, Robinson can be playful about the dangers of love when she reverses the situation as in "The Mower," a clever reworking of Andrew Marvell's "The Mower's Song," the fourth and final of his "mower" poems. In reality, the ballad conveys, love can be dangerous for young men in a society in which love is often linked to material wealth. The agent of this message is a young woman, Nancibel, who, like Marvell's Juliana, has a deleterious effect on the mower who pines for her. In Marvell's poem, the young mower's refrain – "and she / what I do to the grass, does to my thoughts and me" – conveys the mower's addled state of mind. Similarly, Nancibel's council to the mower is to "laugh and quaff" and "think no more" of her, since she is engaged "to a finer man" than any of them (68). Such banter situates the whole poetic discourse in more modern times. Hence, in this metaphysical model, emblematic of shifts in gendered power in seventeenth-century expressions of love, Robinson demonstrates the effectiveness of the ballad form related to its time.

"The Deer and the Prophet" is an interesting choice as a closing poem of this collection, since it is a sophisticated return to the more esoteric theme of faith in an integration of realistic and fantastical elements. This time, discussion of faith unfolds in the context of Eastern mysticism rather than Christianity, again suggesting the influence of James. The moral of this poem about Mahomet, whose principled act of generosity saves a doe's life and leads to the conversion of the hunter about to kill her, is summed up in its last verse – all creatures are "worthy of a Heavenly trust" (88). This is an appropriate closing line for a volume concerned with the fluidity of the transitional spaces between life and death and the tenuous connection between past and present. As poet and historian, Robinson recognized in the ballad the potential for intellectual engagement and accessibility. She was aware of the subtle ways in which the past, whether factual or imagined as legend or myth, informs our perspective on our world, and in the last two decades of the nineteenth century she was able to poeticize her world through old and familiar tales, elements of history, suggestive fragments of legend, and narratives that span centuries. These are narratives that have been heard over and over again, and they connect us to our literary past.

Froissart

It is difficult to believe that the contemplative moments of *Retrospect* had little to do with Vernon Lee, but in every respect this collection reflects Robinson's life with her husband, and Lee, for the first time since the *Honeysuckle* volume, is by and large absent. However, by September 1893 the friendship between the women seems to have at least taken on a physical dimension again, with Lee agreeing to meet in Paris and that Christmas sending Robinson sprays of olive and flaxseed. Robinson not only praised Lee's "Orpheus and the Social Question," but she also invited Lee to write for the *Revue de Paris*, which James was still coediting. However, Lee was clearing out the past in a significant way by returning Robinson's letters to her. In acknowledging the arrival of "a great packet of my poor foolish sad little old letters, so boring," Robinson mentions that her letters to Symonds were still at Davos and she "should never dream of asking for them back."[30]

Although she complained to Gosse 25 October 1893, when she was in London, "I am racking my brain for a dozen rhymes," she was in fact focusing on prose.[31] She was publishing in French with ease by this time and was heavily involved in her work on Froissart, including a long article titled "A La Cour de Gaston Phébus" that she published in the *Revue de Paris* 15 March 1894. Phébus, the author of the medieval text *Le Livre de la Chasse*, was a contemporary of Froissart. Robinson wrote the biography of Froissart in French, and her friend Frances Poynter translated it into English for Fisher Unwin. In his review for *The Historical Review*, James Tait is complimentary about Robinson's ability to write in French, noting, "she has caught the secret of that lightness and grace which is so much a matter of course in French literary *appreciations*, and alas, so often lacking in our own.[32] Robinson's interest in Froissart began with her childhood reading and continued throughout her life. In fact, her final lead article for the *Times Literary Supplement* in 1937 marks six centuries since Froissart's death. In the biography, she refers to secondary and tertiary sources, but she draws on her extensive knowledge of the Middle Ages to compensate for the paucity of primary materials in order to develop an account of this legendary figure that is as accurate and as detailed as possible. Froissart's four books of *Chronicles* appeal to English and French readers, for they tell the story of the days when France and England were one country caught up in civil war. As Robinson points out, the *Chronicles* are not historically grounded because they consist of details that Froissart recorded as he experienced events on his journeys; however, these day-by-day records, albeit not scholarly, do indeed "touch the very core of the history of France" and reveal to us an era long past, she points out (145). The *Chronicles* also reflect Froissart's youth, since he wrote them when he was only about twenty years old, which may be why readers have found them so exciting and engaging.

Robinson weaves together what little we know of Froissart, born, it is thought, in 1337 in Valenciennes, where he lived until he left for London in 1361 with the intention of giving his manuscript on the battle of Poitiers to Philippa of Hainault, then Queen of England but also born in Valenciennes. This manuscript, Robinson suggests, was "no doubt the germ of the *Chronicles*," and although it no longer exists, she is able to reconstruct much of what it contained through her own knowledge of history (13–14). Robinson's biography of Froissart is filled with a great deal of information that attests to her extensive knowledge of the period. For instance, she points out that in fourteenth-century England, any text that qualified as a romance would have been written in French, just as "serious books [were written] in Latin; English was merely a patois without elegance" (14). Froissart would have met Chaucer, who was only a few months younger than he and who was also in attendance at the court during the five years when, beginning in 1362, Froissart became "ditteur" in the service of Queen Philippa until her death in 1369.

Of particular interest in Robinson's time was the *Méliador*, which had been lost in 1440 and discovered in the Archives Nationales by a French scholar, M. Longnon, two years before Robinson published *Froissart*. Now, she points out, "this romance that Froissart read each night at the court of Gaston Phébus, everyone, in the course of a year or two, will be able to read for himself, should he feel so disposed" (69). With humour, she comments on the "absolutely unmixed pleasure" of such a find and the "doubtful joy" of having to read and copy 30,600 lines (70). Robinson suggests that Froissart may have presented a copy of the *Méliador* to the Duke of Orleans, "whom he detested," at the 1393 Congress of Amiens (117). Robinson succeeds in conveying the flavour of the times in which Froissart lived and wrote, but what seems to appeal to her is the poetic way in which Froissart recorded these times. She writes, he had this freshness, this soul, as it were, of a child captivated by the marvelous ... at the same time, the clearest vision, the keenest ear, the most just and discerning mind. His greatest fault – and the fault is one that stamps him as a poet – is, that in contemplating the drama of life he did not perceive the truth, and the truth only. (150)

His *Chronicles* reflect his youthful perspective, a reconciliation of the imaginative inner life of the young with an intellectual craving of the emerging older man for a "truth" about the human condition, certainly ideas related to the transience and impermanence that for Robinson typifies our existence.

We see in *Froissart*, I think, Robinson's latent anxiety that the time of extreme happiness that she was enjoying with James was also subject to the "awful brevity" of life that so terrified Pater. Perhaps it is not surprising that her preoccupation with these ideas intensified in this period, given the always worrisome health of James. Although she wrote to Lee 26 February 1894 to say that James "has never been so well in his life and looks about thirty," the joint editorship of the *Revue de Paris*, which he began in 1893 with the French literary critic and journalist Louis Ganderax, as well as Darmesteter's other scholarly work, was taking its toll. She notes in the same letter that she and James aim to go out socially once a week, but that week they had been out for five nights.[33] Things came to a crisis that June, when both she and James came down with food poisoning. They had recovered by mid-July, and in August her parents were able to visit. Despite her resentment and early conviction that the marriage was inappropriate, Frances Robinson had come to love James, writing to Mabel, "I feel more and more thankful that the marriage which I dreaded so much and which cost me so many tears has turned out so happily. Mary seems as she changed her name since her marriage not only happy but *joyous* and anyone can see that the French life suites her exactly. I do not believe she would be nearly as healthy living in England" [emphasis F. Robinson].[34]

However, on 19 October 1894, Robinson walked into the study of the holiday chalet in which they were staying just outside Paris and found James dead at his desk. Frances expressed to Mabel her deep sorrow at reports that James had suffered from colon cancer, but he seems to have succumbed to a heart attack as an immediate cause of death. Frances admits that she could only wish she had "done more to please him, but he never exacted anything."[35] The Robinsons were truly saddened and worried about Mary in terms of health and finances, and they prevailed upon their daughter to return to England. However, she settled down to her widowhood in Paris, where she would be close to James, for, as she explained in 1895 to Marie Herzfeld, who lived in Vienna and asked for biographical details to accompany Robinson's poetry that would appear in an anthology, "as his widow, I feel my place is in France and intend to remain here, to identify myself more and more with his country and his interests."[36] Despite his increasingly poor health, the death of James was a shock, and Robinson told her friend Maurice Barrès 25 September 1909 that she would never be able to reconcile herself to the loss of James.[37] Not surprisingly, during the next six years, as she tried to reconcile herself to the death of the man she considered her tutelary spirit, she did not publish new poems.

Over the next few years, Robinson kept James's memory alive in the press. She published a tribute to him in the December issue of the *Revue de Paris*, and this essay later became the preface to his *Critique et Politique*, which she saw through publication in 1896.[38] This article, which is titled simply "James Darmesteter," mainly highlights his professional achievements, but it ends with reference to James sleeping peacefully in his grave, his head resting on his mother's Hebrew bible and in his hands the book of Robinson's poetry that had led to their meeting. Gaston Paris's article for the *Contemporary Review*, also titled "James Darmesteter," concludes, "Darmesteter stands out as a Jew and a Frenchman, an honour to his race and his country."[39] Robinson also wrote a preface to Darmesteter's *English Studies*, published simultaneously in English by Fisher Unwin and in French by Calmann Lévy under the title *Nouvelles Études Anglais*. She sent this preface to the English journal *Cosmopolis*, where it appeared as an article in February 1896. The preface is another personal tribute to James and another indication of the mutual respect upon which their love was based. She explains how his love for English literature led him to an understanding of the "instinct, spirit, and tradition" of what was for him a foreign nation.[40] In this preface, Robinson notes that late nineteenth-century English poetry defies convention and rejects "bondage to Mrs. Grundy" and "the tyranny of cant" (394). The transformative English writer for James Darmesteter was George Eliot, in whom he sensed a kindred spirit who felt, as he felt, an "infinite and tender commiseration for human sorrow" and a sincere conviction that "our world is slowly moving towards some greater destiny" (395).

In the years immediately following James's death, Robinson, as she had vowed, worked a great deal in French, publishing several complex and substantive articles in the *Revue de Paris*. "Les Paroles de Lao-Tsé," which appeared in September of 1896, is an account of the transformative meeting between the philosophically polarized young Confucius and the aged, retired archivist and philosopher Lao-Tsé, famous for words condensed by a scribe into *Livre de la Vie Divine*, known in English as *The Way and Its Power*. "Anima Poetae" is a review article of Ernest Hartley Coleridge's edition of the Coleridge notebooks, which Robinson describes as a "treasure" to English readers. However, she cautions, perhaps reflecting some of her own recent decisions about posthumous publication, because the notebooks were not meant to be read, they may not appeal to a more reticent French public at first glance. Therefore, she extracts the details of interest to French readers from a "hodgepodge," literally "drivel" (*gentille bêtise de la vie ordinaire*) of notes. This edition focuses on the fifteen or so years beginning at age twenty-eight, when the mystical poet was unhappy both personally and professionally. Robinson disagrees that Coleridge is in essence a Lake Poet, suggesting that Wordsworth is really the sole claimant to this title.

It was the third article for the *Revue*, "Dante Gabriel Rossetti," that caused her some anxiety because of her close relationship with William Michael Rossetti. Although she had published the *Unsere Zeit* article in 1879 and the memorial article in *Harper's New Monthly Magazine* in 1882, William Rossetti had published a book on his brother titled *Dante Gabriel Rossetti* in 1895, and he sent her a copy as she was preparing her article. She writes in thanks 13 December 1895 to her good friend, telling him, "for years I have read nothing so moving, so sincere, stirring me to such deep admiration, compassion and pity. That is the real way to preserve the memory of the dead; to renew their life, such as they were in the flesh, vivid, human, actual."[41]

However, although she aimed to emulate Rossetti's perspective in her article for the *Revue*, she was clearly nervous about her ability to do so, writing again 4 April 1896 to apologize for the "untidy" proofs that she was sending to him for fact verification. She tried, she tells him, "to make a sort of moral portrait" of his brother because the French reading public is not familiar enough with his work for her to discuss it in detail, and she worried that the portrait "evolved from [her] inner consciousness" rather than the truth. Rossetti's advice seems to have been to delete some personal references so as "to avoid all chance of giving pain" to those still living and, as she says in a second letter of 18 April, she would take his advice so as not to "spice my literature with scandal."[42]

A week or so later, Robinson travelled to London, offering her apartment in Paris to Rossetti should he arrive in Paris before her return three weeks later. "Dante Gabriel Rossetti" finally appeared in the *Revue* 1 June 1896, and Robinson presents the details that she felt would interest French readers – his devotion to Lizzie Siddal, her role as muse and inspiration, and, of course, his long-developing illness that ended tragically. She ends the article with an introduction to Christina Rossetti, who had died in 1894 and who was still "little known in France."[43] Despite all of these exchanges, William Michael Rossetti seems to have held back a scrapbook of family photographs, and when he sent them to Robinson in June of 1901, she comments that she regretted not having the documents before she had written her article.[44] The two remained close friends, as is clear in his dedication of his 1899 published correspondence between Dante Gabriel Rossetti and Ruskin to Robinson and in their frequent correspondence about his children and grandchildren.

Finally, Robinson published an article on John Everett Millais, who died 13 August 1896. This article for the *Gazette de Beaux Arts* in August 1897 was the final of her shorter works in French for the decade. She was busy with a biography of Ernest Renan, but she was also swept up in one of the most divisive and controversial events in modern French history directly because of James Darmesteter's Jewish heritage. Ironically, this difficult and emotionally stressful experience also led to happiness with her second husband, Émile Duclaux, who came to James Darmesteter's rescue when he was attacked posthumously in the press for his characterization of

Jewish history. Darmesteter came under fire as France splintered over what came to be known as the Dreyfus affair, a blot on French history that came between many friendships.

The political crisis that unfolded between 1894 and 1906 began in December, two months after James's death, when the Jewish Captain Dreyfus was convicted of selling military secrets to the Germans. The overtly racist tones of the affair by such as Édouard Drumont, the editor of *La Libre Parole*, fuelled anti-Semitism to the extent that when the identity of the true traitor Ferdinand Walsin-Esterhazy came to light, it took the pro-Dreyfus people, one of them Robinson, a long time to convince the government to bring Esterhazy to trial, and, when he was finally court-martialled in January of 1898, he was acquitted. To make matters worse, Dreyfus found himself before a new court-martial in September 1899, and he was once again convicted. In the eyes of Robinson and other French Dreyfusards, this was a blatant attempt to cover up the army's inadequacy. In 1898, Ferdinand Brunetière, the director of the *Revue des Deux Mondes* and a member of the Académie Francaise, responded to Émile Zola's famous letter attacking the army for its continued mistreatment of Dreyfus by taking the position that Dreyfusard intellectuals who advocated attacks such as Zola's actually undermined French democracy. Zola's letter, which was published with the title "J'accuse," led to his conviction of libel. However, in his response, Brunetière claimed that Jewish intellectuals, particularly James Darmesteter, were ironically the root cause of anti-Semitism because their individualistic thinking was fundamentally antithetical to democratic principles. Robinson's natural graciousness is evident in the obituary article for the *Times Literary Supplement* she wrote when Brunetière died in 1906 in which she describes him as "a man to oppose or a man to follow –'ever a fighter' – and perhaps a man to hate. But every one respected Ferdinand Brunetière."[45] The affair reinforced Robinson's friendship with Ludovic Halévy and his two sons, Eli and Daniel, with whom she would spend time at La Haute Maison at Sucy-en-Brie over the years. She soon invited the Halévy brothers to visit her in London when she went to see her mother and sister. Daniel, who became a famous French historian, was a lifelong friend and confidant, ultimately leaving us a valuable resource in published letters between Robinson and Maurice Barrès, an anti-Dreyfusard with whom Robinson managed to retain a friendship. She also met Henriette Guy-Loë, Eli Halévy's niece, to whom Robinson sent one of her last letters, written 7 January 1944. A cousin of Eli's held successful salons where Robinson became good friends with Marcel Proust.[46] However, the most notable acquaintance of Robinson's at this time was the public and prominent leader of the defence of James Darmesteter, the head of the Pasteur Institute, Émile Duclaux, who Robinson married in 1901.

The Life of Renan

Robinson's poetic tribute to Renan upon his death in 1892 was just the beginning of longer and more sustained tributes, both in prose and in poetry. She met Ernest Renan at the home of a friend of her father's in Venice, the archaeologist Signor Castellani, during the September 1880 European trip with her parents. Within thirty minutes of a gathering that included Henry Layard and his wife, Robinson found herself thinking, as she says in this biography, that she was with a "Man of Genius!" (246). She next visited Renan and his wife while James Darmesteter was at the Collège de France, and through James, she became a good friend of the man whose intellectual ambiguity about religion fascinated her. Renan's most pithy expression of this ambiguity is the claim that "all religions are vain, but religion is not vain" (279). Just as Renan was unable to believe in the Catholic faith in which he had been raised, Robinson had long ago cast off her Anglican heritage; like Renan, however, she remained convinced that there was a place in society for the civilizing influence of love and peace included in a religious package. She published "Monsieur Renan: A Pastel" in the *Albemarle* in May 1892, an article in which she describes Renan as "the man who more than any other has taught the modern generation how to doubt."[47] She admired Renan's sincerity, which in the biography she explains culminated in his development as "the priest of Truth" (177).

Robinson dedicated *La Vie de Renan* to Renan's daughter Noémi Renan, who had become Madame Jean Psichari. She and Robinson had become good friends by this point, and years later her son was a subject of Robinson's "war work" on heroism. Robinson's biography of Renan has some origins in James Darmesteter's address "Notice sur la vie et l'oeuvre de M. Renan," which he delivered at the annual meeting of the Asiatic Society 22 June 1893. Darmesteter had succeeded Renan as president of the Asiatic Society when Renan died, and his speech was first published in *The New World* in September 1893 and subsequently translated by Helen Jastrow and published in *Selected Essays of James Darmesteter*, edited by Morris Jastrow Jr. As Jastrow writes in his preface, this project was in place when Darmesteter died, and when it finally appeared in 1895, it was, therefore, a memorial tribute.[48] Darmesteter's central thesis on Renan in his *New World* essay supports Renan's sense that the human race is "advancing to a higher, more perfect form of being" and that "the supreme happiness of man is to draw nearer to this God to come, contemplating him in science, and preparing, by action, the advent of a humanity nobler, better endowed, and more akin to the ideal Being."[49] It was through Renan that Darmesteter came to admire George Eliot's literary attempts to lead us to our higher "destiny" through our human sympathy.[50] This time, Robinson translated her biography into English herself and published it with Methuen in London in 1898.

Renan was surely the most influential figure in Robinson's increased expressions in her prose and poetry that only in understanding the past might we possibly know how to improve conditions in the present. In her biography, she emphasizes the importance of Renan's personal past on the man he became, particularly the influence for most of his early life of his only sister Henriette, his "true fairy – the guardian angel," who also lost her faith in Catholicism (13). When Renan turned to Orientalism, however, he found himself on common ground with James Darmesteter. Robinson notes, "in five years, Renan had lost two ideals – Christianity and Socialism" (99). However, these losses ultimately had a positive effect on this brilliant man, who became a professor of Hebrew at the Collège de France in January 1862. In 1863 he published the *Life of Jesus*, during the writing of which Henriette died. This is the first of seven books that comprise *The Origins of Christianity* published in 1866. Robinson points to the scholarly research of Renan's work and the impact of it on theology, noting that "while the Prussians were taking up their positions at Versailles and St Cloud, Renan sat down and wrote an open letter to

David Strauss denouncing the war as a crime against civilization" (189).
Renan's final years at the Collège, where he worked until his death in
1892, were difficult, as he struggled with ill health and the emotional
turmoil left by France's defeat in the Franco–Prussian War. *La Vie de
Renan* received good reviews in both the *Revue de Paris* and the *Grande
Review*, as well as in the *Daily Chronicle* in London, and indeed, in
his *Times Literary Supplement* obituary, Morgan points out that this
book was "said by good critics to be the most important of her books
written in French."[51] Robinson was pleased with the reviews in a letter
to her mother 2 June 1900, having just returned from a visit to Sucy
to see Daniel and Marianne Halévy and their new baby. However,
it seems that the reviews did not ensure the book's market success
in English, for she writes a week later to tell her mother that only
fifty copies of the text were sold in England and America during the
whole of 1899. "Isn't it sad," she asks rhetorically.[52] In France, the book
fared better, and she reports to her mother in June 1900 that she had
received "two nice little reviews" in the *Grande Review* and the *Revue
de Paris*.[53] Robinson's second poetic tribute to Renan, "Unum Est
Necessarium," was published in the *Athenaeum* 21 August 1897 and
included in the 1901 *Collected Poems*. Alluding to the biblical context
of Christ's lesson delivered during his visit to Martha and Mary,
Robinson uses it to frame the theme of her poem: the "one thing
needful" is faith. In his 1893 memoriam, Renan's contemporary and
friend Sir Mountstuart Elphinstone Grant Duff reports finding that
Renan had penned "Unum est necessarium, et Mary elegit bonum
partem" in a guest book in a church at Mount Casino that he visited
in Italy in 1850.[54] The inscription baffled Duff at first because it seemed
so out of place coming from the scientifically-focused Renan; however,
he suggests that it is understandable when we realize that for Renan,
it is the quiet, thoughtful Mary rather than the practical Martha who
is best suited to further a scientific pursuit of truth. For Renan, as
Robinson had made clear in her biography, religion was as essential
to the intellectual progress of the human race as was pure science, for
it was religion that brought people together. This movement toward
unity determines the rhetorical process of Robinson's poem from
the first stanza:

I thought that I was ravished to a height
Whence earth was lost with all I once had known;

I saw the stars flash dwindling thro' the night,
Like sparklets from a blackening yule-log thrown;
And nothing else remain'd of all that is
Save the essential life of souls alone. (182)

The process through which the speaker goes has to do with finding a community of souls that counters the isolation the speaker
expresses in the last line of this passage. The stars that "flash" here
suggest moments of insight in which the speaker touches on the
"one thing necessary" for happiness in life – the sense of inclusivity
and belonging to something greater than oneself. This is, of course,
a theme that Robinson had developed in various ways throughout
her poetic life –the outsider in love, the outsider in faith, the outsider
in life itself, all hoping to move inside a community of lovers, of
believers, and of those living in this world. Her speaker in this poem
finds her way into the companionship of "radiant spirits" through
the guidance of

a voice from Heaven, not ours
"This is the Race," it cried, "this is the Race
Of Radiating Souls, the large in heart,
And where they circle is a holy place!" (182)

However, in the next lines, the voice warns the speaker to "look
further," and when she does so, she comes to understand that faith
can be both inclusive and individual:

I pierced the depth of space from part to part,
And lo! adrift as leaves that eddy in vain,
I watched the vacant, vagrant, aimless dance
Of Souls concentrated in their bliss or pain:
Unneighboured souls, the drift of time and chance. (183)

The stars become a metaphor during the course of the poem as the
speaker sees each sparkling individually and yet combining to light
up the night sky. "Be thankful," says the Voice, "and learn that all
men love the Light" (183). The poem ends with an oblique tribute
to the "large in heart" Renan, who, Robinson felt, had revised the
implications of *unum est necessarium*:

And lo! A beam of their transcendent bliss
Who, ever giving, ever losing, move
In self-abandoned bounty through the abyss,
Pierced to my soul with so divine a dart,
I swooned with pain, I wakened to a kiss;
"Blessed," I sang, "are ye the large in heart
Irradiate with the light in alien eyes;
For ye have chosen indeed the brighter part,
And where ye circle is our Paradise. (184)

She elaborates on this theme in a follow-up article titled "Ernest Renan: Dernières Années" for the *Revue de Paris* 15 May 1898, in which she fleshes out in personal reminiscences Renan's service as the head of the Collège de France from 1884 until his death. A second collected poem, "Teste Sibylla," which appeared in both the *Living Age* and the *Athenaeum* on 18 November 1899, suggests the continued influence of Renan. Discarding her clothing as she runs, the "pale, shrieking, mad," Sybil speaks in the language of riddle to predict disaster tomorrow. However, Robinson's Sybil is actually the voice of eternal hope, for what seems "mad" and sounds like words from "a liar" today will be tomorrow's truth, avows this speaker (136). This is the idea that Amy Levy took as her epigraph for "A Dream" when Robinson first expressed it in "Paradise Fancies" in *A Handful of Honeysuckle*.

George Robinson died in 1897, which meant that Frances and Mabel spent more time with Robinson in France; in fact, the three of them spent all of November and December 1898 in Cannes and Nice.[55] Robinson published the lengthy review of Bodley's *France* in the *Contemporary Review* in 1898, an essay in which she expresses her own views on politics and governance. Although she is impressed by Bodley's scholarship, she disagrees with his view that administrative powers ought to remain centralized, as they had been since Napoleon; rather, she argues, power should be defused to the different regions. In "The Social Novel in France," again for the *Contemporary* in 1899, she situates the current socially informed and pointed novels of her contemporaries, Anatole France, Maurice Barrès, Édouard Estaunnié, and Louis Bertrand, in the political context of the late 1890s and the Dreyfus affair. She argues that the novel in France, like the novel in England, has found a niche far from the conventional "roman-à-trois." In Robinson's view, novels have become "something more complex, more earnest, more intellectually stimulating, deeper, too, and more opulent in ideas and information, if less sentimentally interesting, than their immediate forerunners" (813).

The final article for an English audience at this time appeared in the *Edinburgh Review* in July 1900. By this time, Robinson had become close to Émile Duclaux and was introducing him to her English friends, such as the Wards when they visited Paris for the World's Fair. She describes to her mother 17 May 1900 a luncheon she hosted to bring Thomas and Mary Ward together with Émile and his son Jacques, as well other French friends.[56] In September 1900, she and Émile Duclaux decided to marry in the New Year. At this point, she reignited her interest in travel writing, describing in "Paris in 1900" the Champs-Elysées in spring and the Rue de Rivoli, as well as other tourist attractions. The tone in which she describes her adopted city reflects the happiness she was feeling as her love for Duclaux – albeit a love different in nature than the love she had felt for James – matured. "No one in Paris lives or dies to himself alone," she says. "Here the individual is less and the aggregate more than in other places" (118). Robinson found the World Fair of 1900 inspiring because it brought to Paris more art and more beauty than the city had witnessed in some time and that influx seemed promising in its global emphasis. Having described the beauty of the city, of the site of the exhibition, and of several pavilions, Robinson concludes her article with a look forward, a perspective rather unusual for her: "In Paris more than in any other city we realize that before us, not behind us, lies the golden age" (139). She published her article "M. Paul Calmann Lévy" in the *Athenaeum* 17 February 1900. Not only was Lévy, who died in 1891, a founder of the *Revue de Paris* but his firm Pierre Mercieux published a translation of *Margaret of Angoulême* in 1900.

In fact, Robinson was busy with the *Revue* between 1898 and 1900, publishing three substantive, multipart articles on the Brownings, the Brontë sisters, and Thackeray. She collected these articles and added to them her 1896 *Revue* article on Rossetti, publishing the whole in 1901 as *Grands Écrivains d'Outre-Manche*. "Ménage de Poètes," published in two parts in September and October 1898, is a response to Frederic Kenyon's three-volume *The Letters of Elizabeth Barrett Browning*, which had come out in 1897. Although Robinson criticizes what she considers Kenyon's invasion of privacy, she tells her French readers that this story of two poets, who met, fell in love, and lived in a marriage of extreme happiness, is worth reading (296). Browning was "auguste à la fois et simple et paternal," she writes, and she brings Barrett Browning into the story through Browning's memories of the wife to whom he still felt spiritually close (297). Although there is nothing new to English readers in this two-part essay, much of the detail was probably new to her French readers.

Perhaps inspired by this essay, she decided to publish a preface to a new English edition of Barrett Browning's *Casa Guidi Windows* that she had actually written 1 May 1891 but that suits the 1901 edition well. In this brief preface, Robinson pays tribute to the woman "who reconciled in her woman's heart the scholar's knowledge and the poet's mind, she whose verse was a golden ring linking together Italy and England" (vi). However, she also suggests that Barrett Browning's poor health impeded her clear thinking to a certain extent in her support of Louis-Napoleon and the coup-d'état: "she never wholly grasped the situation, never saw the night-side of that treacherous plot, nor heard its sinister echoes of political murder, of unwarrantable exile, of confiscation and violated freedom" (xi). An extended version of this preface serves as the biographical introduction to some of Robert Browning's poetry published in French in 1922, *La Pensée de Robert Browning*. Relying heavily on Mrs Sutherland Orr's study of 1885, Robinson traces Browning's poetic development with a brief mention of each of his major works, thereby sketching out for French readers his developing "genius" after the problematic *Pauline* and his early plays and long poems, particularly the difficult and complex *Sordello*. She says that Browning confided to her that if he had died at age sixty, he would never have become popular (129).

For "Les Soeurs Brontë," which appeared in three parts in December 1899 and January 1900, Robinson draws on *Emily Brontë* and on Elizabeth Gaskell's biography of Charlotte, as well as on the commentary of others, such as the subject of the third essay in this series, Thackeray, who likened Emily Brontë to an "austere Joan of Arc." The first part of the article takes readers up to the end of the Brussels episode in the Brontë lives, after which they became aware, she says, of their superiority as writers (45). The rest of the article covers well-known biographical ground with brief references to fictional works and the protracted death of Branwell. Robinson recounts the fact that doctors warned Charlotte that she was too delicate to withstand a pregnancy and points out that ignoring that warning seems to have led to her death. One cannot help but interpret these remarks in light of Robinson's two marriages undertaken with not having children as an understanding between her and both her husbands. "Thackeray" appeared in two parts in November 1900, and it is her only study of this author. Again, she relies heavily on published work on Thackeray that she could be fairly certain was introductory material for her French readers. The biographical first part of the article outlines the less fortunate aspects of Thackeray's life, including his wife's succumbing to severe postpartum depression. In the second part, she concentrates on *Vanity Fair*, perhaps stimulated by Charlotte Brontë's dedication of the second edition of *Jane Eyre* to Thackeray. Robinson calls *Vanity Fair* both a historical and an analytical novel, telling French readers that Stendhal had not dealt better with the narrative of the English army at Brussels and the Battle of Waterloo (410). Along with the rest of Thackeray's fiction, she discusses his editorship of the *Cornhill*, his resignation of that duty, and his death at Christmas time in 1863. She was implicitly clearing out her drawers and preparing for a new start with Duclaux, when she would turn her attention to several new projects and begin a new volume of poetry.

CHAPTER SIX

Mary Duclaux, 1900–12

The personal risk that Émile Duclaux took in defending James Darmesteter's professional reputation during the Dreyfus affair was the foundation for Robinson's growing respect for Duclaux, and that respect grew into genuine, companionate love. As for Duclaux, his championship of James Darmesteter in the early days had nothing to do with Mary. Most of the Auvergne was anti-Dreyfusard, and Duclaux was called a "traitor" and accused of "selling out" in the city of his birth, Aurillac. Already an unwell man, he felt this pressure tremendously: "His voice was shaky and his eyes sad as he felt himself reviled where he had always been revered."[1] Indeed, the current Lycée Émile Duclaux in Aurillac was built and dedicated to him in 1894. Robinson clearly enjoyed the intellectual and socially shy scientist, and she enjoyed the prestige of his position at the Pasteur Institute. In May 1900, she writes to her mother about attending a housewarming at the newly renovated Pasteur Institute, after which she "came home and made tea for young Baring and Gaston Paris." She writes a week later about attending a fête at the institute in "a new dress which is very pretty, with a soft falling long skirt and a little tucked boléro opening on a fichu of black lace *cramped* over an underbodice of white taffetas."[2] She and Duclaux had friends in common, such as Gaston Paris, and events had moved quickly enough that by 22 June 1900, she was able to tell her mother that Émile's son, Jacques, might accompany her to London, a trip she anticipated making soon to visit Frances and Mabel.[3] She made multiple visits to the Paris World Fair with friends visiting from England, including Hannah Lynch, and Vernon Lee came from Florence. She often visited the site on her own as well.[4] For the second time in her life, Robinson proposed

marriage, and Duclaux, although at first surprised, he told his son
Pierre, accepted. However, he reassured Pierre, at his age, he did not
"need a woman" in the conventional sense.[5] She wrote to tell her
mother and Mabel 1 July 1900, "I am an old person of forty three
who has gone through the best and worst of human experiences. But
life is not over for me yet, and I have just come to a great decision
which I feel I ought to tell you." She continues,

> [Émile] is very fond of me and very anxious I should be
> happy. And life with him will be not only pleasant but useful,
> I hope. I ought to be able to help him with his hospital and
> his *colleges* for working people ... I hope he is telling Jacques
> today, just as I am telling you. So far Jacques is very fond of me
> and thinks all sorts of good and kind things; but will he like
> me as a stepmother? I rather tremble! As for me, I *own* that
> Jacques is a great attraction. I look forward to being gran-
> mamma [*sic*] to his babies! If only he is as pleased with me as I
> with him, we may be a great brightness to each other. We have
> the same sort of *facts* and ideas and get on beautifully together.[6]

Other than immediate family members, Mary and Émile told no one
until the fall. Robinson told Gaston Paris and his wife Marguerite in
September and William Michael Rossetti in October that she and
Émile Duclaux were engaged. "I am happy in the affection of the
best man I know," she wrote to the latter.[7] She explained to Edmund
Gosse in November that although her mother and Mabel were "at
first rather aghast at the idea of my remarrying a 'vivisectionist,'" the
wedding would take place 3 January 1901, adding, I am "quite pleased
with my future and with a feeling of friendship for Mr. Duclaux."[8]
The marriage was happy from the beginning, symbolizing, as she
told her mother in May 1901, a new start in life that had "seemed
just a sort of dead leaf" until she met Émile.[9]

Whereas James had been an orientalist and philosopher, Émile
Duclaux was a scientist, but Robinson's husbands shared the goal
of leaving the world a better place than they found it. Émile was
"superior" to James, Robinson joked to Tissot in 1909, in that he spent
his evenings with the frail Englishwoman who made his late life so
happy.[10] She ventured with passion into an entirely new perspective

on both life and death through natural and scientific readings, which she expressed poetically during her marriage and which she collected for the volume of poetry *The Return to Nature* that she published shortly after Duclaux's death. Although she thoroughly enjoyed entering into Duclaux's Parisian circle of intellectual friends, her letters to her mother show that she retained her sense of humour about the mixed blessing such evenings could be. Since neither Émile Duclaux nor his two sons spoke English, she became increasingly more apt to think and write in French. They were not wealthy, but Émile's position with the institute meant that they lived comfortably, and Robinson was able to be her mother's "extravagant little mouse," as Frances calls her in a letter of 19 February 1903 as she thanks her for a monetary gift and exclaims over the £400 that Duclaux had evidently put into his wife's bank account.[11]

Marriage once again led to heightened productivity for Robinson, and she published poetry and prose in the British journals *Harper's Monthly* and *Living Age*. One moving short lyric "Solitude" that appeared in *Harper's Monthly* was never collected for republication.

> Long miles of wave-worn beach,
> Farther than eye could reach,
> Nor sight, nor sound of living thing –
> Only the sea-bird's screech.
>
> The roar and crash of tide –
> A waste of waters wide;
> A shore, a sea, man ne'er hath known,
> Yet there – doth God abide. (282)

In 1901, in addition to *Grands Écrivains d'Outre-Manche*, she published "Ausone ou l'education des rheteurs" in the *Revue*. This substantial article examines the legacy of Decimus Magnos Ausonius, the Roman poet and teacher of rhetoric in fourth century Autun, a city in Bourgogne-Franche-Comté in eastern France that was famous for its school of rhetoric. She traces the long life of this figure, recounting his place in the political intrigues of the time as Ausonius tutored Gratian, the son of Emperor Valentinian, and gained personal wealth and accolades that left him secure even after

Gratian was assassinated. At the end of the article, she returns to the subject of much of her poetry and pays tribute to the rhetoricians who sleep peacefully in their tombs but who have no place in the modern world (546). In the preface to her *Collected Poems* of 1901, Robinson counts Ausonius as one of the poets who had always given her immense pleasure (viii).

Perhaps inspired by the success of collecting her *Revue* articles for a book publication in 1901, Robinson decided the same year to publish her second collection of previously published poetry, *The Collected Poems Lyrical and Narrative of Mary Robinson (Madame Duclaux)*. The dedication "to the Memory of James Darmesteter: Amori et Dolori Sacrum" tells us a great deal about the origin of most of these poems, about the sympathetic and kind nature of Émile Duclaux, and about Robinson's enduring grief at the loss of James. In the preface to *Collected Poems* dated September 1901, Robinson suggestively untangles the multiple artistic personalities signalled by her name changes. "Mary James Darmesteter has no longer a right to exist," she says. And "as regards the English public, Madame Duclaux has given no proof of her existence; she has, she hopes, before her a modest future of French prose, and leaves her English verses to Mary Robinson" (vii). Robinson continued to write poetry, however, and would publish two more volumes of new poems between writing these words and her death.

The only new poems that Robinson adds to her reprints in *The Collected Poems* are listed under the first two sections titled "Lyrics" and "Songs of the Inner Life." The three new poems of "Lyrics" develop to various degrees the familiar theme of dismay at the brevity of life, but we see reflected in them Robinson's relationship with Émile in her growing interest in natural science as the lens through which she could express this theme. In "Maidens," for instance, she develops an analogy between the determined and reliable brilliance of the stars and young women who, in their vitality and innocence, add brilliance to a troubled world. The poem ends with a final image that compares the young women to almonds growing in the snow, perhaps a reference to Van Gogh's series of flowering almond trees in the south of France, which he painted between 1888 and 1890. "To My Muse" evokes the days spent with Vernon Lee as the speaker defines her muse as a "Tuscan grace," who lives among olives in a "lonely place" (127). In its Romanticist conflation of religious perspective and the natural world, the third new lyric, "Michaelmas," foreshadows some of the poetry of *The Return to Nature*. Just as Michaelmas pays tribute to the archangel credited with ensuring Lucifer's defeat in his rebellion against God and Heaven, the glorious "crystal fire" of autumn evident in sky, trees, and flowers seems to the speaker to be the final and doomed resistance to the coming winter.

Of the new poems of "Songs of the Inner Life," "Foreward," dedicated to "JD," is a poignant testament to Robinson's enduring love for James and perhaps belies the intent of the introduction that signals her transition into a new marriage, a new love, and a new identity as a prose writer. This is not only a poem of memoriam to a husband dead for several years and published in the early days of a second marriage but it is a poem that makes clear his continued positive and strengthening effect on his widow as a woman and as a poet:

> When I die, all alone,
> I shall look at last
> For thy tender face, my own,
> Thy face, belovèd
> So far removèd
> From all our happy past ...
>
> Nay, all day, all day long
> Still thou lingerest here ...
> Halting in its muffled song,
> Thy voice, unaltered,
> Still murmurs, faltered,
> The old words still as dear. (131)

The sestet, with trimetre lines predominating and a lengthened third line, well suits the idea of extended grieving that Robinson aims to convey. This speaker's intense love both haunts her and gives her immense comfort, casting the title of the poem in an ironic light as it situates James as the introduction to the poems that follow. This is Robinson's tribute to the power of James's love for her that continues even as his voice, conventionally the most difficult attribute to remember, remains crisp and clear in her mind. The internal couplet in each of these first two stanzas is formed by diction that is deliberately awkward, perhaps even jarring, to drive home his presence. In the third stanza, the mood created by her sense that she remains "alone" and, with reference to the first line of the poem, waiting to join him in death, is once again intensified by the internal couplet that emphasizes his continued presence in her life:

Thou art dead, years ago,
Dead and in the grave;
I am all alone, I know ...
And yet how often
Thy kind eyes soften,
And smile and guide and save!

Ellipses in each stanza imply that there is so much more that is left unsaid, and they emphasize the continued force of grief in her life. In the final stanza, Robinson's implicit retreat from the "dream" of joining him casts her agnosticism in a painful light, as it undermines the potential of the dream itself:

Smilest thou, angel-ghost? ...
Yet, no heavens ope!
All thou art I had, and lost;
And now remember
O'er life's dull ember
Nor call my dream a hope.

The poem immediately following "Foreward," "The Two Lions," develops the same theme through a poet trapped in the present, unable to move forward and unable to reclaim the past. The titular animals of the "The Two Lions" that block the speaker's way and preclude her escape in any direction, named "Yesterday" and "To-morrow," draw attention to the fact that we live with the present as the only certainty.

The *Collected Poems* of 1901 gather up many loose threads of Robinson's past life, including two poems, "Religions" and "Justice," that are dedicated to M.B., most certainly Maurice Barrès. Although

Barrès and Robinson had known each other for years, Barrès's anti-Semitism and his anti-Dreyfusard stance, as well as his direct opposition to Duclaux and Marcel Proust in gathering signatures for the "Manifesto of the Intellectuals" that Duclaux and Zola drew up the day after "J'accuse" was published, strained the friendship significantly. These poems can be read specifically in the context of Barrès's three-volume philosophical treatise on "le culte de moi" or the humanistic love of the self. In the Petrarchan sonnet "Religions," an abstract dream suggests to the speaker that it is all too easy to hide the truth under something ornate and artificial. However, "Justice" takes aim more directly at the cult of the self and Barrès's defence of prioritizing sensual experience of the world as a means of enhancing society:

> "Lord, what is Justice? Say,
> Shall Man be just?
> Shall mortals strike a ray
> Out of the dust?"

The response to this question comes in language evocative of the Christian ethic of poverty:

> "One sage was just: He spake.
> 'Friend, thine is thine!
> Keep all thou hast, and take.
> Nothing is mine!'" (154)

The passage perhaps echoes Proverbs 27.10 in urging us never to abandon a friend or perhaps Matthew 19.21, in which Jesus suggests that a wealthy young man sell all his possessions and give the money to the poor, thereby enriching himself spiritually as he follows Jesus and prepares for treasure in heaven. In any event, Robinson refutes the philosophical perspective of exclusiveness at the heart of "le culte de moi."

"The Gate of Tears," "The Lost Sheep," and "'Seek and Ye Shall Find'" develop themes of simultaneous yearning for and disappointment in a vision of the afterlife as Robinson's poetic perspective shifts back and forth between relativity and absolutism in matters of religious truth. There is no indication to whom G.A.S. of the dedication refers, but "The Gate of Tears" highlights the physical, unreachable separation between the mourner and the dead. Once again, however, the overall movement of the poem is ironically positive, as the speaker assures the listener that there is comfort and peace beyond the metaphorical "gate" of bereavement and the poem is a conventional depiction of peace after death. In contrast, "The Lost Sheep" expresses the speaker's despair of finding permanent comfort in faith itself. Like a pendulum, Robinson's poetic perspective shifts again in "'Seek and Ye Shall Find,'" with the title from Matthew 7.7 suggesting that the truth is there for us to find if we only search for it. However, Robinson takes this concept out of a Christian context and places it in a pantheistic ideal of faith that reaches toward "the Eternal Mind." In the second half of the poem, references to Faustus, who privileged the present over an uncertain eternity, and Kepler, who studied the planet as a way into heavenly insights, contrast the speaker's advice to "seek on" and in so doing to "forget the Here and Now, and learn / At last to contemplate the whole" (137). Therefore, we see in the new poems of the "inner life" Robinson's intensified yearning for spiritual certainty through a more scientifically grounded philosophical perspective.

Yet, the aestheticist Robinson surfaces in "Beauty," as the speaker initially argues that beauty surely transcends death, until, in recounting instances of beauty in daily life – moments in morning, noon, and night when the earth seems to offer beauty that no imagined heaven could possibly offer – the speaker comes to understand a decadent paradox: if there is no afterlife featuring beauty, then the only relief from this disappointment will be forgetfulness. In eleven sestets of the similarly focused "The Valley," the speaker rejoices at the beautiful scene of "our valley" at Olmet that seems to remain in a state of perpetual beauty that emerged long ago out of the violence of lava and earthquakes that formed the peaceful landscape so full of productive farm life now. Her thoughts of geological and meteorological events conclude with an intuited presence of God within that enables us to comprehend and celebrate the evolution of such beauty:

The patient oxen ploughing through the clod,
The very dragonflies about the stream,
The larks that sing and soar,
Employ the force of that tremendous God
Who lurks behind our thought, beyond our dream,
And whom the worlds adore.

In placing "The Valley" strategically in this volume to follow "Darwinism" from *Songs, Ballads*, Robinson hints at the ways in which daily discourse with Émile had expanded her perspective on "God" that could accommodate Renan's belief in the power of religion in the abstract and her own reluctance to enter into any formal religious society. She traces these moments of insight in "The Road Leading Nowhere" through stages of life situated on a metaphorical road that is "pleasant and even" in the morning but that seems to lead nowhere in the afternoon, until it threatens to "slip out of sight" as the day disappears, and nothing is left but "the dread of the night" (168). The activity of collecting her poems, then, represents not so much a departure point for Robinson, as she implies in the preface, but rather a reinforcement of the aestheticist themes of transience and impermanence that she developed early in life, as well as an even more pronounced sense of finitude as her own past lengthened and her future shortened. Looking back is the only way in which we can find direction on that "road to nowhere" of the future, her poetry suggests.

The third project that involved Robinson in gathering up fragments of her past at this time followed soon after her marriage
and took the form of another round of travel writing, this time
focusing on her life in the Duclaux country home in the Cantal.
Although she complained to Laure Briot, the mother of Duclaux's
first wife, a pleasant woman to whom she had become close, that
she was suffering from rheumatism, and although Duclaux himself
was often unwell, Robinson took much pleasure in her life with him
and managed to get him out and about the countryside as much as
possible. Throughout 1902 and 1903, she consulted Briot frequently
on the best care for Émile, especially after he suffered a stroke a year
after their marriage while he was reading a paper to the League of the

Rights of Men in January 1902. Duclaux was a founding member of the league and his commitment to it, as well as his duties as director of the Pasteur Institute, no doubt exacerbated his poor health, which manifested itself in angina and presumably other physical problems that led to this first stroke. After the stroke, he had to decrease the volume of work drastically, and, for the remainder of the winter and early spring of 1902, Robinson looked after him at home with a stream of colleagues from the Pasteur Institute visiting regularly to keep up his spirits.

Despite these difficulties, Robinson once again turned her attention to writing articles about her life in France for English journals. These articles are written in the same vein as the compelling travel journalism of the early 1890s, when her experience of the French countryside was contextualized by her love for and her happy life with James Darmesteter. This time, since Duclaux's health limited travel to his country home in the Auvergne, Robinson shared that region with English readers, beginning with the house at Olmet. She wrote "A Farm in the Cantal" during the summer of 1902, while Duclaux was recovering from his stroke, and published it in the *Contemporary Review* in December 1902. She describes the stunning views from "our" house and gives in detail "our" farm activities contextualized by their historical and cultural significance. Once again, however, the poet and the prose writer merge in the language she uses to help us to see what she sees, and she stirs the collective imagination of her readers as she gazes out from the terrace (824). The people, the language, and the accent, as well as the visual imagery evoking the splendour of summer hay and autumn harvest, are all delivered to English readers in imagistic language filled with movement and colour that reflect both Mary Duclaux's perfect assimilation into French life and Mary Robinson's continued poetic personality. In fact, these comments are, at times, literally highly imaginative, as records at Olmet reveal that some of what she describes is not visible from the terrace of the house. In his copy of the essay, for instance, Pierre Duclaux, Robinson's younger stepson, annotated the margins with satirical comments on where Robinson's "vision" was less literal and more imaginative.[12] Nevertheless, Robinson successfully situates herself within a circle of people that includes her readers, mentioning Lee, for instance, as someone British patrons would recognize. "When my friend Vernon Lee affords us the pleasure of a visit, we turn to other interests, such as fall in the picturesque and archaeological turn of her imagination" (837). These comments are highly ironic in view of Lee's account of her 1901 visit in a letter to Kit Anstruther-Thomson, to whom she praises Émile at Robinson's expense: "I was very happy seeing that beautiful country with him. I say *with him*, because charming and intelligent as Mary is, and grateful though I am for her magnanimous fidelity to me, I seem to have absolutely not one fibre in common with her, and nothing comes of our intercourse."[13] The harsh words and sarcastic tone disappear in Lee's letters to Robinson during this time, but after Émile Duclaux's death, Lee recalled him as "the man, of all my dear French friends, who represented to me the inner soul of his country."[14]

The region a little farther out from Olmet inspired other touristic style articles, such as the now popular tourist stop, La Commanderie de Ballan, which Robinson highlights under the title "A Manor in Touraine." In this article published in the *Contemporary Review* in March of 1903, Robinson again addresses an educated reader and situates her remarks in terms of French patriotism that she notes "has shown two sides – two faces, if you will; the one aristocratic, desiring the advancement of the nation by means of an *elite* ... the other essentially popular" (344). She traces the development of this paradox through the history of the Knights Templar, the original builders of the "Manor," and the political complications of restoration, as well as in the aesthetic joys of the surrounding French countryside just outside Tours. "It is in the autumn that you should visit the Commanderie," she advises, so that the fruition of the surrounding countryside will complement the graceful structure (346). As she had done in previous years with references to James Darmesteter, she mentions Émile Duclaux, calling him "a great chemist of my acquaintance (in point of fact my husband)," thereby recreating the intimacy of her earlier writing.

Two more articles followed in 1903, another for the *Contemporary* on the history of the French peasantry and an article for the French journal *Revue de l'Art, ancien et modern* titled "Delphine Bernard," the subject of a book by the French painter Jules Breton, known for his own artistic depictions of French peasantry. The two-part essay "The

French Peasant before and after the revolution" was published in its entirety 1 July 1903. As its title suggests, this study of the poor, farming classes of France traces the historical, economic, and political daily lives of the peasantry that Robinson viewed at work from her window at Olmet. Essentially, the article is a plea for decentralization that reiterates the case she makes in *The Life of Renan* that the "general impulse towards a moral and intellectual reform" that followed the Franco–Prussian war would inevitably lead to decentralization as the peasants struggle to look after their own interests. She concludes by urging them to do so through cooperative farming and agricultural syndicates. Her focus on local politics and the socioeconomic structure of the farmlands that she had fairly recently come to know indicates the acute pleasure she took in intellectual activity that had begun as a young child in her father's library and that remained a sustaining principle of her life.

"Delphine Bernard," on the other hand, provided an opportunity for Robinson to return to her interest in art, particularly in pre-Raphaelite art, as the style of the French painter Jules Breton was often termed. In 1847, Breton was at the Louvre copying a Titian near a beautiful young woman copying a Rubens.[15] He did not learn her name until 1897, long after her death in 1864, and when he approached her family and received letters and other documents, including photographs of her in her final year, he learned that she had died of what was probably consumption. She was ill and her beauty gone, but from these photographs he was able to reconstruct her face and paint the beautiful portrait of Delphine for the *Salon* of 1902, where Robinson saw it. This article is a tribute to both Delphine Bernard and Jules Breton, a painter who, she says, created a work in the style of the Florentine Filippino Lippi of the quattrocento, the Florence renaissance (219). The article contains Bernard's self-portrait, as well as Breton's reconstructed painting, and Robinson highlights Bernard's contribution to art, as well as Breton's. What particularly resonated with Breton was Bernard's interest in depicting country workers and peasants, an interest which Robinson shared and had poeticized in *The New Arcadia* and, at this point, was busy working on in poetry that would make up *The Return to Nature*. In the few Bernard paintings that remain, Robinson sees "vigor, a seriousness, a power sober and somber, all qualities rare in a woman" (224). Robinson notes that she seems to have become for Breton a muse as powerful as Beatrice was for Dante or Elizabeth Barrett was for Browning, and, had she lived, Robinson suggests, she may have had an extensive influence on late nineteenth-century French art.

In the late fall of 1903, Robinson gathered all of her travel articles – those she had published to record her travels with James and those she had published about her life in and near Olmet – under the title *The Fields of France*. The book was reissued in 1905 with William Brown Macdougall's coloured illustrations. The appeal of these articles is implied in the subtitle of the collection, "Little Essays in Descriptive Sociology," and in the dedication "To My Dear Mother / Like Me, a Lover of the Fields of France." Robinson seems to have conceived the idea of collecting her travel articles from the beginning of her Olmet life, for *The Fields of France* followed the July publication of the second part of the lengthy "The French Peasant" in the *Contemporary Review*. Some of the earlier essays have title changes: "Private Life in France in the Fourteenth Century" is newly titled "How the Poor Lived in the Fourteenth Century"; "Spring in the Woods of Valois" is newly titled "The Forests of the Oise"; and "Impressions of Provence" is newly titled "A Little Tour in Provence." The fourth article of the Darmesteter years, "The Medieval Country House," retains its title here, as do the three articles for the *Contemporary Review* published in 1902 and 1903. In his review for the *Times Literary Supplement*, James Richard Thursfield comments on Robinson's consistently poetic perspective well suited to prose that conveys "an equally tender and delicate sympathy with human life, with its poetry and its prose, with its romance and its reality, with the shrewd and often pinching frugality of the peasant, with the more liberal and kindly home ways of the leisured but not too wealthy classes," and he goes on to praise Robinson's "unobtrusive scholarship."[16] Robinson did not write any more travel articles after Duclaux suffered his second hemorrhage in January 1904; however, Robinson and Duclaux went to Olmet that spring, and they bought a little car in which she drove him around the countryside while she worked on the volume of poetry that her life in Olmet inspired, *The Return to Nature*. Unfortunately, Émile did not live to see its publication; when his health continued to fail, they returned to Paris, where he died 3 May 1904.

The Return to Nature

In style and substance, this volume of poetry is unlike any of Robinson's other collections; however, as she had done for *The New Arcadia*, Robinson made the people around her poetic subjects. Published under the name "Madame Mary Duclaux," *The Return to Nature* reflects her time spent with Émile and examines the intimate relationship she and he shared with the natural world and their neighbours in the Cantal. In this respect, it has themes in common with "The New Arcadia"; however, this time the context of the world under the poetic microscope is defined by French rather than English cultural mannerisms, and she is closer to the experiences she describes in this highly personal volume. She inscribed one of the copies in circulation online as follows: "Les souvenirs de notre dernier été, Émile et moi." Robinson's study of Rousseau published five years later in *The French Procession* suggests that she was in these days well-schooled in French philosophical ideas about the connections between human society and the natural world. Rousseau's privileging of "a simple, animal life, healthy, placable, and affectionate" emerges from the pages of this volume; however, whereas Rosseau claims that "the man who reflects is an animal depraved," Robinson comes to reflection not through abstraction, as she had tended to do as a younger woman, but through empirical evidence and acute attention to the detail of the country life that she experienced firsthand with her husband (69). Her approach to nature and to life in the natural world as she sees it, therefore, is directly influenced by his scientific perspective.

As Baron Altrincham writes in the *Times Literary Supplement*, these poems "now spring from sheer out-of-door happiness, from that state of open exultation under any sky in which all faculties blend, and shouting or gesticulating, thinking shining thoughts or jumping sunny streams really seem but one and the same thing."[17] Indeed, subtitled "Songs and Symbols," these poems about the people and the countryside of the Cantal not only reflect Robinson's persistent gestures toward pantheism but they also indicate her affinity with Baudelaire in a shared conviction that signifiers in nature enable "correspondence" between this world and an ideal world. Unlike her Platonic wrestling with appearance and reality that provides a unifying thread in much of her aestheticist poetry, these pantheistic poems express her hope that death brings about absorption of the human being by a greater, undefined entity characterized by universality rather than individual systems of rewards and penalties. She had, of course, considered pantheism as a substitute for conventional religion in earlier poetry, but her marriage to a scientist and naturalist and his concurrence that human cycles were subsumed in larger, natural cycles is evident in these poems written in 1902 and 1903 during Duclaux's extended health crises. Her perspective on human mortality that had been influenced so dramatically by the death of James persists in this volume and reflects her fear that Émile was living on borrowed time, a preoccupation that results in poetry that is paradoxically filled with life and vitality in its presentation of the organic unity of life and death. Therefore, while she continues to focus on the larger themes of transience and impermanence, these themes are now grounded in her keen awareness that the entire natural world, including humankind, is moving along a continuum of evolutionary development and that the past must always be integrated into perspectives on the present in order to gain intuitive insight into how the future might unfold. She and Émile's scientist son Jacques were speaking about Einstein one day, and Robinson confided that she had always thought that the world was formed by a series of spheres. Jacques was impressed by her ability to think in these terms when she had never learned the multiplication tables.[18]

Francis Thompson, whose mystical poetry Robinson had long admired, was uncomplimentary about the volume in his review for the *Academy*, suggesting that Robinson's poetry in *The Return to Nature* is "without magic."[19] However, although without Thompson's mysticism and ethereal context, this volume of verse by a poet who finds renewed peace and contentment begun many years ago on her grandfather's farm has "magic" of its own. To focus this "return," Robinson takes her epigraph from Keats's "Meg Merrilies," quoting the third verse to demonstrate her sense that perfect happiness lies not with other people but in living in a "family" of "craggy hills" and "larchen trees" that offer the opportunity to exist "as she did please." A memorial page to Émile Duclaux, with the black bordered announcement of his death and the dedicatory poem that she had written in the month preceding his death, indicate that the poems here speak of "little things" that emerge out of her creative intellect and the material concerns of the scientist:

> For thy brows benign and calm,
> Here I bring no branch of palm,
> Nay, nor oak-leaves red and brown
> Twisted in a civic crown,
> Nor Apollo's shining bay –
> I've no laurel in my posies!
> Here are little things, but roses
> That shall last as long as they.

The poem is particularly poignant because it is dated April 1904, a few weeks before Émile's death and was meant to be a dedication rather than the memorial it became. The five quatrains in couplets that act as a preface to the collection evoke "The New Arcadia" in tone as they situate the collection in the reality of the Auvergne, as the first and fifth quatrains demonstrate:

> Fain would I be the bard who sings
> To show the proof of hidden things.
> Whose dreams o' nights take shape and give
> The world a better way to live.
> …
> And yet my country friends shall praise
> The mirror of my roundelays,
> For – brook and blossom, dove or daw –
> Believe me, what I sing, I saw!

The last line sets the speaker of *The Return to Nature* in stark contrast to the speaker of "Arcadia," who admits in the epilogue, "I cannot show, / I cannot say the dreadful things I see" (107). Instead, the speaker introducing *A Return to Nature* signals a poetic transition from the contemplative *Retrospect* lyrics and ballads to poetry grounded in the natural world around the house at Olmet.

The poems of *The Return to Nature* are organized under the titles "The Village," "A Summer Out of Doors," "One and All," and "Harvest: Two Idylls." Under these titles, Robinson depicts

her daily life at Olmet during the spring, summer, and early fall
of 1902 and 1903. The first two poems of "The Village" suggest the
timelessness of the pastoral ideal, particularly the "The Daydream,"
dated 25 August 1903, as the speaker returns imaginatively to the
resort town of Lioran not far from Olmet:

> Without, the traffic shakes the dusty street,
> I sit entranced; I neither hear nor see 't:
>
> I know a hollow in the mountain-side …
> All round, the forests mantle far and wide. (9)

The scene within the speaker's mind is detailed and rich, with the
senses intermingling as she sees and hears a mountainside waterfall that she longs to actually taste again. However, perhaps one of
the more important poems "An Old Air with Variations," which is
dedicated to E.D., undoubtedly Émile and is dated 2 September
1902, marks the end of the long recuperative summer at Olmet
following Émile's first stroke the previous January. The "variation" is
on Christopher Marlowe's "The Passionate Shepherd to his Love,"
as the first lines, complete with quotation marks, make clear:

> "Come live with me and be my Love,
> And we will all the pleasures prove
> That hills and valleys, dale and field,
> And all the craggy mountains yield." (10)

Robinson's invitation to her husband to live and love in the pastoral
ideal of Olmet is offered in terms of the glories of this simple life – a
day in the countryside followed by dinner made of "the partridge"
they have brought home and the "custard" made of the "peach" and
"plum" that they have gathered. Like the poem that inspired it, "An
Old Air" is an appeal not to emotion but to reason, casting love in
a logical context for such a day and suggesting that, in the language
of Marlowe, "if such delights thy mind may move, / Then live with
me and be my love" (11).

Robinson composed most of the remaining poems in "The Village"
in July and August of 1903, the last summer that she and Émile

spent together at Olmet. These poems invite an expanded understanding of the title of this section, as the poetic eye records specific
elements of the aspects of nature that reinforce the speaker's sense
that scientifically and aesthetically, the natural world and the human
world are integrated in an existence that is defined by transience and
impermanence. In "The Tyrant of the Stream," dated July 1903, for
instance, the speaker's Darwinian fascination with the survival of
the fittest and strongest, in this case a river shark, otherwise known
as a pike, extends over nineteen quatrains of rhymed couplets that
highlight the pike's powers of survival as it descends to the bottom
of the stream to avoid a lightning storm and, after the final quatrain,
a single line sets out the natural instinct of this creature:

A hundred years are as a day
In yonder monster's sight, they say;
And thy behest to all alive,
Thine only gospel is: Survive!

And all of thy commandments: Thrive! (15)

In setting the last line off from the body of the poem, Robinson highlights the Darwinian context within which she viewed nature with
Émile. Other poems featured in this section offer equally significant
comments on the superior ethical structure of the natural world – the
instinctual love for her young of the kestrel of "Mother-Love" and
the right to life of the fox captured by young boys who are persuaded
to release it in "The Fox in Auvergne." These poems were written a
day apart on 4 July and 5 July 1903 at Bois à Avis, thereby suggesting
Robinson's intense engagement with the world around her.

Robinson also makes cautionary tales of poetic intersections with
nature. In the fantasy "Jenny Wren," the lesson of nature to a simple
farmer is to be grateful for what he has, and, in one of the last
poems she wrote for this volume, "The Huntsman," which she wrote
2 February 1904, while she was back in Paris, she offers a more
sophisticated lyrical warning against greed. Perhaps it is the ballad
form of this poem that makes the didactic elements of fantasy more
successful. The balladeer begins, "Children, believe me if you can! /
Elders, believe me if you dare!" The lesson is delivered through the

story of husband and wife who, seeing a crow drinking from waters that magically restore it to a youthful, glossy state, decide to drink themselves. Like the crow, the husband drinks sparing; his wife, however, greedily quaffs more than she needs, and the result is predictable:

> A newborn baby creased and pink
> That shivers in the nakéd blast –
> Great Heaven! and still she seems to shrink! –
> Too small for sight, she breathes her last! (24)

The epigraph in italics that delivers the warning follows:

> *Taste but the spray of fairy springs,*
> *The cream of Life, the fruits that fall;*
> *Remember, in the happiest things,*
> *Excess is worse than none at all.*

Throughout "The Village," Robinson vacillates between the more spiritual and contemplative poet appreciative of the beauty of nature that James recognized in his first encounter with her poetry and the keen and perceptive observer of natural life that she had become with Émile. Throughout *The Return to Nature*, she celebrates the simple events that unfold outside her window, focusing particularly on the farmers in the fields at Olmet from whom she learned not only about farming but also about the culture of country life. Drawing on the same resources that she had used for *The Fields of France*, she poeticizes moments of village life in the joyful ballad "St Peter's Day," written on 5 July 1903, a few days after the holiday celebrated 29 June, and in "The Drowned Shepherd" and "The Old Farmer," she highlights personal and cultural moments of toil and stress. Then in August 1903 she moves away from the activity of daily life as her time at Olmet draws to a close for that summer. In both "Weather," dated 10 August 1903, and "The First Wood-Fire," dated 30 August 1903, setting is directly related to the speaker's mood and to the closing down of the house to prepare for the return to Paris. In "The First Wood-Fire" in particular, which closes "The Village," the seasons suggest not merely transience and impermanence in the passing of summer and the onset of autumn but also a warm and beautiful continuity in the trees of summer transformed into the fires that keep them warm in the fall:

> Till mere and fountain freeze on
> Our moors, and ways are mire, –
> Through all the summer-season –
> The sunshine loves to play
> About our peaks, our trees on,
> With many a burning ray;
> The boughs have kept the ray:
> 'Tis the fire! (28)

Syntax suggests this continuity through unfinished poetic sentences and disrupted word order that convey the fragmented moments in which the flames transfer the warmth of the sun in the final days of August.

The poems of the second section, "A Summer out of Doors," were all written at Olmet during the summer of 1903, when it must have been clear to both Robinson and Émile Duclaux that he was becoming increasingly ill instead of regaining his health. This "summer out of doors" is reflected in poetry that not only emphasizes Robinson's connection with the natural world just outside the doors of her country home but that also conveys her acute awareness of finitude that hovers implicitly in the renewal of spring. The poems in this section become increasingly more elegiac as the poetic voice traces the time from spring, through summer, and into the early fall. "A Mild Day in March" conveys the joyous mood of unexpected warmth and the seven poems that follow it reflect the moving poetic gaze. The whispered discourse in "Tree-Talk," for instance, suggests the intensity of this gaze and the gazer's yearning for complete affinity with these magnificent wonders of the Cantal in summer:

> Might I understand, O Trees!
> Your green and rustling voices:
> All you whisper to the breeze
> With hushing, swishing noises: (31)

The speaker's sense that there is something to "understand" suggests her continued longing for unity with the natural world, but the last lines of the stanza suggest as well that she is excluded from the secrets they "whisper" to the "breeze" that bring about the discourse she overhears but cannot make out. Alliteration and onomatopoeia through "s" sounds draw attention to the range of emotions that the speaker senses in these communications.

> Sorrows of the soughing pines,
> Delight of limes a-flutter,
> Hermit-joys the beech divines,
> Or spells the old oak-woods mutter; (32)

She closes with a pantheistic expression of yearning that takes different forms in the poems that follow:

> Might I share, O talking boughs,
> Your deep mysterious spirit –
> I'd renounce the life, the vows,
> The soul that I inherit! (32)

This final vow, unachievable, of course, indicates the speaker's ambivalence about ever reaching an intuited understanding of the natural world through intellectual study. The speaker's concern perhaps represents the conflict within between her youthful and instinctive affinity with nature and the middle-aged scientific focus of these early twentieth-century poems.

The poetic survey of the countryside defined by the titles "A Riverside in May," "The Magpies," "The Red-Start," and "The Glen," the last which again evokes Marlowe, suggests the expansive range of natural stimuli with which Robinson had to work in her two full summers at Olmet. When the poetic gaze turns inward to become more contemplative and philosophical, as in "Inter Pares," for example, Robinson draws more effectively on her longstanding kinship with Baudelaire and the "correspondences" she senses between the natural world and an abstract, unspecified ideal. On one level, this short lyric is a tribute to the beauty of swallows and skylarks "gliding" and "shooting" through the sky:

Circling swallows skim and fly
On a gliding wing;
Skylarks shooting up the sky
Soar aloft and sing; (36)

Figurative language – alliteration, diction with "ing" verbs denoting movement, and the tetrametre lines – suggest the song and movement of these birds. However, on a philosophical level, this lyric invites us to change the way we think about our relationship with the natural world:

Light as balls of thistledown
Dreamy barn-owls drift;
Like an arrow sharply flown
Speeds the darting swift;

Who shall say what realms unsought,
Flashing, they may find?
Flight may range as far as Thought,
Motion rival Mind!

These are poignant moments in which the poetic speaker reflects with humility on the knowledge about the natural world from which she is excluded. However, in "August Silence," she finds some kinship with nature through the seasonal cliché – that nature's fruition at summer's end also signals the coming autumnal decline – which has become a metaphor for human existence, and in this respect the poems that follow situate the speaker's thoughts more specifically in Robinson's waning time with Émile. "The Strawberry Woods," for instance, begins with an allusion to Adonis, associated with fertility and beauty. The anemones on the floor of the woods are like his blood in one version of the legend in which the goddess Artemis mixes the blood of Adonis, killed by a wild boar, with nectar, and from the soil upon which she sprinkles the mixture, the red anemone takes its colour. In another version of the legend, Adonis dies in the arms of Aphrodite, and her tears of grief take the shape of small red hearts or strawberries. Robinson wrote the poem to commemorate an outing that she and Émile took to pick strawberries, and the reference to

Adonis's short life suggests the anxiety she felt about her husband's deteriorating health. "I never spent serener hours / Than in your craggy wood," she says,

> Yet, as we call from bole to bole,
> The laugh upon my lip
> Dies, and a tremor chills my soul
> To feel the summer slip.

> How sure, how swift, we run our race!
> How soon the best is flown! –
> And one of us may live to pace
> The strawberry-woods alone. (38–9)

Therefore, the second section of *The Return to Nature* closes with a return to thoughts of transience and impermanence: "Nightfall in Harvest-Time," "Autumn Woods," "Sunset in September," "Old Maids in October," and "The Garden in October" all suggest the paradox of autumn as simultaneously a time of bountiful fruition and a time of winding down and waning. The paradoxical joy and pathos that the speaker conveys in the poems of this section collectively comment aptly on human life and anticipate the resolution to which she comes in the next section.

The epigraph in Greek for the third section, suggestively titled "One and All," refers to Gaia, the personified earth as ancestral mother of life. In Aeschylus's *Prometheus*, Prometheus calls on "mother, / Earth (one person, though of various names)."[20] This epigraph, therefore, signals Robinson's growing sense that her spiritual identity lay in a pantheistic unity with nature, even though the poems of this section suggest her continued ambivalence about "Mother Earth." In the titular poem that begins this third section, the speaker is inclined to resolve the issue by positioning herself as a very small part of nature and its cycles. Written at Olmet in August 1902 and published in the *Athenaeum* the same year and in *Living Age* in 1904, this is an expression of the pantheistic concept of unity with nature that takes shape later in the section. The speaker and her companion, who seem to be Mary and Émile, are positioned above a panoramic view of the valley, looking out – on the eagle drinking from a fountain, on

the otter in the stream, and on foxes in their lair. Nature compels us
to "learn how small a thing is Man," says the speaker (48). However,
when she deals with this philosophical platitude more precisely,
as in "Science and Poetry," she situates herself in relation to the
argumentative discourse suggested in the title:

> Nature, O my great Companion –
> Mystic Mother of my soul –
> Must I stand apart, abandoned?
> Watch a rival touch the goal?
> And, ousted from thy breast, desire a beggar's dole? (55)

The alliterative address to the earth as the speaker's "Mystic Mother"
evokes the Promethean concept of mother earth to whom Prometheus
felt he owed a duty far above the duty he owed to the gods. However,
in the stanzas that follow, the speaker once more recognizes the
tension between her inclination to respond to nature aesthetically and
her new sense that she should apply reason instead of emotion to her
experience of natural phenomena. These men have not "sobbed for
joy to note the rose that studs the larch" she says in the second stanza,
"nor, thick i' the beanflower, watched the / wild-bee thrill and hum"
in the third. The difficult and uneven metrics of the poem convey the
speaker's mixed feelings – joy that she experiences nature aesthetically
but simultaneous uncertainty about the veracity of this experience. By
the last stanza, she can only throw herself at the mercy of the power
in which she believes, returning to Renan's perception of truth in the
natural world in terms of what we understand of ourselves through it:

> I, so infinitely distant,
> Flung below thy rolling spheres;
> I, who hear thy forests whisper
> Humbly, as the licken hears –
> Judge between me and them! O Mother, dry my tears. (56)

By 1902, then, before the intimacy with the natural world that she
achieved over two summers in tandem with the scientific perspective
learned from Émile, Robinson had decided how her "return" would
be shaped.

Similarly, the speaker of "Lyric" enters into a Romanticist dialogue with her soul:

Have I not said to my soul:
"Slumber, O Spirit, and sleep!
What thing lures thee forth in the whole,
Out in the dark, so deep?

"Are we not one, Thou and I?
Glide not out of my veins;
Into the stars and the clouds of the sky,
Into the stones of the plains! (56)

In the next two stanzas, the speaker asks her soul to "loiter and dream" and to look no further than the natural world for inspiration. In the concluding lines of the poem, she suggests that poetic inspiration is linked not to the outer world but to her aesthetic response to the natural world around her:

"Sweet is the surface of things –
Ripples adrift on the pond –
Nothing deeper the poet sings;
Look not, O Spirit, beyond!"

Even in this memorial volume to Émile, James is present in the beautiful "The Lark at Pontoise," dedicated to James with "In Memoriam J.D." That the perspective of the poem is Pontoise, a Paris suburb, rather than Olmet, indicates its distinction in her mind from the "return to nature" she enjoyed with Émile. The poem opens with a direct address to James that conveys her conviction that somehow and somewhere, he can hear her, and the details of the event she remembers mark what Robert Browning would call "an infinite moment":

The last time, Belovéd, we listened to the lark
We stood upon the gay green hills that rise above Pontoise –
The last time we listened the soaring note to mark –
And in the windy sunny sky we saw the skylark poise;

The song o'er-rippled hill and vale with such a flood of joys,
The last time, Belovéd, we listened to the lark! (48)

The emphasis is on this moment of complete unity with James through a simultaneous unity with the lovely bird that is the harbinger of new life and a symbol of the dawn. As the second stanza indicates, there was to be a terrible irony in this Easter that was presumably their last together. Repetition and rhyme situate the stanzas in juxtaposition to draw attention to the speaker's loss.

A hint of winter chilled the air, the woods were brown
    and stark,
And yet the corn was ankle-high, and oh! the sun was bright,
From every spur and spar of rock it struck a living spark!
And all that Easter-world of sun and wind was one delight,
While still our shrill glad Angel sang, and still you
    murmured: Hark!
… The last time, Belovéd, you listened to the lark. (49)

The hint of resurrection associated with Easter, as well as their moment of exquisite unity with the natural world, blend to highlight the speaker's characterization of this moment as a spiritual experience. The effect of memory is intensified in the speaker's repetition of the first line of the poem as the last line of the first stanza, and then again as the last line of the poem with the significant change in pronoun from plural to singular to signal the speaker's resignation as the reverie ends and her reality is that James's life has long been over. Perhaps it is not surprising that the "return" to nature that Robinson experienced with Émile Duclaux elicited memories of the man with whom she had first felt such completeness of being and had experienced such happiness, and it is not surprising that the peaceful reconciliation of poet and nature in this volume was inspired by another, albeit it different, state of marital happiness that she had thought impossible after James's death.

There are several other poems in this "One and All" section that record moments of clarity and precision, most having to do with specific instances elicited by the speaker's sense of community with the natural world: with the old lime tree that is as weather beaten as she feels herself in "The Lime on the Crag," with the changing seasons of "Hope" that suggest transitions similar to those that have to be made when one is dealing with adversity, with the nightingale that symbolizes to the speaker the unity of lovers in death in "The New Friend," and with the possibilities below the surface of the pond upon which the titular "Water-Lily" floats, for instance. In these and other lyrics, the speaker singles out specific "signs and symbols," as her epigraph for the volume indicates, to convey her kinship with nature on a spiritual level. In other poems, the connection with nature is shaped by an epiphany in which the speaker intuits that such moments situate her on a continuum specific to the poetic psyche's affinity with the natural world. In "Recurrences" this awareness is suggested by a Wordsworthian concept of preexistence:

> Hush! For a wonder has happened, a miracle, sudden, august.
> How shall I utter the marvel? Listen and understand! ...
> Something stirred in my brain and the centuries stirred in
>   the dust:
> Sudden I knew this hour, of old, in the self-same land.
>
> All have I known before (if the unborn I were I).
> All! And all unchanged – to the star that laughs on
>   the height –
> The scent of the honeysuckle, the course of the moon in
>   the sky,
> The faint sound of the fountains, the hush of an infinite
>   night. (57)

The "miracle" has to do with the speaker's intimacy with natural elements that permeate the Robinson oeuvre: "star," "honeysuckle," "moon," "fountains," and, of course, the "infinite night" that is the subject of so many poetic nocturnes. In this moment, the speaker situates herself within a universal space of poetic immortality.

"In the Barn" depicts an even less abstract moment of epiphany as the speaker peers out from the cool space in a barn to which she has fled to avoid the heat. Her telescopic vision moves from a sweeping view of the natural world to specific elements of nature close to her, and finally to the elements of nature she can only partially see. She understands this narrowing of her perspective to be a metaphor for the paradox that is by now very familiar – the finite human desire for some way to conceive of and express the infinite:

> So, in our twilit cavern of the Soul,
> We spy the brilliant vision of the whole,
> As near, as real, but incomplete and strange:
> The river flows with neither fount nor goal. (58)

Helen Groth likens the speaker's view in this poem to the photographic perspective of Barrett Browning in "Casa Guidi Windows" and points out that Robinson's Bergsonian sense of time and movement and her "privileging of the qualitative heterogeneity of experienced time" is not surprising, given Bergson's appearance in Robinson's *Twentieth Century Writers*, published in 1919 but written before the war held up publication.[21] The analogy introduced in this sixth stanza of "In the Barn" suggests Robinson's Platonic perspective in the speaker's reimagining the confined space from which she views evidence in nature of the limited "time" and "space" through which all life moves. In the opening phrases of the next two stanzas, she addresses directly the Bergsonian elements of "Time" and "Space," and in the concluding stanza brings them together in the kaleidoscopic terms of this vision:

> O moving Life, O world immense and free
> Circling all round in magic mystery,
> When down my wall at last shall crash and fall,
> Grant I may rear a fearless front, and see! (58)

The "wall" is not that of the barn but that of the body, at which point, she hopes, her soul will also be set free from the limitations of earthly life.

The partner poems "All Saints" and "All Souls" close this third section of *The Return to Nature*. Traditionally, All Saints Day celebrates those who have earned a place in heaven and All Souls Day remembers the dead with the promise of heaven before them. These are specifically Christian days of remembrance; however, consistent with Robinson's overall perspective in this volume, the spiritual context of these contemplative poems is pantheistic. The seasonal metaphor of autumnal decay leads the speaker of "All Saints" to intuit a "vaster Presence" in "the brown November wood" than the tableau created by herself and her dog, the birds of winter, the squirrels, and the falling leaves that break the silence of her thoughts (60–1). "All Souls" is the more interesting of the two, not only because it is dated October 1903 at Olmet, the last fall that Robinson spent there with Émile, but also because of its technical attributes, as through imagery and tight rhyming patterns, the speaker, feeling one with the bare and cold woods, reinforces her preoccupation with themes of transience and impermanence – limitation, confinement, and the finality of death. The refrain that ends each stanza addresses the forces of nature that ensure spring renewal and rebirth: "*Turn, turn, thy wheel, O round and rolling Earth!*" (61–2). Italics and the sustained rhyme with "earth" in each stanza emphasize the speaker's growing sense that death is part of a process, and the earth, in turning the wheel of life, moves the speaker toward a different kind of life implied in "a newer green" of the last stanza:

Even now, even here, even in this leafless dene,
The Spirit of Life is rich in everything:
The forest oak shall spring
From this poor drift that was a summer's sheen
And shall be earth and next a newer green ...
O Death, where is thy sting?
Art thou not change and hope? O rolling Earth,
Turn, turn thy wheel, revolving joy and dearth. (62)

Transience, then, is for this speaker not the dire and implicit decay that impermanence suggests; on the contrary, death promises "change and hope." The substitution of "dearth" for "earth" in this last line implies a balance between happiness and disappointment.

The two narrative "idylls" that comprise "Harvest," the fourth and final section of *The Return to Nature*, differ in genre and in theme from the rest of the volume and are closely allied with "The New Arcadia" in their examination of the ways in which individual actions unfold according to specific social and cultural contexts.

While the inhabitants of Arcadia directly reflect Robinson's neighbours in Surrey, these poems originate in her experience of Olmet and its busy country life. "The Quarrel," dated August 1903, and "Too Busy," dated September 1903, were also written at the end of what would be the last summer with Émile, and both poems situate some of Robinson's thoughts about nature and death in didactic narratives – cautionary tales meant to inspire changes in both behaviour and cultural contexts. The disagreement between the elderly farmer Esmond of Ronesque and his carter "young Monsalvy" at the heart of "The Quarrel" arises out of the carter's rebellion against the strict discipline and work ethic that Esmond enforces to run his farm efficiently. When Esmond's competitor, Miller Maurice, entices Monsalvy to work for him instead, Monsalvy's coming of age of begins. Ronesque is actually near Vic-sur-Cère, just down the road from Olmet, and the real-life existence of place invites us to read Robinson herself as the poet. Esmond is "our farmer," she says, who lives on "yon gaunt farm at Olmy-Wood" (65). Esmond with "mild and trustful eyes" has a wife and two "stalwart boys," and Monsalvy is like a third son who, until the interference of Maurice, helps manage a farm in a difficult and, at times, unforgiving climate with a "summer short and violent." Miller Maurice is not only "the merriest farmer ever paid a tithe" but also a "wit, mischief maker, vintner, gossip, wag" (67). The form his mischief takes in this case is to cause hardship to Esmond, who is left to run the farm alone after Monsalvy succumbs to Miller's enticements and his wine. The rest of the idyll deals with the consequences of Monsalvy's act of rebellion: his growing weariness with the lax life he is leading, until, chastened and wiser, he is reconciled with Esmond. The idyll ends not only in forgiveness on Esmond's part but also gratitude, for he has not been able to manage on his own in his advanced years, and Monsalvy is grateful that he is needed. The final line of the poem, "So then and there the quarrel had an end," suggests that this kind of reconciliation and mutual friendship is the normal course of things in this country world (74).

The cautionary tale "Too Busy" has its own elements of realism, for it is based on events that unfolded the previous year at Beaufort, also near Olmet. A farmer working feverishly to get his corn in before a pending storm makes a series of unfortunate decisions to justify turning away from someone in need. He becomes an emblematic anti-good-Samaritan figure motivated by his preoccupation with the economy of his farm. The poet-narrator is careful to tell this story without depicting the farmer as greedy or cruel; he is simply a hard-working man focused completely on his labour. The catalyst for his realization that he must develop a work ethic that accommodates humane behaviour is Fanny Morin, a young girl representative of her time and place, who has had to go out into service and who is now returning home with "her health half-shattered by the servant's lot" (74). The longest section of the poem focuses on Fanny lying under a corn rick in the blazing heat with a broken foot; she is exhausted and, when he finally notices her, the farmer jumps to the conclusion that she has been drinking. This is a convenient conclusion that permits him to continue his work, "for a man's own affairs will aye come first!" says the speaker (79). The poem ends with Fanny's death and a reminder of "our noblest duty," which is that we are our brother's keeper (80). In closing the volume with these didactic narratives, Robinson gives poignancy to the title: the need to return to nature and to a humanity that not only raises us above the beasts in the fields but that also challenges social perspectives on the "nature" of human beings.

In the manuscript copy of Robinson's biography of Émile Duclaux currently held at the Pasteur Institute, there is included a copy of the frontice page of *The Return to Nature* with a quotation from Renan: "La nature agit par progress, *itus et reditus*. Elle passé et revient, puis va plus loin, puis deux fois moins, puis plus que jamais."[22] Although this comment on the cycles of life did not make its way into subsequent publications of *The Return to Nature*, Renan hovers over all four sections of the book as Robinson moves from the more abstract sources of inspiration for her earlier volumes and responds to the immediacy of her material world, a shift in her poetics that reflects her prose interests as well as the education about country life garnered during her time with Duclaux. This poetic perspective would subsequently define the poetry she produced during the years of the First World War.

After Émile Duclaux

By the time Émile Duclaux died, he had regained the respect he had lost in the region during the Dreyfus crisis. Using the papers that Duclaux left and with the help of friends such as Daniel Halévy and Dr Émile Roux of the Pasteur Institute, Robinson wrote the biography of her husband. She and Roux, who became director of the Pasteur Institute upon Duclaux's death, enjoyed what Vincent Duclert described in 1921 as a "rare and intellectual friendship," and Roux carefully edited the book manuscript with her.[23] Roux attended her salons, and they remained friends until his death from tuberculosis in 1933. The library at the Pasteur Institute holds their correspondence that reflects not only their mutual respect but also the delight they took in their deep and comfortable friendship. *La Vie d'Émile Duclaux* is comprehensive and personal in tone, but it is also a careful reconstruction of Duclaux's childhood and upbringing, his studies, his work as a scientist, and his courageous position as a Dreyfusard. Writing to Gosse 29 March 1908, Vernon Lee compliments him on reaching the same sympathy in his treatment of his memoir *Father and Son* as Robinson achieved in this biography: "You have given it that same bright beautiful quality ... that Mary Duclaux gave her life of her husband: the most intimate personal matters become safe," she writes.[24] Thus ended what we might call the third phase of Robinson's life as she entered into her final widowhood and very long old age, moving into a flat close to the Invalides overlooking the gardens of a building that eventually became the Musée Rodin, where Mabel had the flat opposite on the same landing.

After Émile's death, Robinson continued her close relationship with his sons, Jacques and Pierre, as well as with his mother-in-law Laure Briot, and she continued to holiday at the lovely house at Olmet. Émile left her funds in a life estate. She regained her equilibrium, but she also regained her preoccupation with her own health, eliciting from Briot, for instance, suggestions that the "encore suffrante" Robinson get out of bed and, bundling up to compensate for her slenderness, get outside for exercise and fresh air.[25] Robinson wrote and reviewed with a view to earning a living and supplementing the modest income that she and Mabel, along with their mother, enjoyed. She continued to see Lee, and in 1907 she wrote her memoriam article "In Casa Paget" to mark the death of Eugene Lee-Hamilton. She and Lee made plans to meet for a holiday at a cottage in Winkfield for a week in late August or early September of 1908, but they seem not to have crossed paths as often as Robinson would have liked in these years. She notes that she and Lee seemed always to miss each other when they were in the same country.[26] Correspondence between 1908 and 1912 records several of these exchanges, as well as Robinson's travels with Mabel in Germany and Italy in 1911. Lee was not in Italy at this time, but Robinson was expecting her to visit France in 1912. Although the extent to which all of these plans were carried out is not clear, the postcard correspondence in which the plans developed and held now at Somerville College Library indicates that the friendship had recovered significantly.

The French Procession and the *French Ideal*

Robinson's plans for money making involved prose rather than poetry, of course, because her prose tended to sell more widely in England and in France than her poetry. However, the first of two books of prose essays on French writers and philosophers that she published before the outbreak of the First World War was not as well received as she hoped when it was published in 1909. John Cann Bailey wrote a full review for the *Times Literary Supplement* 30 September 1909, in which he expresses his frustration with the brevity of the essays, complaining that it is "as if her magazine or newspaper limits were exhausted."[27] Although Bailey concedes that Robinson casts each author in an interesting and innovative light, he seems to have missed the point Robinson makes with the use of "procession" in the title. Through this metaphor, she offers a glimpse in passing of each of the many French writers who influenced the development of literature in France and elsewhere. The reviewer for *The Common Cause*, on the other hand, understood her intentions in this "procession": "Her strength is not in philosophy, but in the human touch on individual lives. When she is describing writers whom we already know, our memories are revived in the most pleasurable manner; and when she is dealing with those of whom we know little more than the names, she fills us with a desire to read their works and lives."[28] Tissot points out that Robinson is able to render her historical and biographical subjects accurately without judging them.[29] The *Boston Evening Transcript* suggests in its review of 26 November 1909 that "all her critiques are marked by subtle sympathy and insight."[30] Nevertheless, Robinson addressed Bailey's criticism by publishing *The French Ideal* in 1911. This more focused and detailed study limited to four French writers was also only moderately successful, however.

The epigraph of *The French Procession*, which Robinson takes from François-René de Chateaubriand, whose 1802 novel *René* is considered a major influence on British Romanticism, points to the unifying thread of the volume as it evokes those who have had an impact on Western literature: "Que sont devenus ces personnages qui firent tant de bruit? Le temps a fait un pas, et la face de la terre a été renouvellée." In this procession of great French citizens of history, Robinson hopes to inspire a new set of writers, philosophers, and scientists willing to make noise and to bring about change. The dedication to Lee includes a personal letter apologizing for missing a planned visit to Florence in the interests of producing this book, but Robinson says that Lee has "really a right" to this particular piece of work that arises from discussions they had in "those old days in Florence, those times of our girlhood" (viii). The pageant of great French writers marching by on our inner stage, she suggests, "is the continuous genius of a people" (x). Indeed, the table of contents, with its subtitles organizing the essays in chronological order, situates each writer in a position relative to the present, beginning with the early writers who have already passed the poetic eye and are now "in the distance" at the front of the procession in part 1, followed by the more recent "Romantics" in part 2, and concluding with the "Sons of Science," who bring up the rear of the procession in part 3. She makes the point in the introduction that the unifying thread of all humanity is defined by historical chronology, for "each man begins where his predecessor stopped, profits by his acquirements and carries on the message of the race" (ix).

In "French Poetry," the first chapter of the *Procession*, Robinson expresses her regret that readers seem less interested in literature of the past and that English readers also seem less interested in French poetry. Beginning with the fourteenth-century poet Ronsard, she endeavours to provide insight into the ways in which French literature of the past might be pertinent to the English readers of today, prevailing upon them to move past their preference for "Molière (whom we admire as a comic philosopher) and Victor Hugo, whose novels no less than his poems endear him to our romantic heart" (3–4). Although she limits her glimpses into the past to six pages or so, the total "procession" is impressive, and she draws on personal knowledge of all the "Sons of Science" members – Ernest Renan, Hippolyte Taine, Marcelin Berthelot, Gaston Paris, Ferdinand Brunetière, and Anatole France. In every chapter, she highlights the author's connection to "science" in the context of cultural growth and development, and she situates the literature of the time in terms of its contribution to this aspect of society. Writers, philosophers, thinkers – Racine, Fénelon, Rousseau – and their ideas have filtered down not only through the historical pipeline in France but also in Germany through Goethe, Robinson suggests. George Sand, "the chief apostle of the humanitarian movement in Europe," is the lone woman of this procession of twenty-eight writers, and Robinson profiles her mainly through the love letters she exchanged with Alfred de Musset (175).

In her opening discussion of the first poet leading the procession "In the Distance," Ronsard, Robinson introduces the general premise of the collection: "the genius of France is such that its incarnations are almost always social and involve a group associated round an individual" (19). The individuals "marching" with Ronsard have many ideals in common, from the "pure and exquisite" style of Racine, whose poetry "is at the very heart of French literature," through the "more intellectual" Fenélon and Fontenelle (32, 33, 44). The more philosophical and abstract lines of thinking would end in the French Revolution, she points out, but Fontenelle's perspective would result in "the return to Nature and the cult of science," the premise, of course, of the poetry of *The Return to Nature* (54). Voltaire, Rousseau, Bernardin de Saint-Pierre, Laclos, and Liancourt all follow in this lineage as she traces the growth of the French Romantics, with the remaining three authors bringing up the rear of the procession in part 1 – Goethe, Saint-Simon, and Auguste Comte, all at the heart of French Romanticism. Robinson had published a long book review essay with the same title as this chapter, "Goethe in France," in the

Times Literary Supplement 15 April 1904, and many of the details of that essay reappear in this chapter, including Goethe's links to Madame de Staël and August Wilhelm Schlegel, as well as her ranking him a precursor of Darwin (116). The "Two Saviours of Society" who walk with Goethe, Saint-Simon, "the great inventor of Socialism" and Comte, the "man of reason," have left a notable legacy, she argues (120, 123).

Victor Hugo, the leader of the "Romantics," was not only a future subject for a *Times Literary Supplement* essay but also for a biography. Robinson also gives us a good look at George Sand, "walking" behind Hugo in this procession, through letters that Sand exchanged with her lover, Alfred de Musset. Robinson describes these letters as "extraordinarily brilliant as literature," but she concludes that although Sand had significant humanitarian interests, she was "misguided" as well as "passionate" (163, 176). The "shallow Romanticist" Alfred de Musset, on the other hand, "beneath his impertinent airs" showed "fundamental good sense, a logic and a grace, a feeling for tradition and necessity – qualities in your true French classic" (191). Balzac, Robinson suggests, "recreated the modern novel" in that he "sought to represent in his pages, not the beautiful, or the rare, or the morally improving, but the whole of life, good, bad, and indifferent" (181, 182). This is precisely why Vernon Lee in 1883 suggested that "The Rothers" of *The New Arcadia* would be better represented in fiction than in poetry. In contrast, Michelet was not merely an historian but a writer capable of evoking history in all its complexity – he was, Robinson says, the "Wagner of history" (199). Robinson tells the story of his love for a woman thirty years younger than he, adding a personal anecdote of having known Michelet's wife Athénaïs Mialaret herself many years later as "an alert, robust, talkative old lady." With humour, she wonders how the same woman could ever have been "so ethereal, so romantic" as Michelet depicts her (204). The comment implies that in matters of the heart, Michelet, like most of us, was less objective than he was in matters of history.

Flaubert, Baudelaire, and Arthur Comte de Gobineau conclude the Romantics section of the parade, and George Sand receives further attention here, as though she had doubled back to reposition herself in the procession. In addition to drawing on Baudelaire for poetic epigraphs, Robinson reviewed an edition of his letters

7 June 1907 and would subsequently review G. Turquet Milnes's *The Influence of Baudelaire* 13 March 1913, both for the *Times Literary Supplement*. Baudelaire "loves a language precise and technical, and his vocabulary has none of the decent vagueness, the ambiguous generality of a classic," she suggests, although she is disturbed by his failure to find the "loveliness" for which he searches (208). She, like critics since the publication of *Les Fleurs du Mal*, has the uneasy sense that his poetry demonstrates that "the love of the rare may easily become a disease of the soul, for only a line divides the rarity from the monster" (211). The "Prophet" Gobineau was a man limited in vision and, in her view, remiss in not understanding the aestheticist principle that "the conditions, therefore, are never twice identical in relation to the universe. The same man never sits twice in the same spot" (225). On the other hand, she did admire Gobineau's treatment of history in his *Histoire des Perses*, which James Darmesteter admired, and which she calls "boldly impressionist" (226). George Sand, Rossetti's equal with respect to style in Robinson's view, appears as "La Bonne Dame de Nohant," a title that refers to her proprietorship of the beautiful chateau in the Loire countryside in which she could write peacefully and privately. Robinson highlights the ways in which Sand and Flaubert differ in their perspectives on nature: to Sand, nature is "something which fills and perhaps transcends the universe," while to Flaubert, nature "is the raw material of science, something for man to manipulate and perfect, from which, with infinite labour, he may disengage a product superior to himself" (246). George Sand thus becomes an ironic introduction to the "Sons of Science" that make up the third and final group comprising this parade of French literary history.

The essay on Renan, who leads the "Sons of Science" in this procession, is taken directly from Robinson's 1897 biography, which was also the source for "Ernest Renan: Dernières Années," published in the *Revue de Paris* 15 May 1898, and for the lead article for the *Times Literary Supplement* in 1923. Renan is given the honour of first place because "he alone of his generation kept a trace of the optimism and serenity of George Sand," she explains (249). Her focus on Renan's youth is complemented by "The Youth of Taine," an essay on the friend that Renan and Robinson shared. "Of all the figures in this flitting pageant, that pass like shadows across our field of vision, none beckons to me with a gesture more endearing than the remembered phantom of Taine," she writes (264). She reminisces about her own time spent with Taine, admitting that his "fastidiousness of taste and ethics made the majority abhorrent to him" and that he "hated the easy give-and-take of modern democratic life" (292). However, Taine warrants two essays, as though this ghostly participant in the procession has slowed down to take a more extensive shape in her imagination. In the second essay, she focuses on Taine's interactions with those of his time and those figures of history that she has sketched for us earlier in the procession. In his intellectual pursuits, Taine was determined and self-driven to the point of affecting his health, she says, but he was also "a Romantic: a lover of nature and real things, a man who prefers facts and images to ideas and laws, individuals to categories, details to abstractions, and the supple trans-formation of a world in the making to an ideal evolved out of his inner consciousness" (300). Marcelin Berthelot, also the subject of a *Times Literary Supplement* article of 29 March 1907, follows Renan and Taine, even though as Renan's senior he had, as Robinson says, "converted Renan to democracy" (314). Berthelot was not a poet but a chemist; however, he warrants inclusion here, Robinson says, because of his work on explosives during the Franco–Prussian war and his service at that time as minister of Foreign Affairs.

The final three marchers in this procession of French elites are three of Robinson's contemporaries: Gaston Paris, Ferdinand Brunetière, and Anatole France. The "genius of philology," as she calls Gaston Paris, visited Rue Bara often to entertain her and James, and the "only French salon [she] ever knew was Gaston Paris's book-lined library, where Taine and Renan, Sully Prudhomme, Berthelot, Leconte de Lisle, Bourget, France, and many others used to meet on Sunday afternoons" (322, 327). "In those days, at every turn of our ideas or our opinions, we were brought up with a shock against the harsh and rocky dogmatism of Brunetière," Robinson notes (329). This was the same "harsh, involved, long-winded, strenuous, dialectical" man of powerful rhetoric and eloquence rivalled only by Jean Jaurès; he was also the man with whom Émile Duclaux entered into debate in the *Revue des Deux Mondes* and the *Grande Review* during the Dreyfus years (332). The final figure in this section is also the final figure marching past Robinson's window, an irascible man of French letters who was a close friend of James and an admirer of Mary. Anatole France seems to have been a difficult man to like in some ways. Brunetière, she points out, hated him, and even James was irritated with him when he published *Le Lys Rouge* with Robinson and Lee in mind. In this brief description of him, however, Robinson conveys the intimacy of the friendship that developed from when she first met Anatole France immediately after her move to Paris in 1888 and her growing closeness to him as he became the only member of the Académie Française to support Dreyfus, as well as Zola. In his preoccupation with time and history, she writes, Anatole France "is a fatalist; or, if you like it better, he is a determinist philosopher; or (to play a third variation on the same air) he is a classic poet" (341). When he was busy and active, he was cheerful; when he was a "dilettante," his pessimism prevailed (352). Hence, she concludes the "procession" of French writers that she hoped would give English readers a glimpse of the rich culture out of which modern French writers emerged.

When she addressed Bailey's complaint that *The French Procession* left readers hoping for more substance than the metaphorical parade of writers allowed and decided to treat four writers more extensively under the title *The French Ideal*, Robinson aimed to present the four writers that she considered the most influential to the development of modern French culture and thought. They are listed with subtitles that indicate the overall nature of this influence: Pascal, the Pragmatist; Fenélon, the Theosophist; Buffon, the Naturalist; and Lamartine, the Romantic. Two other "ideal" French writers, Saint François de Sales and Baudelaire focus the text epigraphically, the former with his urge to "vivre généreusement" and the latter with the last four lines of the sonnet "Le Goffre" or "The Abyss" from *Les Fleurs du Mal*:

> I see / Only the infinite through all windows,
> And my spirit, haunted by vertigo,
> Envies non-being its insentience.
> Ah! never from beings, numbers to be free![31]

Robinson had alluded to this sonnet in "The Present Age" of *Retrospect*, and its reappearance in this text of 1911 suggests that, like Pascal and Baudelaire, Robinson lived always conscious of the gulf positioned between the world she knew and entrance into a more frightening and disturbing realm. The response of English reviewers to Robinson's choices as her subjects that follow this bleak reminder reflects the currency of French writers in England: Thomas Seccombe highlights only Pascal and Fenélon in his review for the *Times Literary Supplement* 21 September 1911, and the reviewer for *The North American Review* is equally dismissive of Buffon and Lamartine, although praising the volume generally as "essays at once grave and gay, deep and light, readable, and of permanent value."[32] In Robinson's view the four selected writers are "ideal" in the nature of the influence they had on the development of French literature as well.

In the essay on Pascal, Robinson lays the groundwork for her 1927 *Portrait of Pascal*. She stresses here the significance of Pascal's childhood and early life to *Les Pensées*, his "perfect" style and his "sublime and imperfect soul" that conceived of love as "Platonic, an ideal attachment, a sentiment compact of admiration and respect" (4, 39). Robinson refutes Pierre Nicole's suggestion that Pascal was a lover of the trivial and compares him instead to Tolstoi as "a saint with pain and difficulty – a human, faulty saint; a feverish but heroic soul. Physicist, pragmatist, artist in prose, inventor, mathematician, man of the world and saint" (4). In her discussion of Fenélon's *Lettres Spirituelles*, Robinson takes the opportunity to articulate her own complex intersection with his views on death: "Eternity is not a mere persistence in time after the dissolution of the body. It has no relation to time; it has a relation to the Divine Being," she argues. Furthermore, Eternity "is not a continuance, but a manner of life – something entering into our existence and transforming it, which can be realized here and now as well as at any other time or place" (149). She suggests that Fenélon was someone who, "having grasped the interior secret of religion" was able to live "the generous life," thus explaining the epigraph (231).

Her treatment of George Louis de Buffon and Alphonse Lamartine is relatively cursory and undeveloped, arguably deserving of the criticism of the book. She describes Buffon's daily walks in his garden that led him to the conclusion that "Man is no mysterious and terrible enigma, but an animal among other animals"; however, she moves from this note to a general criticism of his proprietorial and dictatorial attitude as the founder of the Jardin des Plantes and his interference in the experiments carried out there (235). The closing chapter on the poet Lamartine focuses specifically on his relationship with Julie Charles, who appears as Elvire in his poetry. Robinson refers in passing to Lamartine's political interests, comparing him to Shelley and highlighting his love for Julie, who was the source of poetry that "expressed in unequalled language the genius of Christianity," an inspiration that had been made clear in the publication of the letters they exchanged in the brief time they had together before Julie died (279). With *The French Ideal* Robinson not only introduces major French literary figures to English readers but she also shapes the way in which English readers might understand the development of French philosophical and literary thinking not possible in the breezy and cursory glimpse she gave in *The French Procession*.

Robinson's familiarity with and love for French writers in these years was augmented by an everyday life enriched by her immersion in French cultural society. Emmanuel Berl was an intense young adolescent when he met Robinson just before the war. He says that he was always intimidated by the "petite fée" and admits that at times he feared her as he feared oral exams.[33] She was to him an enigma: the symbol of everything he most respected, someone who pushed him to work hard at his studies; however, he later came to resent her continued power over him and his inability to stand up to her. Nevertheless, her apartment was "an oasis" with its oriental works of art and other mementoes from James Darmesteter's travels, and she became not only a friend and mentor for twenty years but someone who shaped his life in subtle ways that he really only understood many years later.[34] Mary and Mabel lived comfortably, he says, but not luxuriously; they never discussed money or sexual matters, although they listened patiently as he spoke of his own romantic encounters, and during the war years, they were sympathetic to his distress at what he witnessed and his difficulty in accepting the deaths of his friends. He clearly suffered from a form of what we would call today posttraumatic depression. Given her commitment to and admiration of heroic action during the war years, however, it is difficult to imagine that Robinson could be truly sympathetic with him in his increasing despair. He makes clear his ambivalence about the courage with which she faced the Second World War, for he was taken aback by the fact that nothing could interrupt her "Platonic serenity," that to him seemed both "admirable and monstrous" and that, he says, "fascinated me and disgusted me."[35]

Berl attended Robinson's salons regularly, which, according to John Pollock, were successful in part due to an atmosphere that was uncontrived and spontaneous, thereby enabling friendly, intellectual conversation. Robinson was adept not only at listening to people but also at ensuring that the shyest and quietest had the opportunity to talk.[36] Vernon Lee introduced Berl to Freud and Robinson introduced him to Proust, perhaps with an aim to guiding him in his confusion in both sexual and personal matters.[37] Berl already knew Robinson's close friend Anna de Noailles when he began attending these salons. While de Noailles seemed to him to pretend to know a great deal about art and literature, Robinson truly represented what he terms "an accumulation of culture superimposed," and she had a keen intellect that made her salons interesting and lively.[38] She had a wide circle of friends to offer Berl: Jean Cocteau, George Moore, Maurice Barrès, Noémi Renan, and other French writers less familiar to English readers – Henry de Montherlant, Georges Goyau, Lucie Faure-Goyau, François Mauriac, André Maurois, Raymond Escholier, and Madeleine Saint-René Taillandier, all who attended Robinson's salons regularly hoping for her support and her literary advice. Proust's mother was a regular, along with Mathilde Hecht, a close friend of Proust's mother, and Edith Wharton.[39] Robinson's sister-in-law Mme Arsène Darmesteter, an accomplished painter, was a popular attendee as well, bringing along, when he was in Paris, her brother Sir Philip Hartog.

In the years leading up to the outbreak of the war, then, through her two books on French writers and philosophers, and through her increasingly prolific reviewing work for the *Times Literary Supplement*, Robinson continued her mission to strengthen literary ties between England and France. She continued as well to bring English figures to her French readers, writing a preface in French to Sarah A. Tooley's *La Vie de Florence Nightingale* in 1911, for instance. She situates Nightingale as one of the "chevaliers de l'idéal," a woman of intelligence, devoted to duty, and blessed with "the most tender woman's heart" (xii). However, Robinson's interest in Nightingale as "Theresa of the Sick" is limited; instead, she focuses on the more lasting effects of nursing reform, emphasizing in this preface the achievements of the French feminist Gabrielle Alphen-Salvador, who was not only the founder of the Nightingale School of Nursing in Paris, but who also translated Tooley's biography, along with Robinson's preface, into English (xiv).

The following year Robinson published "Maurice Barrès and His Life and Work" in the *Quarterly Review*, an essay that reflects her friendship with Barrès but that reinscribes what she had said about Barrès in *The French Procession* and *The French Ideal*. She was becoming astute at assessing how she might make the most of her linguistic ambidextrousness and her successful cultivation of two reading audiences. She had become engrossed in the letters of Marie de Rabutin-Chantal, Marquise de Sévigné, a seventeenth-century Parisian noblewoman whose witty and satiric letters, most of them to her daughter, Françoise, the Countess de Grignan, offered insight into a period in French history in which Robinson was interested and about which she was knowledgeable. Many of these letters appeared in contemporary editions after de Sévigné's death, but more letters were discovered in 1873 and a complete edition was subsequently published. Robinson published an essay in the *Revue des Deux Mondes* in 1914 on Madame de Sévigné's son, Charles, in which she presents a sympathetic account of a man who confessed to his mother that everything he attempted seemed to come to naught, including matters of the heart. Robinson wrote an introduction for a new edition of de Sévigné's letters, *Textes Choisis et Commentes* in 1914. She toyed with the idea of writing a biography of de Sévigné, but in 1926 made the decision not to publish a full biography, instead writing a lead article on de Sévigné for the *Times Literary Supplement*. She translated her 1914 edition of the letters, along with her introduction, into an English edition that she dedicated to Lee and published in 1927.

CHAPTER SEVEN

The Belle Époque
and Literary "War Work"

Just after the turn of the century, Robinson met Marie Lenéru, a French writer who lost her hearing and her eyesight as a consequence of scarlet fever when she was just shy of her twelfth birthday. Lenéru rarely spoke in public, primarily because she could not hear her own voice and, therefore, could not control its register. She was so sensitive about this matter that Maurice Barrès, Robinson, and others who knew her well and who influenced her work considerably, did not realize for a long time that she could indeed speak.[1] She eventually regained enough vision to read with a magnifying glass, but she was the Helen Keller of France, and she actually published a study of Keller in the *Mercure* in 1908. Lenéru's tragic story ended when she died of the Spanish Flu 23 September 1918 in Lorient, where she had taken refuge while Paris was under siege.

Lenéru left behind a diary in which she recorded her daily life and in which she expressed her political pacifism during the war, her literary aspirations, and, most touching of all, her despair at the physical circumstances that she felt would make love and marriage impossible. Robinson first appears in the journal as a notation 3 June 1907, when Lenéru had just returned from a visit to her, probably during one of Robinson's salons.[2] In the next entry about Robinson, in October 1910, Lenéru describes her as "perfection" and notes Robinson's aesthetic beauty and Pre-Raphaelite qualities that made her so attractive.[3] Robinson's ability to see things from perspectives contrary to her own and her personal charm and attentiveness seemed to Lenéru to make her unique. On her part, Robinson was supportive of Lenéru's work, but she was also wary of Lenéru's aggressive perspective on and rigid views about many philosophical matters that to Robinson seemed to warrant more flexibility and generosity, as she implies in her 1910 review of Lenéru's play *Les Affranches* for the *Times Literary Supplement*. She writes that the "mind of Mademoiselle Lenéru seems, like an x-ray, to pierce the coverings of things and portray the organic life of her characters"; however, Robinson also notes that Lenéru had little patience with those who disagreed with her sometimes narrow view of how those characters should behave when confronted with adversity.[4] Nevertheless, Robinson's appreciation of Lenéru's work was intense enough that in the same year, when she was serving on the Comité Vie Heureuse, which later became the Comité Femina, she was instrumental in getting the prize for Lenéru for *Les Affranchis*.[5] This prestigious prize was second only to *le Grand Prix du Roman* awarded by the French Académie.

Robinson included Lenéru in her 1919 *Twentieth Century French Writers* and republished this chapter as an introductory essay titled "A Reminiscence" for William Aspenwall Bradley's 1924 English translation of *Le Journal de Marie Lenéru*. She recalls meeting Lenéru when the latter was about twenty-five years old and notes that she did not seem deaf; rather, "she walked with an elastic, almost a bounding step, and brought with her as it were the whiff of a sea-breeze" (49). Robinson learned sign language in order to help Lenéru manage in salon society and, in addition to helping to obtain the prize, she furthered Lenéru's career in practical ways, such as hosting a meeting at her apartment 25 February 1911 between Lenéru and the famous French playwright François de Curel. At this meeting, Lenéru gave Curel the manuscript of *La Maison Sur Le Roc: Pièce en Trois Actes*, which Curel decided had "neither passion nor flexibility."[6] It was, he thought, inappropriate for the theatre, and he declined to support its production. However, Curel wrote the introduction to Lenéru's diary when it was published in French in 1923. Through Robinson, Maurice Barrès became another influence on Lenéru, and he was favourably impressed by her essay "Saint Juste," which appeared in *Le Mercure de France* in 1905 and for which he wrote a preface when it was published posthumously in 1922.

Robinson was the cultural and professional connection between Lenéru and the world, but she was often ambivalent about the ways in which Lenéru's work might be understood by the public. As Cecilia Beach points out, Lenéru wrote in a genre – the play of ideas – that did not always translate well to the stage. The play of ideas resists offering a solution to the dilemma under scrutiny: instead, "the author shows all sides of the debate, allowing the members of the audience to form their own conclusions."[7] Even nine years after Lenéru's death, in her preface to *La Maison sur la Roc*, which she saw through publication in 1927, Robinson was uncertain about Lenéru's depiction of human nature and of the social human being. She calls the play an "amoral, brilliant, pure, 'rigide'" and "absolute tragedy" (110). Vera Louise Peacock describes Lenéru's dramatic style in a similar fashion: "Her appreciation of the classical virtues on clarity, harmony, and symmetry, her sense of formula, her scorn of loose composition and undignified lyricism led her to employ a genre which demanded conciseness and precision." Her drama, Peacock writes, leans toward "a serious analysis of moral and social problems which contrast vividly with the lightness and superficiality of much of contemporary drama."[8] In 1932, Suzanne Lavaud wrote a biography of Lenéru that includes a comprehensive review of her work, and she interviewed Robinson to further her understanding of this unusual playwright. Robinson in turn reviewed Lavaud's book for the *Times Literary Supplement* in September of 1932. Lavaud describes Robinson's graceful smile and gestures, mannerisms that gave Lavaud insight into how and why Robinson had such a dramatic effect on Marie Lenéru.

From Robinson's first intervention on Lenéru's behalf until the spring of 1918, when Lenéru gave Robinson the manuscript for what would be her final drama, *La Paix*, Lenéru depended on Robinson to ease her passage in French literary circles.[9] Unfortunately, the dismay that Robinson felt when she first read *La Paix* had little to do with its flaws in stagecraft and everything to do with what she felt was an inappropriate stance to take during the war. She found it to be a "violent, lyrical debate, rather than a play" and unsuitable for wartime (*Twentieth Century French Writers*, xix). Lenéru's goal in entering into this debate was to fulfill a promise recorded in her diary in December 1915, as she tells the youth of France, "I shall work to keep you from being massacred in the future."[10] Robinson was pragmatic about the destructive consequences of war, writing to Maurice Barrès in February 1915, for instance, to ask him to give advice to her young friend Jean Delebane, who had lost an arm in battle. "Ces pauvres amputés," she says, and urges him to help the young man to find employment.[11] However, although she found much to admire in *La Paix*, Robinson felt that it failed to point to an acceptable resolution to a war that seemed to be winding down by that point, and, by 1919, she was convinced that Lenéru's plays were "meant rather for the student's chair and the fireside lamp than for the glare of the footlights" (*Twentieth Century French Writers*, x). Against Robinson's advice, Lenéru asked the Comédie-Française, which was scheduled to stage her earlier play *La Triomphatrice*, to stage *La Paix* instead; however, the theatre declined, and *La Paix* was finally staged posthumously and without success in 1921 at Théâtre de Odéon.

Images and Meditations: Poetry of War

Robinson's real difficulty with *La Paix* was probably more simply related to the profound disagreement that she felt with the pacifism of Marie Lenéru and Vernon Lee and their expression of that pacificism in print. In her poetry of the war years, which she would include in what would be her last poetry collection, the 1922 *Images and Meditations*, Robinson takes war as its topic, but she has little patience for pacifism as a means to lasting peace. Robinson dedicated this volume to Mabel, "only sister, dearest friend," who, Pollock claims, courageously acted as a courier for those fighting for Irish home rule before the Home Rule Act of 1914.[12] We cannot know for certain whether this story is true; however, both women put themselves to work in various ways during the First World War as volunteers, Mabel at Invalides, which specialized in spinal injuries, and Robinson at Rohan hospital.[13] They saw firsthand the horrific injuries as a result of this terrible war, yet, as Emmanuel Berl, praising them as "tireless" volunteers, notes, Robinson was adamant that the French had to fight until the end. Berl, of course, found Robinson's position in this respect increasingly difficult to accept as he fought his own war-related depression.[14] Robinson contributed several essays to the *Times Literary Supplement* in which she expresses her admiration for those who showed courage in times of war and for the French determination to fight for the causes important to the nation. In "The

New Frenchman," which appeared in January of 1916, for instance, she writes, "the young men in the trenches, the most French of all the French, share naturally in these tendencies to foresight, to self-sacrifice, and to *esprit de corps*" (20).

Robinson had written an obituary essay on the French writer Charles Péguy for the *Times Literary Supplement* when he was killed in action in 1914, and in 1916, she expanded this essay into "A Chaplet of Heroes" for the *Quarterly Review*. In the extended article, she highlights the human and cultural costs of the death of Péguy and four other young men who, having died in the early months of the war, had left France without the literary riches for which she had hoped. However, these five men must be remembered as heroes, she insists, and we must "lay on their tombs the flags of that victory for which they paid the price the day they fell in battle" (72). Using the chaplet or rosary of Catholic practice as a metaphor, Robinson "says her beads," noting that "we Anglicans" might adopt the rosary practice as a means of remembering all those who have died for their country. Ernest Psichari, Charles Péguy, Émile Nolly, Henri-Alain Fournier, and André Lafon "were men of action, doers, not dreamers," she writes, couching her praise in awareness of the insidious hold of war on a generation whose parents had lost the Franco–Prussian war of 1870, leaving a country that "has been vanquished in arms, but has not yet avenged and redeemed that disgrace" (54). She was particularly dismayed by the death of Psichari, who was the grandson of Ernest Renan and the son of her close friend Noémi Psichari.

The sentiments that Robinson expresses in these prose works originate in "The Background of a Victory," an essay that she wrote in English and in French for the 1915 fund-raising *Book of France*. The essay concludes, "No fate, surely, is so worthy of our envy as the glorious death of those who in a joyful sacrifice redeem their country and their race, achieving, not only victory, but the downfall of a tyrant and the triumph of human right and freedom" (118).

Such patriotic rhetoric was consistent with the general sentiment in France and increased her popularity with the reading public in general. She continued to review for the *Times Literary Supplement* throughout the war, including several books on war and others on writing poetry in times of war. She had just finished *A Short History of France* when the war broke out, but publication was held up until March 1918, when the end of the war seemed probable. In the foreword to *A Short History*, which she wrote in November 1917, she says that she "was cut out for this particular form of war-work" (v). Nevertheless, her views on heroism and war positioned her in opposition to both Marie Lenéru and Vernon Lee; on the other hand, these views aligned her with Maurice Barrès and repaired in part the damage to that relationship when Barrès became a leader in the anti-Dreyfusard camp. Although Robinson seemed once again not to feel the rift between the women with the same intensity as did Lee, their "war work" created a new set of tensions between them. As late as 1925 Lee warned her friend Berthe Noufflard not to be influenced by anything that Robinson might say about Lee's "attitude" during the war.[15]

While Lee wrote two lyrical dramas to protest the war, Robinson was inspired by the war to return to lyric poetry, which afforded her an aesthetic form in which she could develop personal "images" of war and articulate her meditations on heroism in a subtle and figurative way. In his review of *Images and Meditations* for *The Times Literary Supplement*, John Middleton Murry makes the case that the emotions of war are so immediate, so heightened, and so reactionary that poetry cannot adequately capture them. However, a striking feature of Robinson's lyric voice in this body of work is its modulation: she resists the range of emotions – shock, despair, and anger – that one might expect in poetry written during and about a crisis of this magnitude. While it is true that she romanticizes heroism at times and criticizes military carelessness at other times, she never wavers from her conviction that war can also draw on the remarkable attributes of human nature, that we need to rise to these circumstances that provide opportunities for us to meet our historical and cultural obligations, and that heroism and valour are worth cultivating and celebrating.

In 1915, she had taken the same position as Murry, commenting in her *Times Literary Supplement* review of Owen Seaman's *Poems in War Time* in July that "very little of the verse occasioned by the war is likely to survive it" because the poetry of war belongs to the time of war (217). However, she also points out that "poetry is the outcome not only of an effort of will, but also of a rare and an imaginative impulse; and, like every other art, it needs some clear peace and quietness of mind, however momentary, for its creation" (217). These moments were few and far between in the war years, but she was alert to moments of clarity when she became less an idealist and more a realist. Her passionate belief in the importance of heroic action seems not to have waned in the post war years. Writing to Lee 30 June 1927 on the publication of Emily Sargent's biography of her brother, for instance, she comments on Emily's sensitive account of the "absorbed, elegant, refined" artist who, "living by his eyes as he was to do all his life, and yet, owing to his strong idea of duty, accepted his appointed destiny as a naval officer without any of the nerves and passion one would have expected."[16] She tellingly does not mention John Singer Sargent's poignant painting of the aftermath of a mustard gas attack, "Gassed," which he completed in 1919 and which perhaps undermines to a certain extent what Robinson praises as his ability to subvert his artistic passions when his country needed him to do so.

Images and Meditations is focused – and perhaps haunted – by the opening poem, "Pavillon du Nord, Maison Lafitte," titled in English simply "The North Pavilion," which was the hunting lodge where Robinson found James dead in the study while they were on holiday. This allusion to James in 1922 indicates his continued presence in her thoughts and gives us some insight into her own experience of suffering that she recasts in this volume to highlight not only the collective pains of war but also the need for fortitude and perseverance in the face of human tragedy. In "The North Pavilion," Robinson expresses the paradox of remembrance that unifies the collection as she relives both the exquisite joy of time spent with James during the summer before his untimely death and her intense and continued grief after his death. This hunting lodge, designed by the seventeenth-century French architect Mansart, remained for her a symbol of perfect happiness, as well as a reminder of the transience and impermanence of life and love, themes appropriate in times of war and in postwar contemplative poetry. In the first few stanzas of this poem of fourteen quatrains, Robinson conveys the intense joy of that last spring and summer that no doubt intensified the tragedy of James's October death:

I
O Spring of Eighteen-ninety-four!
Bright miracle of sun and rain!
Was ever such a spring before?
Will such another dawn again?
...
III
We sought a summer's home in vain
Until at length our fateful stars
Between the forest and the Seine
Espied a marvel of Mansart's (1)

The use of "fateful" to describe the alignment of their stars at this time conveys Robinson's complex emotional attachment to this time and place and suggests her continued sense that there are spiritual forces that determine the patterns of our lives. The rhyming couplets and tetrametre lines contribute to our understanding of these months that seem, in retrospect, to have been a pastoral ideal.

VIII
What months, what days, what hours of bliss
Come floating backward from the Past,
Like birds above a precipice,
And each one lovelier than the last! ... (3)

Diction emphasizes the timeless perfection in which Robinson lived with James in a relatively short expanse of actual time, and, as the simile suggests, memories seem to turn back time for her, as though she were able to experience again the beauty of those days. The ellipses at the end of the quatrain also imply that this is a recurring memory that gives her both joy and pain. The eleventh and twelfth quatrains indicate the transcendental nature of Robinson's love for James after the passage of nearly thirty years that included a second marriage and a World War:

XI
O doubled brain, twin souls, and hearts
That mirror'd each the deepest deep

Where our unconscious Being starts
And murmurs in his dreamful sleep! ... (3)
XII
Some thirty years have come and gone;
I stand and look across the fence ...
It seems a thing to wonder on
That I should be an exile hence. (4)

Perhaps the "fence" suggests her return to the actual pavilion or perhaps it has to do with the barrier between the living and the dead
that memory has enabled her to breech in these moments. Either
way, the image of doubling and twinning to represent Robinson's
companionate, passionate, and very romantic marriage to James
Darmesteter seems to mirror letters to her family and friends and
to James himself. By the last quatrain, the speaker has reached a
moment of aestheticist transcendence through this reminiscence.
In the final stanza she makes it clear that this "return" has been for
her a revelation that on a non-material level, she will always "live"
with James:

XIV
Doubtless in some immortal sphere
(For there we touched Eternity)
We spend the imperishable year:
The North Pavilion, Thou and I. (4)

The influence of Pater lingers in Robinson's hope for union with
James in some form, therefore, even thirty years after James's death. It
is difficult to separate her profound and lasting grief at losing James
from many of her attitudes in later life, including her determined and
resolute treatment of Vernon Lee as though nothing significant had
occurred in their relationship, her decision to marry Émile Duclaux
for the companionship they both needed, her choosing to live with
James's possessions filling her apartment, and her uncompromising
perspective on duty and sacrifice. In a very real sense, James's death
was the worst that was to happen to Robinson in her life, and it
altered the way in which she understood human tragedy. Her war
poetry might be read as an antidote to the emotional turmoil and

grief of epic proportions experienced by ordinary men and women during the Great War, just as poetics enabled her to express her own inner suffering at the loss of James that seems to have remained undiminished over the years. In a paradoxical sense, then, for Robinson, the war served as a reminder that all experience can be transformative in positive ways.

Robinson was in Sucy-en-Brie with her sister and mother when war broke out, and they had to cut short their holiday in the house that Marianne and Daniel Halévy had loaned them while they were away. Fleeing Sucy-en-Brie, the three managed to get as far as Melun, where they had already arranged to rent a house for the month of August. Robinson wrote about these difficult first days of the war in "The Background of a Victory," and she published her first war poem, "Belgium the Barlass," in the *Times Literary Supplement* under the title "Belgia Bar-Lass" on 20 August 1914. This poetic "thank you" to Belgium for taking the brunt of the German invasion and acting as a "bar" between Germany and France tells the story of Catherine Douglas, a lady in waiting to Queen Joan Beaufort, wife of King James I of Scotland. One evening, the story goes, the king and those inside his refuge with him discovered to their dismay that someone had betrayed him and had removed the bolt from the door to allow those intent on killing him to enter. Catherine used her arm as a bolt while he hid. However, the rebels forced the door, breaking her arm in the process. Douglas became known from that point as Katherine Barlass, and Robinson uses her tale as a metaphor to highlight the fortitude of Belgium that allowed time to build trenches to create the Western Front, which was well established by 22 November 1914. The rhyming couplets and formal, iambic pentametre rhythms convey Catherine's bravery, and diction reinforces the fact that it was a woman with her "naked arm" that was "supple, white as milk, and warm" who demonstrated courage in a difficult time (35). These deeds of tremendous and unexpected courage, the speaker reminds us, "are the ransom of our Earth," and in the final couplet of the poem, she praises Belgium for accomplishing what Katherine Barlass was unable to accomplish, describing the country as "Happier than she who saw her monarch fall, / Thine arm, thy heart, thy faith have saved us all!" (36).

Of course, France was a long way from being "saved" in any sense, but Robinson was inspired in these early days of the war and clearly excited by acts of heroism that still seemed fruitful. Poetry, she implies, has a place in celebrating these important moments as the second poem that emerged from the stay in Melun similarly suggests. "A Scotch Reel" records Robinson's experience in the streets with others cheering the arrival of the highlanders. "I felt no fear, only an immense strained curiosity; but I must have been at heart far more afraid than they, for I could not have moved or cried," she explains, as she watched the highlanders march down the street, many of them never to return.[17] She remembers, she says, singing "'Scots wha hae' at the top of my cracked old voice" and the soldiers tipping their hats at her. When she asked a returning soldier on 6 September whether he thought the Germans were on their way, he replied in a mock accent that the Germans "will have been hafing a pit of a set-back," for the allies had advanced toward winning the Marne. The ballad that arose out of this incident reflects both excitement and fear in the dizzying "reel" that predicts the death of these front liners. The repeated poetic address to one highlander, "William," perhaps inspired by the man she described to Pollock – a "demure, douce young Highlander taking his afternoon walk as quietly as if it had been in Glasgow" who gave her the news of the Marne – creates a collective identity for the numerous, individual young men who found themselves suddenly caught up in this whirl of dance and war.[18]

In July 1915, Robinson returned to the area near Sucy-en-Brie in her imagination in "The Wood at Sucy," which begins in the silence of anticipated invasion with the cloudy sky suggesting the calm before the storm:

Warm woods all wet with rain,
Where no winds stir,
Wide heavy boughs of plane,
One tall dark fir
Slanting its crest awry
Black, 'gainst a stormy sky. (44)

The alliterative "w" that conveys the imminent explosion of the humid, sticky air as it moves into the violence of the storm works as a metaphor for the impending outbreak of war. This is a scene of isolation, with the lone tree described in enjambed lines that highlight its importance as a signal of all that is "awry" in the coming destruction. On "the topmost bow" of this tree in the next stanza, a loriot, the golden oriole of Europe, perches on its highest branch to further the contrast between the natural world and the unnatural pending catastrophe as the bird's normally sweet voice seems troubled and sounds "loud, brief, a bugle-note" to foreshadow the German and French forces fighting just beyond the woods (44). In history, the Battle of Soissons, as it is known, was a turning point in the war, but it was a difficult battle with the allies marching through the woods and dealing with very hot weather and drenching thunderstorms. Robinson poeticizes the march abstractly through the poetic consciousness of the tranquil, silent, black woods and the distant sound of bombing that foreshadows the transformation of what had once been a place of repose into a frantic and terrifying arena of war:

> Nay, it is scarce a sound –
> So hoarse, so grave –
> That travels underground,
> Like some spent wave,
> Whose last weak ripples tell
> How, at the mouth of Hell,
> All day the German bombs on Soissons fell. (45)

In this final stanza, the aural and tactile imagery of the blasts moving underground to expand their effect throughout the woods conveys the speaker's sense of damage permeating the deep, once protected woods – there is nowhere to hide from the effects of this expanding "Hell."

In other "war" lyrics, Robinson draws compelling parallels between this disruption of the natural order of things and the fading of Christian certainty in times of war. In "The Two Worlds," written five months later in December 1915, the context for war is Lucifer's uprising that ultimately led to the loss of paradise, and in "Stars Over a Battlefield," graphic imagery and alliteration depict in realistic horror a night sky in which "shattering shock of bomb and shell" replaces the natural stars (49). This imagery comes from experience as Robinson sat on the veranda with her mother at Melun watching the unnatural sight of a sky filled with aircraft ("Background," 115). In her poem to mark this event, she uses the beginning of Psalm 19 in the third stanza in order to situate God into this scene of destruction:

> Ay, *Caeli enarrunt*! ... But whose glory tell
> These earth-born stars that rise and blaze and swell
> And burst in shattering shock of bomb and shell? (49)

In the psalm, the Latin exclamation is translated "the Heavens declare," and what they "declare" is "the glory of God." This thread of an absent, careless God is developed in other war poems as evidence that there simply cannot be a God who would permit such destruction. In the sky over Melun that evening, the unnatural "stars" formed by exploding rockets and gunfire brought to mind for the agnostic Robinson not the glory of God but the carnage and death on the battlefield below. The speaker's outrage and confusion are conveyed again through enjambment as the lines swell in metric rhythm to the explosions they describe. These are the stars of mythic gods, the speaker concludes – Sirius, the star most important to the Egyptians, and Hesper, the Evening star – but they have nothing to do with a Christian God who allows such destruction. The speaker wonders how God could have created the world on "the crystal's perfect plan" only to see it destroyed (50). The answer seems clear: God has disappeared, "gone on some long journey's endless quest" and is perhaps even enjoying the havoc as "He takes His rest / while half a world is weeping" (50). The poem ends with images of hell on earth specific to war:

> Wounded that cry for water in the flames,
> And dying men that murmur women's names:
> Are these a mist of dreams,
> Unreal, through which the Soul in lonely splendour streams? (51)

It is important to note that Robinson's persistent calls for courage in times of war are not to be cast in light of warmongering or approval of war in any sense. She abhorred the destruction of the countries that she loved, and she felt keenly the widespread ripple effect of war. Yet, she casts even the loss of loved ones – and her work with the wounded in the hospital must have exposed her to such grief – in as paradoxically positive a light as she can. It is in poems such as "The Mourners" that we see reinscribed the fortitude that she demanded of herself with the loss of James and that is kept in the forefront by "The North Pavilion" introducing the poetry of this volume. She wrote "The Mourners" in Paris in 1917, when increasingly intense battles had been fought since the previous July, and in this lyric she situates Hell not in general, abstract terms, but in a human context as she speaks to those who have lost loved ones in battle. In the last stanza, she urges them to focus on making their losses significant by seeing them in terms of allied gains:

> So they who in this war have lost their all
> And go in black, head bent, with slow sad feet,
> Shall none the less find England's victory sweet,
> And say: She lives! She lives! There is no death!
> "The drops of blood that from our dear ones fall
> Are seals that sign her freedom and our faith!" (46)

Perhaps the fact that she did not personally lose anyone close to her enabled Robinson to suggest that those left to mourn would inevitably find comfort in winning the war itself. She does write her experience into her poetry in more distanced ways, as in "The Beetroot." The titular symbol accomplishes a similar recasting of tragedy as something positive, but it is more sensitive to the aftereffects of war. Robinson's personal familiarity with this plant from Touraine that marks the graves of the fallen at Flanders and thus pays tribute to the heroes lying beneath also implicitly evokes Émile. Written in Paris 18 January 1916, "The Beetroot" first appeared in *Country Life*, an apt venue for this ironic depiction of the transformation of the plant that in Touraine signals the final harvest bounty into the sinister, yet poignant symbol of a patriotic death in Flanders, where the Battle of Verdun would take place in February 1916.

A feature of Robinson's war poetry, of course, is its link to what would become significant historical events, and she was increasingly adept at determining verse forms best suited for this purpose. In the

lyrical ballad "The Submarine," also dated January 1916, she recalls
an event that occurred 22 September 1914, when she, Mabel, and
Frances Robinson were still in Melun and three ships on patrol in
the North Sea sank quickly when attacked by a German submarine.
This was a disaster of vast political magnitude, not only because the
allies were not yet using submarines themselves but also because
this trio of ships was known collectively as the "livebait squadron"
because they were outdated and poorly maintained. The loss of
1,450 sailors left the English public outraged and distrustful of the
Royal Navy and its concentration on the more immediate strategies
of U-boats. The speaker of this ballad focuses on the human beings
caught up in this terrible event, describing the men peering nerv-
ously at the sea only to find "nothing to right of them, nothing to
left!" (40). Literally, then, those on board the *Cressy*, the *Aboukir*,
and the *Hogue* watch their own demise as the ships are attacked
from underneath the water.

Robinson's war poetry of 1918 reflects the politically complex and
shifting landscape of Europe during what would be the final year of
the First World War. "Cordelia," which she wrote in Paris, concerns
America's late entry into the war on 6 April 1917. In this short poem
of three quatrains, the speaker compares America to Cordelia, the
"dowerless daughter" of King Lear (47). Britain has misunderstood
America's delay, suggests the speaker, for just as Cordelia refuses to
praise and swear loyalty to her father when she feels that he should
simply know that she loves him dearly, America would not join a
war in which it was not fully invested and was not certain was its
business. Cordelia arouses Lear's anger in part because her sisters
Regan and Goneril make false declarations of loyalty and love, and he
believes them rather than the daughter who truly loves him. When
the American Expeditionary Forces did enter the war, it was France
rather than England that welcomed America's aid, points out the
speaker. The poem is interesting because the speaker is English rather
than French, and in the final stanza, she draws on Shakespeare again
to highlight just how remiss England was in expressing resentment
at the tardiness of the American contribution rather than gratitude
for the help:

But when the brunt of battle shook our isles
Our "forlorn soldier that so nobly fought"

> Looked up, and saw, full-armed, in tears and smiles,
> Cordelia, with the legions that she brought! (47)

The second line of this stanza is taken from *Cymbeline* act 5, scene 5 to evoke the image of Cymbeline rewarding his three compatriots, Guiderius, Arviragus, and Belariuse, for their brave deeds in battle as he wonders at the same time what has happened to an unknown peasant who fought for Britain. Ironically named Postumus, this figure brings the poem back to the general theme of self-sacrifice and patriotic duty.

Finally, the historical event that inspired the Petrarchan sonnet "Poland," dated 18 December 1918, was the repatriation of Poland. The octave traces the history of the partitioning of Poland to Austria, which received the first part of Poland 5 August 1772, then to Prussia, which received the second part 23 January 1793, and finally to Russia, which received the third part 25 October 1795. The sestet, drawing on the rhetorical process of the sonnet, celebrates Poland's victory in reunification in light of this history:

> One hundred years, and nearly fifty years
> Reigned Austria, Prussia, Russia, unrebuked,
> Till God's eye glanced their way, pierced through, and looked
> Below the surface for the source of tears ...
> Then, from three graves, arose the Victim, whole,
> Who waited with an undivided soul. (48)

The subtle religious allusion to the resurrection as orchestrated by God gives the reunification a sense of justness and rightness. Perhaps as well, given the date of composition, Robinson has in mind that this political restructuring bodes well for the formation of the peace committee that was meeting at the end of that year.

The "other" poems of *Images and Meditations*

In integrating the war poems with poems that develop some of the aestheticist themes with which she had been preoccupied her entire life, Robinson makes it clear that her "war work" was simply a continuation of her work as a poet. Because this 1922 volume is the final collection of Robinson's published poetry, it offers us insight into how far Robinson had developed as a poet since *A Handful of Honeysuckle*. The noteworthy "Roussel's Sonata," written on 8 May 1922, for instance, although loosely related to the war in that it is a tribute to Albert Roussel (1869–1937), who was an ambulance driver in the war and afterwards lived and composed music in Normandy, stands as evidence of Robinson's technical achievement as a poet. The subtitle "For Piano and Violin" suggests that Robinson was inspired by Roussel's 1922 piano and violin sonata. This classical musician, influenced in his style by the impressionists Ravel and Debussy, in turn had a profound influence on his student Erik Satie. The six verses of Robinson's poem follow the three main sections of the sonata form: exposition, development, and recapitulation. Robinson delineates this musical rhetorical process in poetry, beginning the first three stanzas with an address to "Music," thereby forming the exposition not only through alliteration and repetition, but also through form:

I
Music!
and into the narrowest room
Enters illimitable space!
Visions arise on a boundless horizon,
Vistas of glory and grace,
Vortex of grandeur and gloom!
II
Music!
a universe ampler than ours
Bursts – as a bird that breaks the shell –
Airily swinging upwards and singing;
Bursts – as a bee from the cell –
Full of perfections and powers.
III
Music – sole means to reach the unvisioned sphere
That sheds no ray on Memory's earthy rill,
Free us from Now and Here!
Free us from Want and Will!
And all the fancy dare not dream fulfil! (11)

The effects of the music on the speaker in these stanzas evoke Robinson's earlier music poems as the experience of listening to music becomes transformative; however, since music is the "sole means" of transcendence, it becomes necessary to the spiritual vitality of the speaker. In alliterative tetrametre lines the first three verses trace the exposition of the expansive attributes of music: the "v" alliterations of the first stanza, "visions," "vistas," and "vortex," suggest expanded imaginative sight; the "b" and "p" of the second stanza in "sputter," "burst," and "explode" evoke corresponding moments of musical explosion; and repetition of "Free" in the third stanza emphasizes the restriction signalled by the alliterative "want" and "will." The fourth and fifth stanzas making up the development of this literary sonata indicate the nature of the inner life inspired by music:

IV
I dream of worlds apart
And infinitely far,
Unlike us as a star,
And foreign to the heart.
A wind of music, blowing as it lists,
Whispers: that alien other world exists!
V
Our sages with their schemes
Shall never understand
The strange immortal dreams
A breath of music fann'd –
For all they count or span
The mirage is of Man –
Our shadow as we pass,
Our image in the glass!

Whereas shortened lines of poetry often have a staccato effect, these lines instead suggest the swaying, rhythmic movement of the dreaming speaker led by music into worlds beyond this one. These worlds are implied rather than made concrete through "a wind of music [that] whispers" and "a breath of music [that] fann'd out," such diction suggesting a shimmering "mirage" rather than substance. Diction and metre thus convey not only the aural pleasure of music but its power to stimulate the inner life of the speaker. The final stanza concludes this poetic tour de force with an address to music that brings the speaker full circle, thereby mimicking the effect of music fading out, and repetition of the third stanza word for word signals the speaker's emergence out of this moment of epiphany.

As in previous collections, water functions as an important metaphor in these "meditations," and it is significant that the only prewar poem included in *Images and Meditations*, "The Death of the Wye," which Robinson composed on 1 September 1909 at Ross-on-Wye, well demonstrates her ongoing concern with reaching "the unvisioned sphere" that she imagines in "Roussel's Sonata." The personified waters of the Wye River moving toward "the Unknown," as the speaker describes the river moving toward the Severn Estuary, form an analogy to the course along which we proceed in life (7). This river pauses in calm waters before it joins the Bristol Avon River and then flows through the Bristol Channel and the Celtic Sea until it is subsumed by the Atlantic Ocean, thereby following the trajectory of pantheism. A trajectory toward inclusion in a larger, universal "space" takes place in "The Fountain's Shadow," as alliteration and a couplet following three unrhymed lines create the effect of moving water appearing unexpectedly out of the rock face:

Out of the barren rock
Gushes the laughing water,
Liquid in life ecstatic,
Tossing into the day
Fountains of spray.

Ferns flourish and flowers:
Fairer, this fountain's shadow –
Dancing, alive, prismatic –
Quivers upon the stones,
Lovelier than a rose. (21)

The effect of the couplet is synesthetic in each stanza of this brief lyric, suggesting the water emerging in spray to bring to life everything in its path, including the senses of the speaker. The same effect is produced in "Mediterranean Noon," subtitled "A Cameo" to convey the impression of fragmented moments in this vision of natural unity. Metre and line length suggest the ebbing and flowing of waves in the gentle Mediterranean Sea in the first stanza:

Now the Earth rocks the sea, like a sleeping boy,
In the hollow of her lap –
All the sea!
Drawing close, folding over, the hills that wrap
That slumber of a joy
On her knee! (19)

This image of maternity is complemented in the next stanza by an image of paternity as "the sky, bending down, sees the image of his face," and the poem concludes with a familial tableau that suggests the normalcy of this natural composite of mother, father, "and the child of their embrace, / Fast asleep!"

Although not all of Robinson's "water poems" are technically complex, her increased facility with metaphor and symbol marks her advance from the aestheticist poetry of the 1880s into a modernist mindset thirty years later. "The Demented Mother," dated 23 September 1922, presents a darker side of the maternal through a water metaphor that contrasts that of "Mediterranean Noon." In this Petrarchan sonnet, as the title suggests, the speaker depicts a sick mother who cannot care for her offspring and who meanders instead in the first quatrain from "shore to shore" as she "moans the secret of a mind deranged" (28). The Petrarchan rhyming pattern of the second quatrain emphasizes the unnatural situation of a mother estranged from her children:

Her blue eyes shone at noon, as though to bless
That perished world her memory keeps unchanged,
But now she wails old sorrows unavenged,
Threatens and thunders, storms to obtain redress. (28)

This is an unsettling image, not only of a mother estranged from her children, but, as the sestet makes clear, of children too far removed from their origins to ensure generational continuity:

The sea is old, far older than the land,
Full of strange things we cannot understand;
– The moon-struck, vagrant, and tempestuous deep! …

Introduction of the moon evokes the cycles of womanhood, a symbol of the feminine that Robinson had used successfully in 1886 in the first rispetto of "Tuscan Cypress" to focus the whole sequence. Significantly, as the speaker suggests in the final tercet of "The Demented Mother," we are drawn to the sea through a kind of in vitro memory and intuit a kinship with the sea as an element of nature important to the rhythm of human life:

Yet from her womb our life was multiplied,
And still our veins her salty savours keep
That beat the rhythm of a remembered tide.

"Final Failure," written during the same holiday at Les Fées a week after "The Demented Mother," is a simple reminder that in our eagerness to gain access to knowledge beyond the world, we, like the water crashing against the land along the shoreline, are doomed to fail again and again in our attempts. These poems suggest the continued influence of both the philosopher and the scientist – James and Émile – on Robinson's perspective on this world and on her intuited sense that there must be some form of a world beyond.

In the poetry of this volume as in earlier poetry, Robinson's speakers shift and readjust their perspectives on their world as they draw on Platonic, pantheistic, and Christian ideals. She indicated to Daniel Halévy 6 October 1922, when *Images and Meditations* appeared, that were she to subscribe to a formal religion it would be Catholicism, a religion steeped in aesthetic symbolism and poetic beauty, but not a religion in its common form based on intellectual and empirical investigation.[19] Perhaps this sustained ambivalence about the place of religion in her own life explains the eclectic ways in which it is depicted in this final volume of poetry, designated by its title to belong to the contemplative rhetorical arguments between philosophy and science. *Images and Meditations* reflects the perspective of a woman in later middle life who had experienced

love, who was bilingual and bicultural, and who had lived through
the deaths of two husbands and a devastating war. This body of
poetry returns to the turmoil of all of those defining features of her
life in some way but in an overall tone of calmness and peacefulness.
In "Expression," the speaker warns explicitly that truth depends
on the context of our lives and our times, and that ultimately, as
she concludes in the last lines, "our sincerest words have said /
the truth of yesterday" (59). Similarly, church bells of "The Bell at
Ross" ringing to mark a death seem to chime "lost" one moment
and "wait" the next. The lingering last echo of "wait" that concludes
this poem suggests that uncertainty is the only logical philosophical
perspective on life (62–3). The speaker of "Confessio Amantis," dated
1922, with the title evoking John Gower's 1399 work of the same
name and situating it thus in the tradition of the medieval poetry
of consolation, comes to the same conclusion, confessing in the
first of the three stanzas that as much as she might want to believe
in conventional terms, such belief is elusive, and she remains as
"blind as a mole" (52). In the second stanza, she feels that this lack
of faith makes her of less value to those she loves. However, in the
third stanza, the speaker develops a complex metaphor to express
commitment to a vague and undefined afterlife:

> Yet is it mine
> To fill Thy cup with water or with wine?
> My humbler part
> Is but to burnish and to set apart.
> I grave Thy metal in a lovely line:
> See, round the rim
> The radiant letters of Thy Name I trace –
> Then wait on Him
> Who yet may brim
> The void and brilliant chalice with His grace. (53)

The tone of prayer in this final stanza evokes the reverential moment of
transubstantiation, perhaps the most symbolically powerful moment
of joy and hope in the Catholic liturgy, and implies that, as Marandon
suggests, if grace ever came to her, she would welcome it.[20] This
poetic moment is certainly consistent with her affirmation to Daniel

Halévy that were she to practice any organized method of worship, it would be the most symbolic and aesthetic of Christian practices.

Robinson also pays tribute to a Catholic who was one of her contemporaries in "Père de Foucauld," subtitled parenthetically "Le Bonheur de Dieu." This is the story of a military man who might have found happiness in a conventional life of military heroism and marriage, the speaker suggests in the first two stanzas, but instead, he became a priest. In the third stanza, the speaker wonders whether de Foucauld was truly happy in his vocation or whether he was simply "rapt in the imagined happiness of God?" (58). De Foucauld died in 1916 at hands of bandits, and, when Robinson wrote the poem, the leader of this group of bandits remained at large. He was caught and executed in 1944, and in 2005, Pope Benedict beatified de Foucauld. Robinson's poem explores not only the power of faith but also the potential cost of such faith as it has manifested itself through the centuries. She is at times ambivalent about the positive effects of faith on those who truly seem to believe in God, suggesting in the ekphrastic poem "The Death of David," for instance, that faith can be dispiriting rather than comforting when one has to negotiate the divide between sin and reward at the end of life. Dated 3 May 1921, this poem was inspired by a painting of Ferdinand Bol, a student of Rembrandt, titled "David's Dying Charge to Solomon."[21] This theme is developed through the tension between the aged, dying David and Bathsheba, the young, beautiful woman for whom, he fears at this moment of reckoning, he has compromised his spiritual salvation. In the short poem "Burial," on the other hand, the pragmatic speaker questions the logic of worrying about the decaying body after death when only the lasting soul matters.

When she deals more specifically with aging, Robinson's poetry is poignant. Although "Song" is conventional and didactic in its message to the young to "love ye one another," the rhetorically sophisticated "The Blind Woman" is affective and effective in its merging of two voices – the poetic speaker and a blind woman moaning on her bed. Over the course of the poem, the voices become one to express longing for love long gone and the isolation of waiting for death:

The blind woman lay moaning on her bed:
I held my breath in pity. I heard her groan,

And bent at length to soothe her shuddering head.
And then she smiled and ceased her weary moan:
"Art thou beside me Love?
I thought I wept alone!" (17)

There are, of course, autobiographical implications in the last two lines, and it is very difficult not to see Robinson herself as the blind figure pining for James. In the second stanza the speaker admits that she too has wept at night, "a dear companion gone / who yet may stand beside me out of sight." This stanza ends with repetition of the last two lines of the first stanza, underscoring the pathos of widowhood. "Old Age," another poem written during the holiday at Les Mées, when Robinson was only sixty-four, is similarly inflected with her own experience and with her perception of herself. The speaker's perspective moves from a mirrored reflection of a "wan face and watery eye" to reconstruct and piece together the person she has become. The cumulative effects of old age, as her faculties fade, days "leave" and years gather "dust," are daunting (30). However, she admits that she still feels "fresh and fine" inside, and concludes that like an "old wall, crumbling" that is "full of gilly-flowers" in a new version of itself, so she too will find some kind of renewal through the aging process (31). This poem is a particularly nuanced insight into the paradox of aging – the body changes but the spirit often has difficulty in keeping up with it.

The allegorical poems "The Ball-Room" and "The Circus" are perhaps less compelling, as are the nature poems "Birds" and "The Peacock." However, "The Spider," dated 10 May 1922, develops an effective metaphor through a spider expelling the threads for her web from her breast, the site of the heart and the symbol of mother love and mother sustenance. In other nature poems such as "The Birth of the Rose" and "The Carnation," the titular flowers work as natural symbols of aestheticism, for while their delicate beauty fades and then disappears altogether, their perfumes, like human memory, linger. Memory itself acts as a similar creative power in "The End of Summer," which in the first two stanzas evokes the transitional fall equinox when the full moon, along with the pale sky, the yellowing trees, and falling flower petals, are given new life in the speaker's mind through memory of the previous April, when these elements were markers of anticipation. In the third and final stanza, the speaker takes comfort in her power to evoke memories of spring happiness brought to fruition in summer:

> All that was ours may yet be ours! We choose it
> Out of Life's infinite unordered litter,
> Dip it in memory, embalm it, muse it,
> Doubling each day with one remembered, fitter
> To cheer us; then, if freezing winter's bitter
> We turn to recollection, and refuse it! (61)

As the title implies, the end of summer always leads to beginning anew in the spring, and this is a poet who "chooses" to engage in active "recollection" that she makes permanent in her poetry.

Images and Meditations concludes with "The Awakening," one of the last poems that Robinson wrote for the collection in November 1922, and it complements "The North Pavilion" as the closing book-end. The speaker of "The Awakening" seems to have found the peace for which "The Blind Woman" yearns as she accepts her old age and embraces the power of memory that comes with it.

> Here, in the blue of the dawn, with the first pale glint in
>   the curtains –
> Sudden, I started awake, sitting bemused on my bed,
> Thought I was back (how strange!) a maid in my
>   maiden-chamber,
> Back in the London house, a slip of a girl, unwed. (65)

The metrically uneven lines in this opening stanza emphasize the speaker's struggle to surface from her dream, but it is in the next stanza that she conveys the power of dreams that arises out of memory:

> Forty years of endeavor, love, and lonely bereavement
> Slipped from my shoulders, then; fresh in the morning gleam,
> I was a girl of twenty, alert, with a life before her:
> All my days and my doings nothing more than a dream.

Thomas Hardy told Robinson that this was his favourite poem of the collection "because <u>there you are</u>, & sincerity is the prime virtue in verse, as elsewhere [emphasis Hardy's].[22] That this is clearly an autobiographical lyrical expression makes the reference to the past poignant, but it is the final verse that suggests the true comforting power of dreams, for they record a life well lived and the tone at the end of the poem is not so much reconciliation to the trajectory her life has taken but thankfulness at its configuration. "Well, do you think I was glad," she asks with respect to waking up in the illusion of youth and inexperience? On the contrary, she continues,

> Bitter, acute disappointment
> Struck at the strings of my heart, jangled me out of my sleep;
> Glad to be old, half-blind, a foreigner here, and a widow,
> Since I have known (thank God) all I remember and keep.

The last two lines of the poem situate the touch points of her life as Mary Robinson, Mary James Darmesteter, and Mary Duclaux in a positive light, and the "awakening" of the title refers to the speaker's epiphany: through memory she has found a source of untapped happiness and joy.

More "War Work": French History, French Writers, and a Biography

When their mother died in 1917, Mary and Mabel moved to Rue Varennes, where Edith Wharton was a neighbour. Although the war made correspondence difficult, Robinson remained in touch with old friends in England, including George Moore and, of course, Lee, who happened to be in England when war broke out and was unable to return to Italy until it ended. In addition to writing the poetry for *Images and Meditations* and reviewing for the *Times Literary Supplement*, Robinson completed the manuscript for *A Short History of France: From Caesar's Invasion to the Battle of Waterloo*, which was published in 1918. The timing of the publication was fortuitous, since in the final year of the war there was a great sense of alliance between England and France and hope that their joint war efforts would mitigate some of the historical strife between the two countries. *The Anglo-French Review* jumped into this effort, for instance, publishing a stirring speech given by Paul Deschanel of the L'Académie Française in May of 1918 during the final days of the war, before Deschanel became Président de la République.[23] Conciliatory moments like this strengthened Robinson's position in the Anglo-French community and enhanced the popularity of her work.

Robinson wrote the forward to her condensed and accessible account of this vast period in French history in 1917, explaining that what had been a "hobby for thirty years or more" had become a form of "war-work" meant to educate "the class of cultivated and ignorant men and women to which I myself belong" (v). In a complimentary review for *The American Historical Review*, Charles Downer Hazen calls the book a model for historians writing short histories of large subjects, describing Robinson's fewer than 350 pages as "a history of nineteen centuries told with abounding and varied knowledge, with penetrating and subtle judgment, and with remarkable literary power and charm."[24] In France, this volume was well received, as Daniel Halévy notes in his review in French for the *Anglo-French Review*. It is among the best, he says, by a specialist in these matters.[25] He points out that Robinson is a poet, as well as a follower of Walter Pater and Saint-Beuve, and, therefore, it makes sense that her style is literary as she traces events leading up to and resulting from the French Revolution. Moreover, he says, although she is factual and accurate, what really emerges is her sensibility and French "genius" that reflects her deep understanding of French culture.

Robinson's short history includes four maps and is divided into four sections that span the social and political movements that unfolded in France: "The Roman Tradition," "Feudal Society," "The Centralized Monarch," and "The Revolution and Europe." She offers astute commentary to put facts into context for an English audience, acknowledging the challenges of historicity that make it difficult for us to get a sense of daily life in the Roman Empire (10). One of the most valuable elements of this book is its carefully constructed index. Although she progresses toward the nineteenth century without the judgmental posturing of hindsight, she indicates that the British made some poor decisions with respect to France, particularly with respect to Napoleon's rise to power. The epilogue is really a substantive conclusion that highlights some of the main points in this short history, returning to the 1815 Conference of the Allies, about which Robinson writes, "not since Henry VI of England was crowned King of France in Notre Dame had the great nation suffered a humiliation so entire" (333). She describes Alexander and Wellington as "two unexpected angels, two miraculous champions" who formed the alliance between France, England, and Russia that led to France's excellence in art, science, and industry during the nineteenth century (335, 338). In essence this is a history of France written to demonstrate to English readers the strength of the country that Robinson had taken for her own, and its publication just after the war certainly underscored the common values for which England and France had fought. Appropriately and symbolically, she affixes her maiden name to her married name as author, signalling the integration of English and French cultures in her own life.

When the war broke out, Robinson had nearly finished the manuscript for a second book, this one highlighting contemporary French writers that seemed to her to be representative of the literary transformation occurring in France in the early years of the twentieth century. *Twentieth Century French Writers: Reviews and Reminiscences* contains a photograph of Robinson in 1919, an attractive and stylishly dressed figure probably familiar to her English public at age sixty-two. In the preface, written before the war, Robinson explains that she aimed to present France in terms of its movement away from nineteenth-century literary characteristics but that she had to omit the "critics," by which she meant the "moralists, the biographers, the portrait-painters of a soul, an epoch, or a race" (viii).

In the "Afterwords – Afterwards," written in Paris in April 1919, Robinson explains that when the proofs arrived after a delay of five years, she had to make adjustments when authors had failed to live up to her predictions in some cases and exceeded them in others. Her political stance and patriotism that so annoyed Lee and Lenéru is evident in her choices and in her justification for them. She feels that Maurice Barrès, for instance, lived up to his promise in his inspired and inspiring journal contributions on courage in difficult times; Romaine Rolland, on the other hand, who was not active in "war work" of any kind, has proved to her that "his genius is not French" (xii). Even Paul Claudel, who increased the "volume" of his work in the five years, comes under censure for not changing its "character" (xv). Of all the changes she made, the most significant were those to the section on Péguy. She admits that she had written about him in 1914 in "a mood of freakish pleasantry" that she now finds to be "inappropriate" in speaking of a poet who died a martyr and a hero" (xvi). Perhaps the most poignant comment that focuses this "reminiscence" is attributed to Robinson's friend the Countess de Noailles, to whom she devotes a chapter. Robinson appropriated the substance of this remark for herself in subsequent years: "the terrible enigma – Must I grow old like the others? And, if not, must I die?" (xviii). Years later, in December 1927, she mentions in a letter to her stepson Pierre Duclaux that when she attended a meeting of the Prix Femina committee, she found herself "attacked wonderfully" by de Noailles, who she had not seen for six years. She jokes that Barrès always told her that were he not so in love with her, he would have loved de Noailles.[26]

Each of the eighteen chapters of *Twentieth Century French Writers* profiles a French author, but much of the text is taken directly from previous work, such as the chapters on Charles Péguy, Ernest Psichari, and Emile Nolly, who were all three included in "A Chaplet of Heroes," as well as the chapters on Marie Lenéru and the closing chapters on the French novel in general, taken from the article that she had published in the *Times Literary Supplement*. In the epilogue, Robinson sums up the French writers of her time as both "mystics" and people who "set a high value on action, on social energy" (257). They are "almost all of them Intuitionalists," she says, "and, in almost all of them there is the same reaction from the Individualism of the Nineteenth Century" (258). She ends with a reminder to English readers that France is historically both Celtic and Latin, a duality that is reflected in its literary history (258). However, she did tell Edmund Gosse on 2 March 1919, that although this book might interest him, as well as George Moore and Vernon Lee, she thought that it would interest few others.[27]

The third major publication of this time was the biography of Victor Hugo, which Robinson had also begun before the war with the chapter on Hugo in *The French Procession* of 1909. Basil Williams notes in his preface to the English edition dated July 1920 that Robinson first broached the subject with him in 1914, but then the war prevented further discussion. She incorporated the *French Procession* chapter and a *Times Literary Supplement* article of 8 January 1920 into the full biography, which was published in English in 1921 by the London publisher Constable in a series titled "Makers of the Nineteenth Century," and in French in 1925 by the Paris publisher Plon-Nourrit et Cie, with Robinson herself providing the translation. Dedicated to the friends at whose borrowed house she began her war experience and to whom she had remained close during the war, Daniel and Marianne Halévy, Robinson's *Victor Hugo* tells the story of a writer and poet already well known to and beloved by many English readers. He became an iconic figure in the channel island of Guernsey, where he lived for an extended period, and his work had routinely been translated into English.

Robinson includes biographical details perhaps less familiar to English readers, but she spends most of the biography discussing Hugo's writing, which she argues was always politically and socially focused through themes of royalism, Napoleonism, and democracy (67). She is particularly drawn to his 1826 third volume of *Odes* and his 1828 collection of lyrics published as *Les Orientales*, comparing the latter to some of Swinburne's *Poems and Ballads* (70). However, the eventual breakdown of Hugo's marriage and the ensuing complex triangular relationship with his wife Adèle and his mistress, Juliette Drouet, with whom he had four children, along with the death by drowning of his and Adele's daughter Léopoldine in a boating catastrophe in 1843, took a toll on the man and the writer. Robinson brings out the integrated passions of Hugo's life, pointing out that he "was not without shame, not without a haunting sense of degradation" for his weaknesses. However, she points out, "not all natures are capable of repentance or remorse" (159). It is in "the immortal *Contemplations*," Hugo's six-volume poetry collection, his personal "repentance, redemption, expiation," as Robinson describes it, that we find the best of this passionate man (160). This biography not only reflects Robinson's admiration of Hugo, the man and the writer, but it also served to reignite her interest in biographical writing that would lead to two more full biographies and several biographical articles for the *Times Literary Supplement* during the 1920s.

Through her ongoing engagement in archival retrieval and focus on biographical writing, Robinson also continued her preoccupation with the past, with time passing, and with the recurring theme that Pater articulates in terms of the "awful brevity" of life. She writes to Lee 22 December 1921, "how sad it is to grow old and to see one's friends grow old!" Telling Lee that she feels "very dim and very blurred these dark days" as her eyes continue to give her problems, she also makes clear that it is still Lee who never fails to raise her spirits simply because of "all the love and pleasure and delight with which I often think of you and all you have brought into my life." These remarks follow a long passage of complaint about politics and literature in which she reveals that she does not admire the work of Rudyard Kipling, who she met, with his parents, through James Darmesteter. She agrees with Arthur Myer, "that old fool," who blames politicians for making trouble between France and England.[28] She addresses Lee directly in the 1927 preface to her edition of de Sévigné's letters in English, reiterating the familiar theme of transience: "The worst of a greening old age is that those who live to enjoy it have survived their contemporaries and can with difficulty adapt themselves to the changing spirit of their times" (xxxvii). Yet, Robinson seems to have adapted herself fairly well. Her stance on heroism during the war had not only ruffled Lee's pacifist feathers, but it had also most likely contributed to an activism unusual for Lee. As correspondence between Lee and some of her French friends, including Berthe and André Noufflard, indicates, Lee was unequivocally disappointed in the prowar in the stance of Robinson and Barrès and busied herself handing out antiwar pamphlets at various events.[29] Lee's "war work" took the form of two poetic dramas, *The Ballet of the Nations* in 1916 and *Satan the Waster* in 1920. She also published the poignant essay "In Time of War" in 1917, in which she notes, what "my generation can never see re-made, is the cult of the genius of places: frivolous, of course … but decent and kindly."[30] The letters between Robinson and Lee of 1921 and 1922 avoid political discussion and are limited to exchanges about increasing health issues, which Lee suggested to Noufflard was the only conceivable way to move forward in her friendship with Mary Robinson. On a personal level, this friendship did progress, despite financial difficulties that made travel problematic for both Lee and Robinson. Mabel actually worked with Lee in April 1922 to persuade Robinson to accept some financial help in organizing a trip for Mabel and Robinson to travel to Florence.

She suggests that if Lee were to offer the money, perhaps Robinson would accept, for "one never knows with her. Poets have such fluid minds have they not that one never knows what is at the bottom of them." She points out that Robinson had not visited Florence in thirty-five years.[31]

In May 1922, Lee had to cut her hair rather drastically because of a scalp infection, an action that Robinson calls "extremism" at the age of sixty-five. She reminisces that when she was thirteen, she suffered from typhoid fever and had to take the same measure.[32] Robinson and Mabel managed a trip to stay with Lee at Palermo in July, and afterwards they stayed in London for a time. However, Mary Robinson, the British expatriate, had become more comfortable living as Mary Duclaux, the French patriot, telling Lee in October 1922, after the trip to London, "much as I love England & the dear kindly delicate-minded good humored English, still, still France for me!"[33] She was equally at home writing in English and in French and wrote the preface for a French translation of a selection of Browning's poems by Paul Alfassa and Gilbert de Voisins, which was published as one of Daniel Halévy's *Cahiers Vert*. The preface, which goes over territory well covered by others, particularly Mrs Sutherland Orr, whose *Life and Letters* reached a second edition almost right away in 1891, is titled "La Pensée de Robert Browning" in French and "Robert Browning: A Study on His Thoughts and Life" in English. In both cases, the emphasis is biographical rather than critical. Robinson points out that Orr had been able to interview Browning's sister Sarianna after his death, and notes that her biography remained popular in Britain. She notes as well that although Browning spoke to her often of his wife, he never mentioned his father-in-law, which suggested to her that perhaps Mr Barrett was the inspiration for some of Browning's more evil and diabolical speakers, such as the Duke of Ferrara and Guido Franceschini. In letters to Maurice Barrès at this time she responds to his questions about Browning, telling him 22 August 1922, for instance, of Browning's everlasting awareness of Elizabeth's presence, his continued adoration of his wife, and Robinson's sense that the Barrett/Browning marriage was a success. However, she adds, whether he was always happy is another question, for Elizabeth was rather authoritarian and, as a woman who married late, she was set in her ways.[34] The slightly critical tone is consistent with the preface that Robinson had written for the republication of *Casa Guidi Windows* in 1901.

Robinson's personal life was as busy as ever and included visits with the Halévy family in Sucy-en-Brie, receiving James Darmesteter's nephew Philip Hartog and his family, and helping her stepson Pierre Duclaux, whose wife, the mother of five children, suffered a nervous breakdown. It was actually Mabel who travelled to Toulouse to escort Pierre's wife back to Paris, thereby indicating the extent to which both Robinson and her sister had been integrated into the Duclaux family. Life with the extended Duclaux family continued with visits from "two little granddaughters," Jacques's daughters, staying for five days in February to enjoy the Carnival, and Émile's grandson and namesake who spent some time with her that December before leaving with his father for Indo-China.[35] The family was unhappy about the decision to take the child so far off, she tells Lee 17 December 1923, "but I silently applaud. Bringing up by women, the little chap had got quite out of hand, a good lad but unruly and idle."[36] She was clearly happy in this family life.

Robinson was also as busy as ever writing and reviewing, and her reputation in England was at this time such that, as she told Maurice Barrès in January 1923, she was invited to go to Oxford for the month of May to lecture on French literature. She declined with regret because her weakened voice and eyes would not permit her to carry such a project out, she tells Barrès.[37] The invitation itself, however, is certainly a testament to her continued status as a woman of letters in both countries. She published some new poetry in *Country Life* in 1923 and 1924: "Two Seascapes," "The Limit of Effort," "The Fly-in-Amber," "Partant pour Syrie," and "Dried Cows" in 1923 and in 1924 "A Dirge – Barrès," written for her old friend who died that year. The friendship with Lee seems to have been as repaired as it was going to be, Robinson telling Lee 24 January 1924, that she had "read several of Mrs. Anstruther-Thomson's sketches" and found in them "a sort of second sight," praising particularly the sketch describing the Venus de Medici, although she adds that she had never liked that statue herself. She also points out that Lee's excessive smoking is affecting her laryngitis.[38] She was still corresponding regularly with George Moore and spending time with Berthe and André Noufflard in Paris. Nevertheless, writing

Lee 27 December 1924 to thank her for a Christmas gift of paired stylographs, she says, "I am not sorry to see the end of 1924, which I have always regarded askance with a shy mistrustful eye. For in 1884, I nearly died of the smallpox; in 1894 James left me a widow, and Émile died in 1904; the war broke out in 1914. What next, I kept saying to myself. If there is a rhythm in things, what will happen in 1924?"[39] In this letter, Robinson notes that the portrait that Sargent had painted of her was still in Florence at Lee's home. She asks that Lee show it to the Noufflards when they visit and mentions that Berthe Noufflard had done a portrait of her.[40]

The Life of Racine and Biographical Essays

In the winter of 1923, Robinson was, she confided to Lee, "meditating a life of Racine," a project she brought to fruition in July 1925.[41] When she had finished the project, she wrote to Lee, "why I can be so completely envooulie [bewitched] by a man whose two poles were the Theatre and Salvation (neither of them much in my line) is a mystery to me, but envooulie I am" [emphasis Robinson's].[42] Her passion for Racine seems to have paid off, and reviews of the book are collectively complimentary. Writing for the *Saturday Review of Literature* 24 April 1926 when the book was published in New York by Harper, Ernest Sutherland Bates notes that Robinson "threads her way through the religious controversies of the time with lucid impartiality."[43] In the *Times Literary Supplement*, Cyril Benthan Falls comments 5 November 1925 that the book is more biography than critical study but says that Robinson is an "admirable" critic.[44] The reviewer for the *Spectator* writes that Robinson evokes both the man and his poetry with "a brain finely touched to fine issues," adding that she tells the story of Racine's life "with consummate skill" and that the book "should be read in full."[45] Although Morgan suggested posthumously that Robinson had not written this biography "to popularize Racine in England" and that simply producing "a good book was for her an end in itself," she seems to have earned her share of critical accolades for *The Life of Racine*.[46] The reviewer for *The Northern Whig* perhaps sums up most succinctly that "alike as a biography and a critical study it has great merit.[47]

Using the term that Lee once applied to her, Robinson calls Racine a "born poet," one of those oysters "whose initial grain of sand becomes a pearl" and who are "from a sheer love of perfection, made into something richer and rarer than Nature, no doubt, intended" (248). She acknowledges that Hugo and Racine differ in style and technique, but they are, she says, two of "the greatest of French poets." *The Bookman* reviewer, although disagreeing with Robinson that Racine should be classified with Victor Hugo as one of France's greatest poets, does say that she achieves "a living human portrait" of the man in a time that she evokes with equal colour and skill.[48] This focus on the individual in the context in which he wrote had been a defining feature of Robinson's biographical writing since *Emily Brontë*. Perhaps driven by her own early tendency to give up understanding him and her more recent sense that she should indeed make a greater effort to do so, she writes here as well conscious of the resistance of English readers to Racine.

The titles of the four books that comprise the biography together map out the chronology of Racine's life: "Youth," "The Theatre," "The Prodigal's Return," and "The Poet of the Bible." Each phase of the poet's life is contextualized in terms of the general political and cultural climate of seventeenth-century France, as well as the complicated, often emotionally charged ways in which Racine responded to his surroundings. It is through his letters to his sister Marie, Robinson says, that we see his early artistic development, and these letters, to which English readers did not have ready access, make the book interesting (30). Racine's early abandonment of his first impulse to become a monk, his love of writing poetry, and his introduction to Molière and the world of playwriting contributed to the development of what Robinson terms his "natural bent … in the direction of elegance, distinction, a noble tranquility masking a depth of feeling" (55). She analyzes the major plays, but her real admiration for Racine is rooted in his poetry, particularly *Esther* and *Athalie*, the latter comparable to *Paradise Lost*, she suggests (190, 196).

Robinson was also writing about English authors for French readers, publishing "Souvenirs sur Walter Pater" in the *Revue de Paris* in January 1925. Her reminiscences about her early days with Pater and his sisters in Oxford and on Earl's Terrace seem to have appealed to French readers, perhaps because she gauged their probable interest in his eccentricities. In this essay, she takes exception to the depiction of Pater by his most recent biographer, A.C. Benson, who presents Pater as completely lacking in cheer. On the contrary, she says, Pater was as "sober as a quaker, simple as a philosopher," but he was mischievous as well (341). She recounts an anecdote about her entering the Pater home one Christmas to invite Pater and his two sisters for the festive meal at the Robinson family house a few doors down on Earle's Terrace and finding all three sitting in the parlour anticipating the arrival of a favoured aunt and her sister, who would bring gifts and join them for Christmas. Pater turned to Robinson in the next instant and assured her that the aunt and sister did not exist but were figments of their imagination that they evoked for fun, since their parents were no longer living and their brother William was away. They did join the Robinsons for Christmas dinner, of course, and Pater was rather a different person at these feasts – gentle and pleasant (346). She ventures little into Pater's tumultuous relationship with Benjamin Jowett that ultimately cost him promotion; however, she casts his decision to give up his place as tutor while remaining a fellow as a consequence of his need to spend more time completing *Marius the Epicurean*, even though his move to London meant a commute to Oxford.

Robinson recalls introducing Pater to George Moore and to Vernon Lee, highlighting Lee's appreciation of Pater's eccentricities. Lee herself writes of this meeting in a letter to her mother in August 1882, describing Pater as "a very simple, amiable man, avowedly (almost) afraid of everything," and they did indeed become good friends.[49] The story of Pater's excitement at viewing what from a distance appeared to be beautiful, exotic flowers but that were really just onion flowers provides a segue to a discussion of his Platonic perspective and Robinson's sense that beauty for him was always a divine message. His lifelong belief that childhood experience irrevocably influences the adult, as he outlines in "The Child in the House" and develops as a theme central to *Marius*, is woven into the fabric of his being, she says. He was not overly attracted to women – he had no "faible penchant" – but he was indeed a real epicurean with a need for sensual pleasures and a love of luxury (349, 350). Robinson's critical analysis of *Marius* emphasizes his debt to Renan as a lover of truth, and she points out that the fictional character and Pater lived parallel lives in this respect. However, whereas Marius's thinking was in line with stoics, Pater's was in line with Unitarians, and just as Marius joined the Christians in the catacombs and brought himself to believe, Pater converted to Catholicism (354). The final section of the article deals with her own favourite among Pater's texts, *Plato and Platonism*, a book she compares in style to the rhythms of Bach's music, with its balance of intellectual and technical appeal (355). This book reinstated Pater in Oxford's good graces, she points out, and so he was able to return to Oxford with Jowett appeased, not as Pater the epicurean but as Pater the Platonist, and he lived there until he died of heart failure 30 July 1894.

Year by year, the influence of Pater on Robinson became stronger and stronger, not only with respect to the "awful brevity" of life but also with respect to the aging processes that underscore that brevity. The woman who had been so aesthetically appealing in her youth did not accept the infirmities and flaws that come with aging. "I feel old & blind & deaf and shabby, and very tired – a dreadful muff at going about by myself," she writes to Mabel.[50] In anticipation of an impending visit by Lee, she writes 11 June 1923 that she would not meet Lee at the station, explaining that since she was "such a blind old bat" she "should certainly miss" Lee.[51] Her tone with Lee became easy and relaxed once the war had fallen into history. For instance, she writes, "George Moore is here, and is coming to dinner tomorrow night with the Daniel Halévys and Julien Benda," the latter a popular French author who Lee grouped with the prowar crowd. "The talk will be good – but would be better if you were there. We are always so glad to be together."[52] For her part, Lee did respond to these invitations but with less enthusiasm as her deafness made her seem "dull," she felt, and her own health problems intensified.[53] Their mutual friend Bella Duffy died in early 1926, and on her seventieth birthday 27 February 1927, Robinson tells Lee "how old we are getting, my Dear! In my own rooms, among my books, I do not really feel very different though out of doors my purblind eyes and wobbly ankles keep me well informed of my advancing years. So long as one can enjoy the books one reads and the persons one loves I do not very much mind my infirmities so far."[54]

The truth is that although Robinson was susceptible to bronchial infections and other minor ailments, she actually enjoyed fairly good health and was still able to work six or seven hours each day to produce articles for an income.[55] In addition to the pieces on Madame Sévigné – the introductory essay to *Letters from the Marchioness de Sévigné to Her Daughter*, the letters themselves in English, and a lead article "Madame de Sévigné"in the *Times Literary Supplement* – she republished "Reminiscence" from the English translation of Lenéru's journal as the introduction to the 1926 publication of Lenéru's *La Maison sur la Roc*. She continued to republish the occasional verse, even "Le Roi est Mort" from *A Handful of Honeysuckle*, which appeared in the *Literary Digest* on 1 January 1927. Notably, she was included in the 1926 edition of the *Encyclopedia Britannica* and she continued in her role as a judge for the Prix Femina. In both England and in France, then, she was an influence on literary culture.

Portrait of Pascal

The genesis of *Portrait of Pascal* is the chapter on Pascal in *The French Ideal* of 1911, but the larger project preoccupied Robinson on and off through the years following. She uses the term "portrait"deliberately, she says, admitting in the preface that she was not capable of writing a "life": "I see him only from the outside, as the painter sees his model ... just one side of him, just as much as my intent and patient gaze can absorb ... But I see him very vividly: a noble, enchanting, insupportable being – whom sometimes I adore and sometimes almost dislike" (13). The comment gives us insight into the challenges that this particular subject had for a biographer accustomed to "entering into the genius," to recall Augusta Webster again, of her subject, and it highlights how she had become adept at balancing the disinterest necessary for the biographer with the personal commentary for which she had become known.[56] The "apology" to Lee appears on a card in Lee's presentation copy: "Here is Pascal. I feel sure you will think him stark staring mad – but that is no reason for not liking him. There was a deal more of Descartes and of Montaigne in him than I have quite been able to bring out. But then it is only a profile."[57] Lee's response was that she had finished reading the book and was rereading it with great admiration. Critical reviews are complimentary. In his review for the *Times Literary Supplement*, Arthur Sydney McDowall's only significant reservation has to do with the brevity of the chapter on the *Pensées*, for "if ever the inwardness of Pascal is to be reflected in his 'portrait,' it must be here," writes McDowall.[58] Ernest Benn writes in the *Spectator* that Robinson "always wears her scholarship like a grace," and although he does not share her view that Pascal has much in common with Donne, he admits that "it is difficult to disagree with so distinguished a scholar."[59]

The tone of Robinson's treatment of Pascal is set by the same epigraphic quotation from Baudelaire's "The Abyss" of *Les Fleurs du Mal* that she had used for the chapter on Pascal in *The French Ideal*: "I see the infinite through every window." However, now she pairs this quotation with another one on the concept of redemption taken from Pascal's *Pensées*: "Grace is indeed needed to turn a man into a saint; and he who doubts it does not know what a saint or a man is."[60] The effect of this pairing is to emphasize reliance on inner perceptiveness, a concept that appealed to Robinson as a poet, a philosopher, and a historian. Pascal was born in Auvergne, a region with which she had become extremely familiar and which had changed little in essence since the seventeenth century. She thus had an affinity for this region in common with her subject, and she minimizes the effect of historicity with comments that draw attention to historical and cultural continuity. For instance, she describes the comfortable means of the Pascal family in terms of the "constitutional objection" of the French to paying taxes (31). When she focuses on Pascal himself, she refers to his meditative thoughts housed in archives, but she draws on her own considerable knowledge of history and philosophy to provide religious context for his movement in the final phases of his life from "the extreme rigour" of his Jansenist perspective and the doctrine of predestination to a stance grounded in a gentle awareness of Christian forgiveness. He has left us, she says, "a collection of thoughts richer in soul-stuff than aught save the rare eternal masterpieces of the mind – thoughts which prove that, in this Order, neither abundance, perfection nor coherence is essential, but rather a certain quality, a tone of the voice, a sensitiveness quick to seize and repeat a mysterious echo of Reality which very few perceive" (229). Robinson's *Portrait of Pascal* is an intelligent presentation of the man, with his flaws and his genius exposed in a perceptive and reasoned way, and, as her final

major biography, it is a fitting conclusion to a successful career in
the genre. Although her status as an Anglo-French writer makes it
difficult to assess the extent to which she influenced the development
of biographical writing in either country, the unique stamp she left
on the genre is consistent with her advances in poetry and historical
writing. In her biographies, she fulfils the promise of *Emily Brontë*
in bringing together the poet and the historian through language
and archival work.

As the decade drew to a close, Robinson continued to enjoy life as
a "grandmother" in the Duclaux family circle, and she was still very
active socially. Writing to Lee at Easter 1929, she mentions meeting
two of Lee's friends, Aldous Huxley and D.H. Lawrence, at a tea
party at the home of Daniel Halévy. She had met Huxley previously,
but Lawrence was new to her, and she tells Lee with humour, her
"nice clear English voice" made its way through his deafness. She
goes on to say, "I found Lawrence very sensitive and apprehensive and
interesting without a trace of the coarseness which I had expected
in him, from his books, but I expect he has another side: his ears
are set on at such a Fawn-like slant, and altogether I think he does
look rather like some wild woodland thing disguised as humanity."
She continues in this letter to tell Lee that she and Mabel did not
attend the funeral of Marshal Foch, the renowned French general
of the war, because she hates crowds and Mabel hates generals.[61]

She was thinking about Lee these days with nostalgia, reminding
Lee in a birthday greeting of 8 October 1929 of their first meeting,
when their "minds rushed together in such enthusiasm that all the
ups and downs of fifty years have not really divided what came
together then."[62] Lee responded with a similar letter 21 November
in which she tells Robinson that she too remembers the past vividly
and has carried the framed photograph that Robinson gave her in
1880 in her writing case throughout the years. She describes Robinson
in this photograph, taken in Rome just before they met, in which
she was wearing a "sprigged liberty brocade dress," a cape, and "little
Venetian lace collar," remarking not only on how pretty Robinson
was but also commenting that "the smart little 1929 lady is still one
and the same" and that she looks younger in her "modern clothes."[63]
Robinson herself was not feeling particularly young when she sent
Lee her passport photograph several months later, asking, "what do
you say to this queer old apple woman?"[64]

Times Literary Supplement

Robinson's contributions to the *Times Literary Supplement* between 1902 and 1937 are impressive, not only in number, but also in the breadth and depth of analysis. She reviewed at least 370 books, possibly more allowing for indexing errors, in addition to writing seven "lead" articles, thirteen regular articles, five letters, six lengthy obituaries, and the 1914 poem "Belgia Bar-Lass" included in *Images and Meditations*.[65] Always looking for ways in which she might increase her income, she considered collecting her articles for an edition, a project that George Moore proposed 13 July 1931 to C.S. Evans, the editor of William Heinemann Press.[66] Although Evans initially responded favourably and Moore attempted to facilitate the process, offering six articles on Robinson's behalf, the collection was never printed.[67] Whether Moore's ill health prevented him from writing the preface he had promised or whether Robinson herself was unable to see the project to fruition is not clear.[68] Robinson's reviewing pace must have been daunting at times, particularly in light of her increasingly poor eyesight and growing cataracts, but it provided her with a good income. She reviewed a significant number of books by French writers in her continued efforts to familiarize English readers with contemporary French literature, and the subjects of all of her articles are European, primarily French, either focusing on individuals such as Ferdinand Brunetière, Marcellin Berthelot, Joris Karl Huysmans, Sully Prudhomme, Ludovic Halévy, Charles Péguy, Frédéric Mistral, and Julius Wellhausen, or developing broad subjects on which she had already touched, such as "French Novelists of Today" (1913), "The New Frenchman: (1916), and "The French Novel" (1934).

In reviews impressive for their depth and their diversity, Robinson was able to situate French contemporary literature in the *Times Literary Supplement* in a context that English readers could appreciate. Realistically, few of her readers would have had access to some of the lesser-known authors but others were well known, such as her friends Anatole France, Anna de Noailles, Paul Bourget, Julien Benda, Maurice Barrès, and Daniel Halévy. She reviewed her stepson Jacques Duclaux's 1910 *Chemistry of Life*, chiding him in the review for his tendency to pose questions and wait for answers. "He is a great friend of Truth, a greater still of a happy paradox; and possesses that natural clearness of mind which lends at least a superficial lucidity to the stupendous complication and solemn mystery of Nature," she writes. She reviewed many English authors as well, including Irene Cooper Willis, who was Lee's executor and with whom she would deal upon Lee's death in 1935. She writes with commendable care and precision, investing a great deal of time in reading and writing for which she was rewarded monetarily but not professionally, for as was the custom, these were unsigned reviews and articles. Of course, she too was reviewed in the *Times Literary Supplement* and, upon her death, received a laudatory obituary from Charles Langbridge Morgan.

In addition to her *Times Literary Supplement* work during the 1930s, Robinson kept busy with other writing projects, beginning in 1930 with an introduction for Henriette Renan's *Souvenirs et Impressions*. The following year she republished *An Italian Garden* with sketches that Jacques Beltrand completed from watercolour illustrations by Maurice Denis. She had funds that she had inherited from her parents deposited in a London bank, but she was careful to leave the principal alone and take the interest only. In June 1931, she was hit by a taxicab while she was in Battersea Park in London and suffered significant blood loss as a result, which kept her in London until early July. She describes the incident to Lee 28 July 1931 in reply to Lee's concern about Emily Sargent, who had fallen ill while visiting Florence, evoking the familiar theme: "It's a terrible thing to realize that one's friends are mortal!" She continues with respect to her own recent mishap, "as for myself, I do not mind a bit, and was slipping out of this mortal sphere in beatific indifference when the doctor came in and sewed up that artery."[69]

When George Moore died in January 1933, Robinson wrote a retrospective obituary article, "Souvenirs sur George Moore," for the 1 March issue of the *Revue de Paris*. Moore had been a constant in her life from 1876, and he often stayed at the Robinson country house at Epsom. She integrates recollections and perceptions of Moore into the facts of his life to produce a warm account of a man who, as his good friends acknowledged, could be difficult. He could be eccentric as well, and she describes the very blond haired, blue-eyed Moore's tendency to dress strangely, visiting Mabel and Mary at times in white muslin robes that trailed on the carpet (116). Moore first pursued art, studying at the School of Art at the South Kensington Museum and at the Sorbonne, where he honed his writing skills until he decided to pursue poetry instead. Drawn to Robinson through her poetry, he was also heavily influenced by Pater's *Marius*, suggests Robinson, as well as by Zola, and he treated controversial subjects, such as prostitution and illegitimacy, in a realistic context (119). Robinson suggests that his early upbringing in an Irish manor house, Moore Hall, and his aristocratic heritage informed his successful novel *Esther Waters*, published in 1894 (110–12). In later years, he became increasingly lonely as he quarrelled with friends, but he continued to send his work to Robinson, including *The Lake* in 1905, which she says she admired, even though she had really understood nothing in it (125). About this time Moore sent her a little silver eighteenth-century cake basket that he found in a store window, telling her that its delicacy made him think of her (125).

The Legacy of A. Mary F. Robinson/ Mary James Darmesteter/ Mary Duclaux

Vernon Lee's death on 13 February 1935 was no doubt a terrible loss for Robinson, but she had lost many friends by this point, and she was surprisingly pragmatic about the death of Vernon Lee. She complimented Irene Cooper Willis, Lee's executer, on 18 February on the obituary that Cooper Willis had written on the heels of a less complimentary one that had appeared in the *Times*. "I fear she must have suffered terribly – angina pectoris! I cannot bear to think of it," Robinson writes. "But her life was sad and lonely, sorely hampered by her deafness and pain, – and it was not worth living and we must be thankful that she is now beyond pain. We shall always miss her shall we not?"[1] The tone of her comments gives us some insight into Robinson's state of mind in general and into her resignation at her own waning years. Cooper Willis initially contacted Robinson to say that Lee had left her framed pictures, but Robinson worried that transporting them would be too costly for her. Cooper Willis seems to have taken care of the transport, and when the pictures arrived in Paris, they included the Sargent portrait, which has remained in a private collection. When Robinson received the painting and wrote to thank Cooper Willis, she included her own response to the painting: "what an ugly girl!"[2] In June, she commented to Cooper Willis that although it "looks very well on the wall" reframed in a more attractive gold frame, no one thinks it is "in the least like me." At this point, she also asked for her letters to Lee to be returned to her so that she might consign them to the woodstove the following winter, and to that end, she planned to collect them from Cooper Willis in London in July.[3] This plan was firmed up and, it seems, carried out. However, two years later, Robinson accepted Cooper Willis's offer of a copy of Lee's letters and Celtics, or sketches, which Cooper Willis was thinking of casting into a book despite Lee's request that they be destroyed. These sketches, points out Robinson, were a front study for "Miss Brown" and must be "charming and valuable"; however, she continues, "ought you to print them? The expressed wish of a dead friend is a formidable obstacle." She warns again that it might not be wise to print the book but if it is printed, she says, she would like a copy.[4] Cooper Willis published the sketches privately and circulated the book to a few people. She did publish Lee's letters home in 1937 and, as sole owner of copyright to Lee's estate, began the process of donations to Colby College and other repositories as she dismantled the house in Italy.

At the time of Lee's death, she and Robinson were diminishing in importance in literary circles. Robinson's review of John Middleton Murry's *Jean Racine* for the *Times Literary Supplement* on 23 December 1939 was her final submission, in part because the heightening tensions of the Second World War made contact with England difficult and in part because her worsening cataracts made reading and writing problematic. When the situation in Paris became dangerous, the Duclaux family moved Robinson and her sister to the house at Olmet, where the whole family was taking shelter. Mary Robinson was a French citizen, but Mabel was still a British citizen, and the family worried that she would be at increased risk if left in Paris. During the winter, when snow impeded access to the house at Olmet, Robinson and Mabel lived in an apartment in Aurillac at 6, Rue Transparot, which is located in the centre of town and looks much the same today as it did then. The modern, stylish woman had returned to the fashions of older days, and contemporaries describe the elderly Mary and Mabel walking on the streets of Aurillac with a Victorian air.[5] The last photograph of Robinson does indeed show her with her white hair covered with a lace cap and wearing a nineteenth-century lace fronted dress. Jacqueline Bayard-Pierlot remembered her mother and her grandmother chuckling at the idiosyncrasies of Mary and Mabel as they absorbed mid-twentieth-century social and cultural changes, noting, for instance, that class divisions remained as natural to Mary Robinson as geographical divisions.[6]

Despite her vision problems, Robinson wrote poetry in these years in English and in French, and she left poems that are clearly prototypes for some that she had published in previous collections. Sylvaine Marandon claims that she was gathering poems for a final collection to be titled either *The Interior Dialogue* or *More Ways than One*.[7] This publication did not come about, but some of the poems that she may have meant to include are available in Marandon's *L'Oeuvre Poétique*, along with other poems that Marandon translated into French. Some of these poems clearly belong to the past, but others, written in her final years in Aurillac, develop familiar themes of transience and impermanence in poignantly blind scribbles across the pages and suggest that in her old age, she found some ways in which Christian belief did offer her some relief from her longing for a spiritual life. "Consolation" and "Autumn Twilight," for instance, seem to anticipate "The Blind Woman." "Consolation" in particular offers poignant first-person insight into the terrible suffering of a poet who faces losing her vision completely:

> Poor women, old and blind
> Left all alone,
> What solace shall we find
> To calm an acheing [*sic*] mind?
> What balm so pure and kind
> It stills our moan,
> Though we be old and blind
> And left alone?

In the second, responsive stanza the speaker finds "consolation" in coming to the end of a long life and of feeling in unity with forces stronger than herself:

> A spirit moves in me
> That moves the Sun,
> And sways the tidal sea!
> All rhythmic things that be
> (E'en this poor verse you see)
> Are surely one!
> A spirit moves in me
> That moves the sun.[8]

The humour of the parenthetical aside undercuts the pain of a speaker isolated in an aged body, but it also makes clear that this speaker has found consolation through her gifts as a poet. A third unpublished poem, "All Saints," is clearly a prototype for the longer version she published in *The Return to Nature* as it conflates the seasonal metaphor with the symbolic dimness of twilight to suggest the restricted vision of "a world dissolved in haze," where "nothing is solid, nothing sure," yet "that which must aye endure."[9]

The Petrarchan sonnet "The Lost Child" seems to foreshadow "Mediterranean Noon" of *Images and Meditations* as the speaker imagines that the "Mother" earth "dropt from her arms" the moon, which now hovers like a lost child. Just as the moon is left "dreaming of the warm, close embrace" of mother earth, so the speaker yearns for "the one perfection mirror'd in our mind."[10] It is an awkward metaphor in this prototype but a poignant expression of isolation. In the two quatrains of "The Wild Swan," the poetic voice internalizes the bird's cry as a signal of "an underworld of chaos, storm and change," but the rest of the comparison is undeveloped.[11] On the other hand, in placing ellipses in the title of "A Platonist Despairs ..." Robinson suggests her sustained ambivalence about living life outside the context of religious certainty. In the first two stanzas, the speaker traces a shift in her perspective on beauty from that of a young girl, who thought that beauty on earth was a gift from God, to that of an old woman, who has come to the conclusion that the beauty she sees around her has nothing to do with God. The third and final stanza indicates the paradox of her perspective now, for the beauties of this world are available only as long as one lives:

O Beauty, art thou but a nerve
That quivers in a mortal brain?
The gleam, the glow, the sweep, the curve,
The rapture of delight and pain,
Are these but shadows flung about
Till my poor candle shall go out?[12]

Friends such as Emmanuel Berl would have been surprised at the misery of this speaker, who seems to suffer now, at the end of life, for her life-long devotion to Walter Pater and, implicitly through Pater, for her persistent Platonism. Similarly, in the two short quatrains of "The Mask," the speaker casts her search for faith as a metaphorical mask that makes concrete an object of worship in the first stanza only to lose it to a "wind / that tore it from its place" in the second stanza, "revealing behind / the Void that has no Face."[13] It is impossible to know just when these poems were written, but they are poignant testaments to Robinson's persistent struggle to find some way to situate herself along a meaningful spiritual continuum bookended by birth and death.

The last two unpublished poems deal with poetic expression itself. In "If," the speaker suggests that the broken lute, representing the dead poet, might be heard residually as poetry has the capacity to "repeat / the love, the life, the laughter, / that make our Earth so sweet."[14] A more complex poem titled "Mother-O'-Pearl," with the subtitle "Poetic Creation," conveys the transcendent qualities of poetry with the help of an epigraph from de Vigny that can be translated "Poetry, oh treasure, the pearl of thought." The speaker compares the poet to a pearl alone in a shell that is protective but also isolating, leaving her submersed in something greater than she. Like a pearl in the shell, the poet will eventually "dissolve in the deep"; however, also like a pearl, her poetic creation "shall keep the sum and soul of me."[15] This conceit sums up Robinson's sense that all those years ago Lee's assessment of her was accurate: she was indeed "a born poet." It is interesting that so many of these unpublished poems deal with poetry and the poet, for even though several of them are clearly prototypes for more refined published works, they do attest to the fact that Robinson spent these blind years thinking about the long life of poetry that she had left behind her.

Daniel Halévy includes some of Robinson's unpublished poems written in French in his essay "Les Trois Mary," which is his preface to *Mary Duclaux et Maurice Barrès: Lettres Échangées*.[16] These poems were written, he says, when Robinson was isolated in Aurillac during her final years, and she wrote them for herself rather than for a public audience. Some of these poems are nostalgic, such as the "Ballade de Mes Anciennes Servantes." The women who looked after her in earlier times have disappeared, the speaker says, but they come alive in her poetic memory: Marguerite, an old Bretonne woman, served her a half century ago and is now dead, and Pauline died in the war; Eugenie, with whom she would love to speak has simply disappeared, and Susanne, Marie, Antoinette, "happy women, all three," she hopes "still speak of her now and again."[17] This last poem was found in a notebook with the Latin "Contemplata aliis trader" on the first page, which is the motto of the Dominican order of priests taken from Thomas Aquinas and translated "to give to others the fruit of contemplation." In another poem, "Le Jet D'Eau," the speaker touches on the familiar theme of renewal in nature that makes its way into so much of Robinson's poetry, this time through the beauty of a waterfall whose source is far underground.

As Halévy explains, the visual imagery of poems written between January and October 1943 came from memory, for they preceded her cataract surgery. These are poems of despair by a woman who no longer has the sight on which she depended for reading, for writing, and for taking in the beautiful elements of the natural world that she found so inspiring. Written in English alongside these poems is the exhortation, "So, muse, defend me against the thoughts that kill." Such dark thoughts came to an end with her successful cataract surgery, as a poem written in English that Halévy translates into French, suggests, "Petit psaume de ma deliverance."[18] In this poem, Robinson celebrates the return of her sight and thanks God in whose hand she had placed her "unbelieving hand." He opened the "doors" to admit "Sun, Life, Splendor," she says (36). Perhaps in some way, she managed to find in these final months a measure of comfort in the conventional elements of religious faith that had always eluded her.

Robinson did not have a great deal of time left to enjoy her repaired eyesight and died in the flat in Aurillac 9 February 1944, a few weeks short of her eighty-seventh birthday, thereby ending a life that Marandon describes as characterized by the "three notes" of "endeavor, love, and lonely bereavement."[19] Two final poems written in French indicate that she was prepared for her death, one of them a poignant poem of anticipation and a declaration of love left in her notebook that, as Halévy suggests, could only have been written with James Darmesteter in mind.[20] Fanny Heyman, Pierre Duclaux's daughter, found a second poem in French in a drawer of Robinson's bedside table the night after her death, and I render it here in English:

That I had, that I knew
It seems little to me today
And I love so much this naked tree
Fragrant in June with roses.
Who knows? To die might be better
Than our fugitive fever
Farewell. I dissolve. Farewell
I sink
And I reach the other shore.[21]

Although she would most likely have preferred to be buried with James in Paris, where her name is actually inscribed on Darmesteter's tombstone, the war made this impossible, and she rests now with Émile Duclaux in Aurillac.

Robinson prepared for her death in material ways, writing to Jacques Duclaux about the usufruct, or her access to the Duclaux estate that she had until her death. She had brought to her marriage with Émile about £2,000, made up of earnings and of an inheritance from James. She wanted to ensure that these funds, as well as the house at Olmet, eventually went back to Émile's sons, noting in the letter that she had some modest funds in England, which she had been able to access during the war through Switzerland, as well as an annuity of £200 a year left to her by Emily Sargent for her lifetime only and held at the Bank of Montreal in Place d'Armes, Montreal, Canada. She set out the terms of her will to Jacques, telling him that she planned to leave everything to Mabel; however, should Mabel die first, she would use as a model what Émile did for her, leaving the Duclaux funds in usufruct to Jacques and Pierre for their daughters. In an interesting comment on patriarchal laws, she defends this choice with the explanation that there is not enough money to leave to their sons as well.[22] The *Leamington Spa Courier* for 24 May 1946 reports that Robinson left an estate in England of £5,901.[23]

Tidying up Robinson's affairs just after her death took some strange turns, beginning with a letter from Daniel Halévy 19 June 1944 confirming a conversation he had the previous day.[24] Whether the conversation was with Mabel or with Fanny Heyman, who was ultimately responsible for removing Robinson's books and letters from the apartment, is not clear. However, Halévy is quite desperate in presenting his case that nothing should be destroyed because Robinson left no specific instructions about doing so. He asks that someone be permitted to read everything first and says that his grandson will call Wednesday afternoon to collect the books that have been put aside for him. The Renan books he particularly would like to have, he says, are *Questions Contemporaines; Essais Morale et de critique* and *Marc Aurèle.* He wrote to Fanny Heyman 7 July 1944, again attempting to secure access to Robinson's papers, and this intrusion into the sensitive matter of retaining and destroying letters and other materials is regarded by the family today as unusual and inappropriate.[25]

Because she died during the war in relatively isolated Aurillac, notice of Robinson's death took a few months to get to England, and it was not until 14 April 1944 that an obituary appeared in the *Leamington Spa* and not until 22 April 1944 that Charles Langbridge Morgan's tributary article "Menander's Mirror" appeared in the *Times Literary Supplement.* Morgan, a well-respected novelist and a playwright in both England and France, highlights Robinson's ability to write in both languages, despite, he points out, her friend George Moore's conviction that she negatively affected her career in so doing. Instead, Morgan points to the French critic Louis Gillet's suggestion that Robinson's knowledge and astute assessment of French culture enabled her to speak to French readers about English writers and to English readers about French writers. She retained her British accent during her fifty-six years as an expatriate, speaking French with a pronounced British accent as well. Gillet was particularly impressed, says Morgan, with Robinson's work on Renan, in which she subtly uses the English language to depict Renan with an equanimity that French readers would not have understood. She is "fair" to Renan, whereas French readers tended either to approve or, more commonly, disapprove of Renan. Morgan also comments on Robinson's success as a prose writer, particularly citing the continued relevance of *Emily Brontë* and highlighting Robinson's ability to be "scrupulously fair" as a critic and reviewer for the *Times Literary Supplement* and other journals. Morgan's assessment of Robinson in this article was the last critical assessment of the writer and her work until Sylvaine Marandon completed a doctoral thesis in French on Robinson in 1960. Mabel died in Paris 22 June 1954, but Marandon was able

to speak with Duclaux family members, and she also had Daniel
Halévy's edition of the letters that Robinson exchanged with Maurice
Barrès. In 1967, Marandon turned her dissertation into a critical
study of Robinson as a poet. However, Marandon does not situate
Robinson as influence and she makes no mention of her prose work.

Although she continued to write poetry until her death, Robinson
did not publish poetry after 1927. In February 1937, Monsieur M.A.
Lebonnais asked his audience gathered for the Cercle Français in
Leamington Spa why Robinson's books were so few in the library
of her birthplace and why her name was relatively unknown there.
He pointed out that she had been a respected correspondent for the
Manchester Guardian, the *Times*, and *Times Literary Supplement*, and
he lauded the "easy grace of her style."[26] Marandon suggests that once
James Darmesteter introduced French readers to Robinson with his
translation of *An Italian Garden*, the French took Robinson's poetry
more seriously than English readers, and, in fact, thanks to Enrico
Nencioni and Vernon Lee, she seems to have been more popular
during her lifetime in Italy as well. Of the poets in Miles's anthology,
points out Marandon, Robinson is the only one who seemed in
the 1960s to have been completely forgotten, despite the fact that
Symons, in his entry on Robinson for the Miles edition, claims optimistically, "perhaps no living English poet, after Swinburne, is nearly
so well known [*sic*] abroad."[27] Today, Robinson has reappeared as one
of the "recovered" British women poets of the nineteenth century
who disappeared in a reshaped literary canon in the first half of the
twentieth century. She is represented in all the major anthologies of
Victorian literature and recent anthologies of Victorian women poets.
As I hope this study demonstrates, A. Mary F. Robinson, Mary James
Darmesteter, and Mary Duclaux are identities that signal not only
stages in Robinson's personal life but also stages in her development
as a poet and a prose writer as she became an increasingly important
figure in Anglo-French relations. To say that Robinson wrote prose
for an income and poetry for pleasure does not tell the whole story, for
she succeeded in applying her poetic skills to her prose writing, and
critical responses to Robinson's work in general note the integration
of aestheticism and intellectualism in all of her work.

Robinson's love for France and for the French language seems
never to have waned, and even in the most difficult moments of

her life, she resisted all suggestions that she return to London. She was as at home with Ernest Renan, Maurice Barrès, and Marcel Proust as she was with Oscar Wilde, Henry James, and George Moore. As a poet, she became more sophisticated in expressing the aestheticist view of human life that dominated the fin-de-siècle and characterized the transition from Victorian to modern literature. She was cosmopolitan in her views and committed to achieving intellectual and creative excellence throughout the trajectory of her life. She found happiness through commitment and love in her marriages, first with James Darmesteter and then, albeit in a different form, with Émile Duclaux, and she remained steadfastly loyal to Vernon Lee for the rest of Lee's life after the intense liaison of younger years had settled into a sustainable, mature friendship. She remained very close to her sister from their idyllic and happy childhood through old age.

It is to be hoped that the inner life of Robinson/Darmesteter/Duclaux, as it informs her work, will continue to unfold for critics in the near future. She has left us a legacy through which we might understand a period in our literary history when the world was as complicated as our world seems today. I have had the pleasure and the privilege as a Victorianist to experience a little of that world through the kindness of Jacqueline Bayard-Pierlot, who hosted me in the house at Olmet for several days in June 2016 and who died in that house in February 2021. I worked in what was once Robinson's bedroom and is now a beautiful library, and I stood on the little terrace from which Robinson viewed her "kingdom" for the Cantal articles. I sat in the dining room where Mary Robinson once warmed her feet by the fire, and I was driven up Puy Mary to see the majestic beauty that inspired her work. At the Émile Duclaux Lycée in Aurillac, the common room in which students relax, play quiet games – albeit mainly electronic games today – and read is dedicated to Mary Robinson, the English poetess, complete with pictures and poetry mounted on the walls. Students who do not speak much English know of her and greet her on a daily basis. It is telling that she remains prominent in the place in which she was furthest removed from her roots but where she found deep and abiding happiness, and, of course, it is particularly significant that she is remembered as an English poet.

Notes

✦

Introduction

1 Gosse, "The Ethics of Biography," 144. This article first appeared in *Cosmopolitan* 35 (July 1903): 317–23.

2 Halévy, *Lettres Échangées*, 72. "Toute biographie du genie tourne à l'hagiographie."

3 Morgan, "Menander's Mirror," 195.

4 For a discussion of biography as a framing critical context see Rigg, *Julia Augusta Webster*.

5 Ward, preface to *Baudelaire and the Poetics of Modernity*, ix.

6 O'Connor, "Reading The Biographer's Tale," 387.

7 Hamilton, *Biography*, 2.

8 Loriga, "The Role of the Individual in History," 89.

9 See also the more recent *The Biographical Turn*.

10 Renders, "Biography in Academia," 169.

11 Marandon, *L'Oeuvre Poétique*, 97.

12 Mary Robinson to John Addington Symonds, 4 March 1879, Fonds Anglais 248, ff. 37–40, f. 39. Bibliothèque Nationale de France.

13 Pater, *Studies in the History of the Renaissance*, 211.

14 Hein, "Refining Feminist Theory," 4–5.

15 Vernon Lee to A. Mary F. Robinson, 20 October 1883, Fonds Anglais 245, ff. 93–7, f. 95, Bibliothèque Nationale de France.

16 Beckson, preface to *Aesthetes and Decadents of the 1890s*, xii.

17 Bell-Villada, *Art for Art's Sake*, 3.

18 Harrington, "The Strain of Sympathy," 68.

19 Quoted in Bell-Villada, *Art for Art's Sake*, 70.

20 Thornton, "'Decadence' in Later Nineteenth-Century England," 26.

21 Review of *The Life of Racine, Northern Whig*, 10.

22 Pollock, *Time's Chariot*, 108.

23 Stedman, "Some London Poets," 886.

24 "A. Mary F. Robinson," *The Literary World*, 389.

25 Robinson to Countess Ballestrein, 26 December 1879, Fonds Anglais, 252. ff. 4–5, Bibliothèque Nationale de France.

26 Marandon, *L'Oeuvre Poétique*, 19.

27 Ibid., 19, 20.

28 Robinson to Countess Ballestrein, 26 December 1879, Bibliothèque Nationale de France.

29 Robinson, "Sunset at Kenilworth." A copy of the original, which is dated 5 January 1870, can be found in Fonds Anglais 251, f. 49, Bibliothèque Nationale de France.

30 *Literary World*, 389.

31 Robinson to Countess Ballestrein, 26 December 1879, Bibliothèque Nationale de France.

32 Family Archives of Jacqueline Bayard-Pierlot, Olmet. Bayard-Pierlot, the great-granddaughter of Émile Duclaux, lived in the family home at Olmet near Aurillac, where the family keeps personal papers and photographs of Robinson/Duclaux.

33 Symons, "A. Mary F. Robinson-Darmesteter," www.bartleby.com/293.

34 Mary Robinson to Edmund Gosse, 28 April 1879. Gosse Collection, Brotherton Library.

35 Pollock, *Time's Chariot*, 109.

36 Lynch, "A. Mary F. Robinson," 265.

37 Mary Robinson to John Addington Symonds, 1 January 1879, Fonds Anglais 248, ff. 19–20, f. 20. Bibliothèque Nationale de France.

38 Vernon Lee to Mary Robinson, 26 November 1884, Fonds Anglais 245, ff. 315–21. f. 315. Bibliothèque Nationale de France

39 Marandon, *L'Oeuvre Poétique*, 34.

40 Mary Duclaux to Maurice Barrès, 6 October 1922, in *Lettres Échangées*, 79.

41 Vadillo, "New Woman Poets and the Culture of the *salon*," 27.

42 Mary Robinson to John Addington Symonds, 15 December ny, Fonds Anglais 248, Bibliothèque Nationale de France. The letter is sent from Gower Street and so precedes the family's 1884 move to Earl's Terrace.

43 Diedrick, *Mathilde Blind*, 170.

44 Quoted in Marandon, *L'Oeuvre Poétique*, 26.

45 Robinson (Duclaux), "Souvenirs sur Walter Pater," 339.

46 A copy of this poem can be found in Robinson's letter to Symonds, Fonds Anglais 248 f. 18, Bibliothèque Nationale de France.

47 Prins, "'Lady's Greek' (with the Accents)," 599. See also Prins's more extensive work *Ladies' Greek: Victorian Translations of Tragedy.*

48 Mary Robinson to John Addington Symonds, nd, Fonds Anglais 248, ff. 52–3, f. 53, Bibliothèque Nationale de France.

49 Mary Robinson to John Addington Symonds, 25 February 1879, Fonds Anglais 248, ff. 33–5, f. 33. Bibliothèque Nationale de France.

50 Mary Robinson to John Addington Symonds, 1 December ny, Fonds Anglais 248, ff. 16–17, f. 16. Bibliothèque Nationale de France.

51 Mary Robinson to John Addington Symonds, 4 March 1879, Fonds Anglais 248, ff. 37–40, f. 39. Bibliothèque Nationale de France.

52 John Addington Symonds to Edmund Gosse, 25 November 1878, Ashley Collection 5036 f. 1–2, f. 2, British Library.

53 Grosskurth, *John Addington Symonds,* 223.

54 Ibid., 222; Holmes, "Mary Duclaux," 28.

55 Mary Robinson to Edmund Gosse, 11 April 1884, Gosse Collection, Brotherton Library.

56 Edsal, *Toward Stonewall,* 106.

57 John Addington Symonds to Edmund Gosse, 4 February 1879, in Schueller and Peters, *The Letters of John Addington Symonds,* 583.

58 Mary Robinson to Edmund Gosse, 2 October ny, Gosse Collection, Brotherton Library.

59 The original copy of "A Ballad of Poetesses: To Miss Mary Robinson" is in the Fonds Anglais 251, f. 41–2, Bibliothèque Nationale de France:
    To Miss Mary Robinson
    No fairer names hath time than those
    Of girls who smote the lyre with skill,
    Who dared to climb the cliffs that rose
    Along the steep Parnassian hill,
    Nor paused for rue or daffodil;
    Each shall not lose her godlike share
    Of garlands plucked by Delphi's rill,
    Thin leaves around her silken hair.
    Edmund Gosse (1879)

60 Mary Robinson to Edmund Gosse, 17 March 1880, Gosse Collection, Brotherton Library.

61 Quoted in Berl, *Rachel et autres graces,* 135–6.

62 Colby, *A Literary Biography,* 81.

63 Halévy, "*Les Trois Mary*," 74.

64 Mary Robinson to John Addington Symonds, 9 April 1879, Fonds Anglais 248, ff. 41–4, f. 43, Bibliothèque Nationale de France.

65 This portrait is now in a private collection.

66 Mary Robinson to John Addington Symonds, 25 February 1879, Fonds Anglais 248.ff. 33–5, f. 33, Bibliothèque Nationale de France. She explains in this letter that she and her father had had the conversation about her poetry "a year ago today."

67 Vernon Lee to Matilda Paget, 22 June 1882, in Gagel, *Selected Letters*, Vol. 1, 364.

68 Mary Robinson to John Addington Symonds, 3 February 1880, Fonds Anglais 248, ff. 115–16, f. 115, Bibliothèque Nationale de France.

69 Mary Robinson to John Addington Symonds, 27 December ny, Fonds Anglais 248, f. 15. Bibliothèque Nationale de France. In context of the letter itself, the year is probably 1878.

Chapter One

1 Frederick Macmillan to A. Mary F. Robinson, 28 July 1877, Macmillan Archives, British Library.

2 Lynch, "A. Mary F. Robinson," 262–3.

3 Bright, review of *A Handful of Honeysuckle*, 232.

4 Review of *A Handful of Honeysuckle*, *Saturday Review*, 21.

5 Lang, review of *A Handful of Honeysuckle*, 53.

6 Review of *A Handful of Honeysuckle*, *Spectator*, 1343.

7 Tissot, *Princesses de Lettres*, 311.

8 Marandon, *L'Oeuvre Poétique*, 72.

9 Ibid., 69.

10 Walter Pater to Edmund Gosse, 29 January 1881, Gosse Collection, Brotherton Library.

11 Dante Gabriel Rossetti to A. Mary F. Robinson, 31 May 1878, 78.113.2, Bibliothèque Nationale de France. Thank you to Dr Roger Lewis for sending me this reference.

12 Mary Robinson to Edmund Gosse, 29 January 1881, Gosse Collection, Brotherton Library.

13 Burt and Mikics, *The Art of the Sonnet*, 7.

14 Marandon, *L'Oeuvre Poétique*, 20.

15 Throughout this book, I have cited from the original editions of Robinson's prose and poetry. Since her poetry was published without line numbers, all citations are by page number. The page for this opening sonnet of *A Handful of Honeysuckle* is unnumbered.

16 Lee, introduction to *Belcaro*, 15–16.

17 Ibid., 14.

18 Vernon Lee to A. Mary F. Robinson, 19 November 1880, in *Selected Letters of Vernon Lee*, 270.

19 Vernon Lee, "A Dialogue on Poetic Morality," 706.

20 Vernon Lee, "A Dialogue on Poetic Morality," 232.

21 Ibid., 239.

22 Pater, *Studies in the History of the Renaissance*, 211.

23 Marandon, *L'Oeuvre Poétique*, 85.

24 Review of *A Handful of Honeysuckle*, *Spectator*, 1343.

25 Glaser, "Polymetrical Dissonance," 200.

26 Lang, Review of *A Handful of Honeysuckle*, 53.

27 Review of *A Handful of Honeysuckle*, *Spectator*, 1343.

28 Marandon, *L'Oeuvre Poétique*, 102.

29 For the poem itself, see Margaret Symonds (Vaughan), *Out of the Past* (London: John Murray, 1925), 212 ff.

30 Lynch, "A. Mary F. Robinson," 263.

31 Vadillo, "Immaterial Poetics," 248.

32 Marandon, *L'Oeuvre Poétique*, 135.

33 Bright, review of *A Handful of Honeysuckle*, 232; Lang, review of *A Handful of Honeysuckle*, 53.

34 Marandon, *L'Oeuvre Poétique*, 69.

35 Lang, review of *A Handful of Honeysuckle*, 53.

36 These are titled "The Last Sight of Fiametta" and "Fiammetta Singing." See Jan Marsh, "'The Old Tuscan Rapture,'" 161.

37 Lang, review of *A Handful of Honeysuckle*, 53.

38 Mary Robinson to John Addington Symonds, 1 January 1879, Fonds Anglais 248, ff. 19–22, f.19. Bibliothèque Nationale de France.

39 Mary Robinson to Countess Ballestrein, 26 December 1879, Fonds Anglais 252, ff. 4–5. Bibliothèque Nationale de France.

40 Philip Marston to A. Mary F. Robinson, 31 March 1880, Fonds Anglais 251, ff. 61–4. Bibliothèque Nationale de France.

41 Mary Robinson to Edmund Gosse, 17 March 1880, Gosse Collection, Brotherton Library.

Chapter Two

1 Frances Robinson to George Robinson, 18 October 1880, Fonds Anglais 240, f. 27, Bibliothèque Nationale de France.

2 Colby, *Vernon Lee*, 47.

3 Frances Robinson to George Robinson, 24 October 1880, Fonds Anglais 240, f. 27, Bibliothèque Nationale de France.

4 Mary James Darmesteter to Vernon Lee, nd, nm, 1888, Vernon Lee Collection, Colby College.

5 Vernon Lee to Mary Robinson, 25 January 1881, Fonds Anglais 244, f. 88, Bibliothèque Nationale de France.

6 Vernon Lee to Mary Robinson, 19 February 1881, Fonds Anglais 244, f. 61, Bibliothèque Nationale de France.

7 Vernon Lee to Mary Robinson, 14 August 1881, in Gagel, *Selected Letters*, 344.

8 Colby, *Vernon Lee*, 52.

9 Vernon Lee to Mary Robinson, 10 August 1881, Fonds Anglais 244, f. 181, Bibliothèque Nationale de France.

10 Mary Robinson to Vernon Lee, 8 October 1929, Fonds Anglais 243, f. 99, Bibliothèque Nationale de France.

11 Vernon Lee to Mary Robinson, 21 November 1929, Fonds Anglais, 247, f. 131, Bibliothèque Nationale de France. Given the description, this is most likely Robinson's Carte de Visite.

12 Colby, *Vernon Lee*, 58.

13 Mary Robinson to Emily Sargent, 10 November ny, Vernon Lee Collection, Colby College. Although there is no year associated with the letter, it was sent from Rue Bara in the early days of Robinson's marriage and, therefore, during Lee's collapse.

14 Mary Robinson to Edmund Gosse, 1 July 1881, Gosse Collection, Brotherton Library.

15 Mary Robinson to Marie Herzfeld, nd nm 1895, Herzfeld Collection, MS3152, f. 72. British Library.

16 Mary Robinson to Edmund Gosse, 27 January 1881, Gosse Collection, Brotherton Library.

17 Mary Robinson to Edmund Gosse, 30 April 1881, Gosse Collection, Brotherton Library.

18 "A. Mary F. Robinson," *The Literary World*, 390.

19 Prins, "'Lady's Greek,'" 596.

20 Ibid., 612.

21 Mills, *Euripides: Hippolytus*, 29.

22 Ibid., 26.

23 Symonds, *Studies of the Greek Poets*, 201.

24 Ibid., 205.

25 Mills, *Euripides: Hippolytus*, 33.

26 Sale, *Existentialism and Euripides*, 35.

27 Augusta Webster to John Stuart Blackie, 30 May 1870. Blackie Archives, National Library of Scotland.

28 Lauritsen, foreword to *Oresteia*, 10.

29 Lang, review of *The Crowned Hippolytus of Euripides and new poems*, 8.

30 Carson, introduction to *Grief Lessons*, 163.

31 Prins, "'Lady's Greek,'" 603.

32 Symonds, *Studies of the Greek Poets*, 233, 234.

33 Devereux, *The Character of the Euripidean Hippolytus*, 62.

34 Mary Robinson to John Addington Symonds, 1 January 1879, Fonds Anglais 248, f. 19, Bibliothèque Nationale de France.

35 Mary Robinson to John Addington Symonds, 4 March 1879, Fonds Anglais, 248, f. 39, Bibliothèque Nationale de France.

36 Zeitlin, *Playing the Other*, 252.

37 Tuomy, *A Literal Translation*, 26.

38 Howe, "Hippolytus," 74.

39 Sale, *Existentialism and Euripides*, 135.

40 Tuomy, *A Literal Translation*, 27.

41 Buxton, *Myths and Tragedies in their Ancient Greek Contexts*, 171.

42 Glaser, "Polymetrical Dissonance," 200, 206.

43 Prins, "'Lady's Greek,'" 609.

44 Tuomy, *A Literal Translation*, 33.

45 Arnold, "The Study of Poetry," 176; Rossetti, "Monna Innominata," 58.

46 Mary Robinson to J.A. Symonds, 4 March 1879, Fonds Anglais 248, f. 37. Bibliothèque Nationale de France.

47 Mander, "Pantheism."

48 Gosse, Review of *The Crowned Hippolytus and other poems*, 117.

49 Perkins, *The Suffering Self*, 187.

50 Mary Robinson to John Addington Symonds, Fonds Anglais 248, Bibliothèque Nationale de France.

51 Barr, "Captain Ortis," 551.

52 Gosse, review of *The Crowned Hippolytus*, 117.

53 Glaser, "Polymetrical Dissonance," 210.
54 Mary Robinson to J.A. Symonds, nd. June 1878, Fonds Anglais 248, ff. 11–12, Bibliothèque Nationale de France.
55 Gosse, review of *The Crowned Hippolytus*, 117.
56 Hahn, "Oh for the Wings of a Dove," lyrics by Mary Duclaux (Paris: Heugel, 1904).

Chapter Three

1 Mary Robinson to James Darmesteter, 16 September 1888, Fonds Anglais 249, f. 43, Bibliothèque Nationale de France.
2 Quoted in Gardner, *The Lesbian Imagination*, 168–9.
3 Gardner, *The Lesbian Imagination*, 166.
4 Mary Robinson to Matilda Paget, 27 July 1882, Vernon Lee Collection, Colby College.
5 Vernon Lee to Mary Robinson, 16 October 1882, Fonds Anglais 244, ff. 185–6, Bibliothèque Nationale de France.
6 Mary Robinson to John Addington Symonds, 13 February 1883, Fonds Anglais 248, f. 11, Bibliothèque Nationale de France.
7 Vernon Lee to Robert Browning, 6 November 1882, Browning Collection, Baylor University.
8 Vernon Lee to Mary Robinson, 8 May 1883, Fonds Anglais 245, f. 32, Bibliothèque Nationale de France.
9 Vernon Lee to Mary Robinson, 22 May 1883, Fonds Anglais 245, f. 44. Bibliothèque Nationale de France.
10 Mary Robinson to Edmund Gosse, 28 April 1883, Gosse Collection, Brotherton Library.
11 Gardner, *The Lesbian Imagination*, 171.
12 Cook, review of *Arden*, 633.
13 Saintsbury, review of *Arden*, 326.
14 Gosse, Review of *Arden*, 776.
15 Mary Robinson to Edmund Gosse, 28 April 1883, Gosse Collection, Brotherton Library.
16 Schueller and Peters, *The Letters of John Addington Symonds*, 816–18.
17 Vernon Lee to Mary Robinson, 3 May 1883, Fonds Anglais 245, f. 28, Bibliothèque Nationale de France.
18 Mary Robinson to John Addington Symonds, 2 July 1879, Fonds Anglais 248, f. 61, Bibliothèque Nationale de France.

19 Vernon Lee to Mary Robinson, 22 May 1883, Fonds Anglais 245, f. 44, Bibliothèque Nationale de France.

20 "Literary World," 390.

21 Vernon Lee to Mary Robinson, 20 October 1883, Fonds Anglais 245, f. 95, Bibliothèque Nationale de France.

22 Mary Robinson to Cunningham Graham, 25 September ny, Acc. 11335, no. 83, National Library of Scotland. This letter is signed Mary Duclaux, and Robinson refers to the publication of *Emily Brontë* as occurring twenty-nine years previously, so was probably written in 1912.

23 Quoted in Vine, *Emily Brontë*, 1.

24 Swinburne, review of *Emily Brontë*, 762.

25 Mary Robinson to Swinburne, 15 June 1883, Ashley Collection, ff 34 – 5b British Library.

26 Review of *Emily Brontë*, by A. Mary F. Robinson, *St James's Gazette*, 7.

27 Vernon Lee to Mary Robinson, 3 October 1883, Fonds Anglais 245, f. 74, Bibliothèque Nationale de France.

28 Vernon Lee to Mary Robinson, 22 December 1883, Fonds Anglais 245, f. 136, Bibliothèque Nationale de France.

29 Vernon Lee to Mary Robinson, 12 May 1884, Fonds Anglais 245, f. 230, Bibliothèque Nationale de France.

30 Colby, *Vernon Lee*, 66.

31 Harrington, "The Strain of Sympathy," 85.

32 Watts, review of *The New Arcadia and other Poems*, 141.

33 Vadillo, "New Woman Poets and the Culture of the *salon*," 28.

34 Mary Robinson to Edmund Gosse, 21 May 1884, Gosse Collection, Brotherton Library, Leeds.

35 This copy is available at the University of British Columbia Special Collections, Angeli-Dennis Collection.

36 Schueller and Peters, *The Letters of John Addington Symonds*, 907–8, 910.

37 Vernon Lee to Mary Robinson, 28 October 1883, Fonds Anglais 245, f. 101, Bibliothèque Nationale de France.

38 Vernon Lee to Mary Robinson, 12 May 1884, Fonds Anglais, f. 230, Bibliothèque Nationale de France.

39 Review of *The New Arcadia*, *Spectator*, 19.

40 Glaser, "Polymetrical Dissonance," 199.

41 Ely, "'Not a Song to Sell,'" 101.

42 Harrington, "The Strain of Sympathy," 83.

43 Lee, "A Dialogue on Poetic Morality," 682–707.

44 Ely, "'Not a Song to Sell,'" 102.

45 Mary Robinson to Edmund Gosse, 21 May 1884, Gosse Collection, Brotherton Library.

46 Beeching, review of *The New Arcadia*, 342.

47 Symonds, "Poliziano's Italian Poetry," 180.

48 Watts, review of *The New Arcadia*, 142.

49 Vernon Lee to T.H.S. Escott, 27 August 1883, ADD 58789, British Library.

50 Ker, review of *The New Arcadia*, 308.

51 Schueller and Peters, *The Letters of John Addington Symonds*, 912–14.

52 Ibid., 926–8.

53 Ibid., 938–40.

54 William Watson to Michael Field, 11 November 1884, ADD 46866-67, British Library

55 Schueller and Peters, *The Letters of John Addington Symonds*, 945–6.

56 Symonds, review of *Apollo and Marsyas*, 71.

57 Schueller and Peters, *The Letters of John Addington Symonds*, 948–9.

58 Ibid., 952–3.

59 Vernon Lee to Mary Robinson, 26 November 1884, Fonds Anglais 245, f. 319, Bibliothèque Nationale de France.

60 Mary Robinson to J.A. Symonds, 21 December 1884, Fonds Anglais 248, ff. 141–5. Bibliothèque Nationale de France.

61 Colby, 102.

62 Strackey and Samuels, *Mary Berenson*, 56.

Chapter Four

1 Marandon, *L'Oeuvre Poétique*, 42.

2 Berenson, *Mary Berenson*, 117.

3 Vernon Lee to Mary Robinson, 1 January 1885, Fonds Anglais 246, f. 1, Bibliothèque Nationale de France.

4 Marandon, *L'Oeuvre Poétique*, 75.

5 Mary Ward to Vernon Lee, 17 February 1885, *Colby Library Quarterly* 3, no. 13 (1954): 212–14.

6 Vernon Lee to Robert Browning, 25 April 1886, in *Intimate Glimpses From Browning's Letter File: Selected from Letters in the Baylor University Browning Collection*, assembled by A. Joseph Armstrong Baylor University's Browning Interests, Series Eight, Letter no. 149, 112.

7   Mabel Robinson to Vernon Lee, nd. May 1927, Somerville Library.

8   Mary James Darmesteter to Vernon Lee, nd. nm. 1888, Vernon Lee Collection, Colby College.

9   See Darmesteter, "Preface du Traducteur," ii–iii. "L'auteur est idéaliste, c'est-à-dire que le monde, tel qu'il se réfléchit dans son imagination, n'est que le signe de l'âme, l'âme du poète même, ou une âme suprême ... c'est union étroite des deux dons le plus rarement unis: la lucidité de la pensée dans l'intensité du rêve."

10 Augusta Webster, review of *An Italian Garden*, 517.

11 Review of *Strambotti a Sonetti dell'Altissimo*, 265.

12 Lynch, "A. Mary F. Robinson," 276.

13 Nencioni, "Poeti inglesi moderni," 605–20.

14 Vadillo, "Cosmopolitan Aestheticism," 164.

15   Canzonetta, che passi monti e valli,
        Se trovi l'amor illio, dille che vanga,
        E dilla. Son vinasta iu questi paggi
        Come rimaue la smarrito agnella.

16 Chesnutt, review of *An Italian Garden,* 204–5.

17 Berl, *Rachel et autres graces*, 135.

18 Marandon, *L'Oeuvre Poétique*, 104.

19 Mary Robinson to John Addington Symonds, 17 January 1886, Fonds Anglais 248, f. 137. Bibliothèque Nationale de France.

20 John Addington Symonds to Mary Robinson, Fonds Anglais 248, f. 133. Bibliothèque Nationale de France. The letter is undated, but it is the letter to which Robinson responds on 17 January 1886 to describe the circumstances in which she wrote the sequence.

21 Thank you to my colleague Dr Anna Migliarisi, who kindly translated this rispetto for me from the original Italian.

22 In 1903, "Love Without Wings" was published as a musical score by B. Reynaldo Hahn under the title "I know you love me not." See British Library Music Collections. Tyson MS 24 B, ff. 27-30.

23 This copy is available at The University of British Columbia Special Collections, Angeli-Dennis Collection.

24 McGowan, translator, "The Harmony of Evening," by Charles Baudelaire, 97.

25 Marandon, *L'Oeuvre Poétique*, 88.

26 Review of *An Italian Garden*, 23.

27 Pater, *The Renaissance*, 189.

28 Review of *The End of the Middle Ages, The Cambridge Review*, 214.

29 Review of *The End of the Middle Ages, Spectator*, 24.

30 Review of *The End of the Middle Ages, Cambridge Review*, 214.

31 Review of *The End of the Middle Ages, The Art Journal*, 96.

32 Frances Robinson to Mabel Robinson, 16 June 1888, Fonds Anglais 241, f. 18, Bibliothèque Nationale de France.

33 Robinson, "The Novelists of Naples," 685, 686.

34 Mary Robinson to Vernon Lee, 13 March 1887, Fonds Anglais 243, f. 2, Bibliothèque Nationale de France.

35 Eugene Lee-Hamilton to Mary Robinson, 16 December 1883, Fonds Anglais 251, f. 45, Bibliothèque Nationale de France.

36 These records are in the Vernon Lee collection at Colby College.

37 Mary Robinson to Edmund Gosse, 9 February 1887, Gosse Collection, Brotherton Library.

38 Vernon Lee to Mary Robinson, 12 April 1887, Fonds Anglais 246, f. 320. Bibliothèque Nationale de France.

39 Vernon Lee to Mary Robinson, 25 April 1887, Fonds Anglais 246, f. 325. Bibliothèque Nationale de France.

40 Vernon Lee to Matilda Paget, 24 June 1887, Vernon Lee Collection, Colby College.

41 Vernon Lee to Matilda Paget, 2 July 1887 and 8 July 1887, Vernon Lee Collection, Colby College.

42 Vernon Lee to Matilda Paget, 24 July 1887 and 25 August 1887, Vernon Lee Collection, Colby College.

43 Maltz, *British Aestheticism and the Urban Working Classes*, 224.

44 Pollock, "Mary Duclaux," 204.

45 Vernon Lee to Matilda Paget, 30 August 1887, Vernon Lee Collection, Colby College.

46 Vernon Lee to Matilda Paget, 14 September 1887, Vernon Lee Collection, Colby College.

47 Gardner, *The Lesbian Imagination*, 181.

48 Arthur Symons to James Dykes Campbell, 31 July 1887, ADD 49522 Dykes Campbell Papers Vol 1, British Library.

49 Mary Robinson to William Michael Rossetti, 13 June 1888, Angeli-Dennis Collection, University of British Columbia.

50 Vernon Lee to Matilda Paget, 2 September 1887, Vernon Lee Collection, Colby College.

51 Vernon Lee to Matilda Paget, 24 September 1887, Vernon Lee
    Collection, Colby College.

52 Vernon Lee to Matilda Paget, 29 September 1887, Vernon Lee
    Collection, Colby College.

53 Mary Robinson to James Darmesteter, 1 September 1887, Fonds
    Anglais 249, f. 4, Bibliothèque Nationale de France.

54 Mary Robinson to James Darmesteter, 2 September 1887, Fonds
    Anglais, 249, f. 6, Bibliothèque Nationale de France.

55 Mary Robinson to James Darmesteter, 3 September 1887, Fonds
    Anglais 249, ff. 10 – 12, Bibliothèque Nationale de France.

56 Mary Robinson to James Darmesteter, 13 September 1887, f 15;
    16 September 1887, Fonds Anglais 249, f. 20, Bibliothèque Nationale
    de France.

57 Mary Robinson to James Darmesteter, 4 October 1887, Fonds Anglais
    249, f. 30, Bibliothèque Nationale de France.

58 Mary Robinson to James Darmesteter, 4 January 1888 Fonds Anglais
    249, f. 38, Bibliothèque Nationale de France.

59 Mary Robinson to James Darmesteter, 13 September 1887, Fonds
    Anglais 249, f. 16. Bibliothèque Nationale de France.

60 Frances Robinson to Mabel Robinson, 6 June 1888, Fonds Anglais 241,
    f. 9, Bibliothèque Nationale de France.

61 Mary Robinson to James Darmesteter, nd. June 1888, Fonds Anglais
    249, f. 43, Bibliothèque Nationale de France.

62 Mary Robinson to James Darmesteter, 24 June 1888, Fonds Anglais 249,
    f. 48, Bibliothèque Nationale de France.

63 Mary Robinson to Eugene Lee-Hamilton, 15 June 1888, Vernon Lee
    Collection, Colby College.

64 Mary Robinson to Eugene Lee-Hamilton, 4 August 1888, Vernon Lee
    Collection, Colby College.

65 Mary Robinson to Vernon Lee, nd. nm. 1888, Vernon Lee Collection,
    Colby College.

66 Colby, *A Literary Biography*, 123.

67 Gardner, *The Lesbian Imagination*, 200–1.

68 Marie Spartali Stillman to Vernon Lee, 30 September 1890, Vernon Lee
    Collection, Colby College.

69 Quoted in Gardner, *The Lesbian Imagination*, 202.

70 Darmesteter, *Poèsies*, 111.

71 Mary Robinson to James Darmesteter, 17 September 1887, Fonds Anglais, 249, f. 28, Bibliothèque Nationale de France.

72 Rossetti, "Later Life," in *A Pageant and other poems*, 157.

73 Hughes, *The Cambridge Introduction to Victorian Poetry*, 37.

74 Ledbetter, *British Victorian Women's Periodicals*, 141–3.

75 Wilson, review of *Songs, Ballads, and a Garden Play*, *Athenaeum*, 181.

76 Darmesteter, *Poèsies*, iii.

77 Review of *Songs, Ballads, and a Garden Play*, *Spectator*, 16.

78 Review of *The End of the Middle Ages*, *Spectator*, 23.

Chapter Five

1 Mary Robinson to Emily Sargent, nd. nm. 1888, Vernon Lee Collection Colby College Library.

2 Demoor, "Mabel Robinson," http://www.oxforddnb.com/index/101060276/Mabel-Robinson.

3 "Mabel Robinson," *Islington Times*, 11 June 1889, 6.

4 Lhombreaud, *Arthur Symons*, 66.

5 Mary Robinson to William Michael Rossetti, 26 November 1889, Angeli-Dennis Collection, University of British Columbia.

6 Mary Robinson to William Michael Rossetti, 8 October 1893, Angeli-Dennis Collection, University of British Columbia.

7 Mary Robinson to Vernon Lee, nd. nm. 1889, Fonds Anglais 243 f. 8, Bibliothèque Nationale de France.

8 Frances Robinson to Mabel Robinson, 23 May 1891, Fonds Anglais 241, f. 49; 10 March 1892, f. 56. Bibliothèque Nationale de France.

9 Mary Robinson to Vernon Lee, 9 December 1892, Fonds Anglais 243, f. 25. Bibliothèque Nationale de France.

10 Review of *Lyrics Selected from the Works*, *The Critic*, 222.

11 George Robinson to Mary Robinson, 11 May 1892, Fonds Anglais 240, f. 175. Bibliothèque Nationale de France.

12 Thompson, *Travel Writing*, 99.

13 Lynch, "A. Mary F. Robinson," 268.

14 Review of *Marguerites du temps passé*, *Revue bleue*, 767.

15 Review of *Marguerites du temps passé*, *Spectator*, 33.

16 Marzials, review of *Marguerites du temps passé*, 368.

17 Mary Robinson to George Robinson, 5 November 1890, Fonds Anglais 240, f. 234. Bibliothèque Nationale de France.

18 See *The Renaissance Diaries of Marin Sanudo*, edited by Patricia H. Labalme and Laura Sanguineti White, translated by Linda Carroll (Baltimore: Johns Hopkins University Press, 2007).

19 This copy inscribed to Lee 13 May 1893 is noted in *Bookman's* Catalogue Volume 1.

20 Review of *Retrospect and other poems*, *The Saturday Review*, 246.

21 Review of *Retrospect and other poems*, *The Dial*, 267; Review of *Retrospect and other poems*, *The Bookman*, 118.

22 Watson, Review of *Retrospect and other poems*, *The Academy*, 179–80.

23 Vadillo, "'Gay Strangers,'" http://cve.revues.org/856.

24 Mary Robinson to John Addington Symonds, 4 March 1879, Fonds Anglais 248, f. 37.

25 Mary Robinson to Eugene Lee-Hamilton, 4 August 1888, Vernon Lee Collection, Colby College.

26 Darmesteter, "Ernest Renan," 433.

27 Darmesteter, introduction to *The Zend Avesta*, Part 1, iv.

28 Mary Robinson to Vernon Lee, nd. Fonds Anglais 243, f. 28, Bibliothèque Nationale de France.

29 Review of *Retrospect*, *The Bookman*, 118.

30 Mary Robinson to Vernon Lee, 24 December 1893, Fonds Anglais 243, f. 33. Bibliothèque Nationale de France.

31 Mary Robinson to Edmund Gosse, 25 October 1893, Brotherton Library, Leeds.

32 Tait, review of *Les Grands Écrivains français. Froissart*, *The English Historical Review*, 608.

33 Mary Robinson to Vernon Lee, 26 February 1894, Fonds Anglais 243, f. 40. Bibliothèque Nationale de France.

34 Frances Robinson to Mabel Robinson, nd, July 1894, Fonds Anglais 241, f. 109. Bibliothèque Nationale de France.

35 Frances Robinson to Mabel Robinson, 23 October 1894, Fonds Anglais, 241, f. 120. Bibliothèque Nationale de France.

36 Mary James Darmesteter to Madam M. Herzfeld, nd. nm. 1895, Herzfeld Collection, Egerton MS 3152, ff. 72–5. British Library.

37 Halévy, *Lettres Echangées*. Robinson writes, "Je ne me suis jamais consolée de la perte de James Darmesteter. Il est mort avant l'âge, sans avoir donné sa mesure."

38 "James Darmesteter," *Revue de Paris*, 804–18; *Cosmopolis*, 393–9; "Preface" to *Critique et Politique*, by James Darmesteter, 1–8.

39 Paris, "James Darmesteter," 104.

40 "Preface" to *English Studies*, by James Darmesteter; *Cosmopolis*, 393.

41 Mary Robinson to William Michael Rossetti, 13 December 1895, Angeli-Dennis Collection, University of British Columbia.

42 Mary Robinson to William Michael Rossetti, 4 April 1896, Angeli-Dennis Collection, University of British Columbia.

43 "Dante Gabriel Rossetti," *La Revue de Paris*, 1 June 1896, 581.

44 Mary Duclaux to William Michael Rossetti, 20 June 1901, Angeli-Dennis Collection, University of British Columbia.

45 Mary Duclaux, "Ferdinand Brunetière," 257.

46 Duclert, *Portraits Intellectuels (V)* "Mary Robinson Darmesteter et Émile Duclaux," 77.

47 Mary Darmesteter, "Monsieur Renan: A Pastel," 159.

48 Jastrow, "Introductory Memoir," v–xv.

49 James Darmesteter, "Renan," *The New World*, 433.

50 Mary James Darmesteter, "James Darmesteter in England," 395.

51 Morgan, "Menander's Mirror," 195.

52 Mary Robinson to Frances Robinson, 2 June 1900 and 10 June 1900, Family Archives of Jacqueline Bayard-Pierlot, Olmet.

53 Mary Robinson to Frances Robinson, 2 June 1900, Family Archives of Jacqueline Bayard-Pierlot, Olmet.

54 Duff, *Ernest Renan*, 24. "One thing is necessary, and Mary has made the best choice."

55 Mary Robinson to William Michael Rossetti, 26 December 1898. Angeli-Dennis Collection, University of British Columbia.

56 Mary Robinson to Frances Robinson, 17 May 1900. Family Archives of Jacqueline Bayard-Pierlot, Olmet.

Chapter Six

1 Duclert, *Portraits Intellectuels*, 85.

2 Mary Robinson to Frances Robinson, 17 May 1900 and 27 May 1900, Family Archives of Jacqueline Bayard-Pierlot, Olmet.

3 Mary Robinson to Frances Robinson, 22 June 1900, Family Archives of Jacqueline Bayard-Pierlot, Olmet.

4 Mary Robinson to Frances Robinson, 17 June 1900, Family Archives of Jacqueline Bayard-Pierlot, Olmet.

5 Émile Duclaux to Pierre Duclaux, in Duclert, *Portraits Intellectuels*, 83.

6   Mary Robinson to Frances Robinson, 1 July 1900, Family Archives of Jacqueline Bayard-Pierlot, Olmet.

7   Mary Robinson to William Michael Rossetti, 25 October 1900, Angeli-Dennis Collection, University of British Columbia.

8   Mary Robinson to Edmund Gosse, 29 November 1900, Gosse Collection, Brotherton Library, Leeds.

9   Mary Robinson to Frances Robinson, nd, May 1901, Family Archives of Jacqueline Bayard-Pierlot, Olmet.

10 Tissot, *Princesses de Lettres*, 311.

11 Frances Robinson to Mary Robinson, 19 February 1903, Family Archives of Jacqueline Bayard-Pierlot, Olmet.

12 Family Archives of Jacqueline Bayard-Pierlot, Olmet. Indeed, when one stands on the terrace, there is no possibility of seeing everything recorded in Robinson's Olmet articles.

13 Gunn, *Vernon Lee*, 169.

14 This essay originally appeared in Lee's 1908 *The Sentimental Traveler: Notes on Places*.

15 Lacouture, *Jules Breton*, 188–9.

16 Thursfield, review of *The Fields of France*, *Times Literary Supplement*, 360.

17 Altrincham, review of *The Return to Nature*, *Times Literary Supplement*, 258.

18 Marandon, *L'Oeuvre Poétique*, 93.

19 Thompson, review of *The Return to Nature*, *Academy*. This review is cited in Marandon, 154n4.

20 Many thanks to my colleague Vernon Provençal, professor in History and Classics at Acadia University, for this translation.

21 Groth, *Victorian Photography and Literary Nostalgia*, 214.

22 Robinson offers a graceful translation in *The French Procession*, 245: "Ebbing and flowing, yet ever progressing, the tides of Life creep up the sands of time,"

23 Duclert, *Portraits Intellectuels*, 87.

24 Vernon Lee to Edmund Gosse, 29 March 1908, Gosse Collection, Brotherton Library.

25 Laure Briot to Mary Duclaux, 29 February 1908, Family Archives of Jacqueline Bayard-Pierlot, Olmet.

26 Mary Robinson to Vernon Lee, nd, nm, 1908, Somerville College Library, Oxford.

27 Bailey, review of *The French Possession*, *Times Literary Supplement*, 352.

28 Review of *The French Procession*, *The Common Cause*, 453.

29 Tissot, *Princesses de Lettres*, 273.

30 Review of *The French Procession*, *Boston Evening Transcript*, 7.

31 McGowan, trans. "The Abyss" in *The Flowers of Evil*, 345.

32 Seccombe, review of *The French Ideal*, *Times Literary Supplement*, 337–8; Review of *The French Ideal*, *The North American Review*, 569.

33 Berl, *Rachel et autres graces*, 133.

34 Ibid., 142.

35 Ibid., 154.

36 Pollock, *Time's Chariot*, 115.

37 Ibid., 145–6.

38 Berl, *Rachel et autres graces*, 134.

39 Berenson, *Mary Berenson*, 422.

Chapter Seven

1 Peacock, *The Works of Marie Lenéru*, 24.

2 Lenéru *Journal*, 259.

3 Ibid., 271.

4 Mary Duclaux, review of *Les Affranches*, *Times Literary Supplement*, 183.

5 Peacock, *The Works of Marie Lenéru*, 23.

6 Mary Duclaux, Preface to *La Maison sur le Roc*, by Marie Lenéru, ii.

7 Beach, *Staging Politics and Gender*, 110.

8 Peacock, *The Works of Marie Lenéru*, 23.

9 Lavaud, *Marie Lenéru*, 61, 63.

10 Lenéru, *Journal*, 261.

11 Halévy, *Lettres Echangées*, 52–3.

12 Pollock, *Time's Chariot*, 108.

13 Berl, *Rachel et autres graces*, 144.

14 Ibid., 147–8.

15 Cenni et al, *Violet del Palmerino*, 2014. These are the proceedings of a conference held at Lee's former home, Palmerino, in 2012. Berthe Noufflard's daughter, Geneviève Noufflard, now deceased, attended the conference.

16 Mary Robinson to Vernon Lee, 30 June 1927, Fonds Anglais, 243, f. 83. Bibliothèque Nationale de France.

17 Pollock, *Time's Chariot*, 111. Pollock relies heavily on Robinson's account in "The Background of a Victory."

18 Pollock, "Mary Duclaux," 204.

19 Mary Robinson to Daniel Halévy, *Lettres Echangées*, 79.

20 Marandon, *L'Oeuvre Poétique*, 99.

21 Thank you to Professor Bonnie Rigg at the University of Miami for helping me to sort out the provenance of the painting.

22 Thomas Hardy to Mary Duclaux, 18 March 1923. Thank you to Dr Sophie Geoffrey for sending me this letter from the private notes of Berthe Noufflard.

23 Deschanel, "L'Empire Britannique et La France," 97–101.

24 Hazen, review of *A Short History of France, The American Historical Review*, 661.

25 Halévy, review of *A Short History of France, Anglo-French Review*, 172.

26 Mary Robinson to Pierre Duclaux, 12 December 1927, Family Archives of Jacqueline Bayard-Pierlot, Olmet.

27 Mary Robinson to Edmund Gosse, 2 March ny, Gosse Collection, Brotherton Library, Leeds.

28 Mary Robinson to Vernon Lee, 22 December 1921, Fonds Anglais 243, Bibliothèque Nationale de France.

29 See Cenni, *Violet del Palmerino*.

30 Vernon Lee, "In Time of War," 241.

31 Mabel Robinson to Vernon Lee, 12 April 1922, Somerville College Library, Oxford.

32 Mary Robinson to Vernon Lee, 4 May 1922, Fonds Anglais, 243, ff. 48–9, Bibliothèque Nationale de France.

33 Mary Robinson to Vernon Lee, 10 October 1922, Fonds Anglais 243, ff. 50–1. Bibliothèque Nationale de France.

34 Mary Robinson to Maurice Barrès, 22 August 1922, in Halévy, *Lettres Échangées*, 74.

35 Jacques's daughter, Françoise, was the mother of Jacqueline Bayard-Pierlot.

36 Mary Robinson to Vernon Lee, 17 December 1923, Fonds Anglais 243, f. 27. Bibliothèque Nationale de France.

37 Mary Robinson to Maurice Barrès, 19 January 1923, in *Lettres Échangées*, Halévy, 52–3.

38 Mary Robinson to Vernon Lee, 24 January 1924, Vernon Lee Collection, Colby College Library.

39 Mary Robinson to Vernon Lee, 27 December 1924, Fonds Anglais 243, ff. 45–8, Bibliothèque Nationale de France. Whether the 1884 illness was smallpox, typhoid, or something less threatening is not clear.

40 Noufflard's portrait of Vernon Lee at about the same time is extant, but there is no record of Noufflard's portrait of Robinson. There is a portrait by Noufflard identified as Mabel in the Family Archives of Jacqueline Bayard-Pierlot, Olmet.

41 Mary Robinson to Vernon Lee, 10 February 1923, Vernon Lee Collection, Colby College Library.

42 Mary Robinson to Vernon Lee, 10 July 1925, Fonds Anglais 243, f. 68. Bibliothèque Nationale de France.

43 Bates, review of *The Life of Racine, Saturday Review of Books*, 739.

44 Falls, review of *The Life of Racine, Times Literary Supplement*, 734.

45 Review of *The Life of Racine, Spectator*, 21.

46 Morgan, "Menander's Mirror," 195.

47 Review of *The Life of Racine, Northern Whig*, 10.

48 Review of *The Life of Racine, The Bookman*, 494.

49 Gagel, *Selected Letters of Vernon Lee*, 389.

50 Mary Robinson to Mabel Robinson, 6 September ny. Fonds Anglais 240, f. 282, Bibliothèque Nationale de France.

51 Mary Robinson to Vernon Lee, 11 June 1923, Somerville College Library.

52 Mary Robinson to Vernon Lee, 17 March ny, Fonds Anglais 243, f. 70. Bibliothèque Nationale de France. Given its placement in this string of manuscript letters, this letter was probably written in 1926.

53 Vernon Lee to A. Mary F. Robinson, 8 July 1926, Fonds Anglais 247, ff. 40–2. Bibliothèque Nationale de France.

54 Mary Robinson to Vernon Lee, 27 February 1927, Fonds Anglais 243, f. 73, Bibliothèque Nationale de France.

55 Smith, *The Gender of History*, 162.

56 Augusta Webster to John Stuart Blackie, 30 May 1870. Blackie Archives, National Library of Scotland.

57 This copy is held in the Vernon Lee Collection, British Institute, Florence.

58 McDowall, review of *Portrait of Pascal, Times Literary Supplement*, 123.

59 Benn, review of *Portrait of Pascal, Spectator*, 32.

60 Baudelaire: "Je ne vois qu'infini par toutes les fenetres." Pascal: Pour fair d'un homme un saint, il faut bien que ce soit la grace; et qui en doute ne sait ce que c'est que saint, et qu'homme.

61 Mary Robinson to Vernon Lee, Easter 1929, Somerville College Library.

62 Mary Robinson to Vernon Lee, 8 October 1929, Fonds Anglais 243, f. 99. Bibliothèque Nationale de France.

63 Vernon Lee to A. Mary F. Robinson, 21 November 1929, Fonds Anglais, f. 131, Bibliothèque Nationale de France.

64 Mary Robinson to Vernon Lee, 14 May 1927, Fonds Anglais, 243, f 122, Bibliothèque Nationale de France.

65 A comprehensive list of Robinson's contributions to the *Times Literary Supplement* appears in the bibliography of this book.

66 George Moore to C.S. Evans, 13 July 1931, Fonds Anglais 250, f. 33. Bibliothèque Nationale de France; C.S. Evans to George Moore, 15 July 1931, Fonds Anglais 250, f.32, Bibliothèque Nationale de France.

67 George Moore to A. Mary F. Robinson, 17 July 1931, Fonds Anglais 250, ff. 30–1, Bibliothèque Nationale de France.

68 Marandon, *L'Oeuvre Poétique*, 26.

69 Mary Robinson to Vernon Lee, 28 July 1931, Somerville College Library.

Conclusion

1 Mary Robinson to Irene Cooper Willis, 18 February 1935, Colby College Library.

2 Mary Robinson to Irene Cooper Willis, 10 April 1935, Colby College Library.

3 Mary Robinson to Irene Cooper Willis, 3 June 1935, Colby College Library.

4 Mary Robinson to Irene Cooper Willis, 23 June 1937, Colby College Library.

5 Schuhl, "Carnet de Notes: Mary Robinson (1857–1944)," 377.

6 Bayard-Pierlot. *Mary Duclaux*, 26, 27.

7 Marandon, *L'Oeuvre Poétique*, 64.

8 Quoted in Marandon, *L'Oeuvre Poétique*, 349.

9 Ibid., 350.

10 Ibid., 340.

11 Ibid.

12 Ibid., 344.

13 Ibid., 346.

14 Ibid.

15 Ibid., 342.

16 Halévy, "Trois Marys," in *Lettres Échangeés*, 31–6.

17 Ibid., 32. Robinson wrote this poem in English and Halévy translated it into French.

18 Halévy, "Trois Marys," 36.

19 Marandon, *L'Oeuvre Poétique*, 18.

20   Languissante pour mon ami
    (Je sais son nom, je ne le dis pas)
    Je languis jusqu'à l'aube
    Il ne venait pas.

    Il vint dans la nuit,
    Joie immense, éternelle!
    Il éteignit sa lumière,
    Franchit le seuil.

    Nul salut ne donna,
    Nul baiser ni caresse;
    Un unique mot muet,
    Plus exquis, plus grave.

    Et l'amour brisant
    Les voiles de la presence,
    But comme rosée
    Mon essence vitale.

    Je ne vis son visage
    Ni trace de son passage,
    Par la grâce de Dieu
    J'espère le retrouver.

    Je vis pour mon ami,
    Ma vue ne le peut voir.
    Monde sans fin,
    Un Coeur le peut tenir. (Halévy, "Trois Marys," 21–2)

21 Thank you to Jacqueline Bayard-Pierlot for the original poem written in French:

> Ce que j'ai eu, ce que j'ai su
> Me semble aujourd'hui peu de choses
> Et j'aime autant cet arbre nu
> Que juin tout odorant de roses.
> Qui sait ? Mourir peut valoir mieux
> Que notre fièvre fugitive
> Adieu. Je me dissous. Adieu
> Je sombre
> Et j'atteins l'autre rive. (*Mary Duclaux* 127)

22 Mary Duclaux to Jacques Duclaux, 27 January 1944, Family Archives of Jacqueline Pierlot- Bayard, Olmet.

23 Probate records list the precise amount as £5901 18s 6p, retrieved 9 May 1946 by Mabel's lawyer, Keith Sydney Thompson.

24 This correspondence is held in the Family Archives of Jacqueline Bayard-Pierlot, Olmet.

25 Jacqueline Bayard-Pierlot pointed out to me in September 2017 that it was outrageous that Fanny rather than Mabel, who was in good health, undertook such an important matter as to give away volumes to friends and decide to destroy letters.

26 "A Famous Leamington Poetess and Critic," *Leamington Spa Courier*, 4.

27 Quoted in Marandon, *L'Oeuvre Poétique*, 169.

Bibliography

Primary Sources

LITERARY WORKS: BOOKS

A Handful of Honeysuckle. London: Kegan Paul, 1878.

The Crowned Hippolytus of Euripides and New Poems. London: Kegan Paul, 1882.

Arden. London: Longman's, Green, 1883.

The New Arcadia, & other Poems. London: Ellis and White, 1884.

An Italian Garden: A Book of Songs. London: Fisher Unwin, 1886.

Songs, Ballads, and a Garden Play. London: Fisher Unwin, 1888.

Lyrics Selected from the Works of A. Mary F. Robinson. London: Fisher Unwin, 1891.

Retrospect, & other Poems. London, Fisher Unwin, 1893.

Collected Poems, Lyrical and Narrative of A. Mary F. Robinson. London: T. Fisher Unwin, 1901.

The Return to Nature: Songs and Symbols. London: Chapman and Hall, 1904.

Images & Meditations. London: Fisher Unwin, 1923.

HISTORY AND BIOGRAPHY: BOOKS

The Life of Emily Bronte. London: W.H. Allen, 1883.

Margaret of Angoulême, Queen of Navarre. London: W.H. Allen, 1886.

The End of the Middle Ages; Essays & Questions in History. London: Fisher Unwin, 1889.

Marguerites du Temps Passé. Paris: Armand Colin, 1892.

Froissart. Paris: Hachette, 1894.

La Vie de Ernest Renan. Paris: Calmann-Lévy, 1898.

Grands Écrivains d'Outre-Manche. Paris: Calmann-Lévy, 1901.

The Fields of France. London: Chapman and Hall, 1903; with illustrations
  by W.B. Macdougall. London: Chapman and Hall, 1905.

La Vie de Émile Duclaux. Laval: L. Barnéoud, 1906.

The French Procession. London: Fisher Unwin, 1909.

The French Ideal. London: Chapman and Hall, 1911.

A Short History of France from Caesar's Invasion to the Battle of Waterloo.
  London: Fisher Unwin, 1918.

Twentieth Century French Writers. London: W. Collins and Son, 1919.

Victor Hugo. London: Constable, 1921.

Life of Racine. London: Fisher Unwin, 1925.

Victor Hugo. Paris: Plon-Nourrit et Cie, 1925.

Portrait of Pascal. London: T. Fisher Unwin, 1927.

BOOK CHAPTERS AND JOURNAL CONTRIBUTIONS

"Tennyson." *Unsere Zeit* (1879): 81–93.

"Robert Browning." *Unsere Zeit* (1879): 499–526.

"Dante Gabriel Rossetti." *Unsere Zeit* (1879): 767–78.

"Michael Drayton." *University Magazine* (July 1879): 56–65.

"An Address to the Nightingale." *University Magazine* (November
  1879): 539.

"The Sickness of Phaedra." *University Magazine* (December 1879):
  716–19.

"Mrs Barbauld." *The English Poets*. Edited by T. Humphrey Ward. Vol. 3.
  London: Macmillan, 1880, 576–7.

"Joanna Baillie." *The English Poets*. Edited by T. Humphrey Ward. Vol. 4.
  London: Macmillan 1880, 222–3.

"Felicia Hemans." *The English Poets*. Edited by T. Humphrey Ward.
  Vol. 4. London: Macmillan 1880, 334–5.

"Mary Schonewald: A Study in Prophecy." *Fraser's Magazine* 24
  (September 1881): 358–84.

"Dante Gabriel Rossetti." *Harper's New Monthly Magazine* 65 (1882):
  691–701.

"The Art of Seeing." *The Magazine of Art* 6 (1882): 462–4.

"Goneril." *Fraser's Magazine* 106 (July 1882): 85–98.

"The Malatestas of Rimini." *The English Illustrated Magazine* (November
  1884): 98–109.

"The Beguines and the Weaving Brothers: a study in Medieval Mysticism." *Time: Monthly Magazine of Current Topics Literature and Art* 1 (1885): 177–87.

"The Convent of Helfta." *Fortnightly Review* 40 (1886): 641–58.

"The Novelists of Naples." *National Review* (July 1886): 683–97.

"Valentine Visconti." *Fortnightly Review* 47 (1887): 407–20, 573–86.

"The Flight of Piero de Medici." *Fortnightly Review* 48 (1887): 545–58.

"Vincent Harding." *The Witching Time: Tales for the Year's End*. Edited by Henry Norman. New York: Appleton, 1887, 228–73.

"M. Arsène Darmesteter." *Athenaeum*, 24 November 1888, 699–700.

"Captain Antonio Rincon." *Macmillan's Magazine* 60 (September 1889): 371–80.

"The Three Kings." *Contemporary Review* 56 (December 1889): 848–58.

"The French in Italy and Their Imperial Project." *Quarterly Review* 170 (1890): 443–75.

"The Workmen of Paris in 1390 and in 1890." *Fortnightly Review* 54 (1890): 82–106.

"Rural Life in France in the Fourteenth Century." *Fortnightly Review* 54 (1890): 737–52, 865–77.

"The Ballads of the Dauphine." *Revue bleue* 19, no. 47 (9 May 1891): 587–94.

"Private Life in France in the Fourteenth Century." *Fortnightly Review* 55 (May 1891): 751–61; (August 1891): 244–58; (March 1892): 369–89.

"Monsieur Renan: A Pastel." *The Albemarle* (May 1892): 159–62.

"Impressions of Provence." *Contemporary Review* 62 (November 1892): 647–62.

"The Medieval Country-House." *Contemporary Review* 84 (January 1893): 84–107.

"Spring in the Woods of Valois." *Contemporary Review* 64 (August 1893): 198–211.

"Á La Cour de Gaston Phébus." *Revue de Paris*, 15 March 1894, 109–38.

"James Darmesteter." *Revue de Paris*, 15 November 1894, 804–18.

"Anima Poetae: Pensées Intimes de Samuel Taylor Coleridge." *Revue de Paris*, 1 November 1895, 180–4.

"James Darmesteter in England." *Cosmopolis* 2 (February 1896): 393–9.

"Dante Gabriel Rossetti." *Revue de Paris*, 1 June 1896, 550–82.

"Les Paroles de Lao-Tsé." *Revue de Paris*, 15 September 1896, 350–7.

"John Everett Millais." *Gazette des Beaux-Arts* 17 (1897): 89–104.

"Ernest Renan: Dernières Années." *Revue de Paris*, 15 May 1898, 341–55.

"Bodley's *France*." *Contemporary Review* 74 (1898): 60–74.

"Ménage de Poètes." *Revue de Paris*, 15 September 1898, 295–317; 15 October 1898, 788–817.

"The Social Novel in France." *Contemporary Review* 75 (1899): 513.

"Les Sœurs Brontë." *Revue de Paris*, 6 December 1899, 831–55; 1 January 1900, 153–71; 15 January 1900, 419–34.

"M. Paul Calmann Levy." *Athenaeum*, 17 February 1900, 208–9.

"Paris in 1900." *Edinburgh Review*, 1 July 1900, 117–39.

"Thackeray." *Revue de Paris*, 1 November 1900, 139–63; 15 November 1900, 405–21.

"Ausone ou L'Éducation des Rhéturs." *Revue de Paris*, 1 December 1901, 512–46.

"A Farm in the Cantal." *Contemporary Review* 82 (December 1902): 822–42.

"The Youth of Taine." *Fortnightly Review* 78 (December 1902): 943–61; *Living Age*, 28 February 1903, 545–60.

"A Manor in Touraine." *Contemporary Review* 83 (March 1903): 344–61.

"The French Peasant Before and After the Revolution." *Contemporary Review* 84 (1 July 1903): 349–510.

"Delphine Bernard." *Revue de L'Art ancient et modern* 14 (1903): 217–31.

"Ronsard and La Pleiade." *Times Literary Supplement*, 30 November 1906, 401.

"Ferdinand Brunetiere." *Times Literary Supplement*, 14 December 1906, 257.

"Berthelot." *Times Literary Supplement*, 29 March 1907, 100.

"Joris Karl Huysmans." *Times Literary Supplement*, 17 May 1907, 156.

"Sully Prudhomme." *Times Literary Supplement*, 13 September 1907, 277.

"In Casa Paget: A Retrospect." *Country Life* 22 (28 December 1907): 935–7.

"Ludovic Halévy." *Times Literary Supplement*, 21 May 1908, 164.

"The Mind of Pascal." *Edinburgh Review* 214 (July 1911): 53.

"Theophile Gautier." *Times Literary Supplement*, 24 August 1911, 305.

"Maurice Barrès his life and work." *Quarterly Review* 217 (July 1912): 110–35.

"French Novelists of Today." *Times Literary Supplement*, 30 October 1913, 481.

"Mistral." *Times Literary Supplement*, 2 April 1914, 163.

"Peguy." *Times Literary Supplement*, 26 November 1914, 526.

"Les Coulisses d'une Grande Bataille or The Background of a Victory." *The Book of France*. Edited by Winnifred Stephens. London, Macmillan, 1915. 83–118.

"Poor Nelly." *The Country Life Anthology of Verse*, edited by P. Anderson Graham. London, Country Life, 1915, 93.

"A Chaplet of Heroes." *Quarterly Review* 225 (January 1916): 53–72; *Living Age*, 29 April 1916, 266–78.

"The New Frenchman." *Times Literary Supplement*, 13 January 1916, 20.

"The Hibbert Journal." *Times Literary Supplement*, 24 January 1918, 46.

"Julius Wellhausen." *Times Literary Supplement*, 21 February 1918, 90.

"The House of Victor Hugo." *Times Literary Supplement*, 8 January 1920, 18.

"Prose and Verse: Omond, Thomas Stewart." *Times Literary Supplement*, 3 February 1921, 75.

"Ernest Renan." *Times Literary Supplement*, 1 March 1923, 129.

"Ronsard." *Times Literary Supplement*, 11 September 1924, 545.

"Maurice Barrès: A Reminiscence." *Country Life*, 29 March 1924, 491–2.

"Souvenirs sur Walter Pater." *Revue de Paris*, 15 January 1925, 339–58.

"Lurch." *Times Literary Supplement*, 23 July 1925, 496.

"Madame de Sévigné." *Times Literary Supplement*, 4 February 1926, 69.

"Souvenirs sur George Moore." *Revue de Paris*, 1 March 1933, 110–30.

"The French Novel." *Times Literary Supplement*, 22 February 1934, 113.

"Alfred de Vigny." *Times Literary Supplement*, 12 July 1934, 481.

"Chretien de Troyes." *Times Literary Supplement*, 15 November 1934, 781.

"Miss Emily Sargent." *Times*, 6 June 1936, 14.

"Froissart and his Patrons." *Times Literary Supplement*, 11 December 1937, 933.

POEMS PUBLISHED IN JOURNALS

"Two Lovers." *Athenaeum*, 20 December 1879, 798.

"A Pastoral of Parnassus." *John O'Groat Journal*, 8 January 1880, 3; *Exeter and Plymouth Gazette*, 30 January 1880, 3.

"Shadow Lovers." *University Magazine* 1, no. 2 (1880): 144–5.

"Unequal Souls." *Athenaeum*, 17 April 1880, 502.

"Captain Ortis' Booty." *Cornhill* (May 1880): 612–14.

"Lover's Silence." *Athenaeum*, 11 September 1880, 337.

"Helen in the Wood." *Cornhill* (March 1881): 318–19.

"Stornelli and Strambotti." *Athenaeum*, 4 March 1882, 282.

"Love and Vision." *Athenaeum*, 16 September 1882, 368.

"Spring Under Cypresses." *Athenaeum*, 16 May 1885, 630.

"Invocations." *Athenaeum*, 10 October 1885, 471.

"Remembrance." *Athenaeum*, 21 November 1885, 668.

"A Classic Landscape." *Athenaeum*, 30 January 1886, 166.

"Venetian Nocturne." *The Star*, Guernsey, 1 April 1886, 3.

"Love in the World." *Athenaeum*, 2 October 1886, 432.

"An Orchard at Avignon." *Athenaeum*, 23 October 1886, 533–4.

"Etruscan Tombs." *Athenaeum*, 30 July 1887, 14.

"Versailles." *Athenaeum*, 3 November 1888, 591.

"The Death of the Count of Armaniac." *Athenaeum*, 16 November 1889, 672.

"Springs of Fontana." *Athenaeum*, 21 June 1890, 799; *Living Age*, 2 August 1890, 258.

"Twilight." *Athenaeum*, 2 September 1890, 319.

"Celia's Homecoming." *Living Age*, 21 March 1891, 706.

"Ah Love, I cannot die, I cannot go." *Living Age*, 18 April 1891, 130.

"Pallor." *Critic*, 25 April 1891, 222.

"God Sent a Poet to Reform His Earth." *Living Age*, 2 May 1891, 258.

"Vishtaspa." *Athenaeum*, 30 January 1892, 149.

"Recollection." *Athenaeum*, 20 August 1892, 258.

"Veritatem dilexi: in memoriam E.R." *Athenaeum*, 15 October 1892, 517; *Living Age*, 1 January 1893, 2.

"Frozen River." *Athenaeum*, 18 March 1893, 345.

"Tomorrow or in Twenty Centuries: (The Gospel According to St Peter)." *Dial*, 1 October 1893, 198.

"Vision." *Living Age*, 2 December 1893, 514; *Dial*, 1 October 1893, 198.

"Le Roc-du-Chere" and "Spring and Autumn." *Dial*, 1 November 1893, 267.

"Spring and Autumn." *Dial*, 1 November 1893, 267.

"Souvenir." *Living Age*, 16 December 1893, 642.

"Song: the Flocks that bruise the mountain grass." *Critic*, 9 July 1894, 387.

"Unum est necessarium." *Athenaeum*, 21 August 1897, 256.

"Teste Sibylla." *Athenaeum*, 18 November 1899, 687; *Living Age*, 13 January 1900; *Current Literature* 27 (March 1900): 215.

"Solitude." *Harper's Monthly Magazine* 102 (January 1901): 282.

"Dead Friend." *Living Age*, 17 May 1902, 448.

"Last Night I Met My Own True Love." *Living Age*, 31 May 1902, 576.

"Gate of Tears." *Living Age*, 3 August 1902, 576.

"Return to Nature." *Athenaeum*, 30 August 1902, 287; *Living Age*, 29 October 1904, 320.

"Old Air with Variations." *Athenaeum*, 17 January 1903, 82.

"Belgia Bar-Lass." *Times Literary Supplement*, 20 August 1914, 657.

"Two Seascapes": "I. The Demented Mother. II. The Limit of Effort." *Country Life*, 3 February 1923, 134.

"The Fly-in-Amber." *Country Life*, 14 April 1923, 489.

"Dried Cows." *Country Life*, 25 August 1923, 245.

"A Dirge. For the death of Maurice Barrès." *Country Life*, 19 January 1924, 79.

"Le Roi est Mort." *Literary Digest*, 1 January 1927, 26.

PREFACES AND INTRODUCTIONS

Introduction to *The Fortunate Lovers: Twenty-Seven Novels of the Queen of Navarre*. Edited by A. Mary F. Robinson. Translated by Arthur Machen, 1–54. London: George Redway, 1887.

Preface to *Critique et Politique*, by James Darmesteter, i–xxx. Paris: Calmann Lévy, 1895.

Avant-propos to *Nouvelles Études Anglaises*, by James Darmesteter, 1–11. Paris: Calmann Lévy, 1896.

Preface to *English Studies*, by James Darmesteter, vii–xix. Translated by Mary James Darmesteter. London: T. Fisher Unwin, 1896.

Preface to *Casa Guidi Windows*, by Elizabeth Barrett Browning, v–xiv. London: John Lane, 1901.

Préface á *La Vie de Florence Nightingale*, by Sarah A. Tooley. Translated by Mme. Alphen-Salvador and Mme Brandon-Salvador, vii–xv. Paris: Fischbacher, 1911.

Mme. de Sévigné: Textes Choisis et Commentés by Mme. Duclaux. Paris: Plon-Nourrit, 1914.

"La Pensée de Robert Browning." *Poems de Robert Browning*. Translated by Paul Alfassa and Gilbert de Voisins. 1–129. Paris: Bernard Grasset, 1922.

"A Reminiscence." *The Journal of Marie Lenéru*, 49–59. Translated by
William Aspenwall Bradley. London: Macmillan, 1924.

Introduction to *Letters from the Marchioness de Sévigné to her Daughter,
the Countess de Grignan*, v–xxxix. London: Spurr and Swift, 1927.

Préface á *La Maison sur le Roc: Pièce en trois actes*, by Marie Lenéru, 1–9.
Paris: Plon, 1927.

Introduction to *Souvenirs et Impressions*, by Henriette Renan, 5–21. Paris:
La Renaissance du Livre, 1930.

REVIEWS

Review of *Callirrhöe; Fair Rosamund*, by Michael Field. *Academy*, 7 June
1884, 395–6.

Review of *David Lazzaretti di Arcidossa*, by Di Giacomo Barzellotti.
Athenaeum, 16 May 1885, 628–9.

Review of *Nouveaux Essais de Psychologie*, by Paul Bourget. *Athenaeum*,
31 July 1886, 841–2.

Review of *Strambotti a Sonetti dell' Altissimo*, by Cura di Rodolfo.
Athenaeum, 28 August 1886, 265.

Review of *Dorothy Wordsworth: the Story of a Sister's Love*, by Edmund
Lee. *Athenaeum*, 28 August 1886, 266–7.

Review of *Folk Songs of Italy*, by R.H. Busk. *Athenaeum*, 9 April 1887,
475–6.

Review of *Spanish and Italian Folk Songs*, by Alma Strettel. *Athenaeum*,
30 July 1887, 141–2.

Review of *Modern Italian Poets: Essays and Versions*, by William D.
Howells. *Athenaeum*, 4 February 1888, 141.

Review of *The Makers of Venice*, by Mrs Oliphant. *Athenaeum*, 25
February 1888, 236–7.

Review of the *Court and Reign of Francis 1*, by Julia Pardoe. *Athenaeum*,
28 April 1888, 532.

Review of *Les Revolutions Politique de Florence*, by Gabriel Thomas.
Athenaeum, 4 August 1888, 153.

Review of *Histoire de Charles VII*, by J. Dufresne de Beaucourt.
Athenaeum, 6 October 1888, 443–4.

Review of *Histoire de Charles VII*, by J. Dufresne de Beaucourt.
The English Historical Review 4, no. 13 (January 1889): 161–7.

Review of *Bibliographie de l'Histoire de France, depuis les Origines jusqu'en
1789*, by G. Monod. *Athenaeum*, 20 July 1889, 91–2.

Review of *Histoire de Florence*, by François Tommy Perrens. *Athenaeum*, 27 July 1889, 125–6.

Review of *French Traits*, by W.C. Brownell. *Athenaeum*, 31 August 1889, 277–8.

Review of *L'Illusion*, by Jean Lahor (H. Cazalis). *Athenaeum*, 14 September 1889, 346–7.

Review of *Giovanni Acuto (Sir John Hawkwood): Storia d'un Condottiere.* Translated by G. Temple-Leader. *Athenaeum*, 7 December 1889, 773–4.

Review of *Histoire de Florence*, by François Tommy Perrens. *Athenaeum*, 23 August 1890, 247–8.

Review of *L'Italie Mystique*, by Émile Gebbart. *Athenaeum* 13 September 1890, 346–8.

Review of *Études sur la Politique Religieuse de Règne de Philippe le Bel*, by Ernest Renan. *Athenaeum*, 27 January 1900, 103–5.

"Some Recent French Books." *Times Literary Supplement*, 22 August 1902, 251.

Review of *Histoire Comique*, by Anatole France. *Times Literary Supplement*, 30 January 1903, 31.

Review of *Études sur la Nature Humaine*, by Élie Metchinoff." *Times Literary Supplement*, 22 May 1903, 159.

Review of *Gentilshommes Campagnards de L'Ancienne France*, by Pierre De Vaissière. *Times Literary Supplement*, 31 July 1903, 251.

Review of *La Rochefoucauld-Liancourt, 1747–1827*, by Ferdinand Dreyfus. *Times Literary Supplement*, 25 December 1903, 373.

Review of *Ernest Renan in Bretagne*, by René d'Ye. *Times Literary Supplement*, 26 February 1904, 59.

Review of *Taine: Life and Correspondence, vol 2, Le Critique et Philosophe, 1853–1870. Times Literary Supplement*, 11 March 1904, 76.

Review of *Étude de Littérature Comparée*, by Fernand Baldensperger. *Times Literary Supplement* 15 April 1904, 113.

Review of *Les Français de mon Temps*, by Vicomte D'Avenel. *Times Literary Supplement*, 13 May 1904, 146.

Review of *Correspondence of George Sand and Alfred de Musset*, edited by Félix Decori. *Times Literary Supplement*, 1 July 1904, 201.

Review of *Le Visage Émerveillé*," by Anna de Noailles. *Times Literary Supplement*, 15 July 1904, 220.

Review of *Un Vainqueur*, by E. Rod. *Times Literary Supplement*, 5 August 1904, 244.

Review of *Hobbes*, by Leslie Stephen. *Times Literary Supplement*, 19 August 1904, 257.

Review of *L'enfance de Victor Hugo*, by Gustave Simon. *Times Literary Supplement*, 23 September 1904, 288.

Review of *Sur le Branche*, by de Colvaine. *Times Literary Supplement*, 14 October 1904, 311.

Review of *Correspondance Inédite de Sainte-Beuve avec M. et Mme. Juste Olivier*, edited by Mme. Bertrand. *Times Literary Supplement*, 16 December 1904, 397.

Review of *Promenades Littéraires*, by Remy de Gourmont. *Times Literary Supplement*, 13 January 1905, 12.

Review of *Sur la Pierre Blanche*, by Anatole France. *Times Literary Supplement*, 17 March 1905.

Review of *Unpublished Letters of Choderlos de la Laclos*, edited by Louis de Chauvigny. *Times Literary Supplement*, 24 March 1905, 93.

Review of *Il Était Une Bergère*," by André Rivoire. *Times Literary Supplement*, 26 March 1905, 167.

Review of *Les Obsédés*, by Eugène Frapié. *Times Literary Supplement*, 21 April 1905, 136.

Review of *Marie Donadieu*, by Charles Louis Philippe. *Times Literary Supplement*, 28 April 1905, 136.

Review of *La Troisième Jeunesse de Mme Prune*, by Pierre Loti. *Times Literary Supplement*, 12 May 1905, 152.

Review of *The Life of a Simple Man*, by Émile Guillaumin. *Times Literary Supplement*, 6 June 1905, 193.

Review of *Taine: Sa Vie et Sa Correspondance*. *Times Literary Supplement*, 9 June 1905, 181.

Review of *Le Passé Vivant*, by Henri Régnier. *Times Literary Supplement*, 7 July 1905, 217.

Review of *Sayings of Lao-Tzu*. *Times Literary Supplement*, 14 July 1905, 221.

Review of *Terres Françaises: Bourgogne, Franche Comte, Narbonnaise*, by Norman Fullerton. *Times Literary Supplement*, 21 July 1905, 234.

Review of *L'or des minutes*, by Fernand Gregh. *Times Literary Supplement*, 28 July 1905, 241.

Review of *Précurseures et Révoltés: Nietzsche, Ibsen, Gobineau, etc*, by Edouard Schuré. *Times Literary Supplement*, 11 August 1905, 257.

Review of *Au Service de l'Allemagne*, by Maurice Barrès. *Times Literary Supplement*, 18 August 1905, 262.

Review of *Shakespeare's Christmas*, by A.T. Quiller-Couch. *Times Literary Supplement*, 1 September 1905, 279.

Review of *Amour de Philosophe*, by Jean Ruinat de Gournier. *Times Literary Supplement*, 22 September 1905, 300.

"Four French novels," *Times Literary Supplement*, 29 September 1905, 312.

Review of *Old Provence*, by T.A. Cook. *Times Literary Supplement*, 27 October 1905, 357.

Review of *Fontenelle*, by A. Laborde-Milan. *Times Literary Supplement*, 17 November 1905, 395.

Review of *George Sand et sa fille: D'après leur correspondence Inédite*, edited by Samuel Rocheblave. *Times Literary Supplement*, 15 December 1905, 444.

Review of *Le Bel Avenir*, by René Boylesve. *Times Literary Supplement*, 26 January 1906, 28.

Review of "Vers le Coeur de l'Amérique." *Times Literary Supplement*, 16 March 1906, 89.

Review of *La Rebelle*, by Marcelle Tinayre. *Times Literary Supplement*, 13 April 1906, 222.

Review of *Honoré de Balzac*, by Ferdinand Brunetière. *Times Literary Supplement*, 18 May 1906, 179.

Review of *L'Affair Jean Jacques Rousseau*, by Edouard Rod. *Times Literary Supplement*, 6 July 1906, 240.

Review of *Les Désenchantées*, by Pierre Loti. *Times Literary Supplement*, 7 September 1906, 304.

Review of *Frédéric Mistral: Mss Origines. Mémoires et Récits. Times Literary Supplement*, 12 December 1906, 424.

Review of *Monsieur et Madame Moloch*, by Prévost Marcel. *Times Literary Supplement*, 4 January 1907, 5.

Review of *Dingley, l'illustre écrivain*, by Jérôme et Jean Tharaud. *Times Literary Supplement*, 11 January 1907, 13.

Review of *The Friends of Voltaire*, by S.G. Tallentyre. *Times Literary Supplement*, 8 February 1907, 41.

Review of *L'Homme qui Assassina*, by Claude Farrère. *Times Literary Supplement*, 12 April 1907, 116.

Review of *Jean-Jacques Rousseau*, by Jules Lemaître. *Times Literary Supplement*, 26 April 1907, 132.

Review of *Jean-Christophe* (Vol. 4), by Romaine Rolland. *Times Literary Supplement*, 3 May 1907, 139.

Review of *Elie Greuze,* by Gabriel Trarieux. *Times Literary Supplement,* 10 May 1907, 148.

Review of *Charles Baudelaire: Lettres, 1841–1866,* Mercure Society, and *Charles Baudelaire: Étude Biographique,* by Eugène Crépet. *Times Literary Supplement,* 7 June 1907, 177.

Review of *Les Éblouissements,* by Anna de Noailles. *Times Literary Supplement,* 14 June 1907, 188.

Review of *H. Taine: Sa Vie et Correspondance,* Vol. 4, Librairie Hatchette et cie. *Times Literary Supplement,* 28 June 1907, 201.

Review of *La Romantisme Français,* edited by Pierre Lasserre. *Times Literary Supplement,* 5 July 1907, 212.

Review of *Alfred de Musset,* by Léon Séché. *Times Literary Supplement,* 9 August 1907, 241.

Review of *Discours de Combat,* by Ferdinand Brunetière. *Times Literary Supplement,* 23 August 1907, 256.

Review of *Fenelon and Madame Guyon,* by Maurice Masson. *Times Literary Supplement,* 20 September 1907, 284.

Review of *L'émigré,* by Paul Bourget. *Times Literary Supplement,* 20 September 1907, 285.

Review of *Le Blé qui Lève,* by René Bazin. *Times Literary Supplement,* 31 October 1907, 329.

Review of *La Discorde* by Hermant Abel. *Times Literary Supplement,* 7 November 1907, 340.

Review of *Oxford Book of French Poetry. Times Literary Supplement,* 2 January 1908, 1.

Review of *Un Épisode,* by Daniel Halévy. *Times Literary Supplement,* 23 January 1908, 28.

Review of *Louis XIV,* by Ernest Lavisse. *Times Literary Supplement,* 19 March 1908, 93.

Review of *Vie de Jeanne D'Arc,* by Anatole France. *Times Literary Supplement,* 23 April 1908, 132.

Review of *Arguillis,* by André Corthis. *Times Literary Supplement,* 30 April 1908, 140.

Review of *Memoires d'une vielle fille,* by René Bazin. *Times Literary Supplement,* 4 June 1908, 182.

Review of *Jean Racine,* by Jules Lemaître. *Times Literary Supplement,* 18 June 1908, 197.

Review of *Sainte Melanie,* by George Goyan. *Times Literary Supplement,* 6 August 1908, 253.

Review of *Monsieur le Principal*, by Jean Viollie. *Times Literary Supplement*, 27 August 1908, 277.

Review of *Histoire d'une Société*, by René Beraine, and *Les Grands Bourgeois*, by Abel Hermant. *Times Literary Supplement*, 5 October 1908, 346.

Review of *The Brontës' Life and Letters*, by Clement Shorter, and *Poems of Emily Brontë*, introduction by Arthur Symons." *Times Literary Supplement*, 5 November 1908, 381–2.

Review of *La Vie Secrète*, by Édouard Estaunié. *Times Literary Supplement*, 19 November 1908, 416.

Review of *Les Détours du Coeur*, by Paul Bourget. *Times Literary Supplement*, 3 December 1908, 444.

Review of *Muses Et Bourgeois De Jadis*, by Edmond Pilon. *Times Literary Supplement*, 17 December 1908, 472.

Review of *La Mort de Philae*, by Pierre Loti. *Times Literary Supplement*, 4 February 1909, 40.

Review of *Ragotte*, by Jules Renard. *Times Literary Supplement*, 11 March 1909, 89.

Review of *Paradis Laiques*, by Jules Sageret. *Times Literary Supplement*, 17 June 1909, 221.

Review of *La Femme et l'Amour au XII Siècle, d'après les Poèmes de Chrétien de Troyes*, by Myrrha Borodine. *Times Literary Supplement*, 29 July 1909, 273.

Review of *La Porte Étroite*, by André Gide. *Times Literary Supplement*, 19 August 1909, 300.

Review of *Leconte de Lisle*, by Fernand Calmettes. *Times Literary Supplement*, 23 September 1909, 341.

Review of *La Vie de Frédéric Nietzsche*, by Daniel Halévy. *Times Literary Supplement*, 18 November 1909, 433.

Review of *La Passion d'Abailard et Héloïse*, by Jean Bertheroy. *Times Literary Supplement*, 16 December 1909, 495.

Review of *Hiên le Maboul*, by Émile Nolly. *Times Literary Supplement*, 6 January 1910, 4.

Review of *Chantecler*, by Edmond Rostand. *Times Literary Supplement*, 10 March 1910, 77.

Review of *The Shadow of Love*, by Marcelle Tinayre. *Times Literary Supplement*, 7 April 1910, 120.

Review of *La Vie et La Mort de Fées: Essai d'Histoire Littéraire*, by Lucie Félix-Faure-Goyan. *Times Literary Supplement*, 28 April 1910, 154.

Review of *Les Affranches*, by Marie Lenéru. *Times Literary Supplement*, 19 May 1910, 183.

Review of *La Dame Qui a Perdue son Peintre*, by Paul Bourget, *Times Literary Supplement*, 26 May 1910, 187.

Review of *Ascension*, by Charles de Pomairols. *Times Literary Supplement*, 2 June 1910, 197.

Review of *Le Château de la Belle au bois dormant*, by Pierre Loti. *Times Literary Supplement*, 30 June 1910, 233.

Review of *La Chimie de la Matière Vivante*, by Jacques Duclaux. *Times Literary Supplement*, 14 July 1910, 250.

Review of *Petite Ville*, by Charles Louis Philippe. *Times Literary Supplement*, 21 July 1910, 261.

Review of *Comme tout le monde*, by Lucie Delarue-Mardrus. *Times Literary Supplement*, 4 August 1910, 278.

Review of *Henry Poincaré*, by Jules Sageret. *Times Literary Supplement*, 18 August 1910, 292.

Review of *Marie-Claire*, by Marguerite Audoux. *Times Literary Supplement*, 24 November 1910, 460.

Review of *L'Angleterre Modern*, by Louis Cazamian and *Nouvelles Études Anglaises*, by André Chevrillon; *L'Âme des Anglais*, by Fœmina. *Times Literary Supplement*, 23 March 1911, 114.

Review of *Honoré de Balzac*, by Ferdinand Brunetière. *Times Literary Supplement*, 18 May 1911, 196.

Review of *Fermina Márquez*, by Valery Larbaud. *Times Literary Supplement*, 22 June 1911, 238.

Review of *La prison de verre*, by Gaston Chérau. *Times Literary Supplement*, 6 July 1911, 495.

Review of *Monsieur des Lordines*, by Alphonse Châteaubriant. *Times Literary Supplement*, 12 October 1911, 378.

Review of *L'Imperatrice Eugénie*, by Alphonse-Daudet. *Times Literary Supplement*, 4 January 1912, 6.

Review of *Jean-Christophe: Le Buisson Ardent*, by Romain Rolland. *Times Literary Supplement*, 11 January 1912, 12.

Review of *Le Repentir*, by Charles de Pomairols. *Times Literary Supplement*, 29 February 1912, 86.

Review of *Greco, ou Le Secret de Tolède*, by Maurice Barrès. *Times Literary Supplement*, 11 April 1912, 145.

Review of *La Renommée*, by Gaston Rageot. *Times Literary Supplement*, 18 April 1912, 152.

Review of *L'Élève Gilles*, by André Lafon. *Times Literary Supplement*, 16 May 1912, 202.

Review of *Les Dieux ont Soif*, by Anatole France. *Times Literary Supplement*, 4 July 1912, 272.

Review of *Madeleine, Jeune Femme*, by René Boylesve. *Times Literary Supplement*, 8 August 1912, 314.

Review of *Recollections of Guy de Maupassant by Francois [his valet]*, translated by Mina Round. *Times Literary Supplement*, 22 August 1912, 328.

Review of *Sainte Cantal (1572-1641)*, by Henri Bremond. *Times Literary Supplement*, 26 September 1912, 385.

Review of *Jean Christophe, Part 3*, by Romain Rolland. *Times Literary Supplement*, 24 October 1912, 458.

Review of *L'Ordination*, by Julien Benda. *Times Literary Supplement*, 9 January 1913, 12.

Review of *L'Académie Française 1629-1793*, by Frédéric Masson. *Times Literary Supplement*, 30 January 1913, 40.

Review of *Turqui Agonisante*, by Pierre Loti. *Times Literary Supplement*, 13 February 1913, 60.

Review of *Dernières Pensées*, by Henri Poincare. *Times Literary Supplement*, 20 February 1913, 75.

Review of *La Colline Inspirée*, by Maurice Barrès. *Times Literary Supplement*, 27 February 1913, 87.

Review of *Journal du Comte-Rodolphe Apponyi 1826–1830*, by Ernest Daudet. *Times Literary Supplement*, 6 March 1913, 98.

Review of *The Influence of Baudelaire, by G. Turquet Milnes. Times Literary Supplement*, 13 March 1913, 111.

Review of *La Mort*, by Maurice Maeternick. *Times Literary Supplement*, 17 April 1913, 162.

Review of *Le Maître des Foules*, by Louis Delzons. *Times Literary Supplement*, 15 May 1913, 212.

Review of *La Vie Intérieure de Lamartine*, by Jean des Cognets. *Times Literary Supplement*, 22 May 1913, 221.

Review of *L'appel des Armes*, by Ernest Psichari. *Times Literary Supplement*, 26 June 1913, 276.

Review of *Les Vivants et Les Morts*, by Countess de Noailles. *Times Literary Supplement*, 10 July 1913, 292.

Review of *Un Double Amour*, by Claude Ferval. *Times Literary Supplement*, 17 July 1913, 303.

Review of *Stephanie*, by Paul Adam. *Times Literary Supplement*, 4 September 1913, 362.

Review of *The Renaissance*, by Arthur Gobineau. *Times Literary Supplement*, 16 October 1913, 445.

Review of *Chrétienne*, by Mme. Adam. *Times Literary Supplement*, 27 November 1913, 569.

Review of *À La Recherche du Temps Perdu*, by Marcel Proust. *Times Literary Supplement*, 4 December 1913, 585.

Review of *Les Creux-de-Maisons*, by Ernest Pérochon. *Times Literary Supplement*, 8 January 1914, 15.

Review of *La Poésie Française du Moyen-Age, XIe-XVe Siècles*, by Charles Oulmont. *Times Literary Supplement*, 5 March 1914, 114.

Review of *L'Annonce Faite à Mari*, by Paul Claudel. *Times Literary Supplement*, 14 May 1914, 235.

Review of *Science and Method*, by Henri Poincaré. *Times Literary Supplement*, 28 May 1914, 258.

Review of *La Grande Pitié des Églises de France*," by Maurice Barrès. *Times Literary Supplement*, 23 April 1914, 199.

Review of *Journal du Comte Rodolphe Apponi*, edited by Ernest Daudet. *Times Literary Supplement*, 18 June 1914, 295.

Review of *La Vie d'une Femme*, by Gustave Simon. *Times Literary Supplement*, 2 July 1914, 313.

Review of *Le Démon de Midi*, by Paul Bourget. *Times Literary Supplement*, 30 July 1914, 369.

Review of *Servitude et Grandeur Militaires*, by Alfred de Vigny. *Times Literary Supplement*, 24 December 1914, 580.

Review of *Gérard de Nerval: Le Poète, l'Homme*, by Marie Aristide. *Times Literary Supplement*, 11 February 1915, 45.

Review of *Madame de Staël et Monsieur Necker*, by Comte d'Haussonville. *Times Literary Supplement*, 20 May 1915, 169.

Review of *Songs of Brittany*, by Théodore Botrel. *Times Literary Supplement*, 3 June 1915, 184.

Review of *La Guerre: L'Intoxication d'un Peuple*, by Ernest Denis. *Times Literary Supplement*, 10 June 1915, 190.

Review of *Poems in War Time*, by Owen Seaman. *Times Literary Supplement*, 1 July 1915, 217.

Review of *Sur la Voie Glorieuse*, by Anatole France. *Times Literary Supplement*, 8 July 1915, 237.

Review of *La Veillée des Armes: Le Départ, Aout 1914*, by Marcelle
Tinayre. *Times Literary Supplement*, 15 July 1915, 237.

Review of *Confucianism and Its Rivals*, by Herbert A. Giles. *Times
Literary Supplement*, 26 August 1915, 284.

Review of *L'Union Sacrée*, by Maurice Barrès. *Times Literary Supplement*,
2 September 1915, 292.

Review of *Le Sens de la Mort*, by Paul Bourget. *Times Literary
Supplement*, 18 November 1915, 414.

Review of *La Couronne Douloureuse*, by Fernand Gregh. *Times Literary
Supplement*, 6 December 1917, 595.

Review of *L'Odyssée d'un Transport Torpillé*, by Y. *Times Literary
Supplement*, 24 January 1918, 42.

Review of *Le Bonheur à Cinq Sous*, by René Boylesve. *Times Literary
Supplement*, 31 January 1918, 54.

Review of *Le Président Wilson: Étude sur la Démocratie Américaine,"* by
Daniel Halévy. *Times Literary Supplement*, 14 February 1918, 76.

Review of *Histoire de Gotton Connixloo*, by Camille Mayran. *Times
Literary Supplement*, 21 February 1918, 89.

Review of *Reine Adu: les légendes des journées d'octobre*, by Marc de
Villiers. *Times Literary Supplement*, 21 March 1918, 137.

Review of *L'Effort Économique et Financier de l"angleterre*, by Louis Paul-
Dubois. *Times Literary Supplement*, 18 April 1918, 178.

Review of *L'Attente: Impressions d'un Oficier de Légère*, by Marcel Dupont.
Times Literary Supplement, 25 April 1918, 191.

Review of *L'Incertaine*, by Edmond Jaloux. *Times Literary Supplement*,
10 October 1918, 478.

Review of *The Life of Lamartine*, by H. Remsen Whitehouse. *Times
Literary Supplement*, 20 February 1919, 95.

Review of *Une Vie Romantique: Hector Berlioz*, by Adolphe Boschot.
Times Literary Supplement, 5 February 1920, 82.

Review of *Dansons la Trompeuse*, by Raymond Escholier. *Times Literary
Supplement*, 26 February 1920, 139.

Review of *Saada la Marocaine*, by Elissa Rhaïs. *Times Literary
Supplement*, 11 March 1920, 170.

Review of *La Jeune Fille Verte*, by P.J. Toulet. *Times Literary Supplement*,
15 April 1920, 234.

Review of *Marrakech; ou, Les Seigneurs de l'Atlas*, by Jérôme Tharaud.
Times Literary Supplement, 10 June 1920, 362.

Review of *The Origins of French Romanticism*, by M.B. Finch. *Times Literary Supplement*, 15 July 1920, 451.

Review of *Adorable Clio*, by Jean Giroudoux. *Times Literary Supplement*, 22 July 1920, 470.

Review of *La Réssurrection de la Chair*, by Henry Bordeaux. *Times Literary Supplement*, 29 July 1920, 486.

Review of *Idealism in National Character*, by Sir Robert Falconer. *Times Literary Supplement*, 9 September 1920, 575.

Review of *L'Échéance*, by Paul Bourget. *Times Literary Supplement*, 30 September 1920, 634.

Review of *Souvenirs sur l'Impératrice Eugénie*, by Augustin Filon. *Times Literary Supplement*, 4 November 1920, 713.

Review of *Des Inconnus Chez Moi*, by Lucie Cousturier. *Times Literary Supplement*, 18 November 1920, 756.

Review of *Un Apostolat*, by A. t'Serstevens. *Times Literary Supplement*, 9 December 1920, 819.

Review of *Le Courrier de M. Thiers*, by Daniel Halévy. *Times Literary Supplement*, 6 January 1921, 3.

Review of *Saint François d'Assise*, by Roger Boutet de Monvel. *Times Literary Supplement*, 13 January 1921, 23.

Review of *La Vie d'Elie Metchnikoff*, by Olga Metchnikoff. *Times Literary Supplement*, 13 January 1921, 23.

Review of *Perséphone*, by Marcelle Tinayre. *Times Literary Supplement*, 3 February 1921, 72.

Review of *Un Royaume de Dieu*, by Jérôme Tharaud. *Times Literary Supplement*, 24 February 1921, 124.

Review of *Cancer in Plants: The Bacterial Diseases of Plants*, by Erwin F. Smith. *Times Literary Supplement*, 17 March 1921, 171.

Review of *Madame de Maintenon*, by Mme. Saint-René Taillandier. *Times Literary Supplement*, 7 April 1921, 222.

Review of *L'Épreuve de Fils*, by Camille Mayran. *Times Literary Supplement*, 14 April 1921, 242.

Review of *Marie-Antoinette*, by Marquis Pierre de Ségur, *Times Literary Supplement*, 5 May 1921, 288.

Review of *The Cahiers Verts*. *Times Literary Supplement*, 26 May 1921, 1010.

Review of *Trois Études de Littérateur Anglaise (Kipling, Galsworthy, Shakespeare)*, by André Chevrillon. *Times Literary Supplement*, 16 June 1921, 383.

Review of *La Vie de Maurice Barrès*, by Albert Thibaudet. *Times Literary Supplement*, 14 July 1921, 448.

Review of *Un Drame dans le Monde*, by Paul Bourget. *Times Literary Supplement*, 4 August 1921, 496.

Review of *Suzanne et le Pacifique*, by Jean Giraudoux. *Times Literary Supplement*, 25 August 1921, 544.

Review of *Suprêmes visions d'Orient*, by Pierre Loti and Samuel Viaud. *Times Literary Supplement*, 3 November 1921, 712.

Review of *Le Passage de l'Aisne*, by Émile Clermont. *Times Literary Supplement*, 24 November 1921, 766.

Review of *Un Amour*, by Pernette Gille. *Times Literary Supplement*, 22 December 1921, 856.

Review of *Les Matinées de la Villa Saïd*, by Anatole France, collected by Paul Gsell. *Times Literary Supplement*, 5 January 1922, 11.

Review of *Les Taupes*, by Francis de Miomandre. *Times Literary Supplement*, 9 February 1922, 90.

Review of *Le Baiser au Lépreux*, by François Mauriac. *Times Literary Supplement*, 9 March 1922, 152.

Review of *Aymeris*, by Jacques-Émile Blanche. *Times Literary Supplement*, 13 April 1922, 240.

Review of *Histoire Religieuse de la France*, by George Goyau. *Times Literary Supplement*, 20 April 1922, 252.

Review of *Saint-Just*, by Marie Lenéru, "preface" by Maurice Barrès. *Times Literary Supplement*, 18 May 1922, 320.

Review of *La Maîtresse Servante*, by Jérôme et Jean Tharaud. *Times Literary Supplement*, 8 June 1922, 376.

Review of *Le Voyage de M. Renan*, by André Thérive. *Times Literary Supplement*, 22 June 1922, 410.

Review of *Un Jardin sur l'Oronte*, by Maurice Barrès. *Times Literary Supplement*, 29 June 1922, 922.

Review of *Les Amorandes*, by Julien Benda. *Times Literary Supplement*, 6 July 1922, 442.

Review of *Le Chant du Cygne*, by Duchesse Rohan. *Times Literary Supplement*, 10 August 1922, 518.

Review of *Louis XI, Curieux Homme*, by Paul Font. *Times Literary Supplement*, 7 September 1922, 565.

Review of *La Vie en Fleur*, by Anatole France. *Times Literary Supplement*, 14 September 1922, 581.

Review of *Le Père Hyacinth*, by Albert Houtin. *Times Literary Supplement*, 23 November 1922, 758.

Review of *Silbermann*, by Jacques de Lacretelle. *Times Literary Supplement*, 21 December 1922, 859.

Review of *Priscille Séverac*, be Marcelle Tinayre. *Times Literary Supplement*, 25 January 1923, 52.

Review of *The Poets' Year: An Anthology*, by Ada Sharpley. *Times Literary Supplement*, 1 February 1923, 65.

Review of *Recherches sur la Nature de l'amour*, by Emmanuel Berl, and *Recensement de L'Amour á Paris*, by Gérard Bauer, and La Croix de Roses, by Julian Benda. *Times Literary Supplement*, 29 March 1923, 212.

Review of *Le Français, Langue Morte*, by André Thérive. *Times Literary Supplement*, 5 April 1923, 227.

Review of *La Geôle*, by Paul Bourget. *Times Literary Supplement*, 26 April 1923, 285.

Review of *History of the English People in the Nineteenth Century, Vol. 1*, by Elie Halévy. *Times Literary Supplement*, 26 April 1923, 279.

Review of *Isvor: Le Pays des Saules*, by Princess Bibesco. *Times Literary Supplement*, 31 May 1923, 370.

Review of *Le Chemin de Damas*, by Jérôme and Jean Tharaud and *Yamilé sous les Cèdres*, by Henry Bordeaux. *Country Life*, 2 June 1923, 773.

Review of *Vauban*, by Daniel Halévy. *Times Literary Supplement*, 7 June 1923, 384.

Review of *Ariel; ou, La vie de Shelley*, by André Maurois. *Times Literary Supplement*, 28 June 1923, 437.

Review of *Le Roman des Quatre*, by Paul Bourget. *Times Literary Supplement*, 26 July 1923, 502.

Review of *Le Fleuve de Feu*, by François Mauriac. *Times Literary Supplement*, 23 August 1923, 554.

Review of *La Vigne et La Maison*, by Jean Balde. *Times Literary Supplement*, 6 September 1923, 584.

Review of *Renan et Nous*, by Pierre Lasserre. *Times Literary Supplement*, 20 September 1923, 613.

Review of *Ernest Renan – Henriette Renan: Nouvelles Lettres intimes, 1846–1850. Times Literary Supplement*, 1 November 1923, 718.

Review of *La Nuit*, by Raymond Escholier. *Times Literary Supplement*, 8 November 1923, 749.

Review of *Une Vie: Récit detect par Une Paysanne*, by Leo Tolstoy. *Times Literary Supplement*, 22 November 1923, 788.

Review of *Ariel*, by André Maurois. *Country Life*, 24 November 1923, 726–7.

Review of *Der Koenig*, by Karl Rosner, translated by H. Massoul and G. Massoul. *Country Life*, 8 December 1923, 814.

Review of *Goethe*, by Benedetto Croce. *Times Literary Supplement*, 20 December 1923, 885.

Review of *Genitrix*, by François Mauriac. *Times Literary Supplement*, 7 February 1924, 76.

Review of *Une Enquête aux Pays du Levant*, by Maurice Barrès. *Times Literary Supplement*, 14 February 1924, 93.

Review of *Colin-Maillard*, by Louis Hémoc. *Times Literary Supplement*, 13 March 1924, 156.

Review of *Les Princes Lorrains*, by Albert Thibaudet. *Times Literary Supplement*, 17 April 1924, 231.

Review of *Le Plus Grand Péché*, by André Thérive. *Times Literary Supplement*, 22 May 1924, 317.

Review of *Histoire de France*, by Jacques Bainville. *Times Literary Supplement*, 3 July 1924, 411.

Review of *Le Perroquet Vert*, by Princess Bibesco. *Times Literary Supplement*, 17 July 1924, 446.

Review of *Le Bal du Comte d'Orgel*, by Raymond Radiquet. *Times Literary Supplement*, 14 August 1924, 498.

Review of *Juliette au Pays des Hommes*, by Jean Giraudoux. *Times Literary Supplement*, 20 November 1924, 759.

Review of *Pierre Loti: Sa vie, son Oeuvre*, by N. Serban. *Times Literary Supplement*, 1 January 1925, 8.

Review of *Fra Angelico da Fiesole*, by Edouard Schneider. *Times Literary Supplement*, 29 January 1925, 67.

Review of *Remarques sur Benjamin Constant*, by Guy de Pourtalès. *Times Literary Supplement*, 12 February 1925, 93.

Review of *Le Désert de l'Amour*, by François Mauriac. *Times Literary Supplement*, 26 March 1925, 220.

Review of *Lettres á Mélisande pour son Éducation Philosophique*, by Julien Benda. 9 April 1925, 252.

Review of *Les Premières de Jean Racine*, by Henry Lyonnet. *Times Literary Supplement*, 7 May 1925, 305.

Review of *Rendezvous Espagnols,* by Jérôme Tharaud. *Times Literary Supplement,* 30 July 1925, 502.

Review of *La Vie et la Mort d'Eugénie de Guérin,* by Geneviève Duhamelet. *Times Literary Supplement,* 1 October 1925, 634.

Review of *Paul Louis Courier (Chronique des letters Françaises) by Anatole France,* by Richard Aldington. *Times Literary Supplement,* 15 October 1925, 661.

Review of Méditation sur une Amour défunt, by Emmanuel Berl. *Times Literary Supplement,* 3 December 1925, 830.

Review of *Quand On Conspire,* by Raymond Escholier. *Times Literary Supplement,* 24 December 1925, 896.

Review of *Platon,* by Abel Hermant. *Times Literary Supplement,* 28 January 1926, 55.

Review of *Le Roman et L'Histoire d'une Conversion: Ulirc Guttinguer et Sainte-Beuve,* by Henry Bremond. *Times Literary Supplement,* 18 February 1926, 113.

Review of *Voltaire,* by Richard Aldington. *Times Literary Supplement,* 8 April 1926, 260.

Review of *Notre Chèr Péguy,* by Jérôme Tharaud. *Times Literary Supplement,* 15 April 1926, 278.

Review of *La Chercheuse d'Amour,* by Louis Artus. *Times Literary Supplement,* 1 July 1926, 444.

Review of *Portrait de la France: Paray-le-Monial,* by Henri Régnier. *Times Literary Supplement,* 29 July 1926, 507.

Review of *Victor Hugo Artiste,* by Raymond Escholier. *Times Literary Supplement,* 5 August 1926, 523.

Review of *Les Bestiaires,* by H. de Montherlant. *Times Literary Supplement,* 7 October 1926, 673.

Review of *La Vie Raissonable de Descartes,* by Louis Dimier. *Times Literary Supplement,* 7 April 1927, 247.

Review of *L'Honneur de Souffrir,* by Comtesse de Noailles. *Times Literary Supplement,* 12 May 1927, 333.

Review of *Letters from the Marchioness de Sévigné to her Daughter, the Countess de Grignan. Times Literary Supplement,* 2 June 1927, 387.

Review of *Le Mystère en Pleine Lumière,* by Maurice Barrès. *Times Literary Supplement,* 2 June 1927, 388.

Review of *Le Puritains du Désert,* by André Chevrillon. *Times Literary Supplement,* 8 September 1927, 599.

Review of *Catherine-Paris*, by Princess Bibesco. *Times Literary Supplement*, 29 September 1927, 664.

Review of Sainte Thérèse d'Avila, by Jeanne Galzy. *Times Literary Supplement*, 3 November 1927, 779.

Review of *La Vie Amoureuse de la Grande Catherine*, by Lucien, Princess Murat. *Times Literary Supplement*, 1 December 1927, 903.

Review of *The Seven Strings of the Lyre: Life of George Sand*, by Elizabeth Wheeler Schermerhorn. *Times Literary Supplement*, 5 January 1928, 1.

Review of *Primauté du Spirituel*, by Jacques Maritain. *Times Literary Supplement*, 19 January 1928, 39.

Review of *Montaigne*, by Irene Willis Cooper. *Times Literary Supplement*, 1 March 1928, 143.

Review of *La Légende et la Vie d'Utrillo*, by Francis Carco. *Times Literary Supplement*, 8 March 1928, 164.

Review of *Vallée du Doubs*, by André Beucler. *Times Literary Supplement*, 19 April 1928, 283.

Review of *Remarques sur l'action*, by Bernard Grasset. *Times Literary Supplement*, 26 April 1928, 307.

Review of *Und Montag*, by Hans Sochaevewer (with Karl Parker and Vivyan Eyles). *Times Literary Supplement*, 3 May 1928, 335.

Review of *Mes Années Chez Barrès*, by Jérôme Tharaud. *Times Literary Supplement*, 31 May 1928, 408.

Review of *La Vie de Jean Racine*, by François Mauriac. *Times Literary Supplement*, 21 June 1928, 462.

Review of *La Fayette*, by Joseph Delteil. *Times Literary Supplement*, 5 July 1928, 500.

Review of *Reine d'Arbieux*, by Jean Balde. *Times Literary Supplement*, 26 July 1928, 549.

Review of *La Vie Amoureuse de la Belle Hélène*, by Gerard d'Houville. *Times Literary Supplement*, 2 August 1928, 564.

Review of *Melancholia*, by Léon Daudet. *Times Literary Supplement*, 23 August 1928, 601.

Review of *Histoire d'une Société*, by René Béhaine. *Times Literary Supplement*, 4 October 1828, 702.

Review of *Calendrier Royal pour l'An 1471*, by Pierre Champion. *Times Literary Supplement*, 25 October 1928, 770.

Review of *Les Conquérants*, by André Malraux. *Times Literary Supplement*, 8 November 1928, 822,

Review of *Les Pélerins d'Emmaüs*, by Léon Daudet. *Times Literary Supplement*, 29 November 1928, 925.

Review of *Climats*, by André Maurois. *Times Literary Supplement*, 6 December 1928, 958.

Review of *Jules Michelet*, by Daniel Halévy. *Times Literary Supplement*, 10 January 1929, 22.

Review of *L'Homme qui Ressuscita d'Entre les Vivants*, by Joseph Wilbois. *Times Literary Supplement*, 31 January 1929, 73.

Review of *Les Modèles*, by Jacques-Émile Blanche. *Times Literary Supplement*, 14 February 1929, 111.

Review of *Paris Vécu*, by Léon Daudet. *Times Literary Supplement*, 25 April 1929, 332.

Review of *La Vie de S.A.R. La Duchess de Berry*, by Armand Praviel. *Times Literary Supplement*, 2 May 1929, 353.

Review of *Léviathan*, by Julien Green. *Times Literary Supplement*, 16 May 1929, 400.

Review of *Rue Pigalle*, by Francis Carco. *Times Literary Supplement*, 23 May 1929, 419.

Review of *Les Varais*, by Jacques Chardonne. *Times Literary Supplement*, 27 June 1929, 511.

Review of *Poèmes*, by André Spire. *Times Literary Supplement*, 11 July 1929, 557.

Review of *Vie de Bianca Cappello*, by M. Pierre-Gauthiez, and *Philippe II*, by Louis Bertrand. *Times Literary Supplement*, 22 August 1929, 647.

Review of *Le Dialogue avec André Gide*, by Charles Du Bos. *Times Literary Supplement*, 29 August 1929, 662.

Review of *La Vie de Claude Monet*, by Marthe de Fels. *Times Literary Supplement*, 10 October 1929, 785.

Review of *Mazarin, Soutine de l'État*, by Marcel Boulenger. *Times Literary Supplement*, 14 November 1929, 911.

Review of *L'Ordre*, by Marcel Arland. *Times Literary Supplement*, 12 December 1929, 1055.

Review of *Nietzsche in Italia*, by G. Pourtalès. *Times Literary Supplement*, 16 January 1930, 39.

Review of *Trois Diners avec Gambetta*, by Ludovic Halévy. *Times Literary Supplement*, 30 January 1930, 71.

Review of *Quatre Portraits*, by Princess Bibesco. *Times Literary Supplement*, 13 February 1930, 119.

Review of *Byron*, by Charles du Bos. *Times Literary Supplement*,
13 March 1930, 209.

Review of *Variété II*, by Paul Valéry. *Times Literary Supplement*, 27 March
1930, 268.

Review of *Biographie du Cardinal de Retz*, by Louis Batiffol. *Times
Literary Supplement*, 30 March 1930, 201.

Review of *Molière*, by Harry Ashton. *Times Literary Supplement*, 17 April
1930, 333.

Review of *Mayerling*, by Claude Anet. *Times Literary Supplement*, 1 May
1930, 363.

Review of *Orientalle 1930*, by Lucienne Favre. *Times Literary Supplement*,
5 June 1930, 473.

Review of *L'art et la Pensée de Robert Browning*, by Paul Reul. *Times
Literary Supplement*, 26 June 1930, 530.

Review of *La Royauté Bourgeoise 1830*, by Jean Lucas-Dubreton. *Times
Literary Supplement*, 24 July 1930, 597.

Review of *Le Voyageur sur la Terre*, by Julien Green. *Times Literary
Supplement*, 22 August 1930, 664.

Review of *La République de Monsieur Thiers*, by Robert Dreyfus. *Times
Literary Supplement*, 29 August 1930, 675.

Review of *A Literary History of Religious Thought in France vol II
1590–1620*, by Henri Bremond and translated by K.I. Montgomery.
Times Literary Supplement, 2 October 1930, 773.

Review of *Molière, His Life and Works*, by John Palmer. *Times Literary
Supplement*, 6 November 1930, 897.

Review of *The Prix Concourt: Malaisie*, by Henri Fauconnier. *Times
Literary Supplement*, 1 January 1931, 8.

Review of *Opium*, by Jean Cocteau. *Times Literary Supplement*,
19 February 1931, 130.

Review of *Aventures de Jérôme Bardini*, by Jean Giraudoux. *Times
Literary Supplement*, 26 February 1931, 147.

Review of *Tourguéniev*, by André Maurois. *Times Literary Supplement*,
2 April 1931, 269.

Review of *The Weigher of Souls*, by André Maurois. *Times Literary
Supplement*, 30 April 1931, 343.

Review of *Vie de Saint François d'Assise*, by Paul Sabatier. *Times Literary
Supplement*, 4 June 1931, 436.

Review of *Shakespeare*, by Louis Gillet. *Times Literary Supplement*,
18 June 1931, 486.

Review of *Lettres de Degas*, edited by Maurice Guérin. *Times Literary Supplement*, 13 August 1931, 617.

Review of *Décadence de la Liberté*, by Daniel Halévy. *Times Literary Supplement*, 10 September 1931, 671.

Review of *Monsieur de Staël*, by Jean de Pange. *Times Literary Supplement*, 11 February 1932, 89.

Review of *Le Cercle de Famille*, by André Maurois. *Times Literary Supplement*, 18 February 1932, 109.

Review of *Saint-Saturnin*, by Jean Schlumberger. *Times Literary Supplement*, 14 April 1932, 269.

Review of *Les Vies du Comte de Cagliostro*, by Constantin Photiadès. *Times Literary Supplement*, 26 May 1932, 381.

Review of *Épaves*, by Julien Green. *Times Literary Supplement*, 2 June 1932, 404.

Review of *Mémoires*, by Elizabeth de Gramont. *Times Literary Supplement*, 7 July 1932, 485.

Review of *Staline et Cie*, by Richard N. Coudenhove-Kalergi. *Times Literary Supplement*, 14 July 1932, 506.

Review of *Wallraf-Richartz-Jahrbuch*, with Karl Parker and Vivyan Eyles. *Times Literary Supplement*, 11 August 1932, 569.

Review of *Marie Lenéru sa vie*, by Suzanne Lavaud. *Times Literary Supplement*, 8 September 1932, 623.

Review of *Pays Parisiens*, by Daniel Halévy. *Times Literary Supplement*, 22 September 1932, 658.

Review of *Les Bien Aimées*, by Jérôme and Jean Tharaud. *Times Literary Supplement*, 20 October 1932, 752.

Review of *Les Loups*, by Guy Mazeline. *Times Literary Supplement*, 29 December 1932, 986.

Review of *Undine, and other stories*, by Caroline Birley. *Times Literary Supplement*, 2 March 1933, 142.

Review of *Travels in France during the years 1787, 1788, and 1789*, by Arthur Young. *Times Literary Supplement*, 6 April 1933, 237.

Review of *Madame du Deffand*, by Claude Ferval. *Times Literary Supplement*, 18 May 1933, 347.

Review of *Courrier d'Europe*, by Daniel Halévy. *Times Literary Supplement*, 25 May 1933, 354.

Review of *Les Hauts-Ponts: Les Fiançailles*, by Jacques de Lacretelle. *Times Literary Supplement*, 8 June 1933, 392.

Review of *La Chatte*, by Colette. *Times Literary Supplement*, 10 August 1933, 534.

Review of *Lettres du Centurion*, by Ernest Psichari. *Times Literary Supplement*, 17 August 1933, 548.

Review of *Vieillesse de Chateaubriand*, by Marie-Jeanne Durry. *Times Literary Supplement*, 19 October 1933, 706.

Review of *The Face of Paris*, by Harold Clunn. *Times Literary Supplement*, 7 December 1933, 871.

Review of *Quand Israel n'est Plus Roi*, by Jérôme Tharaud. *Times Literary Supplement*, 21 December 1933, 906.

Review of *France-la-Dolce*, by Paul Morand. *Times Literary Supplement*, 22 March 1934, 211.

Review of *Le Visionnaire*, by Julien Green. *Times Literary Supplement*, 12 April 1934, 258.

Review of *Chateaubriand en Angleterre*, by Jules Deschamps. *Times Literary Supplement*, 10 May 1934, 329–30.

Review of *Le Bourgeousie Françaises*, by Joseph Aynard. *Times Literary Supplement*, 14 June 1934, 418.

Review of *Les Célibataires*, by Henry de Montherlant. *Times Literary Supplement*, 26 July 1934, 525.

Review of *Les Dieux*, by Alain. *Times Literary Supplement*, 10 January 1935, 16.

Review of *Marie Antoinette, Fersen et Barnave*, by Oscar Heidenstam. *Times Literary Supplement*, 7 February 1935, 65.

Review of *La Fin de la Nuit*, by François Mauriac. *Times Literary Supplement*, 21 March 1935, 174.

Review of *Visites aux Paysans du Centre*, by Daniel Halévy. *Times Literary Supplement*, 30 May 1935, 344.

Review of *Madame Elisabeth*, by Jean Balde. *Times Literary Supplement*, 11 July 1935, 445.

Review of *Dans L'Ombre de L'Impératrice de Eugénie*, by Lucien Daudet. *Times Literary Supplement*, 15 February 1936, 121.

Review of *Rodin: sa vie Glorieuse et Inconnue*, by Judith Cladel. *Times Literary Supplement*, 22 August 1936, 674.

Review of *Christine de Pizan*, by Jean de Castel. *Times Literary Supplement*, 31 October 1936, 880.

Review of *La Fin des Notables*, by Daniel Halévy. *Times Literary Supplement*, 22 May 1937, 387.

Review of *Jean Racine (1639–1699): Poet of the Passions of Love: The Discipline of Court Conventions*, by John Middleton Murry. *Times Literary Supplement*, 23 December 1939, 742.

Manuscript and Archival Sources

Accademia Letteraria Italiana, Rome.
Angeli-Dennis Collection. University of British Columbia Library, Vancouver.
Athenaeum Editor's Files. City University London.
British Library Manuscripts.
Browning Collection. Baylor University Library, Waco, Texas.
Dykes Campbell Papers. British Library.
Family Archives of Jacqueline Bayard-Pierlot, Olmet.
Fonds Anglais. Bibliothèque Nationale de France, Paris.
Gosse Collection. Brotherton Library, Leeds.
Huntington Library. San Marino, California.
Macmillan Archives. British Library, London.
Moulton Papers. Library of Congress, Washington.
National Library of Scotland, Edinburgh.
New York Public Library, New York.
New York Public Library for the Performing Arts, Lincoln Center, New York.
Pasteur Institute Library, Paris.
Placci Collection. Marucelliana Library, Florence.
Senate House Library, London.
Somerville College Library, Oxford.
Tate Gallery Archive, London.
Vernon Lee Collection, British Institute Library, Florence.
Vernon Lee Collection, Colby College Library, Waterville, Maine.

Secondary Sources

"A Famous Leamington Poetess and Critic." *Leamington Spa Courier*, 12 February 1937, 4.
"A. Mary F. Robinson." *The Literary World*, 15 November 1884, 389–90.

Altrincham, Baron. "Review of *The Return to Nature*, by Mary Duclaux." *Times Literary Supplement*, 19 August 1904, 258.

Armstrong, A. Joseph, compiler. *Intimate Glimpses from Browning's Letter File: Selected from Letters in the Baylor University Browning Collection.* Baylor University Library.

Armstrong, Nancy. *How Novels Think: The Limits of Individualism from 1719–1900.* New York: Columbia University Press, 2005.

Arnold, Matthew. *Culture and Anarchy.* Edited by J. Dover Wilson. Cambridge: Cambridge University Press, 1932.

– "The Study of Poetry." In *English Poetry and Irish Politics*, edited by R.H. Super. 161–88. Ann Arbor: Michigan University Press, 1973.

Bailey, John Cann. "Review of *The French Procession*, by Mary Duclaux." *Times Literary Supplement*, 30 September 1909, 352.

Barr, Mary A. "Captain Ortis." *Harper's Young People*, 27 June 1882, 551.

Batchelor, John. *John Ruskin: No Wealth But Life – A Biography.* London: Pimlico, 2001.

Bates, Ernest Sutherland. "Review of *The Life of Racine*, by Mary Duclaux." *Saturday Review of Literature*, 24 April 1926, 739.

Bayard-Pièrlot, Jacqueline. *Mary Duclaux 1857–1944: D'Une Rive L'Autre.* Paris: Editions Christian, 2015.

Beach, Cecelia. *Staging Politics and Gender: French Women's Drama, 1880–1923.* London: Palgrave, Macmillan, 2005.

Beckman, Linda Hunt. "Amy Levy: Urban Poetry, Poetic Innovation." In *The Fin-de-Siècle Poem*, edited by Joseph Bristow, 207–30. Athens: Ohio University Press, 2005.

Beckson, Karl. *Arthur Symons: A Life.* Oxford: Clarendon Press, 1987.

– Preface to *Aesthetes and Decadents of the 1890s: An Anthology of British Poetry and Prose*, edited by Karl Beckson, xi–xiii. Chicago: Academy, 1981.

Beckson, Karl and John M. Munro, eds. *Arthur Symons: Selected Letters, 1880–1935.* Iowa City: University of Iowa Press, 1989.

Beeching, Henry Charles. "Review of *The New Arcadia*, by A. Mary F. Robinson." *The Academy*, 17 May 1884, 342.

Bell-Villada, Gene. *Art for Art's Sake & Literary Life.* Lincoln: University of Nebraska Press, 1996.

Benn, Ernest. "Review of *Portrait of Pascal*, by Mary Duclaux." *Spectator*, 12 March 1927, 32.

Berenson, Bernard. *Sketch for a Self-Portrait.* New York: Pantheon Books, 1949.

Berenson, Mary. *Mary Berenson: Self-Portrait from her letters and diaries*, edited by Barbara Strackey and Jayne Samuels. London: V. Gollancz, 1983.

Berl, Emmanuel. *Rachel et autres graces*. Paris: Bernard Grasset, 1967.

Birch, Dinah. "What Teachers Do You Give Your Girls?" In *Ruskin and Women's Education*, edited by D. Birch and F. O'Gorman, 121–36. Basingstoke: Palgrave Macmillan, 2002.

Bloom, Abigail Burnham, ed. *Nineteenth Century British Women Writers: A Bio-Bibliographical Critical Sourcebook*. Westport, Connecticut: Greenwood Press, 2000.

Bloom, Harold, ed. *Selected Writings of Walter Pater*. New York: Signet, 1974.

Bright, Henry Arthur. "Review of *A Handful of Honeysuckle*, by A. Mary F. Robinson." *Athenaeum*, 24 August 1878, 232.

Bristow, Joseph. "Introduction." In *The Fin-de-Siècle Poem: English Literary Culture and the 1890s*, edited by Joseph Bristow, 1–46. Athens: Ohio University Press, 2005.

Burt, Stephanie and David Mikics. *The Art of the Sonnet*. Cambridge: Harvard University Press, 2010.

Buxton, Richard. *Myths and Tragedies in their Ancient Greek Contexts*. Oxford: Oxford University Press, 2013.

Buzard, James. *The Beaten Track: Tourism, Literature, and the Ways to Culture, 1800–1918*. Oxford: Clarendon Press, 1993.

Byerly, Alison. *Are We There Yet? Virtual Travel and Victorian Realism*. Ann Arbor: Michigan University Press, 2013.

Carson, Anne. *Grief Lessons*. New York: New York Review of Books, 2006.

Cenni, Serena, Sophie Geoffroy and Elisa Bizzotto, eds. *Violet del Palmerino: Aspetti della cultura cosmopolita nel salotto di Vernon Lee: 1889–1935*. Florence, Firenze Consiglio regionale della Toscana, 2014.

Cevasco, George A. *Three Decadent Poets, Ernest Dowson, John Gray, and Lionel Johnson: An Annotated Bibliography*. New York: Garland, 1990.

Chesnutt, Charles Waddell. "Review of *An Italian Garden*, by A. Mary F. Robinson." *The Critic* 5 (24 April 1886): 204–5.

Colby, Vineta. *Vernon Lee: A Literary Biography*. Charlottesville: Virginia University Press, 2003.

Cook, Edward. "Review of *Arden*, by A. Mary F. Robinson." *Athenaeum*, 19 May 1883, 632–3.

Cook, E.T. and Alexander Wedderburn, eds. *The Works of John Ruskin*, vol. 36. London: George Allen, 1909.

Darmesteter, James. "Ernest Renan." *The New World: A Quarterly Review of Religion, Ethics, and Theology* 7 (2 September 1893): 401–33.

– "Preface du Traducteur." In *Poesies*, by A. Mary F. Robinson, i–ix. Paris: Alphonse Lemerre, 1888.

– "The Zend Avesta: The Vendîdâd." *Sacred Books of the East*. Part 1. London: Oxford University Press, 1880.

Dellamora, Richard, ed. *Victorian Sexual Dissidence*. Chicago: University of Chicago Press, 1999.

Demoor, Marysa. "Robinson, Frances Mabel." Oxford Dictionary of National Biography. https://doi.org/10.1093/ref:odnb/60276.

Denisoff, Dennis. *Aestheticism and Sexual Parody 1840–1940*. Cambridge: Cambridge University Press, 2001.

– "The Forest Beyond the Frame: Picturing Women's Desires in Vernon Lee and Virginia Wolf." In *Women and British Aestheticism*, edited by Talia Schaffer and Kathy Psomiades, 251–69. Charlottesville, Virginia University Press, 1999.

Devereux, George. *The Character of the Euripidean Hippolytus*. Chico, California: Scholars Press, 1985.

Diedrick, James. *Mathilde Blind: Late Victorian Culture and the Woman of Letters*. Charlottesville: University Press of Virginia, 2016.

Donnay, Albert. "Carbon Monoxide as an Unrecognized Cause of Neurasthenia: A History." In *Carbon Monoxide Toxicity*, edited by David G. Penney, 231–53. London: CRC Press, 2000.

Dowling, Linda. *The Vulgarization of Art: The Victorian and Aesthetic Democracy*. Charlottesville: University Press of Virginia, 1996.

Duclert, Vincent. "Mary Robinson Darmesteter et Émile Duclaux. Le Sens D'Une Rencontre Pendant L'Affaire Dreyfus." In *Portraits Intellectuels (V)*, edited by Jean Juares. No. 145 (26 May 1921): 73–89.

Duff, Sir Mountstuart Elphinstone Grant. *Ernest Renan: In Memoriam*. London, Macmillan, 1893.

Edsal, Nicholas C. *Toward Stonewall: Homosexuality and Society in the Modern Western World*. Charlottesville: University Press of Virginia, 2003.

Ely, M. Lynda. "'Not a Song to Sell': Re-Presenting A. Mary F. Robinson." *Victorian Poetry* 38, no.1 (2000): 94–108.

Entwistle, William J. *European Balladry*. Oxford: Clarendon, 1969.

Evangelista, Stefano. *British Aestheticism and Ancient Greece*. London: Palgrave Macmillan, 2009.

– "Vernon Lee in the Vatican: The Uneasy Alliance of Aestheticism and Archaeology." *Victorian Studies* 52, no.1 (2009): 31–41.

Faderman, Lillian. *Surpassing the Love of Men: Romantic Friendship and Love between Women from the Renaissance to the Present*. New York: William Morrow and Company, Inc., 1981.

Falls, Cyril Benthan. "Review of *Life of Racine*, by Mary Duclaux." *Times Literary Supplement*, 5 November 1925, 734.

Fortunato, Paul L. *Modernist Aesthetics and Consumer Culture in the Writings of Oscar Wilde*. New York: Routledge, 2007.

Gagel, Amanda, ed. *Selected Letters of Vernon Lee 1856–1935*. Vol. 1. (1865–84). London: Routledge, 2017.

Gagnier, Regenia. "The Law of Progress and the Ironies of Individualism in the Nineteenth Century." *New Literary History* 31, no. 2 (2000): 315–36.

Gardner, Burdett. *The Lesbian Imagination (Victorian Style): A Psychological and Critical Study of Vernon Lee*. New York: Garland, 1987.

Glaser, Ben. "Polymetrical Dissonance: Tennyson, A. Mary F. Robinson, and Classical Meter." *Victorian Poetry* 49, no. 2 (2011): 199–216.

Gosse, Edmund. *A Short History of Modern English Literature*. New York: D. Appleton and Company, 1900.

– "Review of *Arden*, by A. Mary F. Robinson." *Spectator*, 6 June 1883, 776.

– "Review of *The Crowned Hippolytus and other poems*, by A. Mary F. Robinson." *Saturday Review* 23 (July 1881): 117.

– "The Ethics of Biography." In *Biography as an Art: Selected Criticism 1560–1960*, edited by James L. Clifford, 113–19. London: Oxford University Press, 1963.

Grieve, Alastair. "Rossetti and the Scandal of Art for Art's Sake in the Early 1860s." In *After the Pre-Raphaelites: Art and Aestheticism in Victorian England*, edited by Elizabeth Prettejohn, 17–35. New Brunswick, NJ: Rutgers University Press, 1999.

Grosskurth, Phyllis. *John Addington Symonds: A Biography*. London: Longmans, Green and Co., 1964.

Groth, Helen. *Victorian Photography and Literary Nostalgia*. London: Oxford University Press, 2003.

Gunn, Peter. *Vernon Lee: Violet Paget, 1856–1935*. London: Oxford University Press, 1964.

Halévy, Daniel. "Les Trois Mary." In *Mary Duclaux et Maurice Barrès: Lettres Échangées*, edited by Daniel Halévy, 13–22. Paris: Grasset, 1959.

– "Review of *A Short History of France*, by Mary Duclaux (Mary F. Robinson)." *The Anglo-French Review* 3, no. 2 (3 March 1920): 172–5.

Hamilton, Nigel. *Biography: A Brief History*. Cambridge: Harvard University Press, 2009.

Hamilton, Walter. *The Aesthetic Movement in England*. (1882). New York: AMS Press, 1971.

Haney, Craig. "Criminal Justice and the Nineteenth-Century Paradigm: The Triumph of Psychological Individualism in the 'Formative Era.'" *Law and Human Behavior* 6 (1982): 191–235.

Harrington, Emily. *Second Person Singular: Late Victorian Women Poets and the Bonds of Verse*. Charlottesville: University Press of Virginia, 2014.

– "The Strain of Sympathy: A. Mary F. Robinson, *The New Arcadia*, and Vernon Lee." *Nineteenth Century Literature* 61, no. 1 (June 2006): 66–98.

Hays, Frances. "Mary Robinson." In *Women of the Day: A Biographical Dictionary of Notable Contemporaries*, 168–9. Philadelphia: J.B. Lippincott and Co., 1885.

Hazen, Charles Downer. "Review of *A Short History of France, from Caesar's Invasion to the Battle of Waterloo*, by Mary Duclaux." *The American Historical Review* 24, no. 4 (July 1919): 660–2.

Hein, Hilde. "Refining Feminist Theory: Lessons from Aesthetics." In *Aesthetics in Feminist Perspective*, edited by Hilde Hein and Carolyn Korsmeyer, 3–18. Bloomington: Indiana University Press, 1993.

Holdsworth, Roger, ed. *Arthur Symons: Selected Writings*. Manchester: Carcanet Press, 1974.

Holmes, Ruth Van Zuyle. "Mary Duclaux (1856–1944)." *English Literature in Transition* 10 (1967): 12–46.

Howe, Julia Ward. "Hippolytus." *America's Lost Plays*, edited by J.B. Russak, 73–128. Princeton: Princeton University Press, 1941.

Hughes, Linda K. "A Woman on the Wilde Side: Masks, Perversity, and Print Culture's Role in Poems by 'Graham R. Tomson'/Rosamund Marriott Watson.'" In *The Fin-de-Siècle Poem*, edited by Joseph Bristow, 101–30. Athens: Ohio University Press, 2005.

– *The Cambridge Introduction to Victorian Poetry*. Cambridge: Cambridge University Press, 2010.

Iser, Wolfgang. *Walter Pater: The Aesthetic Moment*. Cambridge: Cambridge University Press, 1987.

Labalme, Patricia H. and Laura Sanguineti White, eds. *The Renaissance Diaries of Marin Sanudo*, translated by Linda Carroll. Baltimore: Johns Hopkins University Press, 2007.

Lacouture, Annette Bourrut. *Jules Breton: Painter of Peasant Life*. London: Yale University Press, 2002.

Lang, Andrew. "Review of *A Handful of Honeysuckle*, by A. Mary F. Robinson." *Academy*, 20 July 1878, 53.

– "Review of *The Crowned Hippolytus and other poems*, by A. Mary F. Robinson." *Athenaeum*, 2 July 1881, 8.

Lauritsen, John, ed. *Oresteia: The Medwin-Shelley Translation*. Seattle: Pagan Press, 2011.

Lavaud, Suzanne. *Marie Lenéru, sa vie, son journal, son théâtre*. Paris: Edgar Malfère, 1932.

Lee, Vernon (Violet Paget). "A Dialogue on Poetic Morality." *The Contemporary Review* 39 (1 January 1881): 682–707.

– *Belcaro: Being Essays on Sundry Aesthetical Questions*. London: W. Satchell, 1881.

– "Christmas Legends: A Nativity by Fra Filippo Lippi." *The Contemporary Review* 56 (December 1889): 844–7.

– "In Memoriam Émile Duclaux." In *Le Lycée Émile Duclaux*, edited by Veronique Visy, 114–15. Aurillac, France: Éditions Maisons des Lycées, 2012.

– "In Time of War." In *The Golden Keys and other essays*, by Vernon Lee, 241–50. London: John Lane, 1925.

Leighton, Angela. *On Form: Poetry, Aestheticism, and the Legacy of a Word*. London: Oxford University Press, 2007.

Lenéru, Marie. *Le Journal de Marie Lenéru*, edited by François Curel. Paris: Éditions G. Crès, 1922.

Lewis, Melville. *The Life of William Makepeace Thackeray*. 2 vols. London: Hutchinson, 1899.

Levey, Michael. *The Case of Walter Pater*. London: Thames and Hudson, 1978.

Lhombreaud, Roger. *Arthur Symons: A Critical Biography*. London, Unicorn Press, 1963.

Livesey, Ruth. *Socialism, Sex, and the Culture of Aestheticism in Britain, 1880–1914*. London: Oxford University Press, 2007.

Loriga, Sabina. "The Role of the Individual in History." In *Theoretical Discussions of Biography: Approaches from History, Microhistory, and Life Writing*, edited by Hans Renders and Binne de Haan Brill, 75–93. New York: Edward Mellen Press, 2013.

Lynch, Hannah. "A. Mary F. Robinson." *Fortnightly Review*, 1 February 1902, 260–76.

MacLeod, Kristen. *Fictions of British Decadence: High Art, Popular Writing, and the Fin de Siècle*. Basingstoke: Palgrave Macmillan, 2006.

Macrae, Donald, ed. *The Man Versus the State*, by Herbert Spencer (1884). London: Pelican, 1969.

Madden, William A. *Matthew Arnold: A Study of the Aesthetic Temperament in Victorian England*. Bloomington: Indiana University Press, 1967.

Maltz, Diana. *British Aestheticism and the Urban Working Classes, 1870–1900: Beauty for the People*. Basingstoke: Palgrave Macmillan, 2006.

Mander, William. "Pantheism." In *The Stanford Encyclopedia of Philosophy*, edited by Edward N. Zalta. (Winter 2016). https://plato.stanford.edu/archives/win2016/entries/pantheism/.

Mannocchi, Phyllis F. "Vernon Lee: A Reintroduction and Primary Bibliography." *English Literature in Transition, 1880–1920* 26, no. 4 (1983): 231–67.

– "Vernon Lee and Kit Anstruther-Thomson: A Study of Love and Collaboration between Romantic Friends." *Women's Studies* 12, no.2 (1986): 129–48.

Marandon, Sylvaine. *L'Oeuvre Poétique de Mary Robinson 1857–1944*. Bordeaux: Imprimerie Pechade, 1967.

Marsh, Jan. "'The Old Tuscan Rapture': The Response to Italy and Its Art in the Work of Marie Spartali Stillman." In *Unfolding the South: Nineteenth-Century British Women Writers and Artists in Italy*, edited by Alison Chapman and Jane Stabler, 159–82. Manchester: Manchester University Press, 2003.

Marzials, Frank. "Review of *Marguerites du Temps Passé*, by Mary James Darmesteter." *The Academy and Literature* 41 (16 April 1892): 368.

Matthews, Alison Victoria. "Aestheticism's True Colors: The Politics of Pigment in Victorian Art, Criticism, and Fashion." In *Dress Culture in Late Victorian Women's Fiction: Literacy, Textiles, and Activism*, edited by Christine Bayles Kortsch, 172–91. London: Routledge, 2016.

McComb, A.K., ed. *The Selected Letters of Bernard Berenson*. Boston: Houghton Mifflin, 1964.

McCormick, Jerusha. "Engendering Tragedy: Toward a Definition of 1890s Poetry." In *The Fin-de-Siècle Poem*, edited by Joseph Bristow, 47–68. Athens: Ohio University Press, 2005.

McDowall, Arthur Sydney. "Review of *Portrait of Pascal*, by Mary Duclaux." *Times Literary Supplement*, 24 February 1927, 123.

McGowan, James, trans. *The Flowers of Evil*, by Charles Baudelaire. Oxford: Oxford University Press, 1993.

Mercieux, Pierre, trans. *La Reine de Navarre*, by Mary James Darmesteter. Paris, Calmann Levy, 1900.

Miller, George Morey. *The Dramatic Element in the Popular Ballad*. Cincinnati: University Press, 1905.

Mills, Sophie. *Euripides: Hippolytus*. London: Duckworth, 2002.

Morgan, Charles Langbridge. "Menander's Mirror." *Times Literary Supplement*, 22 April 1944, 195.

Morris, William. "Modern Manufacture and Design." In *The Two Paths: Being Lectures on Art and its Application to Decoration and Manufacture Delivered in 1859*, 78–112. New York: John Wiley and Sons, 1886.

Munro, John M. *Arthur Symons*. New York: Twayne, 1969.

Nencioni, Enrico. "Poeti inglesi moderni: Nuovi canti di Mary Robinson." *Nuova Antologia*, 16 June 1886, 605–20.

Newman, Sally. "The Archival Traces of Desire: Vernon Lee's Failed Sexuality and the Interpretation of Letters in Lesbian History." *Journal of the History of Sexuality* 12 nos.1/2 (2005): 51–75.

Noble, James Ashcroft. "Review of *Emily Brontë*, by A. Mary F. Robinson." *Academy* 19 May 1883, 340.

O'Connor, Erin. "Reading *The Biographer's Tale*." *Victorian Studies* 44, no. 3 (2002): 379–87.

Ojala, Aatos. *Aestheticism and Oscar Wilde*, Part 2 (1954). Helsinki: Folcroft Library Editions, 1971.

Orel, Harold. *Victorian Literary Critics*. New York: St Martin's Press, 1984.

Ormesson, Jean. *Tant que vous penserez à moi: Jean Ormesson d'Emmanuel Berl*. Paris: Grasset, 2003.

Paris, Gaston. "James Darmesteter." *Contemporary Review* 67 (1895): 81–104.

Pater, Walter. *Studies in the History of the Renaissance*. London, Macmillan, 1873.

– *The Renaissance: Studies in Art and Poetry* (1893), edited by Donald L. Hill. Berkeley: University of California Press, 1980.

Peacock, Vera Louise. "The Works of Marie Lenéru." PhD diss., Cornell University, 1930.

Pemble, John. *The Mediterranean Passion: Victorians and Edwardians in the South*. Oxford: Clarendon, 1987.

Perkins, Judith. *The Suffering Self: Pain and Narrative Representation in the Early Christian Era*. London: Routledge, 1995.

Pollock, Sir John. "Mary Duclaux." *Contemporary Review* 167, 1 January 1945, 201–8.

– *Time's Chariot*. London: John Murray, 1950.

Potolsky, Matthew. *The Decadent Republic of Letters: Taste, Politics, and Cosmopolitan Community from Baudelaire to Beardsley*. Philadelphia: University of Pennsylvania Press, 2013.

Poynter, E. Frances, trans. *Froissart*, by Mary Darmesteter. London: Fisher Unwin, 1895.

Prettejohn, Elizabeth. *After the Pre-Raphaelites: Art and Aestheticism in Victorian England*. New Brunswick, NJ: Rutgers, University Press, 1999.

Prins, Yopie. "Greek Maenads, Victorian Spinsters." In *Victorian Sexual Dissidence*, edited by Richard Dellamora, 43–81. Chicago: University of Chicago Press, 1991.

– "'Lady's Greek' (with the Accents): A Metrical Translation of Euripides by A. Mary F. Robinson." *Victorian Literature and Culture* 34, no. 2 (2006): 591–618.

– *Ladies' Greek: Victorian Translations of Tragedy*. Princeton: Princeton University Press, 2017.

– "Patmore's Law, Meynell's Rhythm." In *The Fin-de-Siècle Poem*, edited by Joseph Bristow, 261–84. Athens: Ohio University Press, 2005.

Psomiades, Kathy Alexis. "'Still Burning from This Strangling Embrace': Vernon Lee on Desire and Aesthetics." In *Victorian Sexual Dissidence*, edited by Richard Dellamora, 21–41. Chicago: University of Chicago Press, 1999.

– "Whose Body? Christina Rossetti and Aestheticist Femininity." In *Women and British Aestheticism*, edited by Talia Schaffer and Kathy Psomiades, 101–18. Charlottesville: University Press of Virginia, 2000.

Renders, Hans. "Biography in Academia and the Critical Frontier in Life Writing." In *Theoretical Discussions of Biography: Approaches from History, Microhistory, and Life Writing*, edited by Hans Renders and Binne de Haan Brill, 169–76. Lewiston, NY: Edward Mellen Press, 2013.

Renders, Hans and Jonne Harmsma, eds. *The Biographical Turn: Lives in History*. London, Routledge, 2016.

Rigg, Patricia. "A. Mary F. Robinson." In *The Encyclopedia of Victorian Literature*, edited by Dino Franco Felluga. Hoboken, NJ: Wiley-Blackwell, 1st ed., 1 August 2015.

– "A Mary F. Robinson's *The New Arcadia:* Aestheticism and the Fin-de Siècle Social Problem Poem." *Papers in Languages and Literature* 51, no. 2 (2015): 170–94.

–*Julia Augusta Webster: Victorian Aestheticism and the Woman Writer.* Madison, NJ: Fairleigh Dickinson University Press, 2009.

–"'Tell me a story, dear, that is not true': Love, Historicity, and Transience in A. Mary F. Robinson's *An Italian Garden.*" *Australasian Victorian Studies Journal* 17, no.1 (2012): 1–14.

– "'War Work' and the Philosophy of Heroism: A. Mary F. Robinson Duclaux's Friendly Fire with Marie Lenéru and Vernon Lee." In *Vernon Lee and Radical Circles*, edited by Sophie Geoffrey. Paris: Michel Houdiard, 2016.

Robbins, Ruth. "Vernon Lee: Decadent Woman?" In *Fin de Siècle/Fin du Globe: Fears and Fantasies of the Late Nineteenth Century*, edited by John Stokes, 139–61. London: Macmillan, 1992.

Robertson, Eric S. Review of "The New Arcadia." In *English Poetesses*, by Eric S. Robertson, 376–81. London: Cassell, 1883.

Rossetti, Christina. "Later Life." In *A Pageant and Other Poems*, by Christina Rossetti, 144–71. London: Macmillan, 1881.

– "Monna Innominata." In *A Pageant and Other Poems*, by Christina Rossetti, 44–58.

Rudy, Jason, R. "Rapturous Forms: Mathilde Blind's Darwinian Poetics." *Victorian Literature and Culture* 34, no.2 (2006): 443–59.

Ruskin, John. "Modern Manufacture and Design." In *The Two Paths: Being Lectures on Art and Its Application to Decoration and Manufacture Delivered in 1859*, by John Ruskin, 78–112. New York: John Wiley and Sons, 1886.

Saintsbury, George. "Review of *Arden*, by A. Mary F. Robinson." *Academy*, 12 May 1883, 325–6.

Sale, William. *Existentialism and Euripides: Sickness, Tragedy and Divinity in the Medea, the Hippolytus and the Bacchae.* Victoria, Australia: Aureal Publications, 1977.

Saville, Julia F. "The Poetic Imaging of Michael Field." In *The Fin-de-Siècle Poem*, by Joseph Bristow. 178–206. Athens: Ohio University Press, 2005.

Schaffer, Talia. *The Forgotten Female Aesthetes: Literary Culture in Late-Victorian England*. Charlottesville: University Press of Virginia, 2000.

Schueller, Herbert M. and Robert L. Peters, eds. *The Letters of John Addington Symonds. Volume II 1869–1884*. Detroit: Wayne State University Press, 1968.

Schuhl, P.M. "Carnet de Notes: Mary Robinson (1857–1944)." *Revue Philosophique* 3 (1976): 376–7.

Seccombe, Thomas. "Review of *The French Ideal*, by Mary Duclaux." *Times Literary Supplement*, 21 September 1911, 337–8.

Smiles, Samuel. *Self-Help: with illustrations of Character, Conduct, and Perseverance*. New York: Harper & Brothers, 1900.

Smith, Bonnie G. *The Gender of History: Men, Women, and Historical Practice*. Cambridge, MA: Harvard University Press, 1998.

Spencer, Robin. "Whistler, Swinburne and Art for Art's sake." In *After the Pre-Raphaelites: Art and Aestheticism in Victorian England*, edited by Elizabeth Prettejohn, 59–89. Manchester: Manchester University Press, 1999.

Stedman, Edmund Clarence. "Some London Poets." *Harper's New Monthly Magazine* 64 (May1882): 874–92.

Stewart, Susan. *Poetry and the Fate of the Senses*. Chicago: University of Chicago Press, 2002.

Strackey, Barbara, and Jayne Samuels, eds. *Mary Berenson: Self-Portrait from her letters and diaries*. London: V. Gollancz, 1983.

Swart, Koenraad W. "'Individualism' in the Mid-Nineteenth Century (1826–1860)." *Journal of the History of Ideas* 23, no.1 (1962): 77–90.

Swinburne, Algernon Charles. "Review of *Emily Brontë*, by A. Mary F. Robinson." *Athenaeum*, 16 June 1883, 762–3.

Symonds, John Addington. "Poliziano's Italian Poetry." *Fortnightly Review* 14 (1873): 165–88.

– "Review of *Apollo and Marsyas*, by Eugene Lee-Hamilton." *Academy*, 31 January 1885, 71.

– *Studies of the Greek Poets*. London: Smith, Elder & Co., 1873.

Symons, Arthur. "A. Mary F. Robinson-Darmesteter." In *Women Poets of the Nineteenth Century: Joanna Baillie to Katharine Tynan*, edited by

Alfred E. Miles (London, Routledge, 1907). Bartleby.com, 2011. www.bartleby.com/293.

– "The Decadent Movement in Literature." *Harper's New Monthly Magazine* 26 (1893): 851–68.

Tait, James. "Review of *Les Grands Écrivains français. Froissart*, by Mary James Darmesteter." *The English Historical Review* 10, no. 39 (July 1895): 608–10.

Thompson, Carl. *Travel Writing*. London: Routledge, 2011.

Thompson, Francis. "Review of *The Return to Nature*, by Mary Duclaux." *Academy* 2 July 1904, 12.

Thornton, R.K.R. "'Decadence' in Late Nineteenth-Century England." In *Decadence and the 1890s*, edited by Ian Fletcher and Malcolm Bradbury, 15–29. London: Edward Arnold, 1979.

Thursfield, James Richard. "Review of *The Fields of France*, by Mary Duclaux." *Times Literary Supplement*, 11 December 1903, 360.

Tissot, Jules-Ernest. *Princesses de Lettres*. Lausanne: Librairie Payot, 1909, 249–312.

Tomlinson, Mary, trans. *A Medieval Garland*, by Mary Duclaux. London: Lawrence & Bullen, 1898.

Traill, H.D. "Our Minor Poets." *Nineteenth Century* 31 (January 1892): 61–72.

Tuomy, Martin. *A Literal Translation of Euripides's Hippolytus and Iphigenia*. Dublin: Trinity College, 1790.

Tylee, Claire. "Introduction to *La Paix*, by Marie Lenéru." In *War Plays by Women*, edited by Claire Tylee et al., 46–9. London: Routledge, 1999.

Vadillo, Ana Parejo. "A. Mary F. Robinson (Darmesteter Duclaux) 1857–1944." In *Nineteenth-Century British Women Writers: A Bio-Bibliographical Critical Sourcebook*, edited by Abigail Burnham Bloom, 336–9. Westport, CT: Greenwood Press, 2000.

– "Aestheticism 'At Home' in London." In *London Eyes: Reflections in Text and* Image, edited by Gail Cunningham and Stephen Barber, 59–78. New York: Berghahn Books, 2007.

– "Cosmopolitan Aestheticism: The Affective 'Italian' Ethics of A. Mary F. Robinson." *Comparative Critical Studies* 10, no. 2 (2013): 163–82.

– "'Gay Strangers': Reflections on Decadence and the Decadent Poetics of A. Mary F. Robinson." In *Cahiers victoriens et édouardiens* 78 (September 2013). http://cve.revues.org/856.

– "Immaterial Poetics: A. Mary F. Robinson and the Fin-de-Siècle

Poem." In *The Fin-de-Siècle Poem,* edited by Joseph Bristow, 231–60. Athens: Ohio University Press, 2005.

– "New Woman Poets and the Culture of the *salon* at the *fin de siècle.*" *Women: A Cultural Review* 10, no.1 (1999): 22–34.

– "The Crownless A. Mary F. Robinson." *Studies in Walter Pater and Aestheticism* 2 (2016): 71–83.

Vicinus, Martha. *Intimate Friends: Women Who Loved Women, 1778–1928.* Chicago: University of Chicago Press, 2004.

Vine, Steve. *Emily Brontë.* Woodbridge, CT: Twayne, 1998.

Virgil. *The Eclogues. The Internet Classics Archive.* 11194-2009. 1 September 2013.

Visy, Veronique, ed. *Le Lycée Émile Duclaux.* Aurillac, France: Éditions Maisons des Lycées, 2012.

Ward, Patricia A. "Preface." In *Baudelaire and the Poetics of Modernity,* edited by Patricia A. Ward, ix–x. Nashville: Vanderbilt University Press, 2001.

Watson, William. "Review of *Retrospect, and other poems,* by Mary James Darmesteter." *Academy,* 21 February 1891, 179–80.

Watts, Theodore. "Review of *The New Arcadia, and other poems,* by A. Mary F. Robinson." *Athenaeum.* 2 August 1884, 141–2.

Webster, Augusta. "Review of *An Italian Garden,* by A. Mary F. Robinson." *Athenaeum,* 17 April 1886, 517.

Wilson, H.F. "Review of *Mary Robinson: Poesies traduites de l'Anglais,* by James Darmesteter." *Athenaeum,* 11 August 1888, 181–2.

– "Review of *Songs, Ballads, and a Garden Play,* by A. Mary F. Robinson." *Athenaeum,* 11 August 1888, 181–2.

"World Biographies: A. Mary F. Robinson." *The Literary World,* 15 November 1884, 389–90.

Zeitlin, Froma I. *Playing the Other: Gender and Society in Classical Greek Literature.* Chicago: University of Chicago Press, 1996.

Unsigned Reviews of Robinson's Work

"Review of *A Handful of Honeysuckle,* by A. Mary F. Robinson." *Saturday Review,* 21 January 1878, 21.

"Review of *A Handful of Honeysuckle,* by A. Mary F. Robinson." *Spectator,* 26 October 1878, 1343.

"Review of *The Crowned Hippolytus and other poems*, by A. Mary F. Robinson." *Athenaeum*, 2 July 1881, 8.

"Review of *Emily Brontë*, by A. Mary F. Robinson." *Spectator*, 26 May 1883, 678.

"Review of *Emily Brontë*, by A. Mary F. Robinson." *St James's Gazette*, 28 August 1883, 6–7.

"Review of *Arden*, by A. Mary F. Robinson." *Spectator*, 16 June 1883, 776.

"Review of *The New Arcadia and other poems*, by A. Mary F. Robinson." *Athenaeum*, 2 August 1883, 141.

"Review of *An Italian Garden*, by A. Mary F. Robinson." *Spectator*, 4 September 1886, 23.

"Review of *Songs, Ballads, and a Garden Play*, by A. Mary F. Robinson." *Spectator*, 2 July 1888, 16.

"Review of *The End of the Middle Ages: Essays and Questions in History*, by Mary James Darmesteter." *Athenaeum*, 29 December 1888, 873–4.

"Review of *The End of the Middle Ages: Essays and Questions in History*, by Mary James Darmesteter." *The Art Journal* (1889): 96.

"Review of *The End of the Middle Ages: Essays and Questions in History*, by Mary James Darmesteter." *The Cambridge Review*, 14 February 1889, 214.

"Review of *The End of the Middle Ages: Essays and Questions in History*, by Mary James Darmesteter." *Spectator*, 2 March 1889, 23–4.

"Review of *The End of the Middle Ages: Essays and Questions in History*, by Mary James Darmesteter." *English Historical Review*, 15 July 1889, 600.

"Review of *Lyrics Selected from the Works*, by Mary James Darmesteter." *The Critic*, 25 April 1891, 222.

"Review of *Retrospect, and other poems*, by Mary James Darmesteter." *The Critic*, 9 June 1893, 387.

"Review of *Retrospect, and other poems*" by Mary James Darmesteter. *The Bookman* (July 1893): 118.

"Review of *Retrospect, and other poems*, by Mary James Darmesteter." *The Saturday Review*, 26 August 1893, 245–6.

"Review of *The Collected Poems, Lyrical and Narrative*, by A. Mary F. Robinson." *Athenaeum*, 21 June 1902, 778.

"Review of *The Return to Nature*, by Mary Duclaux." *Athenaeum*, 30 August 1904, 287.

"Review of *The French Procession*, by Mary Duclaux." *The Common Cause*, 2 December 1909, 453.

"Review of *A Short History of France*, by Mary Duclaux (Mary F. Robinson)." *The Anglo-French Review* 3, no. 2 (3 March 1920): 172–5.

"Review of *The Life of Racine*, by Mary Duclaux." *Spectator*, 13 March 1926, 21.

"Review of *The Life of Racine*, by Mary Duclaux." *The Bookman*, 26 June 1926, 494.

"Review of *The Life of Racine*, by Mary Duclaux." *Northern Whig*, 30 January 1926, 10.

Index